W. G. Brock

This is the first of three volumes containing papers presented in the invited symposium sessions of the Seventh World Congress of the Econometric Society. The papers summarize and interpret key recent developments and discuss current and future directions in a wide range of topics in economics and econometrics. They cover both theory and applications. Authored by leading specialists in their fields these volumes provide a unique survey of progress in the discipline.

Econometric Society Monographs No. 26

Advances in economics and econometrics: theory and applications

Volume I

Advances in economics and econometrics: theory and applications

Seventh World Congress
Volume I

Edited by

DAVID M. KREPS

and

KENNETH F. WALLIS

CAMBRIDGE
UNIVERSITY PRESS

Published by the Press Syndicate of the University of Cambridge
The Pitt Building, Trumpington Street, Cambridge CB2 1RP
40 West 20th Street, New York, NY 10011-4211, USA
10 Stamford Road, Oakleigh, Melbourne 3166, Australia

© Cambridge University Press 1997

First published 1997

Printed in Great Britain at the University Press, Cambridge

A catalogue record for this book is available from the British Library

A catalogue record is available from the Library of Congress

ISBN 0 521 58011 0   hardback
ISBN 0 521 58983 5   paperback

VN

Contents

Contributors

Paul Krugman
Massachusetts Institute of Technology

Elhanan Helpman
University of Tel Aviv

Roger B. Myerson
Northwestern University

John Sutton
London School of Economics and Political Science

Eddie Dekel
Northwestern University

Faruk Gul
Princeton University

John D. Hey
University of York

Vincent P. Crawford
University of California, San Diego

Kandori Michihiro
The University of Tokyo

Ramon Marimon
European University Institute, Florence

Preface

This book contains papers presented in the invited symposium sessions of the Seventh World Congress of the Econometric Society, held at Keio University, Tokyo in August 1995, for which we were Program Co-Chairs. The papers summarize and interpret key recent developments and discuss current and future directions in a wide range of topics in economics and econometrics. These were chosen on the basis of their broad interest to members of the Society and so cover both theory and applications, and demonstrate the progress made in the period since the previous World Congress. The program also reflected the fact that this was the first World Congress held outside Europe and North America. The authors are leading specialists in their fields, yet do not overemphasize their own research contributions. In one case, the two speakers in the session have combined their papers into a single chapter for this book – a long one, needless to say.

The more general objectives are reflected in the presentation of all the papers in a single book under a general title, with joint editorship, thus departing from the previous practice of separate "economic theory" and "econometrics" books. The size of the book has necessitated its division into three volumes, and thematic connections have suggested the contents of each volume. Within each volume the papers appear in the order of their presentation in Tokyo, which we hope will help readers who were there to remember what a marvellous occasion the Congress was.

We are grateful to the members of our Program Committee for much valuable advice, to the Chairs and discussants of the invited symposium sessions for their contributions, and to Patrick McCartan at Cambridge University Press for his guidance during the preparation and production of this book. More generally we wish to acknowledge the steadfast support we received in our task form Robert and Julie Gordon, respectively Treasurer and Secretary of the Society, and from Masahiro Okuno-Fujiwara, Chair of the Local Organizing Committee for the Congress.

David M. Kreps
Kenneth F. Wallis

CHAPTER 1

Trade and wages

Paul Krugman

Many influential people are firmly convinced that the growth of the world trade and especially the growing exports of manufactured goods from developing countries are the main cause of declining wages and rising unemployment in the west. Widely quoted publications, like the World Economic Forum's *World Competitiveness Report*, state flatly that western prosperity is no longer sustainable in the face of increased global competition; even the European Commission's 1993 White Paper *Growth, Competitiveness, Employment* asserts that the most important cause of rising European unemployment is the fact that "other countries are becoming industrialized and competing with us – even on our own markets – at cost levels which we simply cannot match."

It is not surprising that the idea of a close link between growing trade and declining wages has become widely accepted. The image of global competition – for markets and for capital – that undermines the position of labor is a simple and compelling one, which makes intuitive sense to businessmen and politicians. Moreover, the attribution of domestic woes to international competition appeals strongly to what one might call the fashion sense of policy intellectuals. Not only does the mere use of the world "global" help to convey an image of worldly sophistication; a story that links together the growth of world trade, the rise of Asia, the fall of Communism (which has opened up new outlets for capital and converted new nations to capitalism), and the decline of the west has a sweep and glamour that ordinary economic analyses lack.

But is the story true? Has growing trade really been a major cause of declining wages?

It is important to realize that most people who believe in the link between globalization and declining wages have not tried to put their thoughts in the form of a testable model. Indeed, to an important extent the debate over globalization and its impacts is a debate between those who believe in mathematical and quantitative modeling of economic issues and those who do not, and the ferocity of the debate is driven in part by hostility to the scientific pretension of economists in general as opposed to their views on this particular subject. Nonetheless, the impact of trade on wages is an issue that can and should be addressed with clearly thought out and quantifiable models, and we must try to test hypotheses against the data even if their advocates will not.

In this chapter, then, I will try to answer two questions: "Has trade driven down wages? Will it drive wages down in the future?" I will try to represent various arguments that assert that trade has driven wages down, or will do so in the future, by a series of four models, in order of increasingly possible validity. Each of these models is, it turns out, possible to quantify at least roughly from readily available data.

To preview the conclusions: two widely held views, that international competition has driven down aggregate western incomes and that it has shifted the distribution of income against labor, can be flatly rejected from the data. A third view, that trade deficits have reduced incomes via "deindustrialization," may have some validity for the United States, but this effect cannot have reduced average wages by more than a fraction of a percentage point. The only serious contender is the idea that trade has shifted the distribution of income from less to more skilled workers; this effect is almost certainly there, but it has proved elusive in actual data, and a best guess is that it accounts for only a small fraction of the large recent increase in income inequality.

1   TRADE AND AGGREGATE INCOMES

It seems obvious to many people that the diffusion of technology to newly industrializing nations, and the entry of new players in the world market, are harmful to advanced nations. After all, more competitors means more intense competition, doesn't it?

The answer, of course, is "not necessarily." When one's trading partners experience economic growth – whether because of diffusion of technology, or for any other reason – the effect cannot simply be described as a matter of increased competition. To make the simplest point, growth abroad also expands the size of the world market – in fact, since world spending always equals world income, growth always expands markets by exactly the amount by which it expands production.

In other words, the simple assertion that growth abroad means increased competition and thus lower real income is a partial equilibrium story, applied in a context where general equilibrium analysis is crucial.

None of this should be news: the analysis of the effects of foreign growth on a trading economy goes back to classic papers by Hicks (1953) and Johnson (1955). This literature leads to three key conclusions:

1 The effect of foreign growth on domestic real income is ambiguous; it depends on the *bias* of the growth. Growth abroad that is biased toward goods we export hurts us, but growth that is biased towards goods we import raises our real income.

2 Any adverse effect works via the *terms of trade*: foreign growth hurts us if and only if the price of our exports falls relative to that of our imports. (Strictly speaking, there is another possibility: that foreign growth might interact with market failures in the domestic economy in such a way as to aggravate domestic distortions. I turn to that issue in section 3).

3 The size of any adverse effect via the terms of trade can be quantified: the percentage reduction in real income (by which, for those who want to be careful, I mean the size of the reduction in income at initial prices that would reduce welfare by the same amount as the terms of trade shock) from a deterioration in the terms of trade is equal to the percentage reduction in those terms of trade multiplied by the share of trade in income. In other words, a 1 percent fall in the terms of trade will ordinarily reduce real income by much less than 1 percent.

So, has the fact that, as the European Commission puts it, "other countries are becoming industrialized and competing with us" been a significant drag on OECD real income? We need not get into the issue of trying to determine the bias of growth in the newly industrializing economies (NIEs). Instead, we can look directly at the terms of trade of the advanced nations. And what we see is . . . nothing. The terms of trade of major advanced nations have shown no discernible trend either way. Figure 1.1 shows the ratio of the US implicit deflator for exports to that for imports since 1970: while there was a decline in 1970–3 due to the devaluation of the dollar and the oil crisis, since then the terms of trade have fluctuated with no visible trend. And, if one bears in mind that trade averaged only about 10 percent of US income over the period, one immediately sees that fluctuations in the terms of trade of the magnitude shown cannot have had any large impact on real income. The same is true for all other major economies over the period.[1]

So the claim that international competition has been a major drag on aggregate real incomes in advanced countries can be flatly rejected on the

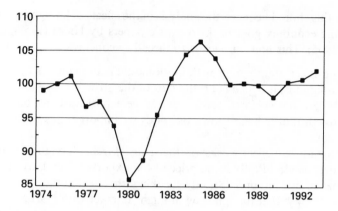

Figure 1.1 US terms of trade

basis of readily available data. It is indeed shocking, and a dismal comment on the success of our profession at communicating even basic ideas, that this simple point has not been appreciated in public debate.

But this is a point about the past, rather than the future. Could competition from newly industrializing countries be a major drag on OECD incomes in the future?

The answer is that it seems unlikely. In the first place, it is far from obvious that growth in the NIEs will be biased toward OECD exports. Indeed, other arguments – like the claim, discussed below, that growing NIE exports will hurt low-skilled workers – seem to require the assumption that NIE growth will be biased toward OECD *imports*. But, in any case, the crucial point to realize is that despite the rapid growth of exports from the newly industrializing economies, such exports remain only a small fraction of OECD expenditure – even now less than 2 percent. That is, the trade share of the OECD viewed as an aggregate is still quite low.

What this means is that even a large deterioration in the terms of trade will have a small impact on real income. Suppose that OECD imports from NIEs are 3 percent of GDP, and suppose that the terms of trade deteriorate by 10 percent, then the reduction in real income is only 0.3 percent. It would take a catastrophic deterioration in the terms of trade to reduce real income in the advanced world by as much as 2 or 3 percent.

One might ask, in this case, why so many people – like the authors of the *World Competitiveness Report* – are convinced that competition from NIEs will have a devastating impact on OECD living standards. Why is their view different? Based on considerable informal empirical research, I would assert that the answer is sheer ignorance of both the concepts and the numbers.

2   CAPITAL VERSUS LABOR

While some commentators believe that competition from low-wage nations has or will hurt both capital and labor in advanced countries, another influential view holds that growing international trade and capital mobility have shifted the terms of the bargain between capital and labor within advanced countries, perhaps raising overall income but benefiting capital at labor's expense.

In principle, trade economists should be sympathetic to this view, for at least three reasons. First, the logic of the Stolper–Samuelson theorem tells us that trade will normally have strong effects on income distribution, actually reducing the real incomes of scarce factors. Second, international capital mobility should, in principle, also tend to benefit capital but hurt labor in the capital-exporting country. Finally, there are clearly some industries where rents due to market power are in effect shared by capital and labor; international trade could surely change the terms of that bargain in some cases.

But it is one thing to accept the possible validity of an argument in principle; it is another to accept its importance in practice. As a practical matter, redistribution from capital to labor simply cannot have been an important factor in declining wages, at least so far.

How do we know this? Again, by the straightforward use of very simple statistics.

The Stolper–Samuelson story obviously requires that there be a rise in the share of capital and a fall in the share of labor in national income. And this simply has not happened. Figure 1.2 shows the share of compensation in US national income since 1973; there have been some small fluctuations, associated mainly with the business cycle, but no visible trend.

The export of capital could reduce real wages without altering labor's share, because diversion of capital to foreign markets could lower the marginal product of labor even with a constant share (for example, if the aggregate production function is approximately Cobb–Douglas). However, exports of capital from high-wage to low-wage countries have been very small compared with the size of the OECD economy. The United States, of course, has been a net *importer* of capital since 1981. And developing countries as a group were net *exporters* of capital for most of the 1980s. With the emerging market boom of the 1990s, some capital began flowing, but the numbers were not large. In the peak years of 1993 and 1994 net capital flows to newly industrializing economies – which can be measured by their combined current-account deficits – amounted to about $60 billion per year. This amounted to about 0.3 percent of the combined GDP of the OECD economies, and about 2 percent of their gross investment. Overall, the flow of

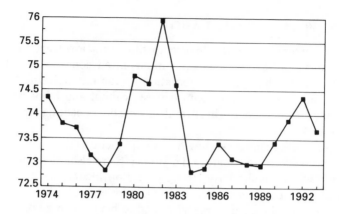

Figure 1.2 Compensation as percent of income

capital to emerging markets since 1990 seems unlikely to have reduced advanced-country wages by as much as 0.1 percent.

That is the past; but what about the future? Could capital exports become much larger (assuming that the markets eventually shake off the nervousness caused by the Mexican crisis)?

The key point here is to realize that any export of savings from advanced to low-wage countries must have as its counterpart a current-account surplus by the OECD and a current deficit in the emerging economies. If that export of savings is large, the current-account imbalances will have to be equally large.

So suppose, for example, that we hypothesize that over the next 10 years the OECD exports enough capital to leave its capital stock 10 percent lower than it otherwise would be. (If we assume a stable labor share of 0.7, this would therefore leave real wages 3 percent lower than they otherwise would be). The current capital stock of the OECD is on the order of $60 trillion; so this scenario, which falls far short of the apocalyptic language often used to describe the likely impact of global capital mobility on wages, would require that the OECD as a whole run an average annual current-account surplus of $600 billion – and that the NIEs run a corresponding deficit. These numbers seem implausibly large (among other things, they would require the *average* NIE to run a current deficit exceeding 10 percent of GDP), and they seem even larger when one bears in mind that the same people who warn of large-scale movements of capital to developing countries also often warn about trade deficits leading to deindustrialization in the advanced nations.

The claim that international trade has already had a major impact on the distribution of income between capital and labor is easily rejected; it is baffling, even to a hardened cynic like myself, that the fact that labor's share in national income has not declined seems to have had no impact on the beliefs of policy intellectuals. The prospect that capital mobility will reduce wages in the future is not so easily dismissed, but once one has realized the size of the capital flows that would be needed to justify alarmist concerns, such concerns seem implausible.

Again, one may ask why so many people hold a different view. And again the answer is, sadly, that would-be sophisticates do not understand even basic accounting identities.

3   DEINDUSTRIALIZATION

Once upon a time, American workers had good jobs at good wages: as steelworkers or autoworkers making $20 an hour, they were members of the middle class. Now, however, most of those good jobs have been lost to imports, and once-proud workers are flipping hamburgers and making minimum wage.

Or so the story goes. The idea that imports have eliminated high-paying manufacturing jobs has been widely accepted by American opinion, and to a certain extent in Europe as well; even in Japan there are now fears about "hollowing out."

Although few of those who tell this story are aware of it, the claim that trade-induced loss of high-wage jobs is a prime cause of lower wages – what we might call the "deindustrialization hypothesis" – is in fact a particular variant of the "wage differentials" argument for protection, an argument thoroughly analyzed a generation ago (see, in particular, Bhagwati and Ramaswami (1963) and Johnson (1965)).

Suppose that we imagine that an economy has two sectors. And suppose that for some reason, such as union power, equivalent workers in one sector are paid more than their counterparts in the other. Then we immediately have the possibility that international trade, if it leads to a decline in high-wage employment, will reduce rather than increase real income. The point is that trade plays into the therefore aggravates the consequences of a pre-existing domestic distortion.

Textbook trade theory tells us, of course, that even if trade has an adverse effect because of a domestic distortion, protection is not the first-best response. It is always better instead to deal with the distortion directly – eliminating wage differentials if possible, offsetting them with taxes and subsidies if not. But let us leave aside the policy response and simply ask whether the story is good a description of what has actually happened.

It is in fact the case that American workers in the manufacturing sector are paid more than seemingly equivalent workers in other parts of the economy. It is also true that the United States has run substantial trade deficits in manufacturing since 1980 which have undoubtedly left manufacturing employment lower than it would otherwise have been. So in qualitative terms the deindustrialization hypothesis seems plausible. But how important is it in reality?

In a recent analysis (Krugman (1995b)) I tried to give an answer, using a model designed to be easy to quantify; I deliberately chose the assumptions to give the deindustrialization hypothesis as favorable a hearing as possible. The model is set up as follows:

Technology The production structure is the simplest possible: a Ricardian framework in which one factor, labor, can be used to produce two goods: manufactures and services. This assumption means, of course, that the model cannot address issues of income distribution; but these are dealt with in section 4 of this chapter.

International markets Breaking with the usual practice in simple trade models, the model economy is not assumed to be a price-taker. Instead, it faces a rest-of-world offer curve. This assumption may be justified simply by noting that the United States is indeed a large economy. There is also, however, a crucial issue of modeling convenience. If one wants to avoid corner solutions – and, as we will see, the reality of US trade experience is very much *not* a corner solution – then one must either build decreasing returns out of the foreign offer curve (on this, see Brecher (1974)). So if the technology is Ricardian, it is a great help to adopt a large-country approach to trade.

Nature of the shock How should we model the shock that is supposed to cause deindustrialization? Most people, including professional economists, would grant that over the past generation there has been a process of "globalization" of the US economy, whose measurable impact is a sharp rise in the share of both exports and imports in GDP. Surprisingly, however, it is quite hard to be explicit about the sources of this increased trade share. A country might be induced to engage in more international trade if given an incentive to do so, that is, if its terms of trade improve – but US terms of trade, at least as measured, have if anything deteriorated slightly over the past generation. Or there could be a fall in transport costs, which would raise the ratio of f.o.b. to c.i.f prices – but while there has indeed been a decline in transport costs for goods, even a generation ago these costs were so low that their continuing decline cannot explain the rapid growth in trade. The same is true of trade liberalization, which has reduced tariffs, but from an initial level that was fairly low by historical standards.

What, then, is the nature of globalization? The best available answer seems to be that it involves the reduction of invisible transaction costs in international trade, a reduction that is presumably due to improvements in communication and information processing – that is, we invoke the magic of silicon to explain trade trends. And how should this be modeled? The easiest way is simply to imagine that some goods and services that were previously non-tradable become tradable.

In the context of a two-sector model, this boils down to starting with a situation in which the United States is in autarky, and then opening up the possibility of trading services for manufactures; the result is then a trade deficit in manufactures, which implies a contraction of manufacturing employment.

The objections to this description are obvious. In particular, for the most part the US deficit in manufactures has not had service exports as a counterpart, but rather has been reflected in a current-account deficit.

This objection amounts to saying that we cannot deal with the issue of deindustrialization except in terms of an intertemporal model. Indeed, the advocates of the deindustrialization hypothesis are notably unconcerned about the implications of intertemporal budget constraints, and sometimes seem to imagine that the United States can run trade deficits forever. It is therefore a charitable gesture to represent their views by imagining that the country exports something to pay for its imports of manufactures. As an empirical matter, we may play somewhat dirty and argue that there are substantial unrecorded US service exports; or we may claim that "services" are a proxy for the export of IOUs, to be repaid at a later date with a future trade surplus in manufactures. This raises some obvious questions about the interpretation of what must then be a transitory deindustrialization, but let us ignore that issue.

Finally, then, we are prepared to lay out the model, which after all that will be very simple. We imagine a two-sector economy, in which one factor, labor, may produce either manufactures or services under constant returns to scale. For some reason, say the existence of unions, workers in manufactures must be paid a higher wage than those in services; let the ratio of the manufactures to the services wage be $w > 1$. We consider an initial equilibrium in which no trade is allowed, and a subsequent equilibrium in which services may be traded for manufactures, with the rest of the world represented by an offer curve.

Figure 1.3 then shows the pre- and post-trade equilibria. The line PF shows the economy's production possibility frontier. In a one-factor model, the wage differential will not put the economy inside that frontier, but it will distort the prices consumers face: the autarky relative price of manufactures will be w times the opportunity cost of manufactures in terms of services.

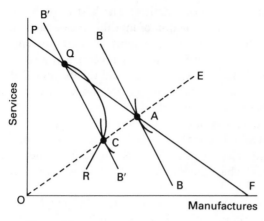

Figure 1.3

Thus the autarky equilibrium will be at a point such as A, with BB the perceived budget line.

Now we allow trade with a rest of world, whose import demand/export supply is represented by the offer curve QR. As long as the country remains non-specialized, the relative price of manufactures must be the same after as before trade (which also implies, incidentally, that even an undistorted economy would not gain from trade – in other words, this model is biased toward producing losses). But the possibility of manufactures imports leads to a decline in manufactures production; the production point shifts to Q. Consumption C must be on the new budget line B'B', and the implied trade vector QC must be a point on the rest-of-world offer curve. (One can think of finding the new equilibrium by sliding Q north-west along PF until C lies on the consumption expansion path OE which passes through A.)

It is immediately apparent that welfare is reduced. The opening of trade, which should make the country better off or at least no worse off, instead leads to a decline in income because it pushes workers out of the high-wage manufacturing sector into the low-wage service sector. The interaction of trade with the pre-existing domestic distortion leads to losses.

Figure 1.3, then, offers what appears to be a rationale for the deindustrialization hypothesis. But it is one thing to show that something can happen in principle; it is something quite different to show that it is an important effect in practice. *How large* is the negative impact of trade implied in figure 1.3?

To assess the welfare loss from deindustrialization, it is useful to define two functions which are implied by the utility function. First, let us define the indirect utility function

$$U = N(y, p), \tag{1}$$

where y is income in terms of services and p is the relative price of manufactures. Second, let us write an expression for expenditure on manufactures (measured in terms of services),

$$E_M = E(y, p). \tag{2}$$

We may also note that income y arises entirely from wage earnings. Let L be total employment, L_M and L_S employment in the two sectors, and choose units so that one unit of labor produces one unit of services. Then we have

$$\begin{aligned} y &= L_S + wL_M \\ &= L + (w - 1)L_M. \end{aligned} \tag{3}$$

Finally, note that income earned in manufactures is total expenditure on manufactures, less spending on manufactures imports

$$wL_M = E(y, p) - E_{IM}. \tag{4}$$

In the situation depicted in figure 1.3, what happens when we move from A to C? Given the assumption there is no change in the relative price p, all that happens is that the budget line shifts in, that is, there is a reduction in y. The driving force behind this change is y is the diversion of some demand for manufactures to imports, that is, a rise in E_{IM}. So all we need to do is analyze the effects of a rise in E_{IM}.

It is easiest (though not essential) to do this by considering a small change so that we can use calculus. From (2), (3), and (4), we easily find that

$$\frac{dy}{dE_{IM}} = -\frac{w - 1}{w - \mu(w - 1)}, \tag{5}$$

where μ is the marginal propensity to spend on manufactures. The welfare effect is then

$$\frac{dU}{dE_{IM}} = -\frac{\partial N}{\partial y}\left(\frac{w - 1}{w - \mu(w - 1)}\right). \tag{6}$$

And that's it: the term in brackets in equation (6) is the compensating variation for the welfare loss from one dollar of expenditure on imports (which in the contest of this model should be interpreted as one dollar of manufactures trade deficit).

To estimate the quantitative importance of the actual deindustrialization, then, we need only three numbers, First, we need a value for w. Proponents of the deindustrialization hypothesis, such as Lester Thurow, often use the figure of 30 percent for the wage premium in manufacturing. This is actually the difference in weekly earnings between manufacturing and non-manufacturing workers; but since manufacturing employees work more hours, the hourly differential is only a bit more than 10 percent. It is thus a good bet that 30 percent is a substantial exaggeration of the true premium, but let us accept it for now.

Second, we need the trade-induced fall in expenditure on manufactured goods, E_{IM}, which we will tentatively identify with the trade deficit in such goods. In the 1990s to date the US trade deficit in manufactured goods has averaged about 1.5 percent of GDP; let us use this as a baseline, with the understanding that it is very easy to scale the calculation up or down if you regard the structural deficit as smaller or larger.

Finally, we need the marginal propensity to spend on manufactured goods. Manufactures account for about 18 percent of US value added; together with a trade deficit of 1.5 percent, this gives an average propensity to spend of about 0.2. Lacking any particular reason to suppose that the marginal is very different from the average, we may therefore assign a value of $\mu = 0.2$.

Substituting $w = 1.3$, $E_{IM} = 1.5$, and $\mu = 0.2$ into (6), we therefore arrive at an estimate of the real income loss due to the trade-induced loss of high-wage manufacturing jobs: 0.36 percent.

To put this estimate in context, consider what the proponents of the deindustrialization hypothesis believe that it explains. Depending on the particular measure used, ordinary workers in the United States experienced something between stagnation and a 15 percent fall in their wages between 1973 and 1993, compared with a 60 percent rise over the previous 20 years. The deindustrialization hypothesis assigns *primary* responsibility for that deterioration in performance to the loss of high-wage jobs to imports. Instead, our estimate finds that the negative impact of trade is well under a half of 1 percent – not one but two orders of magnitude too small to bear the weight being placed on it.

Moreover, as discussed at length in Krugman (1995b), there are a number of reasons to imagine that even this estimate is considerably too high. There may be a grain of truth to the deindustrialization hypothesis, but it is a small grain.

4   THE SKILL PREMIUM

International economists have an occupational failing: they tend to give their critics too much credit. Because sophisticated ideas like the Hicks (1953)–Johnson (1955) analysis of trade and growth – or for that matter comparative advantage – have been around for a very long time, it is natural to suppose that all intelligent people understand them. And thus the normal reaction of economists, when confronted with statements of concern about the impact of free trade, is to imagine that these statements are based on some realistic appreciation of the limits of our standard models.

If one remains in public discussion for any length of time, however, sooner or later there comes a moment of revelation. The seemingly sophisticated American intellectual sharing the podium says something like "In the end, we're talking about a struggle over who gets the jobs"; or the suave European asserts that "the problem is that the Asians won't allow us to maintain our standard of living"; and you suddenly realize that they don't understand anything at all about the most basic concepts, or have even a vague sense of the actual magnitudes.

Up to this point I have presented three stories about the supposed adverse effects of trade on advanced economies that are easily and flatly rejected – or at least are shown to be of minor importance. It is crucial, as a practical matter, to understand that the vast bulk of public concern about the effects of trade, including that originating from people who regard themselves as experts, involves one of these stories. In short, most critics of growing trade are people who, in the words of John Maynard Keynes, "do not know *at all* what they are talking about."

Nonetheless, there is one serious concern about the effects of growing trade: most economists agree that it has played some role in the growth of wage inequality in the United States, and perhaps in the growth of unemployment in other countries where inequality has not been allowed to increase to the same extent.

The logic is simple: if a country with an abundant supply of skilled workers increases trade with another country in which unskilled workers are abundant, one expects to see some convergence of wages – which for the advanced country means higher wages for the skilled, lower for the unskilled. And, since there has in fact been a sharp widening of the skill premium in the United States since the 1970s, theory and the crude facts seem to be in accord.

The crucial issue is one of measurement: how much of the increase in wage inequality can be attributed to growing trade?

This turns out to be a difficult issue to resolve, because of a mixture of conceptual and empirical problems. I do not want to review the fairly tangled literature in this chapter (see Lawrence 1995 for an excellent survey). Instead I want to describe a particular approach – introduced in Krugman (1995a) – which seems to me to offer a useful way to think about both the theory and the evidence.

I imagine a world that consists of only two regions, one intended to represent the OECD as a whole, the other to represent the aggregate of NIEs. All transactions within each aggregate are ignored, as is the existence of other types of countries like oil exporters. The two regions produce and consume two goods.

A major question in all of the economics literature on trade and wages has been how to model the shock. Many studies have treated trade flows as exogenous; but this makes little sense in terms of any fully specified model. Trade theorists would prefer to treat relative prices as the exogenous variable, but this has not turned out to be a very good route either, for several reasons. First, the OECD is not a small, price-taking economy; trade prices are just as endogenous from the OECD's point of view as trade volumes. Second, observed changes in world prices are presumably the result not only of growing world integration but of other forces, such as technological change. If what we want is what Deardorff and Hakura (1994) have called a "but-for" analysis – what would have happened to relative wages, but for the effect of increased global integration? – looking at what actually happened to prices is not much help. Finally, available data on trade prices, as opposed to trade volumes, show no discernible movement.

The answer I adopted in Krugman (1995a) was the same as that used in the model in section 3: to envision the shock as taking the form of opening of trade between the aggregate OECD and a trading partner who was, in effect, not there before. That is, the shock is the appearance of a rest of the world, which provides an offer curve against which the advanced nations can trade.

Since the focus of this analysis is on labor-market developments in the OECD, it is necessary to have some explicit treatment of the factor markets. I make several strategic simplifications. First, the only productive inputs are skilled and unskilled labor; capital is left out of the story. The main reason for doing this is the fact, already emphasized in section 2, that the distribution of income between capital and labor has been quite stable.

Second, production is assumed to take place under constant returns to scale. Economies of scale are surely important in understanding both the causes and effects of trade with the OECD, but probably play a smaller role in north–south trade.

For the same reason, markets are assumed to be perfectly competitive. This is likely to raise some strong objections. One common story about the effects of international trade on wages is that it has weakened the bargaining power of workers; this story only makes sense if one supposes that workers and employers are struggling over the division of some rent, presumably created by the market power of the firm. One may question whether such stories can be a large part of the picture: they seem to predict a shift in the distribution of income between capital and labor, which has not happened, rather than between different types of labor, which has; and the story applies only to those workers in traded-goods industries, whereas the rise in income inequality has been pervasive throughout the economy. In any case, for this model competition is assumed to be perfect.

How should the OECD's trade with the NIEs be modeled? It is common in trade theory to work with small economies, which face given world prices; and some writers on the effects of changing world trade still use this assumption. For the OECD as a whole, however, this is a deeply unrealistic assumption; worse yet, it is analytically awkward, leading to excessively "bang-bang" solutions in some cases. It thus makes sense to regard the OECD as having substantial market power *vis-à-vis* the NIEs. As in section 3, this can be represented by assuming that the OECD faces a rest-of-world offer curve.

Luckily, it turns out not to be necessary to model the inside workings of the newly industrializing countries: they can simply be summarized by their offer curve. Their growth and increased integration with the world economy is then captured simply by an outward shift in that offer curve. In fact, since their manufactured exports were negligible in 1970, we can approximate the effects of their emergence by contrasting an initial period in which the OECD did no external trade, with a subsequent period in which it faces an offer curve that leads to the observed trade volumes. That is, in the model we analyze the effects of globalization by contrasting the current situation with one of autarky for the OECD as a whole.

Or to be more precise, we can answer the "but-for" question by asking the following question: *How much lower would the relative price of skill-intensive goods and the relative wage of skill-intensive labor have to be in order to make the OECD choose not to trade?*

To answer this question, of course, we must have a quantitative model. In Krugman (1995a) I offered a miniature two-sector CGE model, based on a mixture of actual data and guesswork, which allows us to calculate an answer. The details of that model are, without question, highly unreliable. The results, however, are driven by one fairly robust observation and one simple fact.

The robust observation is that, for plausible factor shares and elasticities of substitution in production and consumption, the OECD offer curve is quite flat. That is, substantial trade can be elicited at relative prices only moderately different from autarky prices.

The simple fact, which we come back to repeatedly, is that trade between the OECD and the newly industrializing economies is still not very large as a share of OECD GDP.

Putting these together, we come up with the conclusion that relative prices would not have to be very different from their autarky values to elicit the amount of trade we actually see. Or to put it the other way around, "but-for" relative prices – the relative prices that would prevail in the

OECD but for the existence of the NIEs to trade with – cannot be very different from the actual prices. Indeed, in Krugman (1995a) I conclude that the existence of the NIEs leads the relative price of skill-intensive goods to be only 1 percent higher than it would be if there were no north–south trade in manufactures.

Because of the magnification effect associated with Stolper–Samuelson changes in income distribution, the effect of trade on the relative wages of skilled and unskilled workers is larger than the effect on relative prices, but it is still modest: 3 percent in the back-of-the-envelope calculation in Krugman (1995a).

To repeat: these are not truly solid estimates. But only unrealistically low elasticities of substitution would allow the still quite modest volume of north–south trade to be consistent with very large changes in relative factor prices. At the very least, I would challenge those economists who maintain that trade has in fact had large impacts on wages to produce an illustrative CGE model, with plausible parameters, that is consistent with that view. I claim that it cannot be done.

5   LOOKING TO THE FUTURE

Although claims that international trade has had a severe adverse impact on wages in advanced countries generally melt away when seriously confronted with data, many people – including economists – find it difficult to shake the suspicion that whatever may have happened so far, "we ain't seen nothing yet." After all, are there not now billions of extremely low-paid workers available to produce for the world market? How can Japan and the West continue to pay high wages when there are Asians, Latin Americans, and even Africans able and willing to do the work for far less money?

This argument sounds compelling; yet it is misguided, for several reasons.

First, there is the basic fallacy – which even trained economists easily fall into – of thinking of world demand as if it were a given, and therefore imagining that adding new players to the world market necessarily hurts those already there. In fact, if billions of people are entering the global market place, they will increase world demand by just as much as they increase world supply. There is no presumption that the effect will be to reduce the aggregate incomes of advance nations; if anything, the presumption runs the other way.

Second, if one is worried about the effect of international trade on the income distribution within advanced countries, it is important to remember what may seem a narrow technical point: that Stolper–Samuelson effects apply only if a country is non-specialized. If there comes a point at which a country no longer produces traded goods that use unskilled labor intensively – a point at which all unskilled workers are employed either in producing goods that are either skill-intensive or non-traded – then further changes in the relative price of traded goods will not affect relative wages. It is arguable that the United States is already fairly close to that point: labor-intensive goods like apparel already employ fairly few workers. And for what it is worth, semi-realistic CGE models, like that in Krugman (1995a), suggest that there are fairly narrow limits on the possible range of trade-induced changes in relative wages.

The most important point to realize, however, is that the vision of billions of low-wage workers descending on the world market *gets the metaphor wrong*. The images seem to be one in which 4 billion Martians have suddenly landed on Earth, desperate for work. But the workers in developing countries have not suddenly arrived from someplace else: they have been there all along. (OK, some of them were in effect locked up inside Maoist China; but they were released some time ago.) What made them invisible to the world market was that despite their numbers, they did not have much economic weight because they had low productivity.[2] Now their productivity is rising – but then why should we expect their wages to stay low? It is easy to get awed by the sheer size of the developing world – to find it unbelievable that so many people could actually be paid a decent wage. But economic analysis should not be based on what the evolutionist Richard Dawkins calls "the argument from personal incredulity." We should not abandon our models when they conflict with our gut feelings, still less when they contradict what influential people find convenient to believe. On the contrary, it is precisely when the conclusions from our models surprise us, and irritate powerful people, that economic theory is most useful.

Notes

1 One way to make this point is to compare the growth rate of real GDP with that of "command GDP," which divides exports by the *import* deflator, and therefore measures the rate of growth of purchasing power rather than output. The two rates are nearly identical.

2 It is instructive in this context to consider the recent work of Trefler (1993), who shows that trade patterns are best explained by a model in which labor and other factors are allowed to differ in their productivity across countries. In that case, however, the huge international differences we see in raw factor abundances become far smaller differences in effective capital–labor ratios.

References

Bhagwati, J. and Ramaswami, V. K. (1963). "Domestic distortions, tariffs, and the theory of optimum subsidy." *Journal of Political Economy*, 71 (February).

Brecher, R. (1974). "Optimal commercial policy for a minimum-wage economy." *Journal of International Economics*, 4: 139–49.

Deardorff, A. and Hakura, D. (1994). "Trade and wages – what are the questions?" In Bhagwati, J. and Kosters, M. (eds.), *Trade and Wages: Levelling Wages Down?* Washington, DC: American Enterprise Institute.

, Hicks, J. R. (1953). "The long-run dollar problem." *Oxford Economic Papers*, 2: 117–35.

Johnson, H. G. (1955). "Economic expansion and international trade." *Manchester School of Social and Economic Studies*, 23: 95–112.

  (1965). "Optimal trade intervention in the presence of domestic distortions." In Caves, R. *et al.* (eds.), *Trade, Growth, and the Balance of Payments*. New York: Rand McNally.

Krugman, P. (1995a). "Domestic distortions and the deindustrialization hypothesis." Mimeo, Stanford University.

  (1995b). "Growing world trade: causes and consequences." *Brookings Papers on Economic Activity*, 1: 327–62.

Lawrence, R. (1995). 'Single World, Divided Nations? International Trade and OECD Labor Markets'. Mimeo, OECD.

Trefler, D. (1963). "International factor price differences: Leontief was right!" *Journal of Political Economy*, 101: 961–87.

CHAPTER 2

Politics and trade policy

Elhanan Helpman

1   INTRODUCTION

Economists have devoted much effort to the study of *efficiency* properties of
trade policies. These efforts have produced a coherent body of literature
that describes how trade policy instruments – such as tariffs, export
subsidies, quotas, or voluntary export restraints – affect economies that
trade with each other. And they produced empirical models that have been
extensively used to evaluate the efficiency losses from trade policies, on the
one hand, and prospective gains from trade reforms, on the other. Recent
examples include quantitative studies of the single-market program in
Europe (e.g., Flam (1992)) and of NAFTA (e.g., Garber (1993)).

At the same time another strand of the literature has examined possible
explanations for prevailing trade policies. Here efficiency considerations
have not played center stage. Many policies – such as quotas and voluntary
export restraints – impose large burdens on society. Therefore research
looked for objectives of the policymakers other than overall efficiency in
order to explain them. This literature emphasizes distributional considerations. It views trade policy as a device for income transfers to preferred
groups in society. And it explains the desire of a policymaker to engage in
this sort of costly transfer by means of political arguments in her objective
function (see Hillman (1989) for a review).

Political economy explanations of trade policies are important, because
they help to understand the structure of protection as well as major public
policy debates. It would be impossible, in fact, to understand such debates
without paying close attention to political considerations. Recent examples
include the debate about NAFTA in the USA, in which special interests –
such as the sugar industry – were able to effectively voice their concerns in
Congress. Or the debate about the Uruguay round in France, that brought
farmers out into the streets. Quite often countries design their trade policies

in a way that yields to pressure from special interest groups, and trade negotiations at the international arena respond similarly.

As important as the political economy of trade policy seems to be, however, there exists no coherent theory to explain it. Models that underline some features of the policy formation process have been designed by economists and political scientists. But they do not add up as yet to a coherent theory. One reason for this state of affairs is that there exists no agreed-upon theory of domestic politics. This reflects partly the fact that there are many channels through which residents convey their desires to policymakers, and these ways differ across issues and across concerned groups in society. Moreover, political institutions vary across countries and they affect the ways in which influence works through the system. As a result there are potentially many modes of interaction that require close scrutiny. Special interest politics are prevalent, however, and economists need to understand these processes in order to better predict policy outcomes and to better design feasible policy options.

My purpose is to describe in this chapter a number of political economy approaches that have been developed to explain trade policies. I present these approaches in section 2, using a unified framework that helps to identify the key differences among them. These comparisons revolve around tariff formulas that are predicted by the political equilibria. A typical formula explains cross-sectoral variations in rates of protection as well as differences in average rates of protection across countries. Section 3 then reviews a set of results that emerge from a new approach to the interaction of international economic relations with domestic politics. Importantly, there are two-way interactions in such systems, as pointed out by Putnam (1988). They link the formation of trade policies in the international arena with the activities of domestic special interest groups. The use of a framework of this sort is essential for a proper analysis of a host of important problems, such as negotiations about tariff levels or the formation of free trade areas. Recent studies have developed suitable tools for this purpose, as I will argue in section 3.

2   POLITICAL ECONOMY APPROACHES

I briefly describe in this section some of the leading political economy approaches to the formation of trade policies.

2.1   Direct democracy

Wolfgang Mayer (1984) proposed to view trade policy as the outcome of majority voting over tariff levels. There are, of course, very few countries in which direct democracy is applied to a broad range of issues, Switzerland being the prime example. Nevertheless, there exists a view that in representative democracies policy outcomes are reasonably close to what is supported by a majority of the voters. In such cases the simple analysis of majority voting serves as a good approximation. There remain, of course, the difficulties involved in voting over multi-dimensional issues, that have not yet been resolved (see Shepsle (1990)). And these difficulties apply to trade policies, which are often multi-dimensional in character. Witness, for example, the various rounds of trade liberalization under the auspices of the GATT (the Uruguay round being the last one), in which the removal of many tariffs and other trade barriers were negotiated simultaneously. Nevertheless, we may be able to learn something useful from the direct democracy approach.

The essence of Mayer's approach is quite simple. Suppose that a country has to decide the level of a particular tariff rate. We shall denote by τ_i one plus the tariff rate on product i.[1] Then we can derive a reduced-form indirect utility function for each voter j, $\hat{v}_i(\tau_i, \gamma^j)$, where γ^j is a vector of the voter's characteristics. These characteristics may include his endowment (such as his skills, his ownership of shares in companies) or parameters describing his preference for consumption. Naturally, the shape of $\hat{v}_i(\cdot)$ depends on various details of the economy's structure. If individual j was asked to choose the tariff level that he prefers most, he would choose τ_i that maximizes $\hat{v}_i(\tau_i, \gamma^j)$.[2] Let $\hat{\tau}_i(\gamma^j)$ describe the solution to this problem as a function of the individual's characteristics. The assumption that $\hat{\tau}_i(\cdot)$ is a function means that individual preferences over tariff rates are single peaked. Under these circumstances voting over pairs of alternative tariff rates leads to the adoption of τ_i^m, which is most preferred by the median voter. Namely, it is the tariff rate that has the property that the number of voters that prefer a higher rate equals the number of voters that prefer a lower rate. As a result no other tariff obtains more votes in a competition with τ_i^m.

Mayer studied properties of the equilibrium rate of protection τ_i^m in a Heckscher–Ohlin type two-sector two-factor economy, in which all individuals have the same homothetic preferences, every sector produces a homogeneous product under constant returns to scale, and people differ in their relative endowment of the two factors. Taking labor and capital to be the two factors, γ^j represents the capital–labor ratio owned by individual j. Then, assuming that tariff revenue is redistributed to the public in proportion to income, he was able to derive the most preferred tariff rate of the median voter and to study its characteristics.

As an example of tariffs determined by direct voting, I now develop a model that will also be used for future purposes. Consider an economy with a continuum of individuals. Each individual has the utility function

$$u(c) = c_0 + \sum_{i=1}^{n} u_i(c_i), \tag{1}$$

where c_i is consumption of product i and $u_i(\cdot)$ is an increasing concave function. Population size equals one.

Let there be labor and a sector-specific input in each sector i. Aggregate labor supply is normalized to equal one. Individual j owns the fraction γ_L^j of labor.[3] The numeraire good, indexed 0, is produced only with labor, using one unit of labor per unit output. Each one of the remaining goods is produced with labor and the sector-specific input. We shall measure all prices in terms of the numeraire. Then the wage rate equals one and the reward to the sector-specific input in sector i, $\Pi_i(p_i)$, is an increasing function of the producer price of product i, p_i. Now normalize all foreign prices to equal one. Then $p_i = \tau_i$. Next let γ_i^j represent the fraction of the sector-i specific input owned by individual j.[4] Finally, suppose that the government redistributes tariff revenue in a lump-sum fashion and equally to every individual. It then follows that the reduced-form indirect utility function is given by

$$\hat{v}(\tau, \gamma^j) = \gamma_L^j + \sum_{i=1}^{n} (\tau_i - 1)M_i(\tau_i) + \sum_{i=1}^{n} \gamma_i^j \Pi_i(\tau_i) + \sum_{i=1}^{n} S_i(\tau_i), \tag{2}$$

where $M_i(\tau_i)$ represents aggregate imports of product i.[5] The first term on the right-hand side represent labor income. The second term represents income from the government's transfer and the third term represents income from the ownership of sector-specific inputs. The last term represents consumer surplus.

It is evident from (2) that individual j's preference for the tariff rate in sector i depends only on his fraction of ownership of the sector-specific input in that sector. This preference function can be represented by $\hat{v}_i(\tau_i, \gamma_i^j) = (\tau_i - 1)M_i(\tau_i) + \gamma_i^j \Pi_i(\tau_i) + S_i(\tau_i)$.[6]   As   a   result   we   have $\partial \hat{v}_i(\tau_i, \gamma_i^j)/\partial \tau_i = (\tau_i - 1)M_i'(\tau_i) + (\gamma_i^j - 1)X_i(\tau_i)$, where $X_i = \Pi_i'$ represents the output level in sector i. Since imports decline with the tariff, it follows that individuals with above-average ownership of the sector-specific input vote for a tariff while individuals with below-average ownership vote for an import subsidy.[7] And an individual's most preferred tariff is higher the larger his ownership share of the sector-specific input. It follows that voting on the tariff level in sector i leads to a tariff rate that is most preferred by the individual with the median value of γ_i^j. The larger this median value γ_i^m, the higher the resulting tariff rate. When the median voter's most-preferred tariff rate is not on the boundary of the feasible set, it can be calculated from the condition $\partial \hat{v}_i(\tau_i, \gamma_i^m)/\partial \tau_i = 0$, which yields the following formula for the equilibrium tariff[8]

$$\tau_i - 1 = (\gamma_i^m - 1)\frac{X_i}{(-M_i')}. \tag{3}$$

The tariff rate is higher when the median voter's share of ownership of the sector-specific input is higher, and it also is higher the larger the sector in terms of output and the smaller the slope of the import demand function. Larger output levels imply higher stakes for the industry, which makes it more profitable to have a high tariff (as long as γ_i^m is above average), while the less elastic the import demand function, the lower the excess burden of a tariff. Part of this excess burden is born by the median voter. Therefore he prefers a higher tariff rate the lower this marginal cost. This is, of course, a standard consideration in Ramsey pricing.

One last point should be noted concerning equilibrium tariff rates in a direct democracy. My discussion assumed that the ownership of the sector-specific inputs is thinly dispersed in the population. Occasionally (or perhaps even often) this is not the case. So consider the other extreme case, in which, say, the ownership of the sector-specific input in sector k is highly concentrated, up to the point that it is owned by a negligible fraction of the population. Under these circumstances a member of this minority group, who owns a finite amount of the sector-specific input, wants the tariff rate to be as high as possible. On the other hand, an individual who has no ownership of this input whatsoever wants an import subsidy. Since the latter type of people represent almost 100 percent of the voters, the median voter most prefers to subsidize imports. More generally, it is clear from this example that under majority voting we should not observe tariffs but rather import subsidies in sectors with a highly concentrated ownership. If anything, the opposite seems to be true. As argued by Olsen (1965), however, in sectors with a highly concentrated ownership it is relatively easy to overcome the free-rider problem and to form pressure groups whose purpose it is to protect sector-specific incomes. Therefore we need to consider the role of such organizations in the shaping of trade policies, to which we will turn at a later stage.

2.2   Political support function

An alternative approach was proposed by Hillman (1982). Borrowing from the theory of economic regulation, as developed by Stigler (1971) and Peltzman (1976), he suggested that we could view the choice of a tariff rate as the solution to an optimizing problem in which the government trades off political support from industry interest against the dissatisfaction of consumers. Industry interests provide more support the higher the industry's profits, while the government gains more support from consumers the lower the consumer price. In the event, by raising domestic prices higher tariffs bring about more support from industry interests – whose profits rise – and less support from consumers – whose real income declines. And the government chooses a tariff level that maximizes aggregate support.

Hillman postulated a reduced-form aggregate support function for a tariff in sector i, $P_i[\Pi_i(p_i) - \Pi_i(p_i^*), p_i - p_i^*]$, in which the first argument represents the gain in profits from a trade policy that raises the domestic price from the free-trade price p_i^* to p_i, while the second term represents the loss in consumer welfare that results from the same price increase. Political support rises in the first argument, and it declines in the second argument for $p_i^* < p_i$. Hillman used this approach to study the trade policy response to a declining foreign price. In particular, he showed that under mild assumptions a decline in the foreign price leads to higher domestic protection, but the resulting tariff increase does not fully compensate for the fall in the foreign price. As a result, the decline in the foreign price leads to a decline in the domestic price as well, but to a lesser degree.

I will now reformulate the political-support-function approach in order to derive a formula for equilibrium tariff rates that is comparable with (3). For this purpose suppose that the economic structure is the same as in section 2.1. In this event we can use (2) to calculate aggregate welfare, by integrating the individual welfare functions over the entire population. The result is

$$W(\tau) = 1 + \sum_{i=1}^{n} (\tau_i - 1)M_i(\tau_i) + \sum_{i=1}^{n} \Pi_i(\tau_i) + \sum_{i=1}^{n} S_i(\tau_i). \qquad (4)$$

Next, suppose that the government's political support for a policy is an increasing function of the income gains of sector-specific inputs and of the aggregate welfare gain. For simplicity assume that this function is linear;[9] i.e.

$$\hat{P}(\tau) = \sum_{i=1}^{n} \frac{1}{a_{pi}} [\Pi_i(\tau_i) - \Pi_i(1)] + [W(\tau) - W(1, 1, \ldots, 1)]. \qquad (5)$$

The parameter a_{pi} represents the marginal rate of substitution in the government's political support function between aggregate welfare and profits of special interests in sector i. These parameters are allowed to vary across sectors. The larger a_{pi}, the more willing is the government to give up profits of sector-i interests in exchange for aggregate welfare. The government chooses rates of protection to maximize its political support, as measured by $\hat{P}(\tau)$. Using (4) and (5), an interior solution to this maximization problem implies the following tariff rates[10]

$$\tau_i - 1 = \frac{1}{a_{pi}} \frac{X_i}{(-M_i')}. \tag{6}$$

Comparing this formula with (3), we see that they are the same, except for the fact that the parameter $1/a_{pi}$ replaces $(\gamma_i^m - 1)$. Namely, in both cases the tariff is higher the larger the sector's output level and the flatter the import demand function. Importantly, however, while the political-support function approach implies that each sector in which special interests count (i.e., in which a_{pi} is finite) will be protected and no sector will be afforded negative protection, direct voting over tariff rates brings about positive protection in sectors with median ownership of sector-specific inputs larger than the average, but negative protection in sectors in which median ownership of sector-specific inputs falls short of the average. It follows that in a direct democracy the distribution of ownership has an important effect on the structure of protection, while in a representative democracy – in which the government evaluates a political-support function in its design of trade policy – the political-support function's marginal rates of substitution between the well being of consumers and sectoral interests importantly affect the structure of protection. Evidently, building on the political-support function's approach, a better understanding of the forces that shape the structure of protection requires some insights on what determines the marginal rates of substitution between aggregate welfare and special interest profits. Unfortunately, the theory is not particularly helpful on this critical point.

2.3   Tariff-formation function

The political-support function summarizes a tradeoff between the support that a government obtains from special interests, on the one hand, and the support of consumers, on the other. Under this approach, a government designs its trade policy so as to balance the conflict between these opposing groups in a way that serves it best. Considerations of this sort are, of course, quite common in representative democracies, and even in totalitarian regimes rulers tend to listen to the concerns of the general public. But competition for preferential treatment very often takes on an active form, rather than the passive form envisioned in the political support function approach. Lobbying for the protection of real incomes is prevalent, and many interest groups participate in this process.

To deal with the active seeking of protection of real incomes, Findlay and Wellisz (1982) proposed the use of tariff-formation functions. A function of this sort describes the level of protection afforded to an industry as depending on the amount of resources devoted to lobbying by a group of supporters of protection, on the one hand, and by the lobbying efforts of opposers, on the other. According to this view, the level of protection reflects the outcome of a contest between interest groups on the opposing sides of the issue.[11] More precisely, let $T_i(C_i^S, C_i^O)$ describe the tariff formation function in sector i, where C_i^S represents the lobbying expenditure of the pro-protectionist interest group and C_i^O represents the lobbying expenditure of the antiprotectionist interest group. The resulting rate of protection is higher the larger the expenditure of the former group and the lower the expenditure of the latter. In the political equilibrium $\tau_i = T_i(C_i^S, C_i^O)$.

In order to derive the equilibrium level of protection, we need to describe the incentives of the various interest groups. So suppose that the benefits of the pro-protectionist lobby are given by the increasing function $W_i^S(\tau_i)$ while the benefits of the opposition are given by the declining function $W_i^O(\tau_i)$, both measured in terms of numeraire income. Then the lobbying expenditure levels are determined as the Nash equilibrium of a non-cooperative game in which each interest group chooses its lobbying expenditure so as to maximize net benefits, which are $W_i^S[T_i(C_i^S, C_i^O)] - C_i^S$ for the pro-protectionist lobby and $W_i^O[T_i(C_i^S, C_i^O)] - C_i^O$ for its rival. Findlay and Wellisz developed a two-sector specific-factor model, in which the owners of the specific factor in the import-competing industry lobby for import protection while the owners of the specific factor in the exporting industry oppose protection. As is well known, in an economy of this type the former group gains from protection while the latter group loses (see Jones (1971)), therefore they naturally take the opposite sides of the protection issue. In this framework Findlay and Wellisz have investigated the determinants of the equilibrium rate of protection. Given that the results depend on the shape of the tariff formation function, however, and the fact that their theory has little to say about this shape, they were unable to derive sharp predictions.

In order to relate this approach to my previous discussion, let us consider a somewhat different variant of the tariff formation model. Suppose that the economy is the same as in section 2.1. Also suppose that the owners of the sector-i specific factor form an interest group that lobbies for protection. The purpose of the lobby is to maximize the individuals' joint welfare. Joint welfare maximization is suitable whenever the interest group can resolve its internal conflicts, such as ensuring the participation of all factor owners and the distribution of the burden of the lobbying expenses among them. If these owners constitute a fraction α_i of the population, then the joint welfare that they derive from sector i can be represented by (see (2)):[12]

$$W_i^S(\tau_i) = \Pi_i(\tau_i) + \alpha_i[(\tau_i - 1)M_i(\tau_i) + S_i(\tau_i)].$$

The first term on the right-hand side represents income of the sector-specific input while the second term describes the share of the lobby in the tariff rebate and in consumer surplus. So this describes the benefit function of the protectionist lobby. Marginal benefits of protection equal $W_i^{S'} = (1 - \alpha_i)X_i + \alpha_i(\tau_i - 1)M'_i$, which are positive for values of τ_i that are not too large.

Next suppose that there exists a lobby that opposes protection, which consists of all the other individuals in the economy.[13] The joint welfare that this group derives from a given tariff level equals

$$W_i^O(\tau_i) = (1 - \alpha_i)[(\tau_i - 1)M_i(\tau_i) + S_i(\tau_i)].$$

Namely, they obtain a fraction $1 - \alpha_i$ of the tariff rebate and the same fraction of consumer surplus. To this group the marginal benefit of protection equals $W_i^{O'} = (1 - \alpha_i)[-X_i + (\tau_i - 1)M'_i]$, which is negative for positive rates of protection (i.e., for $\tau_i > 1$).

Finally, consider an interior equilibrium to the non-cooperative game between the interest groups. The first-order conditions for the choice of lobbying expenditures that maximize net benefits are given by $[(1 - \alpha_i)X_i + \alpha_i(\tau_i - 1)M'_i]T_{is} = 1$ for the protectionist lobby and by $(1 - \alpha_i)[-X_i + (\tau_i - 1)M'_i]T_{io} = 1$ for its rival. T_{is} and T_{io} represent partial derivatives of the tariff formation function with respect to the spending levels of the pro-protectionist lobby and the antiprotectionist lobby, respectively. In the first condition, the left-hand side represents the marginal benefit of an additional dollar spent to promote protection, which consists of the product of the marginal benefit of protection and the marginal gain in protection from a dollar of spending. The right-hand side represents the marginal cost. A pro-protectionist lobby chooses its spending level so as to balance costs and benefits at the margin. A similar interpretation can be given to the second condition, which applies to the interest group that opposes protection. Together these conditions yield

$$\tau_i - 1 = \frac{(1 - \alpha_i)(b_i - 1)}{\alpha_i b_i + (1 - \alpha_i)} \frac{X_i}{(-M'_i)}, \tag{7}$$

where $b_i = -T_{is}/T_{io} > 0$ represents the marginal rate of substitution between the spending levels on lobbying in the tariff-formation function.[14] When $b_i > 1$, a marginal dollar of spending on lobbying by·the pro-protectionist interest group raises the tariff by more than it declines as a result of an extra dollar of spending on lobbying by the antiprotectionist interest group. We see from this equation that the sector is protected if and only if $b_i > 1$. And if a marginal lobbying dollar of one interest group is as effective as a marginal lobbying dollar of the other interest group, then there is free trade. Importantly, whenever the sector is protected, the rate of protection is higher the more effective is a lobbying dollar of the pro-protectionist interest group relative to a lobbying dollar of the antiprotectionist interest group, and the smaller the fraction of people that belong to the former group. The last result implies that the more highly concentrated is the ownership of a sector-specific factor, the higher will be the rate of protection afforded to this sector. This result – which is just the opposite from the prediction of the direct voting model – stems from the fact that the fewer the owners of the sector-specific input, the less account does the lobby take of the excess burden produced by protection. In the extreme case, when the entire population has a stake in the sector, free trade prevails, because the lobby internalizes all welfare considerations. Finally, as in the previously discussed cases, the rate of protection is higher the larger the output level and the flatter the import demand function.

Formula (7) results partly from the assumption that the opposition to the pro-protectionist lobby consists of all the other individuals in the economy. This is obviously not the typical case. The important point is, however, that the welfare of at least some fraction of the general public counts in the design of a trade policy. Those members of society may be represented by an organized group or by the government itself. In the latter case the government's motivation may be the desire to do good or just cool political calculus. Indeed, Feenstra and Bhagwati (1982) have used a tariff formation function with a government that cares about welfare of the general public. Under these circumstances the desire to minimize excess burden plays an important role.

2.4   Electoral competition

Unlike most other approaches to the politics of trade policy, Magee, Brock, and Young (MBY) (1989) advocate an emphasis on electoral competition.[15] According to this view interest groups give contributions to political parties and candidates in order to improve their chances of being elected. This contrasts with the tariff-formation function approach in which contributions influence policy choices. For this reason MBY construct a model in which two parties compete in an election. Each one commits to a policy *before* the choice of contributions by special interests. As a result, the choice of contributions does not affect policy choices and their only role is to improve the likelihood of one or the other party being elected. Anticipating the electoral motive in campaign giving, however, the parties – which are interested in maximizing their electoral prospects at the polls – choose policies that correctly anticipate future campaign contributions.

Somewhat more formally, suppose that there are two political parties and two lobbies. Each lobby is aligned with one part. In MBY there is a pro-capital party with which the lobby of capital owners is aligned and a pro-labor party with which labor is aligned. Other alignments are of course possible, depending on context. For present purposes let us be agnostic about the precise interpretation of these allegiances, and let us have party A and party B, and lobby 1 and lobby 2. Lobby 1 is aligned with party A while lobby 2 is aligned with party B. Party A gets elected with probability $q\left(\sum_{i=1}^{2} C_i^A, \sum_{i=1}^{2} C_i^B, \tau^A, \tau^B\right)$, where C_i^K stands for the contribution of lobby i to the political campaign of party K and τ^K is the trade policy of party K. This probability is higher the more contributions party A amasses, the less contributions party B amasses, the less distortive is the trade policy of party A and the more distortive is the trade policy of party B.

In the second stage of the game, after the parties have committed to their trade policies, the lobbies decide on campaign contributions. Let $W_i(\tau)$ be the benefit function of lobby i when the trade policy is τ. Then this lobby expects the benefit level $W_i(\tau^A)$ with probability $q(\cdot)$ and the benefit $W_i(\tau^B)$ with probability $1 - q(\cdot)$. Lobbies choose their contributions non-cooperatively. Therefore, contributions are a Nash equilibrium of the game in which each lobby maximizes its expected net benefit. Namely, the best response of lobby i to the contribution levels of the other lobby is given by the solution to the following problem

$$\max_{C_i^A \geq 0, C_i^B \geq 0} q\left(\sum_{i=1}^{2} C_i^A, \sum_{i=1}^{2} C_i^B, \tau^A, \tau^B\right) W_i(\tau^A)$$

$$+ \left[1 - q\left(\sum_{i=1}^{2} C_i^A, \sum_{i=1}^{2} C_i^B, \tau^A, \tau^B\right)\right] W_i(\tau^B) - \sum_{K=A,B} C_i^K.$$

In the resulting Nash equilibrium the contribution levels are functions of the tax policies. Substituting these functions into $q(\cdot)$ yields a reduced-form probability function that depends only on the trade policies, $\tilde{q}(\tau^A, \tau^B)$. The function $\tilde{q}(\cdot)$ anticipates the contribution game that will be played by the lobbies for each policy choice by the parties. In the first stage the parties play a non-cooperative game. Each one chooses its policy so as to maximize its probability of winning the election. Therefore party A chooses τ^A so as to maximize $\tilde{q}(\tau^A, \tau^B)$ while party B chooses τ^B so as to maximize $1 - \tilde{q}(\tau^A, \tau^B)$. The Nash equilibrium of this game identifies the equilibrium levels of the rates of protection.

Mayer and Li (1994) have re-examined the MBY analysis, using probabilistic voting theory as the microfoundations. Probabilistic voting allows for preferences of voters that depend on economic policies as well as on other attributes of political parties, such as their positions on social issues or political ideology. Preferences over non-economic issues are diverse and parties know only their distribution in the voting population (see Coughlin (1992)). Mayer and Li also assume that voters are not sure about the economic policy stance of the parties, and that each party can use campaign contributions in order to clarify its position. Each party chooses its policy so as to maximize the probability of being elected.

Their analysis supports some of MBY's conclusions, but not all. For example it supports the result that a lobby will contribute to at most one political party; i.e., lobbies specialize in campaign giving. Unfortunately, this result does not fare well on empirical grounds; it is quite common in parliamentary systems for lobbies to contribute to the two major political parties (e.g., Israel). On the other hand, Mayer and Li find that both lobbies may end up contributing to the same political party, while MBY *assume* that each lobby is aligned with one party only. My conclusion from the Mayer–Li analysis is that it is indeed important to develop more detailed models in order to deal satisfactorily with the role of the electoral motive for campaign contributions in the political economy of trade policies. More about this in the next section.

2.5   Influence-driven contributions

Political contributions that influence election outcomes are a desirable feature of trade policy models. They seem to emphasize, however, a motive for contributions that is at most secondary. To be sure, from the point of view of politicians and their political parties the total amount of contributions serve an important role in enhancing their chances of being elected or re-elected. But this does not mean that the individual contributors view the improved chance of a candidate as a major consideration in their giving. For one thing, there typically exist many contributions with the contribution of each one being small relative to the total. This is particularly true in countries with legal limits on contributions, but not only in countries of this type. As a result, each contribution has a marginal effect on the election outcome. Under these circumstances it is more likely that contributions are designed to influence the choice of policy than to influence election outcomes. Namely, having a choice between an emphasis on the electoral motive for contributions (as in MBY) and an influence motive, the latter seems to be more attractive on theoretical grounds. This point is made explicit in the detailed model of electoral competition and special interest politics by Grossman and Helpman (1996), in which they show that with a large number of organized interest groups the electoral motive for campaign contributions is negligible.[16]

At the same time the empirical literature also supports the view that the influence motive is more prominent. For example, Magelby and Nelson (1990) report that: (a) Political action committees (PACs) in the US gave more than three quarters of their total contributions in the 1988 Congressional campaign to incumbent candidates. (b) Not counting elections for open seats, incumbents receive over six times as much as challengers. (c) Over 60 percent of the campaign contributions by PACs occurred in the early part of the election cycle, often before a challenger had even been identified. (d) PACs switch their contributions to the winner even if they supported the loser to begin with. In addition, in parliamentary democracies, interest groups often contribute simultaneously to more than one major political party.

Relying on these considerations, Grossman and Helpman (1994) have developed a theory that puts the influence motive at the heart of campaign contributions. According to this approach, interest groups move first, offering politicians campaign contributions that depend on their policy stance. Special interests seek to maximize the well being of their members. Then the politicians choose policy stances, knowing how their contributions depend on the selected polices. Politicians seek to maximize a political objective function that depends on contributions and on the well being of the general public.[17]

A political objective function that depends on contributions and the well being of voters is consistent with electoral competition. Grossman and Helpman (1996) have shown that it emerges in a political system in which special interests design contributions in the above described way, and two parties compete for seats in parliament.[18]

So suppose again that the economy is the same as in section 2.1, but that the policymaker's objective function is $C + aW$, where C stands for campaign contributions that he amasses, W represents aggregate welfare (or per capita welfare), and a is a parameter that represents the marginal rate of substitution between welfare and contributions. The larger a, the more weight is placed on the well being of voters relative to contributions.[19] Contributions depend on the policy choice and so does welfare, and the policymaker maximizes this political objective function.

Now consider the special interest groups. Suppose that in some subset of sectors, denoted by $\mathscr{L} \subset \{1, 2, \ldots, n\}$, the owners of the sector-specific inputs form lobby groups. Let α_i represent (as before) the fraction of people who own the input in sector i. Also assume that each person owns at most one type of sector-specific input. Then the aggregate well being of the individuals that belong to lobby i is given by

$$W_i(\tau) = l_i + \Pi_i(\tau_i) + \alpha_i \sum_{j=1}^{n} [(\tau_j - 1)M_j(\tau_j) + S_j(\tau_j)]. \tag{8}$$

The first term on the right-hand side represents their share in labor supply, the second term represents their income from the sector-specific factor, and the last term represents their share in tariff rebates and in consumer surplus.[20] The lobby's purpose is to maximize $W_i(\tau) - C_i$, where $C_i \geq 0$ is the contribution of lobby i. How should the lobby design its contributions?

Interest group i takes the contribution functions $C_j(\tau)$ of all the other interest groups $j \neq i$ as given. Therefore it knows that if it does not lobby, the policymaker will attain the political welfare $G_{-i} = \max_\tau[\Sigma_{j \neq i}C_j(\tau) + aW(\tau)]$; i.e., the policymaker will choose a policy vector τ that maximizes its objective function, disregarding lobby i's preferences.[21] It follows that if lobby i wishes to affect the policy outcome, it needs to offer a contribution function that induces a policy change and provides the policymaker with at least G_{-i}. Namely, its contribution function has to satisfy

$$C_i(\tau) \geq G_{-i} - \left[\sum_{j \neq i} C_j(\tau) + aW(\tau) \right] \tag{9}$$

in order to implement τ. This is the standard participation constraint in principal-agent problems. Naturally, the interest group has no desire to give the policymaker more than necessary in order to induce a policy change. Therefore it choose a contribution function that satisfies (9) with equality at the equilibrium point. The policy vector that maximizes the lobby's objective function $W_i(\tau) - C_i$ is then

$$\tau^i \in \arg\max_\tau W_i(\tau) + \left[\sum_{j \neq i} C_j(\tau) + aW(\tau) \right].$$

The contribution function is designed to *implement* this policy vector, and there typically exist many contribution functions that do it. Although lobby i is indifferent as to which contribution function it uses in order to implement this policy vector, its choice may affect the decision problems of other lobbies. Therefore there often exist many combinations of contribution functions that implement the equilibrium policy vector as well as equilibria with different policy vectors (see Bernheim and Whinston (1986)). An equilibrium consists of feasible contribution functions $\{C_j^o(\cdot)\}_{j \in \mathscr{L}}$ and a policy vector τ^o such that: (a) $\tau^o \in \arg\max_\tau W_i(\tau) + [\Sigma_{j \neq i}C_j^o(\tau) + aW(\tau)]$ for all $i \in \mathscr{L}$; (b) $C_j^o(\cdot)$ implements τ^o for all $j \in \mathscr{L}$; and (c) $\Sigma_{j \in \mathscr{L}}C_j^o(\tau^o) + aW(\tau^o) = G_{-i}$ for all $i \in \mathscr{L}$.

To illustrate some of the relevant considerations, first suppose that there is only one organized interest group, say in sector i. Then the equilibrium policy vector maximizes $W_i(\tau) + aW(\tau)$. Using (4) and (8) this implies

$$\tau_j - 1 = \frac{I_j - \alpha_i}{a + \alpha_i} \frac{X_j}{(-M'_j)},$$

where I_j equals one for $j = i$ and zero otherwise. First note that only sector i, which is represented by an organized interest group, is protected. All other sectors are afforded negative protection. The reason is that the special interest group lobbies the policymaker for high prices in sector i, in which it is a net seller, and for low prices in all other sectors, in which it is a net buyer. The rate of protection in sector i is higher the more concentrated is the ownership of the sector-specific factor in that sector (because the less the lobby cares then about excess burden), the less weight the policymaker places on welfare relative to contributions (because the cheaper it is then to influence the policymaker with contributions), the larger the output level of the sector (because it raises the benefit of the influence motive), and the flatter the import demand function (because the lower is then the excess burden imposed on society, about which the policymaker cares). Observe that the effects of output and slope of the import demand function are the same as in the formulas that we derived from the direct democracy approach, the political support function approach, and the tariff formation function approach. In addition, the effect of the degree of concentration of ownership is similar to the tariff formation function approach, while the role of the marginal rate of substitution between welfare and contributions plays a similar role to the marginal rate of substitution between welfare and profits in the political support function approach. These analogies are not accidental. I have purposely constructed variants of the other approaches that enable us to draw these analogies with the influence–motive approach.

What happens when there is more than one organized interest group? Grossman and Helpman (1994) have shown that if we restrict the contribution functions to be differentiable around the equilibrium vector τ^o, then they have to be locally truthful; i.e., the gradient of $C_i^o(\cdot)$ has to equal the gradient of $W_i(\cdot)$ at τ^o. This leads to the tariff formula

$$\tau_j - 1 = \frac{I_j - \alpha_{\mathscr{L}}}{a + \alpha_{\mathscr{L}}} \frac{X_j}{(-M'_j)}, \tag{10}$$

where $\alpha_{\mathscr{L}} = \Sigma_{j \in \mathscr{L}} \alpha_j$ stands for the fraction of people that own sector-specific inputs. The difference between this formula and the previous one, which was derived for the case in which only one sector had an organized lobby, is the replacement of α_i with $\alpha_{\mathscr{L}}$. Therefore the interpretation remains very much the same. Importantly, now all sectors with organized pressure groups enjoy protection while sectors without lobbies are afforded negative protection. In the extreme case, when all sectors have organized pressure groups and every individual has a stake in some sector, there is free trade. Under these circumstances the lobbies battle for protection of their own interests and neutralize each other in the process. Despite the fact that none of them succeeds in securing higher prices for their clients, they typically spend resources in the process (as can be confirmed from the participation constraint). The role of the contributions in this case is to avoid being harmed by the other lobbies.

Formula (10) describes the resulting rates of protection when each lobby conditions its contributions on the entire tariff vector. In practice this may not be the case. A lobby of the textile industry is obviously very much concerned with the protection of textiles, but its interest in subsidizing imports of tea is much smaller. In the event it may choose to neglect the conditioning of its contributions on the policy toward tea, especially if it is costly to spread the lobbying effort across a large number of policy instruments. A complete model of the political process should include a specification of the lobbying technology, which will then determine relative costs of lobbying. We would then expect pressure groups to focus on their core activity and get involved in the design of other policies only when the direct or indirect benefits from doing so would be large or when the marginal cost of doing so would be small. To see what difference a focused lobbying effort can make, suppose that the lobby of sector i conditions its contributions only on τ_i, for $i \in \mathscr{L}$. In this event there will be free trade in each sector that does not have an organized interest group while in the sectors with pressure groups the rates of protection will be

$$\tau_j - 1 = \frac{1 - \alpha_j}{a + \alpha_j} \frac{X_j}{(-M'_j)} \text{ for } j \in \mathscr{L}.$$

We see that the effects of the sector's size and the slope of its import demand function are the same as in the other formulas. Compared with the case in which pressure groups lobby for all policies, however, there are two major differences. First, now unorganized sectors are not protected while in (10) they are afforded negative protection. Second, now the rate of protection of an organized sector depends on the fraction of voters who have a stake in the industry (i.e., α_i) while in (10) it depends on the fraction of voters who belong to any lobby, not necessarily the lobby of the industry under consideration (i.e., $\alpha_{\mathscr{L}}$). The implication is that now the degree of concentration of ownership in a sector has a direct effect on its rate of protection;

sectors with higher concentration of ownership attain higher protection. This is a desirable feature, as it finds support in reality.

My discussion has focused on trade taxes. It should be clear, however, that the same tools of analysis can be applied to other policy instruments as well.[22] There is a major question, however, concerning the choice of instruments of protection. Why use tariffs rather than output subsidies, for example, when the latter instrument is more desirable on efficiency grounds? Partial answers, based on political economy considerations, are provided by Rodrik (1986) and Grossman and Helpman (1994). But as Rodrik (1995) argues forcefully, the choice of instrument is a central question that has received only limited attention. Since good answers to this question are not yet available, I shall proceed to the next topic.

3   DOUBLE-EDGED DIPLOMACY

We have so far examined situations in which trade policies are pursued by a single country facing constant world prices. This simplification helped us to focus on the internal politics; i.e., the interaction between lobbies and policymakers. Much of trade policy is effected, however, by international constraints. As a result, even when a country sets its own trade policy agenda it has to consider the international repercussions. This is particularly so for large countries. But countries also negotiate trade rules, tariff reductions, voluntary export restraints, free trade areas, and other items. Therefore an analysis of the formation of trade policies is incomplete without paying attention to international interactions.

In view of these remarks it is only appropriate to consider the formation of trade policies in a framework that emphasizes two levels of strategic interaction. On the one hand, governments set trade policies facing each other in the international arena. On the other hand, each government has to deal with its internal political system. This type of two-level interaction produces a simultaneous dependence between the internal and the external politics. A government that, say, negotiates a free trade agreement, is aware in its dealings with the foreign government of the domestic consequences of such an agreement. At the same time, domestic pressure groups that wish to influence the policy outcome are aware of the negotiation process, and of the pros and cons of alternative results. These dependencies are the source of the title of this section, which is taken from the title of a book by Evans, Jacobson, and Putnam (1993). Their book describes a series of case studies, building on the conceptual framework that was developed by Putnam (1988), in order to study situations of this sort. In the rest of this section I describe three examples that build on two-level interactions: non-cooperative tariff setting, negotiated tariffs, and negotiated free trade agreements.

3.1   Trade wars

Grossman and Helpman (1995a) have extended the influence-driven contributions approach to a setting with two countries that set trade policies non-cooperatively. In each country the economy is structured as in section 2.1, pressure groups lobby the domestic policymaker in the manner described in section 2.5, and the policymaker maximizes a political objective function that is linear in contributions and aggregate welfare.[23] Both the lobbies and the policymaker take as given the policy vector of the other country. But they do take into account the fact that domestic policies affect the terms of trade. In particular, denoting the countries by A and B and the international price by π_i, the world market-clearing condition for product i, $\Sigma_{K=A,B} M_i^K(\tau_i^K \pi_i) = 0$, defines implicitly the international price as a function of the trade policies in the two countries. Using this relationship, it is possible to derive a set of contribution schedules and a domestic policy vector that are the political response to the trade policy of the other country. A similar political response can be defined for the other country. An equilibrium consists of contribution schedules and a policy vector for each country, such that the contribution schedules and the policy vector of each country represent a political response to the trade policy of the other country. These equilibrium trade policies satisfy

$$\tau_j^K - 1 = \frac{I_j^K - \alpha_{\mathscr{L}}^K}{a^K + \alpha_{\mathscr{L}}^K} \frac{X_j^K}{(-\pi_j M_j^{K\prime})} + \frac{1}{e_j^L} \text{ for } K, L = A, B \text{ and } L \neq K, \tag{11}$$

where e_j^L is the export supply elasticity of country L in sector j (this elasticity is negative if the country imports the product). This formula has two parts: a political power index that is identical to (10) and a second part that captures terms of trade considerations. The latter, which is well known from Johnson (1953/4) and the now standard optimal-tariff formula, states that a tariff should be higher the less elastic is the foreign export supply function.

The tax rate of country K in sector i, as given by (11), depends on the trade policy in the other country (i.e., it depends on it through the international price π_j). This interdependence has some interesting implications. In particular, for constant elasticity import demand and output supply functions, it implies that a lower weight on welfare relative to contributions in the political objective function of the importing country leads it to take a more aggressive policy stance. As a result its terms of trade improve, its tariff is higher – and sufficiently so as to secure a higher domestic price for the protected industry – and the domestic price in the exporting country is lower. It follows that the same industry in the exporting country receives less protection, or that it is afforded more negative protection. This example demonstrates how a change in the political environment in one country affects the resulting degree of protection in each one of them. Evidently, this type of analysis helps to see how trade policies of one country depend on the political environment in the other.

3.2 Trade talks

In section 3.1 trade taxes were set non-cooperatively. As a result, policymakers inflicted deadweight loss not only on the residents of the two countries, but also on each other. To avoid some of this political damage they can set trade policies cooperatively, as governments often do.

When governments negotiate trade policies they are aware of the political repercussions at home, including those that are related to special interest groups. These repercussions affect their strategy. At the same time campaign contributions of special interest groups are designed differently when they expect the policymakers to negotiate than when they expect them to set policies non-cooperatively. In anticipation of negotiation a lobby designs its contribution schedule so as to tilt the agreement in its favor. The best schedule depends on the institutional framework in which the negotiations take place. As shown in Grossman and Helpman (1995a), however, as long as the negotiating procedure allows policymakers to choose from the outcomes that are efficient from their own perspective, the resulting equilibrium policy vectors satisfy

$$\tau_j^A - \tau_j^B = \frac{I_j^A - \alpha_{\mathscr{L}}^A}{a^A + \alpha_{\mathscr{L}}^A} \frac{X_j^A}{(-\pi_j M_j^{A\prime})} - \frac{I_j^B - \alpha_{\mathscr{L}}^B}{a^B + \alpha_{\mathscr{L}}^B} \frac{X_j^B}{(-\pi_j M_j^{B\prime})}. \qquad (12)$$

This formula determines only the relative values τ_j^A/τ_j^B, which are independent of the negotiation procedure. They ensure that the outcome is on the efficiency frontier of the governments. It is then possible to use the levels of these policy variables, or direct transfers between the governments (as in the Common Agricultural Policy in Europe) to select a particular distribution of gains on the efficient frontier.[24] Which particular distribution the governments choose depends on the negotiation procedure, as well as on a variety of economic and political variables.[25]

Importantly, an industry is protected in country A but not in B if and only if the political power index of this industry is larger in A. Negotiations over trade taxes bring special interests of an industry from the two countries to take opposing sides of the issue; each one of them wants to be protected at the expense of the other. As a result they exert opposing pressures on the negotiating parties and the winner is the lobby with the larger political clout. Thus, for example, if the textile industry is organized in country A but not in B, textiles will obtain positive protection in A and negative protection in B, relative to free trade. Formula (12) also shows that the governments will agree on free trade in textiles (or the same internal price in both countries) if and only if the political power indexes of the textile lobbies are the same in both countries.

Finally, observe that contrary to (11), no export supply elasticities appear in (12). This stems from the fact that in a trade war each government is using trade taxes to better its nation's terms of trade. When the governments negotiate, however, the use of terms of trade as a means of income transfer is politically inefficient. Therefore they do not use them in the cooperative design of trade taxes.

3.3   Free trade agreements

Another important example of negotiated trade policies is provided by free trade agreements (FTAs). Unlike negotiated trade taxes, however, FTAs involve discrete choices (although some continuity is available via the specified terms). The GATT article of agreement XXIV allows countries to form a free trade area in exception to the "most favored nation" clause if the agreement eliminates duties and restrictions on "substantially all trade" among the contracting parties. Grossman and Helpman (1995b) have studied the political economy of such agreements when interest groups that represent various industries express their concerns by means of campaign contributions. Each interest group can voice its support or opposition to an agreement by contributing money in case an FTA forms or in case the FTA is rejected.

First suppose that a country contemplates joining a free trade area with well-specified terms that it cannot affect. Each sector is represented in the debate over the agreement, and the representatives of an industry seek to maximize the return to the sector-specific input. The government seeks to maximize $C + aW$, as in section 2.5. The economic model is the same as in section 2.1. In these circumstances the policymaker has to choose one of two regimes: regime F; i.e., joining the free trade area, or regime N; i.e., not joining. Sector-specific income in regime $R = F, N$ equals Π_{iR} in sector i and welfare is given by W_R. Lobby i offers a pair of contributions (C_{iF}, C_{iN}), the first one representing an offer in case regime F is adopted and the second one representing an offer in case regime N is adopted. One of the offers equals zero.

The first question to ask is what types of political equilibria arise in these circumstances? Grossman and Helpman show that two types may arise. If the regime that provides the higher aggregate welfare level generates a large enough welfare gain relative to the alternative, then there exists a political equilibrium in which the welfare superior regime is chosen by the government and all lobbies contribute zero. The welfare gain is large enough for this purpose if the product of a with the welfare gain exceeds the largest loss that a single-sector experiences when the welfare superior regime is selected.[26] Clearly, with no contributions the government selects the welfare superior regime. The point is, however, that under the specified circumstances no lobby stands to gain enough from inducing the government to choose the welfare inferior regime in order to make it worthwhile for the lobby to contribute the required minimum that induces the policymaker to switch regimes. Evidently, this equilibrium builds on a lack of coordination among the lobbying groups, and each one separately does not have a big enough stake to induce a switch of regimes on its own.

Minimal coordination by pressure groups, in the form of non-binding prior communication about preferable outcomes, leads to an equilibrium that is *coalition proof*. In such equilibria the policymaker chooses the regime that provides the highest joint welfare to the organized interest groups and the government.[27] Moreover, every equilibrium in which contributions by at least one lobby support the selected regime is of this nature. In these equilibria contributions by opposing interest groups make the government just indifferent between the alternative regimes. The implication is that a delicate balance prevails in these equilibria, in the sense that about equal political strength supports each side of the issue.[28]

These results can be used to examine what pairs of countries are likely candidates for free trade agreements. An agreement requires both countries to select regime F in the political equilibrium. For this purpose enough support in favor of the agreement has to be amassed in each country.

Now, support for an agreement can come from one of two sources. Either F provides higher welfare, in which case the government will be happy to sign an agreement in order to please its voters. Or potential exporters to the free trade area, who expect to sell at higher prices in the partner country, are willing to contribute enough money in order to open those markets. Sectors that expect to face fiercer import competition in the free trade area oppose the agreement.

If the initial rates of protection reflect a political balance of power of the type described in section 2.5, then each country needs enough potential exporters that support the FTA in order to overcome the opposing political pressures. This means that the imbalance of trade between the countries has to be small enough, because one country's exports into the free trade area are the other's imports. Unfortunately, potential exporters that support the agreement do so because they expect to be able to charge higher prices, and higher prices are bad for welfare. As a result free trade agreements are most viable in situations in which the two countries are most likely to suffer joint welfare losses.[29]

Both countries are more likely to endorse an FTA if some politically sensitive sectors can be excluded from the agreement and allowed to maintain the original rates of protection. If, given a choice, each country prefers to exclude sectors for whom the free trade area produces the largest joint loss of welfare and lobby income per unit of the overall constraining factor, where the constraining factor represents the interpretation of the term "substantially all trade" in article XXIV. Examples of the constraining factor include the fraction of industries that can be excluded from the agreement or the fraction of trade that takes place in exempted products. All sectors can be ranked according to this criterion and the cutoff point then determined by the overall constraint.[30]

It is quite unlikely, however, that both countries will have the same ranking of sectors according to this criterion. Under these circumstances a conflict arises over the set of exemptions and the countries need to reach a compromise in order to enact an FTA. Grossman and Helpman show that if the two governments engage in Nash bargaining over the exemptions, then they agree to exclude a set of sectors that is ranked according to a weighted average of the criterion that each country would like to use on its own.[31] The weights reflect the relative bargaining powers of the two governments. And a cutoff point is determined by the overall constraint imposed by the term "substantially all trade."

These examples show the power of an approach that emphasizes two-way interactions between internal politics and international economic relations. They also show that – complications generated by such interactions notwithstanding – this approach yields interesting insights about important policy issues. Further enrichment of this framework is needed, however, in order to address problems of institutional design that are at the heart of the current debate about rules concerning trade, direct foreign investment, and intellectual property rights.

Notes

Tel Aviv University and the Canadian Institute for Advanced Research. I am grateful to the NSF for financial support and to Gene Grossman and Alan Winters for comments.
1 When τ_i is larger than one and the good is imported, we have a proper tariff.

Alternatively, when τ_i is smaller than one and the good is imported, we have a subsidy to imports. If the good is exported and τ_i is larger than one we have an export subsidy and if τ_i is smaller than one and the good is exported we have an export tax.

2 Depending on context, it may be necessary to limit the choice of τ_i to some feasible set. Obviously, it has to be non-negative. But some upper limit may also exist as a result of political constraints or international agreements.

3 The discussion in the text assumes that the distribution of the ownership of labor and sector-specific inputs is atomless; i.e., it is thinly dispersed in the population. As a result, γ_L^j is treated as the measure of labor owned by individual j, implying $\int_j \gamma_L^j dj = 1$.

4 I.e., $\int_j \gamma_i^j dj = 1$ for every $i = 1, 2, \ldots, n$.

5 When there are trade taxes only, the consumer price equals the producer price. As is well known, the utility function (1) has an associated standard indirect utility function $v(p, E) = E + \Sigma_{i=1}^n S_i(p_i)$, where E represents total spending and $S_i(p_i) = u_i[d_i(p_i)] - p_i d_i(p_i)$ is the consumer surplus from product i, where $d_i(p_i)$ is the demand function for product i. Imports of product i are given by $M_i(\tau_i) = -[S_i'(\tau_i) + \Pi_i'(\tau_i)]$.

6 Namely, the reduced form indirect utility function (2) is given by $\hat{v}(\tau, \gamma^j) = \gamma_L^j + \Sigma_{i=1}^n \hat{v}_i(\tau_i, \gamma_i^j)$.

7 I use the term "tariff" to mean $\tau_i > 1$ independently of whether the good is imported or exported. Also observe that under our normalization of the population size; i.e., that the population equals one, the average ownership share of a sector-specific input equals one.

8 Output and the slope of the import demand function depend on the tariff rate, but these arguments have been suppressed in the following formula for convenience.

9 The assumption of linearity is inconsequential for our purpose. With a non-linear political support function the formula of the tariff rate has a marginal rate of substitution a_{pi} that depends on the levels of income of sector-specific inputs and on aggregate welfare.

10 Observe that by substituting (4) into (5) we obtain an objective function in which every dollar of real income obtains a weight of 1, except for income from a sector-specific input that obtains a weight of $1 + 1/a_{pi}$. These differential weights on different sources of real income drive the results. Long and Vousden (1991) have proposed a somewhat different approach to the formulation of political support functions, in which the weights vary across individuals rather than across sources of income.

11 Feenstra and Bhagwati (1982) take a similar approach, except that they view the government as the defender of the public interest. As a result, the lobbying costs of the pro-protectionist coalition rise with the price distortion. We will come back to this point at a later stage.

12 I exclude the constant term for labor income from this formula.

13 It is, of course, not realistic to assume that the antiprotectionist lobby consists of all other individuals in the economy. But it simplifies the exposition.

14 If only a fraction $\alpha_i^o < 1 - \alpha_i$ of individuals belong to the antiprotectionist lobby, then the first term on the right-hand side of (7) should be replaced with $[(1 - \alpha_i)(b_i - 1) + 1 - \alpha_i - \alpha_i^o]/(\alpha_i b_i + \alpha_i^o)$.

15 Electoral competition is implicit in both the political-support function and the tariff-formation function approaches, while in the Magee, Brock, and Young (1989) approach it plays center stage.

16 The influence motive generates benefits to the lobbies that are of the same order of magnitude as their contributions. This feature makes it desirable to exploit this motive for contributions even when there exists a large number of interest groups.

17 The political-support function approach can be interpreted as a reduced form of the influence-driven contributions approach. For some purposes the details of the influence-driven contributions approach are not needed. For other purposes, however, they are essential.

18 Each party seeks to maximize its expected number of seats. The probability of successfully promoting a policy depends on the number of seats in command. A party uses contributions from special interests to influence the voting pattern of uninformed or "impressionable" voters. On the other hand, each informed voter casts her ballot on the basis of whichever party commits to a policy that she most prefers. Except that each voter may have preferences between the parties that are based on other considerations as well, such as their positions on non-economic issues. This leads to probabilistic voting. In this framework a party can choose a policy that is desirable to the general public and thereby secure the support of informed voters. Instead it can tilt its policy position in favor of special interests in order to gain campaign contributions. In this event it loses the support of some of the informed voters, but it can use the contributions to gain support from the impressionable voters. This tradeoff between the support of the two groups of voters, and a party's objective to attain as many seats as possible in parliament, translate into a desire to maximize an objective function that is increasing in contributions and in the well being of the general public. This function is linear when the distribution of preferences over non-economic issues is uniform. The parameters of the political objective function depend on the degree of dispersion of these preferences, on the non-economic bias in the preferences of voters, the number of informed relative to uninformed voters in the population, and the effectiveness of campaign spending in attracting impressionable voters.

19 As explained in the previous footnote, in the Grossman and Helpman (1996) model of electoral competition with special interests a depends on a variety of the underlying parameters.

20 Observe that unlike the example of the tariff formation function here we include contributions to welfare by all goods, not only the product of sector i. The reason is that we shall allow each interest group to lobby for trade taxes in all sectors (i.e., not only in the sector in which they have a stake in the sector-specific factor). More on this point later.

21 In order to simplify notation, I use $\Sigma_{j \neq i} C_j(\tau)$ as a short hand for the sum of

contributions of all organized interest groups other than i.

22 See, for example, Dixit (1995) for an application to commodity taxation. Similar methods can be used to deal with quotas and other forms of quantitative restrictions.

23 It is also possible to allow pressure groups to lobby foreign governments, as shown in Grossman and Helpman (1995a).

24 See also Mayer (1981) on this issue.

25 See Grossman and Helpman (1995a) for an example.

26 Let R be the welfare superior regime; i.e., $W_R > W_K, R \neq K$. Then there exists an equilibrium in which contributions are zero and the government chooses R whenever $a(W_R - W_K) \geq \max[0, \max_i(\Pi_{iK} - \Pi_{iR})]$.

27 Regime R is selected in this case if $\Sigma_{j \in \mathscr{L}} \Pi_{jR} + aW_R \geq \Sigma_{j \in \mathscr{L}} \Pi_{jK} + aW_K$.

28 The fact that NAFTA has barely passed during the vote in US Congress can be interpreted as a reflection of this sort of equilibrium.

29 In this statement welfare is measured by W, and it does not include the well being of the government.

30 Suppose there exists a continuum of sectors and that the overall constraint is given by $\int_{i \in E} T_i di \leq T$, where E represents the set of exempt sectors, T_i represents the contribution of sector i to the overall constraint, and T represents the overall constraint. If, for example, the overall constraint is on the number of sectors that can be granted an exemption, then $T_i = 1$ for every sector and T stands for the largest measure of sectors that are allowed to be excluded from the FTA under article XXIV. On the other hand, if the constraint is on the trade volume, then T_i stands for the trade volume in sector i and T represents the maximum trade volume that can be excluded from the agreement. The ranking of industries builds on the index $g_i = (a\Delta W_i + \Delta\Pi_i)/T_i$, where ΔW_i represent the welfare gain in sector i from the FTA and $\Delta\Pi_i$ represents lobby i's income gain from the FTA. Indexing the sectors in an increasing order of g_i, the government wants to exclude the sectors for which g_i is negative, up to the constraint permitted by $\int_{i \in E} T_i di \leq T$.

31 Namely, sectors are ranked according to $\omega^A g_i^A + \omega^B g_i^B$, were ω^K is the weight of country K. The overall constraint remains the same as in the previous footnote.

References

Bernheim, Douglas B. and Whinston, Michael D. (1986). "Menu auctions, resource allocation, and economic influence." *Quarterly Journal of Economics*, 101: 1–31.

Coughlin, Peter J. (1992). *Probabilistic Voting Theory*. Cambridge: Cambridge University Press.

Dixit, Avinash (1995). "Special-interest lobbying and endogenous commodity taxation." Mimeo, Princeton University.

Evans, Peter, Jacobson, Harold, and Putnam, Robert (eds.) (1993). *Double-Edge Diplomacy*. Berkeley: University of California Press.

Feenstra, Robert C. and Bhagwati, Jagdish N. (1982). "Tariff seeking and the efficient tariff." In Bhagwati, Jagdish N. (ed.), *Import Competition and Response.* Chicago: University of Chicago Press.

Findlay, Ronald and Wellisz, Stanislaw (1982). "Endogenous tariffs, the political economy of trade restrictions, and welfare." In Bhagwati, Jagdish N. (ed.), *Import Competition and Response.* Chicago: University of Chicago Press.

Flam, Harry (1992). "Product markets and 1992: full integration, large gains?" *Journal of Economic Perspectives,* 6: 7–30.

Garber, Peter M. (ed.) (1993). *The Mexico-US Free Trade Agreement.* Cambridge, MA: MIT Press.

Grossman, Gene M. and Helpman, Elhanan (1994). "Protection for sale." *American Economic Review,* 84: 833–50.

(1995a). "Trade wars and trade talks." *Journal of Political Economy,* 103: 675–708.

(1995b). "The politics of free trade agreements." *American Economic Review,* 85: 667–90.

(1996). "Electoral competition and special interest politics." *Review of Economic Studies,* 63: 265–286.

Hillman, Arye L. (1982). "Declining industries and political-support protectionist motives." *American Economic Review,* 72: 1180–7.

(1989) *The Political Economy of Protection.* London: Harwood.

Hillman, Arye L. and Ursprung, Heinrich (1988). "Domestic politics, foreign interests, and international trade policy." *American Economic Review,* 78: 729–45.

Johnson, Harry G. (1953/4). "Optimal tariffs and retaliation." *Review of Economic Studies,* 21: 142–53.

Jones, Ronald W. (1971). "A three factor model in theory, trade and history." In Bhagwati, Jagdish N. *et al.* (eds.), *Trade, Growth and the Balance of Payments: Essays in Honor of C. B. Kindleberger.* Amsterdam: North-Holland.

Long, Ngo Van and Vousden, Neil (1991). "Protectionist responses and declining industries." *Journal of International Economics,* 30: 87–103.

Magee, Stephen P., Brock, William A., and Young, Leslie (1989). *Black Hole Tariffs and Endogenous Policy Formation.* Cambridge, MA: MIT Press.

Magelby, David B. and Nelson, Candice J. (1990). *The Money Chase: Congressional Campaign Finance Reform.* Washington, DC: The Brookings Institution.

Mayer, Wolfgang (1981). "Theoretical considerations on negotiated tariff adjustments." *Oxford Economic Papers,* 33: 135–53.

(1984). "Endogenous tariff formation." *American Economic Review,* 74: 970–85.

Mayer, Wolfgang and Li, Jun (1994). "Interest groups, electoral competition, and probabilistic voting for trade policies." *Economics and Politics,* 6: 59–77.

Olsen, Mancur (1965). *The Logic of Collective Action.* Cambridge, MA: Harvard University Press.

Peltzman, Sam (1976). "Toward a more general theory of regulation." *Journal of Law and Economics,* 19: 211–40.

Putnam, Robert (1988). "Diplomacy and domestic politics: the logic of two-level games." *International Organization,* 42: 427–60.

Rodrik, Dani (1986). "Tariffs, subsidies, and welfare with endogenous policy." *Journal of International Economics*, 21: 285–96.

(1995). "Political economy of trade policy." In Grossman, Gene M. and Rogoff, Kenneth (eds.), *Handbook of International Economics*, Vol. III. Amsterdam: North-Holland.

Shepsle, Kenneth A. (1990). *Models of Multiparty Electoral Competition*. London: Harwood.

Stigler, George (1971). "The theory of economic regulation." *Bell Journal of Economics*, 2: 3–21.

CHAPTER 3

Economic analysis of political institutions: an introduction

Roger B. Myerson

The phrase "political economy" has come to mean very different things in different places. In political science departments, it generally means the study of how economic forces affect politics. As such, the phrase often has Marxist implications, because of the particular importance that Marxist theory places on economic forces for explaining political events. In economics departments, however, political economy is often taken to mean the study of political forces that affect economic activity.

In classical social philosophy, the study of markets was not so separate from the study of government. The phrase "political economy" was taken from Greek words meaning "housekeeping of city-states," and it was applied to describe the study of how civilized societies are organized. So the classical goal of political economy was to explain the functioning of all social institutions.

The successful development of price theory forced a separation between the study of markets and the study of government. Price theory describes market competition well, but it cannot be applied to political competition. So a separation of *political science* from *economics* was necessary when price theory was the only general analytical methodology in economics. Thus economics has developed around a core analytical methodology, whereas descriptive methodologies have been more dominant in political science.

Today, with game theory alongside price theory, it makes less sense to separate the study of politics from economics. Game theory is an analytical methodology that can be applied to political competition as well as to market competition. Game theory allows theorists to recognize the interconnections between economic and political institutions. So we can now reclaim the original broad scope of political economy, without abandoning a rigorous analytical approach.

We must approach such a reunion between economic theory and political theory with careful respect for both academic traditions. Economists have much to teach political scientists about the analysis of incentives in competitive systems. But economists need to learn from political scientists about what are good questions to ask about political competition. It is good to pursue questions about how politics can affect economic variables, but our concern should not be limited only to economic variables.

To be able to guide the writing of antitrust laws, economists have invested generations of work in trying to understand the ways that different market structures may shape the conduct and performance of competing oligopolists. Political competition for control of governments is surely no less important to us than economic competition for profits. Furthermore, the range of explicit structural variables that need to be analyzed is greater in political competition, because rules of political competition are written in constitutions and electoral codes.

So we should study constitutional structures as the rules of the political game, defining an incentive system for politicians. To be able to guide writing of constitutions, we need to understand how constitutional structure may shape the rational conduct of politicians and the performance of government.

The analytical study of political processes, using the rational-choice modeling methodology of economic theory, is now commonly called *formal political theory* (or *positive political theory*) by political scientists. Unfortunately, interest in formal political theory has not been widespread among political scientists outside of the United States, and the result has been a disproportionate focus on American political institutions. A broader multi-national effort could greatly enrich this literature, because each nation's unique political history may suggest different questions and conjectures about the functioning of political institutions.

In this chapter, I will try to offer some introduction to the range of game-theoretic models that can be valuable in the study of political institutions. I will make no attempt here to survey the whole literature of formal political theory. Instead, I will focus on just four selected models.

Such a selection of models inevitably reflects the author's particular interest and tastes, but I have tried to make this selection with two broad criteria in mind. I have tried to select theoretical models that can offer practical insights into the questions of constitutional design and cross-national comparison of democratic institutions. And I have tried to select models that focus on different aspects of the political process.

The first two models here focus on electoral systems. The first electoral model (based on Cox (1987b, 1990) and Myerson (1993b)) seeks to evaluate the impact of the electoral system on the diversity of political positions that would be taken by any given number of parties or candidates that are taken seriously by the voters. The other electoral model (taken from Myerson (1993a)) analyzes the impact of potential entry into (and exit from) the set of parties that are taken seriously by the voters in game theoretic equilibria.

The third model in this chapter (taken from Diermeier and Myerson (1995) and Groseclose and Snyder (1996)) looks at the legislature, to see why bicameral or presidential systems may induce different forms of legislative and party organization than unicameral parliamentary systems. The fourth model (due to Austen-Smith and Banks (1988)) is a multi-stage model that includes both electoral competition and legislative bargaining to show how anticipation of post-election bargaining may affect rational voters' behavior in a multi-party parliamentary democracy.

I hope that these four models may suffice for an invitation to the economic analysis of political institutions (see also Myerson (1995)). But much more would be needed for a comprehensive survey of the wide and growing literature of formal political theory. General introductory texts include Riker (1982a), Mueller (1989), and Shepsle (1991). For more on theoretical analysis of electoral systems, see Osborne (1995), Riker (1982b), Feddersen (1992), Cox (1994), Myerson and Weber (1993), Ledyard (1984), and Feddersen and Pesendorfer (1996). The literature in theoretical models of legislative organization includes Baron and Ferejohn (1989), Shepsle (1979), Shepsle and Weingast (1994), Weingast and Marshall (1988), Cox and McCubbins (1993), Gilligan and Krehbiel (1990), McKelvey and Riezman (1992), Alesina and Rosenthal (1995), Huber (1992), Laver and Schofield (1990), and Laver and Shepsle (1996).

My main concern here is with analytical theory. However, we must not overlook the importance of empirical studies of comparative political institutions. Our best hopes for real progress in the understanding of political institutions must be based on a complementary development of both empirical comparison of existing political systems, and theoretical comparison of equilibria in game models of different political systems. For an introduction to the empirical literature on comparison of electoral systems, see Rae (1971), Grofman and Lijphart (1986), Lijphart (1990, 1994), and Taagepera and Shugart (1989). For more on presidential and parliamentary forms of government, see Shugart and Carey (1992), Lijphart (1992), Moe and Caldwell (1994), and Laver and Shepsle (1994).

Model 1: Diversity of candidates in symmetric equilibria of election games

Many papers in formal political theory build on the model of spatial competition of Hotelling (1929). Hotelling's formal analysis was focused on a duopoly game played by two shops choosing their location on Main Street, with customers distributed uniformly along the street. After arguing that the two shops would rationally choose to locate together at the location of the median consumer, Hotelling went on to extend the interpretation of his model to the analysis of politics. Like the two shops converging in the middle of the town, the Democrats and Republicans of American politics seemed in 1929 to converge in the middle of the political spectrum.

Hotelling's paper stands as a classic in both oligopoly theory and formal political theory, but there is a sense in which it sets a bad example. Doing one model for two different applications can obscure the important differences between the two applications. Notice, for example, that welfare analysis may be very different in these two applications. In the oligopoly game, separating the two shops could decrease the total of consumers' transportation costs, because each consumer's transportation cost depends on the location of the shop to which he gives his business. In the political game, however, each voter's welfare depends on the policies of the party that wins the election, not of the party to which he gives his vote, and so there is no aggregate welfare benefit from separating the two parties. So the negative connotation that Hotelling gave to "excessive sameness" may be inappropriate in political competition, even if it has some merit in oligopolistic competition.

Much attention has been focused on relaxing the assumption of two parties in Hotelling's discussion (see Shepsle (1991)). But when we extend our analysis to multi-party or multi-candidate elections, we must recognize the great diversity of multi-candidate electoral systems that can be used. In oligopoly theory, it is reasonable to assume that each consumer will generally give all his business to the store that offers him the best terms, when price and location are taken into account. But in politics, some electoral systems allow or require voters to distribute their votes in various ways across different candidates. And, even in electoral systems that require voters to choose one candidate, a voter might rationally choose to vote for his second favorite candidate, if the most likely way of his vote influencing the election's outcome is in a close race between his second favorite and his third favorite candidates. So we need to explicitly compare different electoral systems, and we need to consider strategic theories of rational voting in which voters take account of each other's predicted voting patterns.

To introduce this literature, I focus here on a simplified version of the model of Cox (1987b, 1990). Cox developed his model in the one-dimensional policy space of the Hotelling model, but I simplify the analysis here by considering just a two-point policy space (see also Myerson (1993b)).

So suppose that there is just one political question on which the various parties or candidates may differ: say, whether our nation should ratify some regional free trade agreement. On this question, each candidate must choose one of two policy positions: "Yes" (for ratifying the treaty) or "No" (against ratifying the treaty). The voters have some known distribution of preferences. Let Q denote the fraction of the voters who prefer the "Yes" position. Assuming that no one is indifferent, the remaining fraction $1 - Q$ of the voters all prefer the "No" position.

In this simple game, we can safely assume that voters of each type will vote for the parties that endorse their favored position. But with multiple candidates, we must address the question of how voters might distinguish among two or more candidates who adopt the same policy position. Following Cox (1987), let us for now apply an assumption of symmetry in this regard. That is, we assume for now that voters of each type will (in aggregate) treat candidates at the same position symmetrically. (This *symmetry assumption* will be dropped in the next section.)

Given these assumptions about voters' behavior, let us now analyze a simple model of an electoral game in which the candidates for some political office choose their policy positions. For now, let us assume that there is some given number of candidates, which we denote by K. Suppose that the candidates choose their policy positions simultaneously and independently, each with the goal of maximizing his chances of winning the election.

In this game, if the fraction Q of voters who favor the "Yes" policy is very close to 1, then we would expect all K candidates to adopt the "Yes" policy. Similarly, if the fraction Q is very close to 0, then we would expect all K candidates to adopt the "No" position. Now, let us ask, what is the highest Q such that there is a symmetric equilibrium of this game in which all candidates choose the "No" position? This largest minority that could be ignored by all candidates in a symmetric equilibrium is the *Cox threshold* of candidate diversity, and we denote it here by Q^*.

Cox's analysis shows that different electoral systems yield different thresholds of diversity. The common system of *plurality voting* stipulates that each voter must give one vote to only one candidate, and the candidate with the most votes wins (even if he has less than a majority). Under plurality voting, the Cox threshold is $Q^* = 1/K$, which goes to zero as K becomes large. Thus, when there are many serious candidates under plurality voting, we may expect to find candidates who advocate small minority positions and have a positive probability of winning the election.

But now consider a very different system called *negative plurality voting*, which stipulates that each voter must vote for all except one of the candidates, whom the voter "rejects." The candidate who has been rejected by the fewest voters wins. Under negative plurality voting, the Cox threshold is $Q^* = (K - 1)/K$, which goes to one as K becomes large. This result may seem very strange, because it allows an absolute majority $(Q > 1/2)$ to be ignored by all candidates. To see how this can happen, consider the case of $K = 10$, which gives us $Q^* = 0.9$. Suppose that 81 percent of the voters (an overwhelming majority) favor the "Yes" policy, but all of the ten candidates are expected to choose the "No" position. If one candidate deviated alone to the "Yes" position, then he would be rejected by 19 percent of the voters, whereas the other nine candidates would each be rejected by only 9 percent of the voters, because the 81 percent "Yes" majority must split their rejection-votes among nine different "No" candidates; and so the deviating candidate would lose. Thus, when there are many serious candidates under negative plurality voting, we may expect to find them clustered around a shared policy position, which may be a position that is opposed by a large majority of the voters.

This result might seem a minor academic curiosity, because negative plurality voting is not used in any major democratic system. But the point is that this analysis enables us to see why negative plurality voting may be an undesirable system, even without trying it. Our theoretical model gives us a diagnostic tool for predicting some qualitative aspects about the performance of an electoral system.

Let us consider two more systems: Borda voting and approval voting. *Borda voting* stipulates that each voter must give 0 points to one candidate, 1 point to another, 2 points to another, and so on up to $K - 1$ points for the voter's highest-ranked candidate; and then the winner is the candidate with the highest total number of points from the voters. *Approval voting* stipulates that each voter must give either 0 or 1 point to each candidate, with no restriction on the number of candidates getting a point from the voter, and again the winner is the candidate with the highest total number of points. Borda voting and approval voting both have Cox thresholds of $Q^* = 1/2$, for any number of candidates. Thus, approval voting and Borda voting can guarantee that, in a symmetric equilibrium with any number of candidates, all potentially winning candidates choose the policy favored by the majority.

Model 2: Barriers to entry and non-symmetric equilibria of election games

The analysis in the preceding section used an assumption that candidates or parties that adopt the same policy position will be treated identically by the voters. This is a common assumption, but it should be severely questioned. In no democratic system could I really hope to get as many votes as a leading politician simply by announcing that I favor the same policies!

Simply filing a candidacy petition and announcing policy positions would not necessarily make me a serious candidate in the eyes of the voters. There are other barriers to entry into politics that need to be considered.

Some of these barriers arise from the basic problems of credibly communicating a candidate's credentials and promises to a mass electorate, and these communication problems would arise under any democratic system. But other barriers are created by the game-theoretic properties of the electoral system itself. In particular, some electoral systems define a game for the voters that has multiple non-symmetric equilibria. In such non-symmetric equilibria, it often happens that one candidate may get no support from the voters merely because each voter expects that the other voters will give this candidate no support. When such equilibria exist, the perception of not being a serious candidate can become a self-fulfilling prophecy which acts as a barrier to entry against new parties.

Political scientists have long observed that, when elections are run under the system of winner-take-all plurality voting, there tend to be only two major parties. This observation is known as *Duverger's law* (see Riker (1982b) and Duverger (1954)). In contrast, democracies that use proportional representation electoral systems often have many more parties that win substantial representation in the legislature. So the number of major parties should be an endogenous variable to be explained by analysis of electoral systems, not just an exogenous parameter.

Economic theorists should be particularly sensitive to the questions about how the number of large competitors is determined, because such questions are very important in oligopoly theory. It is widely appreciated that barriers to entry of new competitors may be the most important determinant of long-run profits in an oligopolistic market. From this perspective, Duverger's law looks like a statement about high barriers to entry in democracies that use plurality voting. So, when we study the degree to which electoral systems might raise or lower barriers to entry against new parties, we should ask whether such barriers to entry might have some effect on the extent to which the leaders of the existing major parties can exploit their privileged positions and take profits from government. Such political profit-taking is called corruption.

So let us consider a voting game (from Myerson (1993a)) in which voters are allocating seats in a legislature among parties that have different levels of corruption. To be specific, for each party r, suppose that there is some number $c(r)$, called the *corruption level* of party r, such that each voter will have to pay $c(r)$ in extra taxes for each seat that party r wins in the legislature. We want to focus on the question of how the amount of corruption that is allowed by individually rational voters may depend on the game-theoretic properties of the electoral system. So we assume that the parties' corruption levels are all publicly known to the voters. Given that voters pay the costs of this corruption and get no benefits from it (it goes only to the politicians, who are a negligible fraction of the electorate), one might guess that rational voters would never vote to give any seats to a more corrupt party. In fact, we shall show that this guess may be wrong, depending on which electoral system is being used.

There is one minor wrinkle that needs to be addressed first. Consider the simple case of one corrupt party versus one non-corrupt and otherwise identical party, in a single-seat winner-take-all election. If there are many voters and they all expect everyone else to vote for the corrupt party, then there is no reason for any voter to do otherwise, because there is no chance of one vote changing the outcome of the election. To eliminate this perverse equilibrium, we can either use a dominance argument, or we can add some uncertainty about the number of voters. So let us assume that each voter has an independent $1/1,000$ probability of forgetting to vote (but if everyone forgets to vote then the election will be reheld the next day). Then each voter has a positive probability of affecting the outcome, and no one votes for the corrupt party in equilibrium.

But this result, that known corrupt parties do not win in equilibrium, depends crucially on the assumptions that there are only two parties and that parties differ only in their corruption levels. Once we admit three or more parties that differ even over a two-point policy space, then the ability of rational voters to deter corruption becomes very dependent on the details of the electoral system.

For a specific example, consider a winner-take-all election by plurality voting. As in the preceding section, suppose that there are two policy alternatives: the "Yes" policy and the "No" policy (on the ratification of a regional trade treaty). Suppose that there are four parties. Parties 1 and 3 advocate the "Yes" policy, and parties 2 and 4 advocate the "No" policy. Suppose that there are ten voters, including five voters who prefer the "Yes" policy, and five voters who prefer the "No" policy, and suppose that each voter would gain 1 unit of money from the implementation of his preferred policy rather than the other policy alternative. But suppose also that parties 1 and 2 are known to be corrupt, with corruption levels $c(1) = c(2) = \gamma$, where γ is some positive number. Parties 3 and 4 are known to be clean parties, with corruption levels $c(3) = c(4) = 0$. So each voter would lose γ from the victory of a corrupt party instead of the clean party that has the same policy position.

As above, let us assume that each voter has an independent $1/1,000$ probability of forgetting to vote, so that each voter perceives some chance of affecting the outcome of the election. From Myerson (1993a), ties are assumed to be broken by a tie-breaking ballot from a randomly sampled voter. Most importantly, we assume here that each voter chooses his vote to optimize his expected payoff from the outcome of the election, to the extent that his vote may influence who wins, taking account of how other voters are expected to vote in equilibrium. (This last assumption is called *instrumental* or *strategic* voting, in contrast to another common assumption that voters vote merely to express their sincere preferences over the candidates.)

In this example, then, plurality voting admits a Nash equilibrium in which all the "Yes" voters plan to vote for party 1, and all the "No" voters plan to vote for party 2, and so one of these corrupt parties will win. Given that ties will be broken by randomization, this equilibrium gives each voter a probability of almost $1/2$ (over 0.495) that he can affect the outcome of a tie between parties 1 and 2 by voting for party 1 or 2. But a single voter's out-of-equilibrium vote for party 3 or 4 could enable a non-corrupt party to win only if at least seven other voters forget to vote (so that parties 1 and 2 each get at most one vote), which has probability less than 10^{-19}. So even if the cost of corruption γ were as high as 10^{19}, each voter would find it rational to vote for the corrupt major party that he prefers, rather than waste his vote on a clean minor party.

Of course there is another equilibrium of this game in which nobody votes for the corrupt parties. So we could hope that the voters might focus on the equilibrium that they all prefer. But suppose that the clean parties 3 and 4 are new parties, and so history operates as a countervailing focal factor in favor of the corrupt equilibrium. Then the perception that this election is likely to be a close race between parties 1 and 2, as in past elections, can become a self-fulfilling prophecy.

The problem is that getting voters to coordinate their expectations on the equilibrium that they prefer may require some coordinating leadership, and they already have leaders in parties 1 and 2 who prefer to maintain the old equilibrium. The need for coordinating leadership to guide blocs of like-minded voters in plurality elections seems particularly problematic when we recognize that the whole point of democratic elections is to select our leaders. Thus, the need for coordination in plurality voting can create a barrier to entry which can sustain the profit-taking of corrupt parties.

If we change electoral systems, then the analysis of this example becomes very different. Under approval voting, it can be shown (see Myerson (1993a)) that, in a class of games that includes this example, corrupt parties cannot have any positive probability of winning any legislative seats. To see why, consider again the scenario in which every voter is expected to vote for party 1 or 2. It can be easily shown that a voter might gain, and could not possibly lose, by adding a second approval vote for his most-preferred clean party. But no one needs to vote for a corrupt party when all like-minded voters are voting for the most-preferred clean party. The crucial difference is that, under approval voting, adding a vote for party 3 or 4 does not reduce a voter's ability to affect the electoral outcome in the case of a close race between parties 1 and 2. Thus, under approval voting, a perception that it will probably be a close race between parties 1 and 2 cannot so easily become a self-fulfilling prophecy.

Myerson (1993a) has found that proportional representation systems also yield good sets of equilibria in these games. In our simple conceptual example, proportional representation (in its ideal sense) would mean that each voter can allocate an equal fraction of the legislative seats (1/10 when everyone votes). We assume here that the realized government policy will depend on whether the "Yes" parties or "No" parties have a majority (with a tie going to the status quo, say the "No" side). So even if a voter who favors "Yes" expected all other "Yes" voters to vote for the corrupt "Yes" party 1, he would prefer to vote for the clean "Yes" party 3, because doing so would reduce the corruption cost without affecting the "Yes/No" balance in the legislature. Thus under proportional representation, in any equilibrium of this game, every voter should vote for a non-corrupt party that advocates the policy which the voter prefers.

Myerson (1993a) has shown that Borda voting (like plurality voting) allows equilibria in which corrupt parties win with positive probability, in spite of the fact that non-corrupt parties with the same policy positions are on the ballot. To see why, consider again the above four-party example, but now suppose that the election is winner-take-all, with Borda voting. If it were certain that only parties 3 and 4 could have any chance of winning the election, then all the "No" voters would prefer to maximize their impact on the race between 3 and 4 by ranking party 3 on the bottom of their Borda ballots and party 4 at the top. Similarly, all "Yes" voters would put party 4 at the bottom of their Borda ballots, and party 3 at the top. But then the total Borda score for parties 1 and 2 must equal the total Borda score for parties 3 and 4, and so at least one of the corrupt parties must be a contender to win!

Essentially, the problem with Borda voting here is the opposite of the problem with plurality voting. Under plurality voting, if a party is perceived as a likely loser, then rational voters tend to not give it electoral support, which can function as a barrier to entry against clean parties. Under Borda voting, when a party is perceived as a likely loser, then some voters may rationally give it more support (moving it up so that some other more serious contender can be moved to the bottom of their Borda ballots), and this effect acts as a barrier to exit which protects the corrupt parties. Approval voting and proportional representation perform well in these games because perceptions of electoral strength or weakness have relatively less impact on voters' rational behavior under these systems.

To compare this model with the model from the preceding section, it may be useful to mention Riker's (1982a) discussions of "liberal" and "populist" theories about the functional goals of democracy. Populist theories, in Riker's sense, emphasize the problem of aggregating the diverse preferences and beliefs of voters. From this populist perspective, the success of a democracy should be judged by its ability to generate reasonable compromises among the conflicting interests of different groups of voters. Liberal theories, in contrast, emphasize the problem of deterring the leaders of government from abusing their power. From this liberal perspective, the success of a democracy should be judged by its ability to deter government corruption, by threatening to turn corrupt leaders out of office. Models that focus exclusively on the choice among policy positions favored by different voters, like the first model in the preceding section, could be classified as populist in Riker's scheme. The model in this section, with its focus on corruption of political leaders, might be classified as liberal in this scheme (for other theories of corruption in politics, see Galeotti and Merlo (1994)).

Model 3: Party discipline and legislative organization

The essence of constitutional government is a separation of powers among many elected officials who must then interact and compromise to govern between elections. The structure of the constitutional separation of powers defines a complex game of policy determination, to be played by legislators and other elected officials. To understand how constitutional structures may influence political behavior, we need to look beyond the election and study models of the post-election legislative games. So in this section, we consider a simple example of such a legislative model.

Legislatures in different countries have developed very different forms of internal organization and leadership. The Congress of the United States has a much weaker central leadership than the British House of Commons. In the United States, congressmen regularly make individual decisions about whether to support legislation, independently of their party leadership. Congressional committees have substantial negative power to block legislation in their domain of jurisdiction, but a favorable report by a committee does not guarantee passage on the floor of the American House or Senate. In the British House of Commons, however, it is generally understood that all members of the governing legislative coalition will follow the lead of the Cabinet in supporting any given legislative proposal or bill.

This distinction is often explained by the fact that political parties in Britain have much more cohesion and discipline than political parties in America. But there is reason to suspect that this "explanation" might reverse the cause and effect. To begin, we should be careful to distinguish electoral party discipline from legislative party discipline. Here *electoral party discipline* may be taken to mean that voters tend to choose a party and then support candidates only according to the endorsement of their party. *Legislative party discipline* means that legislators of any given party are expected to regularly vote their party's line in the legislature.

There is an obvious interconnection between legislative party discipline and electoral party discipline. If voters are expected to vote purely along party lines, then a party's nomination becomes a candidate's principal asset, and a candidate's record of independent action can do little to improve his electoral prospects. Conversely, if legislators are expected to vote in the legislature purely along party lines, then voters have little reason to ask more about a candidate than his party affiliation. But as Cox (1987a) has observed, this leaves us with a chicken-and-egg question: Which came first, legislative party discipline or electoral party discipline?

There is good reason to expect that electoral party discipline can be affected by the electoral system; see Carey and Shugart (1995). In particular, a high degree of electoral party discipline is forced by closed-list proportional representation, in which candidates can run only as names on a general party list. But the United States and Great Britain both elect legislators by plurality voting in single-member districts, and legislative candidates appear as individuals on the voters' ballots. So the electoral system cannot be the cause of the different levels of party discipline in these two countries. Furthermore, Cox (1987a) finds that, in Victorian Britain, legislative party discipline seems to have developed ahead of electoral party discipline.

So if we are to find a structural explanation of the different levels of legislative party cohesion in Britain and the USA, then we should look instead at the different constitutional structures of these legislatures. In Britain, legislation requires only a simple majority of the House of Commons. In the USA, legislation requires a majority of both the House and the Senate, plus the approval of the President (or 2/3 supermajorities in each chamber). The American constitution explicitly gives each legislative chamber control over its internal procedures, and terms of office are staggered to maintain a sense of separation between the two chambers. Building on the work of Groseclose and Snyder (1996) (see also Snyder (1991)), Diermeier and Myerson (1995) have developed a simple model to show how these constitutional structures might account for the different levels of legislative party discipline that have evolved in the USA and Great Britain.

The crucial assumption of the Diermeier–Myerson model is that legislators want to maximize the expected value of the favors or bribes that they get from outside interest groups who want to pass or block legislation. Within each chamber, legislative institutions are cooperatively designed to maximize the expected value of these favors to members of the chamber, but separation is assumed to prevent full cooperation across legislative chambers.

To give an overview of the model, let us begin by considering a simple unicameral legislature, in which the legislators are considering different forms of internal organization for their chamber. To illustrate their options, let us explicitly consider three organizational options. One option is *independent majority voting*, in which the legislators vote independently, using simple majority rule for any bill that anyone proposes. A second option is to have a system of *blocking committee chairs*, which stipulates that each bill must go first to a committee in which the chairman has negative power to block any proposed bill, but each legislator still votes independently on proposals that are approved and reported out by the committee. A third organizational option is to have a system of *full delegation to leadership*, in which all legislative power is delegated to a leader of the chamber, who can both approve and reject legislation in the name of the whole chamber. Among these three organizational alternatives, it may be intuitively apparent that the full-delegation option would make it easiest to pass legislation, while the blocking-committee system would make it hardest to pass legislation.

Groseclose and Snyder's lobbying model provides one simple way of quantifying and verifying this intuition. In their model, there are two lobbying agents who may offer favors and money to legislators. Agent 1 wants to pass a specific bill and is willing to spend up to W units of money to get it passed. Agent 2 wants to block this bill and is willing to spend up to V to block it. For simplicity, it is assumed that agent 1 must move first, offering bribes to legislators if they can get the bill passed. Then agent 2 can either pay counterbribes sufficient to block the bill, or he can pay nothing and acquiesce to its passage.

Analyzing this as a game with perfect information, Groseclose and Snyder showed that, with independent majority voting, agent 1 pays $2V$ to the legislators if $W > 2V$, but the legislators get nothing if $W < 2V$. The total bribes needed to pass a bill are $2V$, because any lower amount would allow agent 2 to pay less than V and bribe some 50 percent of the legislators who were together offered less than V by agent 1.

With a blocking-committee system, the analysis is similar, except that agent 1 needs to offer bribes that are at least $3V$ to pass the bill, because agent 2 would block the bill if either the committee chairman or some 50 percent of the backbenchers in the chamber were getting less than V from agent 1. That is, with a blocking-committee system, the legislators get a total of $3V$ from agent 1 if $W > 3V$, but they get nothing if $W < 3V$.

With a full-delegation system, the price of passing legislation drops to $1V$. If $W > V$ then agent 1 pays V to the leader to pass the bill, and otherwise the leader gets nothing.

Diermeier and Myerson use the term *hurdle factor* to refer to this multiple of V that agent 1 must pay to pass a bill. So the hurdle factor is 1 with full delegation, 2 with independent majority voting, and 3 with a blocking committee system. Of course, this is just a simple model, but the point is that a reform of the organization in a legislative chamber can be viewed as a change in the price for lobbyists to get legislation passed. From the legislator's point of view, the optimal price or hurdle factor should depend (like any producer's price) on the demand curve. In this case, assuming that the legislative organization must be chosen before any specific values of V and W are determined, the demand curve is a function $D(r)$ that represents the expected value of a random variable that is equal to V if $W > rV$ and is equal to 0 if $W < rV$. Then with a hurdle factor r, the expected total value that the legislators get is $rD(r)$. When other forms of legislative organization are considered, any hurdle factor above 1 can be achieved by some form of legislative organization. The maximal expected value for the legislators is achieved by a hurdle factor r_0 which, at an interior optimum, must satisfy the following optimality conditions

$$D(r_0) + r_0 D'(r_0) = 0 \text{ and } D'(r_0) < 0.$$

Now let us separate the legislature into a House and Senate, which determine their internal organizations separately. Let s denote the hurdle factor in the House, and let t denote the hurdle factor in the Senate. Then the expected total payments to the members of the House is $sD(s + t)$. So the marginal value to the House of increasing its own hurdle factor is

$$D(s + t) + sD'(s + t),$$

which is strictly positive if $s + t = r_0$ and $t > 0$. This is, if the two chambers tried to set hurdle factors that jointly maximize their gains from lobbyists, then members of each chamber would have an incentive to unilaterally increase their own hurdle factor.

Giving veto power to an independently elected president similarly increases the incentives for higher hurdle factors in the legislature. Diermeier and Myerson consider an example where the variables V and W are independently drawn from an exponential distribution with mean 1, and in this case $D(r) = 1/(r + 1)^2$. Then the optimal hurdle factor r for a simple unicameral legislature would maximize $rD(r) = r/(r + 1)^2$; and this maximum is achieved by $r_0 = 1$, that is, by full delegation to leadership. Adding a president with veto power adds 1 to the overall hurdle factor, and so the expected total value for the legislators becomes $rD(r + 1) = r/(r + 2)^2$; and this expected value is maximized by $r_0 = 2$, that is, by independent majority voting in the legislative chamber. In general, adding more hurdles to legislation outside of a legislative chamber can incite the chamber to increase its own internal hurdle factor.

The essential idea is that, in bicameral and presidential systems, when the members of one chamber delegate full legislative powers to the leadership of a disciplined majority coalition, they are lowering their legislative hurdle factor. The resulting increased legislation benefits must be shared with the president and other legislative chambers (if they exist). But the costs of decreased attention from lobbyists (for each bill that would have passed anyway) is entirely borne within this chamber. From this perspective, we see how presidential vetoes and bicameral separation can erode the incentives for legislators to form disciplined coalitions with strong leadership.

Model 4: An integrated model of elections and legislative bargaining

Thus far, we have considered two models of electoral politics and one model of legislative processes. It is convenient to make a conceptual separation along these lines, but at some point we must recognize that pre-election campaigning and post-election governing are interconnected phases of the overall political process. Voters' behavior in the election depends on their perception of how the winners will behave in the post-election processes of government. Conversely, the behavior of elected officials in legislative voting and coalition formation is largely determined by their perceptions of how decisions in government will affect behavior of voters in future elections. So we should conclude by considering an example of a model that looks at these two phases of politics in an integrated way. The best such model is due to Austen-Smith and Banks (1988).

Proportional representation has been advocated as a way of generating a legislature that is a mirror of the people, giving seats proportionately to each bloc of voters that has an organized party to express its interests. But if many voters do not give their votes to the parties that they truly prefer, then it is not clear that any party should be viewed as a true expression of the interests of the voters who supported it in the election. Austen-Smith and Banks (1988) show how this can happen.

As in the Hotelling model, the space of policy options in their model is the interval from 0 to 1. There are many voters, and each voter has a type θ that has been independently drawn from a uniform distribution over this interval $[0, 1]$. A voter with type θ gets payoff $-(y - \theta)^2$ when y is the policy position that is chosen by the government.

There are three parties, numbered 1, 2, 3 in the game. At the first stage of the game, the three parties independently choose policy positions x_1, x_2, x_3 in the interval $[0, 1]$. At the second stage, the voters vote for parties in a simple proportional representation system with a minimum vote share requirement of α. For now, let us suppose that $\alpha = 0.05$, so that any party must get at least 5 percent of the vote to earn any seats. Seats are allocated to parties that exceed this 5 percent quota in proportion to their respective vote totals. (Assume that integer-rounding problems can be avoided by dividing seats.)

After the election, the parties try to form a government. Forming a government here means choosing a policy position y in the interval $[0, 1]$ and choosing a distribution of the transferable benefits of power (g_1, g_2, g_3) such that $g_1 + g_2 + g_3 = G$, where G is the given total value of the perquisites of power (ministerial offices, etc.) that are available to whoever controls the government. The payoff to any party i in the legislature is then $g_i - (y - x_i)^2$. It is assumed that the parameter G is a large positive number.

If one party has a majority of the legislature, then that party controls the government and chooses (y, g_1, g_2, g_3). Otherwise, the parties must bargain to form a government. Let us assume that a coalition with a majority of the legislature can implement any feasible (y, g_1, g_2, g_3) satisfying $y \in [0, 1]$ and $g_1 + g_2 + g_3 = G$, except that no g_i can be made negative without the consent of party i.

Following actual practice in many countries, Austen-Smith and Banks assume that the largest party (the one that has the most seats in the legislature) makes the first offer to form a government, proposing a plan (y, g_1, g_2, g_3) to be implemented if another party accepts the offer. If this first offer is not accepted by any other party, then the second-largest party gets to make an offer. If this second offer is not accepted by any other party, then the smallest party gets to make an offer. Finally, if no party's offer has been accepted by any other party, a non-partisan caretaker government is formed, and all three parties get payoff 0. To complete the specification of the game, we also assume that any party that fails to get any legislative seats gets a payoff -1 (worse than anything that can happen when it is in the legislature).

Assuming that G is sufficiently large, Austen-Smith and Banks show that, in any sequential equilibrium of this bargaining game, if the largest party does not have a majority then it makes an offer that is designed to be accepted by the smallest party. If the smallest party rejected this offer, then the second-largest party would make an offer aimed at the largest party (because the largest party, having used up its opportunity to offer, would be most eager to reach agreement). Anticipating being thus excluded at the second stage makes the smallest party most eager to reach agreement at the first stage. In equilibrium, the largest party's initial offer is accepted by the smallest party, and so they will form the government.

A simple efficiency argument shows that the policy chosen by a governing coalition will be the average of their promised x_i positions. If 1 is the largest and 3 is the smallest party, then choosing $y = (x_1 + x_3)/2$ minimizes the $\{1, 3\}$-coalition's total breach-of-promise cost $(y - x_1)^2 + (y - x_3)^2$, and the greater bargaining power of party 1 can be rewarded by increasing g_1 at the expense of g_3. (Of course g_2 will be 0 when 1 and 3 form a governing coalition.)

Austen-Smith and Banks find many equilibria of the overall game, but we discuss here just one particularly interesting equilibrium. In this equilibrium, party 1 chooses a "leftist" policy position $x_1 = 0.20$, party 2 chooses a "rightist" position $x_2 = 0.80$, and party 3 chooses a "centrist" position $x_3 = 0.50$.

Given these positions, if everyone voted for the party that has the position that he most prefers, then the expected vote shares would be 35 percent for party 1, 35 percent for party 2, and 30 percent for party 3, with party 3 getting the votes of all voters whose type is between 0.35 and 0.65. There would be some small randomness around these expected shares, because the voters' types are random variables, but the law of large numbers would make shares close to these very likely. So the voters would anticipate that no party would get a majority, and party 3 would be the smallest party, and so the governing coalition would be formed either between parties 1 and 3 or between parties 2 and 3. Thus, the government policy position y would almost surely be either $0.35 = (x_1 + x_3)/2$ or $0.65 = (x_2 + x_3)/2$, depending on whether party 1 or party 2 gets more votes. But then voters would recognize that the crucial question is whether party 1 or party 2 will get more votes, and voters for party 3 would recognize that they have no impact on this crucial question. So the voters whose types are between 0.35 and 0.50 would prefer to deviate and vote for party 1, while the voters whose types are between 0.50 and 0.65 would prefer to deviate and vote for party 2. So party 3's support should be diminished by the greater incentive to vote in a way that can influence the crucial race among the two big parties (expected to be parties 1 and 2) to form the governing coalition.

The rational defections from party 3 to parties 1 and 2 do not stop until party 3 is in serious danger of being eliminated from the legislature, that is, when the expected vote share for party 3 drops to the representational quota $\alpha = 0.05$. So only the voters whose types are between 0.475 ($= 0.50 - \alpha/2$) and 0.525 ($= 0.50 + \alpha/2$) should vote for party 3, while all voters with types below 0.475 vote for party 1, and all voters with types above 0.525 vote for party 2. In this scenario, a voter with type 0.475 recognizes that voting for party 1 instead of party 3 might have the beneficial effect of moving government policy from 0.65 to 0.35 (by making party 1, rather than party 2, the leader of a coalition with party 3); but voting for party 1 instead of 3 might also have the undesirable effect of moving government policy from 0.65 to 0.80 or from 0.35 to 0.20, by driving party 3 out of the legislature and allowing party 1 or 2 to form a more extreme one-party government.

To complete the description of this equilibrium, it remains to consider the first stage and explain why the parties do not want to deviate to other policy positions. The answer is that the subgame after the first stage has many equilibria. For any two parties at different positions, the subgame after the first stage has an equilibrium in which every voter votes for his more preferred among these two parties, knowing that a vote for the third party (having 0 expected votes) would be wasted. So the parties may feel constrained to choose $x_1 = 0.20$, $x_2 = 0.80$, and $x_3 = 0.50$ by the perception that, if any one party announced another policy position then the voters' expected behavior would shift to the equilibrium in which nobody votes for this party.

Thus, studying the post-election legislative bargaining game together with the electoral game enables us to see that voters should be concerned about which major party will get to lead the post-election coalitional bargaining. This concern may cause a voter, even in a proportional representation system, to rationally vote for a party other than the one whose policy position he most prefers. The result can be a proportional representation legislature that has disproportionately large parties near the extremes of the political spectrum, while small centrist parties hover at the brink of extinction. Reducing the minimal representation quota α actually exacerbates this effect, because the small party's vote share decreases with α in equilibrium.

The four models in this chapter make different assumptions and reach different conclusions. The goal here has not been to create a unified theory of politics. Our goal has been rather to illustrate the range of political questions into which theoretical analysis can offer valuable insight. Many more theoretical models and empirical studies are needed, to help us better understand how political behavior of voters and politicians may be shaped by the structures of democracy.

References

Alesina, A. and Rosenthal, H. (1995). *Partisan Politics, Divided Government, and the Economy*. Cambridge: Cambridge University Press.
Austen-Smith, D. and Banks, J. (1988). "Elections, coalitions, and legislative outcomes." *American Political Science Review*, 82: 405–22.

Baron, D. and Ferejohn, J. (1989). "Bargaining in legislatures." *American Political Science Review*, 83: 1181–206.

Carey, J. and Shugart, M. (1995). "Incentives to cultivate a personal vote: a rank ordering of electoral formulas." *Electoral Studies*, 14: 417–40.

Cox, G. (1987a). *The Efficient Secret*. Cambridge: Cambridge University Press.

(1987b). "Electoral equilibrium under alternative voting institutions." *American Journal of Political Science*, 31: 82–108.

(1990). "Centripetal and centrifugal incentives in electoral systems." *American Journal of Political Science*, 34: 903–35.

(1994). "Strategic voting equilibria under single non-transferable vote." *American Political Science Review*, 88: 608–21.

Cox, G. and McCubbins, M. (1993). *Legislative Leviathan*. Berkeley: University of California Press.

Diermeier, D. and Myerson, R. (1995). "Lobbying and incentives for legislative organization." Northwestern University Discussion Paper.

Duverger, M. (1954). *Political Parties: Their Organization and Activity in the Modern State* (B. North and R. North, trans.). New York: Wiley.

Feddersen, T. (1992). "A voting model implying Duverger's law and positive turnout." *Amerian Journal of Political Science*, 36: 938–62.

Feddersen, T. and Pesendorfer, W. (1995). "The swing voter's curse." Forthcoming in *American Economic Review*.

Galeotti, G. and Merlo, A. (1994). "Political collusion and corruption in a representative democracy." *Public Finance*, 49: 232–43.

Gilligan, T. and Krehbiel, K. (1990). "Organization of informative committees by a rational legislature." *American Journal of Political Science*, 34: 531–54.

Grofman, B. and Lijphart, A. (eds.) (1986). *Electoral Laws and Their Political Consequences*. New York: Agathon Press.

Groseclose, T. and Snyder, J. (1996). "Buying supermajorities." *American Political Science Review*, 90: 303–315.

Huber, J. (1992). "Restrictive legislative procedures in France and the United States." *American Political Science Review*, 86: 675–87.

Laver, M. and Schofield, N. (1990). *Multiparty Government: Politics of Coalition Formation in Europe*. Oxford: Oxford University Press.

Laver, M. and Shepsle, K. (1994). *Cabinet Ministers and Parliamentary Government*. Cambridge: Cambridge University Press.

(1996). *Making and Breaking Governments*. Cambridge: Cambridge University Press.

Ledyard, J. (1984). "The pure theory of large two-candidate elections." *Public Choice*, 44: 7–41.

Lijphart, A. (1990). "The political consequences of electoral laws, 1945–1985." *American Political Science Review*, 84: 481–96.

(1992). *Parliamentary versus Presidential Government*. Oxford: Oxford University Press.

(1994). *Electoral Systems and Party Systems in Twenty-Seven Democracies, 1945–1990*. Oxford: Oxford University Press.

McKelvey, R. and Riezman, R. (1992). "Seniority in legislatures." *American Political Science Review*, 86: 951–65.

Moe, T. and Caldwell, M. (1994). "Institutional foundations of democratic government: a comparison of presidential and parliamentary systems." *Journal of Institutional and Theoretical Economics*, 150: 171–95.

Mueller, D. (1989). *Public Choice II*. Cambridge: Cambridge University Press.

Myerson, R. (1993a). "Effectiveness of electoral systems for reducing government corruption." *Games and Economic Behavior*, 5: 118–32.

(1993b). "Incentives to cultivate favored minorities under alternative electoral systems." *American Political Science Review*, 87: 856–69.

(1995). "Analysis of democratic institutions: structure, conduct, and performance." *Journal of Economic Perspectives*, 9(1): 77–89.

Myerson, R. and Weber, R. (1993). "A theory of voting equilibria." *American Political Science Review*, 87: 102–14.

Osborne, M. (1995). "Spatial models of political competition under plurality rule." *Canadian Journal of Economics*, 28: 261–301.

Rae, D. (1971). *Political Consequences of Electoral Laws*, 2nd edn. New Haven: Yale University Press.

Riker, W. (1982a). *Liberalism against Populism*. San Francisco: Freeman.

(1982b). "The two-party system and Duverger's law." *American Political Science Review*, 76: 753–66.

Shepsle, K. (1979). "Institutional arrangements and equilibrium in multidimensional voting models." *American Journal of Political Science*, 23: 27–59.

(1991). *Models of Multiparty Competition*. Chur: Harwood Academic Publishing.

Shepsle, K. and Weingast, B. (1994). "Positive theories of congressional institutions." *Legislative Studies Quarterly*, 19: 149–79.

Shugart, M. and Carey, J. (1992). *Presidents and Assemblies*. Cambridge: Cambridge University Press.

Snyder, J. (1991). "On buying legislatures." *Economics and Politics*, 3: 93–109.

Taagepera, R. and Shugart, M. (1989). *Seats and Votes*. New Haven, Yale University Press.

Weingast, B. and Marshall, W. (1988). "The industrial organization of congress." *Journal of Political Economy*, 96: 132–63.

CHAPTER 4

Game-theoretic models of market structure

John Sutton

1 GAME THEORY AND INDUSTRIAL ORGANIZATION: AN ABC

It has become a familiar observation in recent years that the literature on game-theoretic models in industrial organization faces a serious dilemma. The richness and flexibility of this class of models provide a framework within which we can "rationalize" a huge range of possible "equilibrium outcomes." Whatever the phenomenon, we seem to have a model for it. Should we see this as a success, or as an embarrassment? Does this body of theory allow *any* outcome to be rationalized? After all, the content of a theory lies in the set of outcomes which it excludes. Judged on these terms, is the enterprise empty?[1]

The huge range of outcomes that can be rationalized can be traced to two features of these models. First, many of the models in this literature have multiple equilibria. Second, the appropriate specification of the model is rarely obvious. (Is competition to be à la Bertrand, or à la Cournot? Should entry be modeled as simultaneous, or sequential?) Sometimes it is possible, by referring to the observable features of some particular market, to decide in favor of one model specification over another. In other cases, however, the features that distinguish candidate models must be treated as unobservables, at least from the point of view of the modeler. Both these features tend to widen the set of outcomes that may be rationalized as equilibria (figure 4.1).

These observations lead to two conclusions:

(1) It will not usually be possible, by reference to observable market characteristics, to specify a unique outcome as "the equilibrium outcome." We may have to be content with placing limited restrictions on the space of outcomes, partitioning

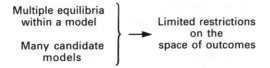

Figure 4.1 The dilemma: game theoretic models are flexible, but do they have content?

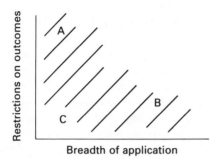

Figure 4.2 A trade-off

outcomes into those that can be supported as equilibria of some admissible model, and those that cannot.

(2) Insofar as part of the problem arises as a result of the influence of observable characteristics that vary across industries, it follows that the range of candidate models may be narrowed by restricting attention to one industry, or set of cognate industries. In other words, a tradeoff may appear between the breadth of application of a theory, and the tightness of the restrictions that it places upon the set of outcomes.

The tradeoff between breadth of application and tightness of restrictions motivates the currently popular literature on "single industry studies." Here the aim is to analyze a specific market, relying on special (institutional or other) features of that market to motivate assumptions. In figure 4.2, A is for Auctions. Here, the strategy of focusing on a highly specific context comes into its own. The institution of the auction specifies explicitly the rules of the game. We know the actions available to players, and specifying the strategy space poses few problems. Here, we avoid almost all the unpleasant arbitrariness in specifying the game: the rules of the auction (almost) specify the game itself. Moreover, in some settings the model gives precise, non-trivial, and pleasing predictions. At its most impressive, the theory delivers convincing explanations of patterns in the data that would be hard to account for in terms of some alternative models (see, for example, Hendricks and Porter (1988)).[2]

But a narrowing of the domain does not always lead to such happy results. The classic problem area in this respect is that of dynamic oligopoly models and in particular the analysis of cartel stability. Here we are at point C in figure 4.2. Many quite different cartel models are available. Case studies of cartels show that different cartels do indeed behave in quite different ways.[3] But even if we narrow the domain to a specific cartel over a specific period, we still fall short of any precision of predictions. The best we can hope for there is a "model selection" exercise. This problem arises more generally throughout the whole area of "dynamic oligopoly models" (see, for example, Gasmi, Laffont, and Vuong (1990)).

The opposite end of the tradeoff arises in the bounds approach to market structure (Sutton (1991)). Here, at point B in the figure, the idea is to turn away from the now-dominant emphasis on single-industry studies and to return to the traditional emphasis on mechanisms that appear to be relevant across the general run of industries. The price we pay for widening the domain of application is that the set of candidate models that we must admit is now wider, and the constraints on outcomes that hold good for all these candidate models are correspondingly weaker. The aim is not to identify some unique "equilibrium outcome" but rather to place some bounds on the set of outcomes that can be supported as equilibria.

This chapter looks at one area of the recent Industrial Organization (IO) literature, the part concerned with "explaining market structure," from the perspective displayed in figure 4.2. No attempt is made to be comprehensive; rather, the aim is to discuss some examples of current research from this perspective. With that in mind, we begin with the quest for "general" properties (point B), before turning to studies which narrow the domain in order to sharpen the constraints on outcomes (B → A). In the final section, we look at the inherent limits of this kind of approach. Here, part of the problem lies in the fact that, however narrow the scope of inquiry, the presence of multiple equilibria and the problem of unobservables place serious limits on the extent to which we can impose constraints on the space of outcomes (point C).

2   STRONG MECHANISMS I: PRICE COMPETITION AND THE MARKET SIZE–MARKET STRUCTURE RELATIONSHIP

Much of the recent IO literature on market structure has been formulated within the framework of multi-stage games. Over a series of stages, firms make choices that involve the expenditure of fixed and sunk costs, whether by entering a market by constructing a plant, by introducing new products or building additional plant capacity, or by carrying out advertising or research and development (R&D). In a final stage subgame, all the results of such prior actions are summarized in terms of some "space of outcomes," i.e., the final configuration of plants and/or products that emerges at the penultimate stage of the game. A description of this "outcome" enters as a set of parameters in the payoff function of the final stage (price competition) subgame, and so the "outcome" of the entry process, together with a specification of the nature of price competition, determines the vector of final stage profits, and of market shares.

In order to circumvent the problems posed by multiple equilibria, and by the role of unobservables, it is of interest to develop propositions that hold good across some suitably defined *class* of models. This class should encompass a range of models between which we cannot hope to distinguish empirically. We might, for example, want to look at propositions that hold good independently of the nature of price competition (Bertrand, Cournot), the entry process (simultaneous, sequential), and so on. It is possible to identify several "mechanisms"[4] that operate in a fairly robust way across a wide class of models, and in what follows we focus attention of these "strong" mechanisms.

The most elementary mechanism examined in recent literature rests upon the assumption that equilibrium price falls (strictly, is non-increasing) with entry. This assumption is well founded, both theoretically and empirically. At the theoretical level, it holds good in a wide class of standard models, including elementary one-shot oligopoly models and various product differentiation models. In the dynamic oligopoly (cartel stability) literature, where multiple equilibria are the norm, some corresponding statements can be made regarding the maximum price, or profit per firm, that can be sustained at equilibrium. Such a robust result invites attempts to construct counterexamples, and these are indeed available. It is a measure of the robustness of the result that such examples are rather contrived, involving for example a carefully constructed distribution of consumer tastes over the space of product characteristics (Rosenthal (1980)). At the empirical level, too, direct evidence on entry and price is strongly supportive of the assumption; the most important body of evidence is the volume edited by Weiss (1989).

What concerns us here are the implications of this assumption for equilibrium market structure. These implications are non-trivial, and they throw some interesting light on certain arguments regarding competition policy.[5] The most important implications relate to the relationship between the size of a market and equilibrium market structure. In describing these implications, we confine attention, in this section, to the class of "symmetric" product differentiation models. These models share the property that each product variety enters into the consumers' utility function(s) in the same way, so that the firms' profits depend only upon the number of product varieties offered by each firm.[6]

We confine attention in this section to models in which the cost of entering the market, or of introducing a new product, is fixed exogenously. (There is no advertising, or R&D.) Consider, first, a setting in which N firms enter, each with one product, at an entry cost of $\varepsilon > 0$.[7] Symmetry ensures that all prices are equal at equilibrium. We summarize the properties of the final stage subgame by expressing equilibrium price as a function $p(N \mid \theta)$, where p is price, N is the number of firms, and θ is a shift parameter indexing the "toughness of price competition." It is assumed that firms operate with constant marginal cost, and that increases in market size occur by way of successive replications of the population of consumers, so that the distribution of tastes remains constant. Under these circumstances, the vector of equilibrium prices is independent of market size, S, and equilibrium profit can be written in the form $S\pi(N \mid \theta)$, where the function $\pi(N \mid \theta)$ is the "solved out" profit function of the final stage (price competition) subgame. The function $\pi(N \mid \theta)$ is decreasing in N. A rise in θ, by definition, leads to a fall in equilibrium price, for any given N. If we assume that the profit per firm is also decreasing in price for all prices below the monopoly level, then an increase in θ implies a fall in profit per firm.

If we define the equilibrium number of firms, N^*, as the largest integer satisfying

$$S\pi(N^* \mid \theta) \geq \varepsilon$$

then N^* rises with S, leading to a fall in concentration, measured by $1/N$, as market size increases.

Once this argument is extended to a multi-product firm setting, in which each firm is free to enter any number of distinct product varieties, at a cost of ε per product, this functional relationship is replaced by a lower bound relation. At a given S, we may have a large number of single product firms, or a smaller number of firms, each with several products (Sutton (1991, chapter 2)).

The parameter θ captures the effect of exogenous influences, such as legal restraints on competition, or changes in transport costs that intensify competition between remote firms. Changes in such factors lead to a shift in the functional relationship between equilibrium price and profit, for any *given* market structure. The phrase "toughness of price competition" refers to this functional relationship. For any fixed value of S, an increase in the

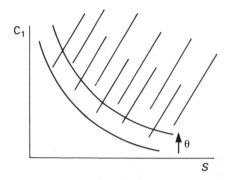

Figure 4.3 Increasing the toughness of price competition

toughness of price competition shifts the lower bound to concentration upwards (figure 4.3).

The "price competition" mechanism can be observed empirically by looking at certain "natural experiments" in which the institutional factors affecting the toughness of price competition underwent a substantial change at some point. For example: in Sutton (1991), the histories of the salt and sugar industries are examined by reference to changes in transport costs, and to shifts in competition policy, both across countries, and over time. The structural shifts and cross-country differences in structure appear to be closely in line with the operation of this mechanism. A major shift in competition policy occurred in the UK in the 1960s, with the outlawing of various restrictive agreements between firms. This allows a comparison of structural shifts between the group of industries so affected, and a control group of industries in which no such agreements had existed prior to the legal changes. It has been known for some time that concentration appeared to have increased in those industries that were affected by this increase in the toughness of price competition. A recent detailed comparison of the two groups of industries by Symeonidis (1995) offers strong support for this view.

Narrowing the domain

The preceding results turned on the assumption that profit per firm was decreasing in N. In the special setting in which firms offer homogeneous products, and in which all firms earn equal profit at equilibrium, a stronger assumption can be justified: that total industry profit is decreasing in N. In other words, we replace our earlier assumption that $\pi(N \mid \theta)$ is decreasing in N, by the stronger assumption that $N\pi(N \mid \theta)$ is decreasing in N. This assumption is not quite so restrictive as might appear to be the case at first glance. If, for example, products are differentiated, and if each firm offers a single variety, this assumption remains valid so long as total industry sales respond only weakly to the introduction of new products, prices being held constant, i.e., the "market expansion" effect is weak, in the terminology of Shaked and Sutton (1990). In this form, the assumption can be justified for an interestingly wide range of markets. One important example is where each firm operates a single retail outlet within a small town. Since no customer is very far from any store, the market expansion effect from adding stores is small.

This stronger property implies that, as we increase the size of the market (by way of successive replications of the population of consumers), *the equilibrium number of firms increases less than proportionally with the size of the market.* To see this, define the minimum ("threshold") market that can support N sellers as S_N, via the equation

$$S_N \pi(N \mid \theta) = \varepsilon$$

whence

$$\frac{S_N}{N} = \frac{\varepsilon}{N\pi(N \mid \theta)}.$$

The assumption that $N\pi(N \mid \theta)$ is decreasing in N now implies that the threshold size S_N rises more than proportionally with N. In other words, an increase in market size leads to a less than proportionate increase in the number of sellers.

Bresnahan and Reiss (1987, 1990) analyze this effect by reference to a set of "isolated towns" across the United States. They look at the number of retail establishments of a specific kind, such as gas stations, as a function of the size of the market, measured by population (together with some ancillary variables whose influence is minor).

A central focus of interest lies in comparing the threshold size of market at which entry by a monopolist becomes profitable with the threshold size that suffices to support a duopoly. Given data on town population and the number of sellers present, the authors proceed to estimate these threshold sizes.

The basic specification used by the authors is as follows: firms move simultaneously. Entrants have the same profit function. Fixed cost is unobservable, and is different for each firm, the realization of fixed cost being independent draws from the same normal distribution. This allows the model to be estimated using an ordered probit model.[8]

This analysis is extended in Bresnahan and Reiss (1987) to various types of retailers (or sellers of professional services) and to larger towns supporting several outlets or sellers. The most striking result to emerge is that the price competition effect is exhausted once three to five sellers are present; thereafter, an increase in market size leads to a proportionate increase in the number of sellers.

It seem, then, that the predicted "less-than-proportional" increase in the number of sellers is indeed borne out in the data. But this observation begs an obvious question: Could this less-than-proportionate increase be explained by reference to a simple alternative story, quite independently of the price competition effect? Suppose some sellers are more efficient than others, so that a pool of potential entrants of varying efficiency levels is available. Markets of small size attract the most efficient entrant. If efficiency levels differ greatly, a large increase in size is needed before the second firm will enter, even if there is no fall in price after entry.

How can this "heterogeneity of firms" interpretation of the "less-than-proportional" increase in the number of sellers be distinguished from the "competition effect" interpretation? Berry (1992) shows how this problem can be tackled by reference to a set of markets across which the same group of firms (potential entrants) are active. His study relates to airlines servicing 1,219 routes between 50 US cities. It is known that substantial efficiency differences exist between different airlines, and that their relative efficiency levels may differ across markets (routes). This context is a natural one in which to tackle the 'heterogeneity of firms" issue.

The unit of analysis (individual market) in this case is a city pair. Each airline is either "active" or "inactive" in any market. This allows the same form of "single product" model to be used, as was used in the Bresnahan–Reiss study.

Bresnahan and Reiss modeled firms' fixed cost (or profits) as independent draws from some underlying distribution and proceeded to estimate entry thresholds for $1, 2, 3 \ldots$ firms, without restricting the form of the relation between firm numbers and profit levels. Berry, on the other hand, posits a particular (logarithmic) form for the relationship linking profits to the number of firms, but he goes beyond the Bresnahan–Reiss specification by introducing a firm-specific contribution to profits. The profit of firm i in market k is written as

$$\pi_{i,k}(N) = X_i \beta - \delta \ln N + Z_{i,k} \alpha + \rho u_{i,0} + \sigma u_{i,k}.$$

Here X_i is a vector of market characteristics, N is the number of firms, $Z_{i,k}$ is a vector of firm characteristics, while β, δ, α, ρ, and σ are parameters to be estimated.

The unobserved component $\rho u_{i,0} + \sigma u_{i,k} = \varepsilon_{i,k}$ is a combination of a market-specific contribution $u_{i,0}$ and a firm-specific term $u_{i,k}$ that is unobserved by the econometrician, but is known to the firm.

One could, in principle, proceed by partitioning the space of $\varepsilon_{i,k}$ into regions corresponding to different equilibrium outcomes, and writing down a likelihood function. However, once we have a large number of entrants that differ in their observed characteristics, this partitioning involves a very large number of irregularly shaped zones. Writing down an explicit representation of the likelihood function is infeasible, and the author uses simulation estimators to get around this difficulty. The estimates are then compared with those obtained by ignoring firm heterogeneity and applying an ordered probit model. The results obtained in the two cases differ substantially.[9]

The preferred model, which allows for firm heterogeneity, indicates a substantial price competition effect, and this is consistent with the Bresnahan–Reiss interpretation of the observed "less-than-proportional" increase in the number of sellers.[10]

3   STRONG MECHANISMS II: ESCALATION AND NON-CONVERGENCE

Once we turn to those industries where advertising and R&D play a significant role, a second type of mechanism appears, which shares the "robust" features of the price competition mechanism. The basic theorem is again stated relative to the class of multi-stage games, in which each firm incurs a fixed and sunk cost F in some early stage(s), and thereafter earns ("gross" or "post-entry") profit $S\pi$ in some final stage (price competition) subgame, where S denotes market size and π is a function of the vector of products entered (and so of the fixed costs incurred) by all firms in earlier stages.

The main theorem is as follows (Shaked and Sutton (1987)):

> suppose: for some constants $a > 0$ and $K > 1$, a firm that spends K times as much as any rival on fixed outlays will earn a final stage payoff no less than aS;
> then: there is a lower bound to concentration (as measured by the maximal market share of the largest firm), which is independent of the size of the market.

The idea is this: as market size increases, the incentives to escalate spending on fixed outlays rises. Increases in market size will be associated with a rise in fixed outlays by at least some firms, and this effect will be sufficiently strong to exclude an indefinite decline in the level of concentration.

The lower bound to concentration depends on the degree to which an escalation of fixed outlays results in profits at the final stage and so on the constants a and K via the ratio $a/(1 + K)$. If we choose the pair (a, K) which maximizes this ratio and write the maximal value of the ratio as α, then each industry can simply be labeled by the scalar index α.

The main empirical problem lies in the fact that there is no direct way of measuring α and so predicting the value of the lower bound to concentration. One way forward lies in making the bold hypothesis that for some group of (advertising – or R&D – intensive) industries, α lies above some minimal positive level, so that for the pooled sample of industries, the empirically estimated lower bound to concentration lies above some strictly positive value.

How can such a prediction be tested? One line of attack would be to look at the same industry across a series of countries. A problem of interdependence across countries arises where some firms operate in more than one country. In the case of advertising-intensive industries, this may not be a serious problem, since the firm must spend fixed outlays to create its "brand image" in each country. For R&D-intensive industries, this problem is fatal to cross-country studies, for products need only be invented once. In R&D-intensive industries, we need to think in terms of a single global market for each product.

If cross-country studies of the same industry are ruled out, what of studies based on a comparison of different industries within a single country? In pursuing this second line of attack, one problem is to control for the "exogenous" element of fixed outlays, which may crudely be identified with the cost of constructing a production plant. Measuring market size in units equal to the cost of constructing a single m.e.s. plant offers a crude way of controlling for this. This is clearly more attractive at very low levels of aggregation, where we are dealing with industries in which all firms produce the same range of products using similar production methods.

Both these lines of attack have been pursued in the recent literature. Sutton (1991) presented evidence for 20 food and drink industries across six countries, splitting the sample into a (very) "low advertising" group and a "high advertising" group. Robinson (1993), using the PIMS dataset for the US examined 1,880 observations on businesses, classifying the industries in which the businesses operated into advertising-intensive, R&D-intensive, and others. Most recently, a consortium of European economists have assembled a large dataset for three-digit industries across four European countries, and have looked at both advertising-intensive and R&D-intensive industries (Matraves (1992), Lyons *et al* (1995)) All these studies indicate that the "non-convergence" property appears to hold good for advertising-intensive and R&D-intensive industries.[11]

The non-convergence property might seem at first glance to represent a fairly weak constraint on the data. It is interesting, therefore, to ask what this relationship implies for the older "regression analyses" of the determinants of concentration. In these studies it was assumed that observed concentration levels might be "explained" by certain "Barriers to entry" that might be proxied by measures of scale economies, advertising intensity, and R&D intensity. Regressions of concentration on these variables indicated that scale economies and advertising intensity were associated with higher levels of concentration.[12] An interesting implication of the lower bound property is that the presence of this bound is sufficient to *imply* that the elementary regressions of concentration on scale economies and advertising intensity, which under this theory are a misspecification, would indeed yield the positive correlations that were observed by Hart and Clarke (1980); in other words, the bounds results encompass these basic regression results (Sutton (1991, p. 124, 127–8)).

One important feature of the game-theoretic approach is that its claims can be tested in a direct and powerful way by turning to case-history evidence. In contrast to "Walrasian" models based on a fictitious "auctioneer," any model based on a Nash equilibrium concept makes a claim about *how* disequilibrium situations are resolved. If an outcome cannot be supported as a Nash equilibrium, then it follows by definition that some "profitable deviation" is available to some firm. The empirical content of any game-theoretic model lies in a claim that certain outcomes will not be observed, and the model of necessity provides us with a qualitative description of the kind of deviation which will be profitable in such a configuration. This feature of the game-theoretic approach greatly enhances the scope for testing: if the theory is correct, then it should be possible in case studies to show such "profitable deviations" at work. The escalation mechanism carries a fingerprint that should be observed in case histories under certain well-defined circumstances. The fingerprint of an escalation process involves a combination of rising advertising–sales or R&D–sales ratios, together with declining profit–sales ratios, leading in due course to the shakeout of all but a small group of leading firms. Examples of this process at work have been documented, for example in Sutton (1991, chapters 8, 10, 12, and 13).

Narrowing the domain

The non-convergence property places a lower bound on concentration. In other words, a small number of firms will dominate the market at any time.

Will this group be stable over time, or will its composition change from one product generation to the next? To proceed further, we must narrow the domain of analysis, and focus attention on features of the market that are highly industry specific.

In general, it is extremely difficult to say anything about patterns of industry leadership across successive product generations. Extreme patterns have attracted much attention in the literature ("persistence of dominance" versus "leapfrogging"). Yet the factors determining whether such patterns will emerge are notoriously sensitive to the beliefs of agents, the nature of price competition, and other factors which are notoriously difficult to measure[13] (Beath, Katsoulacos, and Ulph (1987), Vickers (1986), Budd, Harris, and Vickers (1993)). Only in quite special circumstances can we hope to make any progress on this issue.

One interesting set of circumstances is that in which learning effects are large and the spillover of benefits to rival firms is relatively small, so that the influence of learning effects on the evolution of market structure is important. Games which feature learning effects have been widely studied in the literature (see for example, Spence (1981), Cabral and Riordan (1994)). When this feature is combined with a strong carryover of the private benefits of learning from one product generation to the next, then a leadership position today generates an advantage which consolidates that leadership position tomorrow. In this setting, some conclusions can be drawn for the evolution of leadership over time (Gruber (1994)).

An industry that has been much studied in recent years is the market for semi-conductor memory chips during the 1970s and 1980s.[14] Here, the role played by learning effects is known to be very large. Learning is measured by changes in the proportion of chips that are "satisfactory," initial wastage rates being as high as 80 percent and final rates being as low as 20 percent, the latter figure being achieved within a couple of years – a time period which is large compared with a product generation. Moreover, the carryover of learning benefits across successive generations of chips appears to be very substantial.

An unusual "natural experiment" is afforded by a comparison of the evolution of the markets for two types of memory chips during the 1970s and 1980s, as reported in Gruber (1994). Chips of the EPROM type differ from those of the DRAM type in two relevant respects. As Gruber remarks:

> Production engineers maintain that the learning curve at the firm level is very similar for single generations of DRAMs and EPROMs. Because of the larger market for DRAMs, a DRAM producer can learn faster than an EPROM producer. On the other hand, DRAM producers have to defend their market share within a given generation for a longer time before the availability of a new generation gives them scope for (vertical) product

differentiation. In other words, DRAM producers have to compete for a long period while sitting on a flat part of the learning curve. Cost advantages would be possible if there were economies of scale to exploit. EPROM producers, on the other hand, require much more time to complete learning because of the smaller market. Moreover, once a firm has moved down the learning curve, then after not too long the next generation is already coming out. Because of the relatively slow learning, firms tend to differ in the position on the learning curve. Competition in the EPROM market is therefore more likely to be driven by learning curve effects.

Now if learning effects matter, as in the case of EPROM chips, it follows in Gruber's model that an equilibrium pattern of market shares may persist over time, in which one firm operates as a "leader" over successive generations, entering each generation early, and exiting early also. This firm enjoys high profits as the sole producer of new generation chips for a short period during which price is very high. It then switches its production to the next generation as entry occurs and prices fall. Other firms may follow one or other of two strategies. They may choose to enter later than the leader, incurring lower fixed costs, as a result of learning spillovers or slower R&D programs, but remain active longer than the leader within each generation. On the other hand, a firm may choose to spend even less on fixed outlays, and enter late, eventually becoming the sole remaining supplier of "old generation" chips (for which some residual market will remain, after all rivals have switched their production capacity forward to new generations). Within any given generation of chips, the "leader" firm will have a market share that declines over time, while a firm following the "late entry" strategy will have a market share that rises over time. Firms following an intermediate strategy will have a share that rises and then falls.

The evolution of market shares in the EPROM market follows this pattern, with Intel as "leader" and with Texas Instruments as one of a number of "second tier" suppliers, while AMD plays the third "late entrant" strategy. The leadership pattern is not completely stable (for example, Texas led Intel in 64K chips, and its market share for this category declined rapidly over time). Nonetheless there appears to be a strong pattern in the market share profiles, with Intel's share in each segment falling rapidly, while AMD's starts late and rises over time. That this pattern can indeed be traced to the role of learning effects seems to be well established by direct evidence on differences in learning effects as between EPROMs and DRAMs, and by the fact that this stable pattern of market shares over successive generations did not appear in the DRAM market (Gruber (1994, p. 67)).

But is this a "test of theory?" As with most attempts to narrow the domain of analysis with a view to obtaining tighter restrictions on outcomes, this exercise falls short of providing a test of the kind we have been discussing in earlier sections. The model incorporates the market-specific features of learning effects which carry over across product generations. But it is not the case that any model with these features will necessarily generate the "three-strategy" pattern of Gruber's equilibrium. The emergence of this "realistic" feature of the market turns on the exact design of the model, and on parameter values that cannot be estimated directly. In other words, the model illustrates a possible pattern of events that meshes well with what we see in practice. Even the best of single-industry studies may be able to progress no further than this. The problems we face in such single-industry studies are typical of the more general class of problems posed by "unobservables," to which we turn in the next section.

4.   THE LIMITATIONS OF GAME-THEORETIC MODELS

Unobservables and history

If a process of narrowing the domain by reference to observable industry characteristics could be extended indefinitely, then we might move up the frontier shown in figure 4.2, arriving eventually at a point where we had "one true model" which specified a single "equilibrium structure" for each industry. If this were so, then empirical studies of market structure could be forced back into the traditional ("regression analysis") model, in which observable market characteristics are assumed to determine a unique equilibrium structure, up to some "random error" term.

But a central message of the game-theoretic IO literature is that such a program is infeasible. The presence of multiple equilibria, and – more importantly – the role played by unobservable features of the market rules out any such goal. What kinds of feature must be regarded as "unobservables?" It is useful to distinguish between two types of candidate. The first is a feature that is simply hard to identify, measure or proxy within available datasets. Consider, for example, the kind of "strategic asymmetry" which we model as a "first-mover advantage." This kind of asymmetry is subtle. Even if we have detailed historical information for a particular industry, it may be difficult to decide whether a firm chose its plant capacity on the basis of a correct belief that some rival firm would adjust its planned capacity accordingly. And yet we can, in rare and special circumstances, be lucky. Sometimes the world throws up natural experiments in which accidents in the timing of market entry are such that we can confidently assert that a "strategic asymmetry" was present. Better still, we may be able to find examples where such an asymmetry was present in some countries, but absent in others. The infamous "margarine laws," which inhibited the sale of retail margarine in the United States up to the 1950s, afford an unusual and instructive natural experiment of this kind (Sutton (1991, chapter 9)). Notwithstanding such happy accidents, however, it would be a hopeless business to try to incorporate the influence of such subtle but important influences on structure into a cross-industry study, except by way of exploring particular industry histories in the hope of uncovering occasional natural experiments.

The second kind of feature that must be treated as unobservable relates to the beliefs held by agents. Here, we are dealing with an aspect of the market that is not merely difficult to measure, but one which is intrinsically unobservable as far as the researcher is concerned. Yet the influence of such beliefs can be far-reaching, as the game-theoretic models insist.

The nature of the difficulty is well illustrated by the events surrounding a sudden and substantial jump in concentration in the U.K. Bread and Flour industries in the 1960s, which are documented in Sutton (1991, pp. 166–8). In these industries, a wave of acquisitions in both industries was set off by a shared belief among (upstream) flour millers and (downstream) bread-bakers that other firms were going to engage in acquisitions, and this stimulated others to move quickly in order to avoid "foreclosure." The interesting thing about this incident is that it was precipitated by a quarrel between two firms, and the actions that followed hinged on the fears of each firm that if it failed to acquire, someone else would. What is remarkable about the incident is that its effects on structure were far-reaching, and have persisted for three decades. Moreover, these events were peculiar to the UK market, and appear to be without parallel in other countries. It would seem that any attempt to "explain" this shift in concentration by reference to the pattern of technology and tastes in the industry must be implausible.

As this example makes clear, the roles of "unobservables" is closely intertwined with the claim that "history matters." Business historians continually emphasize the role of accident and personality in shaping the evolution of firms and industries. What the game-theoretic approach does is to push us into a middle ground, in which dialogue becomes easier. It tells us that economic mechanisms related to observable industry characteristics place important but limited constraints on outcomes, while leaving ample room for the accidents of history to influence what happens within such bounds. The economist is free to extend the list of relevant economic influences on outcomes, but only at the cost of introducing more subtle influences than we can hope to control for, by reference to any objective measures of "industry characteristics."

Independence effects

While the problem posed by unobservables is intrinsic and unavoidable there is a second problem which, though central, is more tractable. This relates to the presence of "independence effects."

Any industry will contain clusters of products or plants that compete closely. But an industry, as conventionally defined in official statistics, will usually contain more than one such cluster; it will be possible to identify pairs, or sets, of products that do not compete directly. What is at issue here is that a firm's profit function may be additively separable into contributions deriving from a number of "remote" products.[15] Any real market in which products are spread over either some geographic space, or some space of attributes, will tend to exhibit this feature. In other words, most conventionally defined industries exhibit both some strategic interpendence, and some degree of independence across submarkets.

The game-theoretic literature has been concerned with exploring strategic interdependence, and this program involves characterizing the full set of "equilibria" for the corresponding model. Once separate submarkets are present, however, it is natural to ask whether some combinations of outcomes are more or less "likely" to occur.[16]

The reason for emphasizing the importance of this issue, in the present context, is because of the ubiquity in the standard game-theoretic models of "least concentrated" outcomes in which N firms each have the same minimal (unit) size. These "symmetric" outcomes play a central role in the theoretical literature, especially in relation to the definition of lower bounds to concentration. Such "symmetric" outcomes are rarely, if ever, encountered in practice; rather, it is well known that the size distribution of firms in an industry is normally rather skewed. One way of seeing why this is so, and thereby bringing game-theoretic models into a closer mesh with empirical evidence, lies in building game-theoretic models of markets that consist of separate submarkets, in which the roles of strategic interdependence, and of independence effects, can be combined. By doing so, we might build a bridge between the modern game-theoretic literature, in which strategic interactions are the sole focus of attention, and the older IO literature on the "Growth of Firms," which appealed to independence effects in order to account for the skewed nature of the size distribution of firms. This point is developed in Sutton (1996b).

5   CONCLUDING REMARKS

Five years ago, it was widely claimed that the game-theoretic approach was "empty," because everything depended on the details, and no useful constraints were placed upon the data. Nowadays, such criticisms are becoming rare. In following the logic of the game-theoretic approach, we have been led in a natural way to a new set of theories, and there seems to be some basis for the claim that these theories "work." This has in turn led to a new kind of criticism. Since we emphasize the primacy of a few strong mechanisms, the huge scaffolding of the game-theoretic literature appears to collapse into a simply articulated theory, which captures the first-order effects in the data, together with a rich menu of models corresponding to "special cases." A criticism we now hear is: why bother with the game-theoretic structure at all? Why not just write down the simple (general) models directly?

This argument is unpersuasive. For thirty years, empirical research focused heavily on the study of cross-sectional regularities. In looking at such regularities, researchers could have turned to the kind of structure used, for example, in the bounds approach. In fact, however, they turned to quite different structures. Moreover, the regression relationships they looked for, and reported, are not the ones to which we are led by the game-theoretic approach.

I have, however, a deeper reason for being uneasy about the claim that the simple theory could have been "written down directly." My unease comes from the fact that the lesson we were forced to learn from a decade of game-theoretic models was a painful one, to which there was a long history of resistance in the profession (Sutton (1993)). A tradition stretching from Marshall to Samuelson emphasized the value of attacking the data "as if" it was generated by some "true model." A minority view, which can be traced to Edgeworth, questioned whether this approach was always justified. But so long as our list of reasonable "candidate models" remained manageably small, it was easy to dismiss this minority view. If several candidate models were available, we could "let the data decide" by carrying out some kind of model-selection exercise. What the game-theoretic literature did was to make this response sound hollow: the sheer unmanageability of the class of "reasonable models" forced a change of tack. The only way to obtain any empirically useful constraints on the data was either to confine attention to some very narrow domain where the number of candidate models was small, or else to look at strong mechanisms that held good over some very broad class of candidate models. These approaches have indeed led us back to theories whose structure is pleasingly simple; but these theories are not only different in their detail, but in their form, from what went before. Had some researcher written down these theories in 1970, without reference to game-theoretic models, this would have invited an obvious line of criticism: why stop at these few restrictions? Why these mechanisms rather than others? Why not add more mechanisms, or more structure, or additional assumptions in order to make the model "richer," or more "realistic," or to get "more interesting (tighter) predictions?" And this would simply bring us back to the issues with which I began.

Notes

This chapter was prepared for the World Congress of the Econometric Society, Tokyo, 1995. I would like to thank Alison Hole for her helpful comments on an earlier draft. My thanks are also due to my discussant, Jacques Cremer, for his very helpful suggestions. The financial support of the Economic and Social Research Council and the Leverhulme Trust is gratefully acknowledged.
1 For comments on this dilemma, see Shaked and Sutton (1987), Fisher (1989), Sutton (1990), and Pelzman (1991). The dilemma is not special to industrial organization, although much recent comment suggests that it is. The dilemma is in fact as old as economics: Edgeworth called it the "problem of indeterminacy." The issue is whether the operation of the market mechanism pins things down so tightly that we can model its operation using a set of assumptions which lead to a unique equilibrium outcome. For a discussion of the Edgeworth–Marshall debate and later developments, see Sutton (1993).
2 Unfortunately, this is not always the case. In many settings, the outcome is driven by unobservable distributions of buyers' valuations, and the theory does not constrain the data to any useful degree. For a recent review of these issues, see Laffont (1996).
3 Contrast, for example the (various) mechanisms that have been considered in discussing the JEC cartel (Porter (1983), Ellison (1994)) with the quite different type of story appropriate to the Bromine cartel (Levenstein (1993)).
4 The word "mechanism" is used loosely here; it is possible to formalize this notion, and the related idea of a "Natural Experiment," but to do so requires that we first redefine equilibrium directly on the space of "outcomes;" see (Sutton (1995)).
5 They suggest, for example, that attempts to reduce market concentration in order to increase the intensity of price competition may be ineffectual.
6 These models include the "linear demand model" (Shubik and Levitan (1980)) and the model of Dixit and Stiglitz (1977). They exclude "Hotelling-type" location models.
7 Matters are much more complicated once endogenous sunk costs (such as advertising or R&D) are introduced (Symeonidis (1995)).
8 In specifying an appropriate econometric model, some assumption is needed on the appropriate error specification. Various forms are experimented with in Bresnahan and Reiss (1990), but the choice makes little difference to the estimates. Alternative assumptions were also tried regarding the appropriate form of the entry game. The main results were not sensitive to these changes.
9 It turns out that allowing for the presence of heterogeneity has a major effect on the estimated parameters of the model. A specification that assumes homogeneity of the firms does not, in this setting, lead to the predicted form of the relation

between firm numbers and market size, in the sense that the coefficient δ is not significantly different from zero.

10 The restriction introduced by Berry on the functional form of the profit/numbers relation appears not to be unduly restrictive. To explore the robustness of results in this regard, the model was estimated with separate intercept terms for $N = 1, 2, 3, 4$ and with profit declining linearly with N for $N > 4$. The results were qualitatively similar to those obtained with the restricted form, and the restricted specification could not be rejected against the more general model.

11 These studies all involve the notion that α lies above some minimal level for all industries in the advertising- or R&D-intensive group. Observed levels of the advertising–sales ratio or the R&D–sales ratio are used to partition the sample. This is a crude assumption, and in the case of R&D-intensive industries is problematic. Sutton (1996a) notes that the value of α may be arbitrarily close to zero for some types of technology, even though the equilibrium R&D–sales ratio is high, and describes a method of attack which circumvents this problem.

12 The results regarding R&D intensity are more complex (Sutton (1996a)).

13 They are also very sensitive to factors that are usually "assumed away" in the IO literature, relating to interdivisional conflicts within firms (Foster (1986)).

14 The evolution of market structure in the semi-conductor industry has been widely studied, notably by Flaherty (1984) and Dorfman (1987). Recent studies of learning effects include Irwin and Klenow (1994).

15 Consider, for example, the standard Hotelling model where products are placed along a line. A firm offering a set of non-neighboring products has, at equilibrium, a profit function which is additively separable into contributions from each product.

16 A serious theoretical issue arises in this setting. Game-theoretic models of markets containing independent submarkets will usually have many equilibria. Some of these equilibria will involve strategies in which actions taken in one market are conditioned on earlier actions taken in another. Indeed, equilibria of this kind do seem to be empirically relevant in some cases, as, for example, in the "chain-store" paradox literature. Yet, in practice, this kind of "strategic interdependence" is probably not very common across the general run of markets. A focus on "listing all the equilibria," if used as a general device, may lead us to overstate the scope of strategic interdependence, and to ignore the role played by independence effects. The introduction of "independence effects" within game-theoretic models demands that certain restrictions be placed on the strategy space of the game, a move which runs counter to current practice in this area.

References

Beath, J., Katsoulacos, Y., and Ulph, D. (1987). "Sequential product innovation and industry evolution." *Economic Journal* (supplement), 97: 32–43.

Berry, S. (1992). "Estimation of a model of entry in the airline industry." *Econometrica*, 60: 889–917.

Bresnahan, T. and Reiss, P. (1987). "Do entry conditions vary across markets?" *Brookings Papers on Economic Activity*, 3: 833–81.

(1990). "Entry in monopoly markets." *Review of Economic Studies*, 57: 531–53.

(1991). "Empirical models of discrete games." *Journal of Econometrics*, 48: 57–81.

Budd, C., Harris, C., and Vickers, J. S. (1993). "A model of the evolution of duopoly: does the asymmetry between firms tend to increase or decrease?" *Review of Economic Studies*, 60: 543–74.

Cabral, L. M. B. and Riordan, M. H. (1994) "The learning curve, market dominance and predatory pricing." *Econometrica*, 62: 1115–40.

Dixit, A. K. and Stiglitz, J. E. (1977). "Monopolistic competition and optimum product diversity." *American Economic Review* 67: 297–308.

Dorfman, N. S. (1987). *Innovation and Market Structure: Lessons from the Computer and Semiconductor Industries*. Cambridge, MA: Ballinger Publishing Company.

Ellison, G. (1994). "Theories of cartel stability and the joint executive committee." *Rand Journal of Economics*, 25: 37–57.

Fisher, F. M. (1989). "Games economists play: a noncooperative view." *Rand Journal of Economics*, 20: 113–24.

Flaherty, M. T. (1984). "Market share determination in international semiconductor markets." Harvard Business School Working Paper.

Foster, R. N. (1986). *Innovation: The Attacker's Advantage*, New York: Summit Books.

Gasmi, F., Laffont, J. J., and Vuong, Q. H. (1990). "A structural approach to empirical analysis of collusive behavior." *European Economic Review*, 34: 513–23.

Gruber, H. (1992). "Persistence of leadership in product innovation." *Journal of Industrial Economics*, 40: 359–75.

(1994). *Learning and Strategic Product Innovation: Theory and Evidence for the Semiconductor Industry*. Amsterdam: North Holland.

(1995). "Market structure, learning and product innovation: evidence of the EPROM market." *International Journal of the Economics of Business*, 2: 87–101.

Hart, P. E. and Clarke, R. (1980). *Concentration in British Industry, 1935–75*. Cambridge: Cambridge University Press.

Hendricks, K. and Porter, R. J. (1988) "An empirical study of an auction with asymmetrical information." *American Economic Review*, 14: 301–14.

Irwin, D. A. and Klenow, P. J. (1994). "Learning-by-doing spillovers in the semiconductor industry." *Journal of Political Economy*, 102: 1200–27.

Laffont, J. J. (1996). "Game theory and structural economics: the case of auction data" (Marshall Lecture, European Economic Association 1995). *European Economic Review*, forthcoming.

Levenstein, M. (1993). "Price wars and the stability of collusion: a study of the pre-World War I bromine industry." NBER Working Paper No. 50, Cambridge, MA.

Lyons, B. and Matraves, C. (1995). "Industrial concentration and endogenous sunk costs in the European Union." Economics Research Centre Discussion Paper No. 9505, University of East Anglia.

Pelzman, S. (1991). "The handbook of industrial organization: a review article," *Journal of Political Economy*, 99: 201–17.

Porter, R. (1983). "A study of cartel stability: the joint executive committee 1880–1886." *Rand Journal of Economics*, 14: 301–14.

Roberts, M. J. and Samuelson, L. (1988). "An empirical analysis of dynamic nonprice competition in an oligopolistic industry." *Rand Journal of Economics*, 19: 200–20.

Robinson, W. (1993). "Are Sutton's predictions robust?: empirical evidence on price competition, advertising and the evolution of concentration," University of Michigan, unpublished.

Rosenthal, R. J. (1980). "A model in which an increase in the number of sellers leads to a higher price." *Econometrica*, 48: 1575–9.

Shaked, A. and Sutton, J. (1987). "Product differentiation and industrial structure." *Journal of Industrial Economics*, 36: 131–46.

　(1990). "Multiproduct firms and market structure." *Rand Journal of Economics*, 21: 45–62.

Shubik, M. and Levitan, R. (1980). *Market Structure and Behavior*. Cambridge, MA: Harvard University Press.

Spence, M. A. (1981). "The learning curve and competition." *Bell Journal of Economics*, 12: 49–70.

Sutton, J. (1990). "Explaining everything, explaining nothing? Game theoretic models in industrial organization." *European Economic Review*, 34: 505–12.

　(1991). *Sunk Costs and Market Structure*. Cambridge, MA: MIT Press.

　(1993). "Echoes of Edgeworth: the problem of indeterminacy." *European Economic Review*, 37: 491–9.

　(1995). "One smart agent." STICERD Discussion Paper No. EI/8, London School of Economics.

　(1996a). "Technology and market structure." (Schumpeter Lecture, European Economic Association, September 1995). *European Economic Review*, forthcoming.

　(1996b). "Gibrat's legacy." *Journal of Economic Literature*, forthcoming.

Symeonidis, G. (1995). "Competition law and market structure: a study of the effect of restrictive practices legislation in the UK, 1960–1975." Unpublished.

Vickers, J. S. (1986). "The evolution of market structure when there is a sequence of innovations." *Journal of Industrial Economics*, 35: 1–12.

Weiss, L. (ed.) (1989). *Concentration and Price*. Cambridge, MA: MIT Press.

CHAPTER 5

Rationality and knowledge in game theory

Eddie Dekel and Faruk Gul

1   INTRODUCTION

The concepts of knowledge and rationality have been explicitly applied by economists and game theorists to obtain no-trade results and to characterize solution concepts of games. Implicitly these two concepts underlie much recent work in these fields, ranging from information economics through refinements to attempts to model bounded rationality. Our discussion of the game theoretic and economic literatures on knowledge and rationality will focus on these foundational issues and on the characterizations of solution concepts. Our discussion builds on Harsanyi's (1967) foundation for games of incomplete information and Aumann's (1976) model of common knowledge, on the one hand, and, on the other hand, Bernheim's (1984) and Pearce's (1984) characterization result that, if rationality is common knowledge, then in normal-form games players will choose strategies that survive iterated deletion of strongly dominated strategies.[1]

We begin in section 2 by responding to recent explicit and implicit criticisms of this research agenda. These criticisms are based on the idea that various paradoxes demonstrate that common knowledge of rationality is a problematic notion. We argue instead that these paradoxes are the result of confusing the conclusions that arise from (equilibrium) analysis with assumptions about behavior.[2] A simple example concerns the paradox of cooperation in the Prisoners' Dilemma. Clearly the outcome of the PD will be symmetric. Thus, some have argued, the non-cooperative outcome cannot be the consequence of common knowledge of rationality since, by symmetry, if a player chooses to cooperate so will her opponent. This confuses the conclusion that equilibrium play is symmetric, with the presumption that when a player considers deviating from equilibrium she can assume that all others will symmetrically deviate with her.[3] The section examines this and other paradoxes in more detail. We do not intend to argue that rationality is an uncontroversial assumption, and we agree that an important agenda is to understand its role better and to consider alternative assumptions. Nevertheless, we do claim that rationality is a fruitful assumption and that, in fact, it sheds much light on these paradoxes.

The second fundamental issue we examine is the underpinnings for the basic model of asymmetric information in economics and game theory. (This is the topic of section 3; this section is rather abstract and, except for subsection 3.1 and 3.3.1, can be skipped with (almost) no loss of continuity.) The very definition of common knowledge, and hence its applications to characterizations of solution concepts, requires that there is a model of the environment, including a state space and information partitions, that is common knowledge among the players. We ask what are the justifications for this assumption and what are the limitations of these justifications. We address these questions using both the Bayesian model familiar to economists, and the syntactic models which have been recently introduced into economics; we also examine the connection between the syntactic view of knowledge as information and the Bayesian notion of knowledge, belief with probability 1, which we call certainty. One limitation we point out is that the justifications for assuming a commonly known model do not imply that the assumption that players have a prior belief on the state space is warranted. Thus, we raise a concern with notions such as *ex ante* efficiency and the common prior assumption (CPA), which rely on the existence of such a prior.

Sections 4 through 6.2 are the heart of the chapter; here we characterize solution concepts, using the model of knowledge and certainty developed in section 3, in terms of assumptions concerning the players' knowledge/certainty about one another and their rationality. We begin in section 4 by appending normal-form games to the model of knowledge and certainty and we review both the equivalence between common knowledge of rationality and iterated deletion of strongly dominated strategies, and characterizations of other equilibrium concepts. Due to our concerns about the CPA and other assumptions, and their necessity in some characterizations, we conclude with dissatisfaction with these epistemic justification of certain solution concepts, such as Nash equilibrium.

Section 5 examines extensive-form games. Several papers have obtained different, apparently contradictory, conclusions concerning the implications of assuming common knowledge/certainty of rationality in extensive-form games. These conclusions include that standard models are incomplete (Binmore (1987–8), Samet (1993), Stalnaker (1994)), that common knowledge of rationality is problematic or inconsistent in extensive-form games (Basu (1990), Bicchieri (1989), Bonanno (1991)), that backwards induction is implied by common knowledge of rationality (Aumann

(1995a)), and that backwards induction is not implied by common certainty of rationality (Reny (1993), Ben Porath (1994)). We show that the model of knowledge and belief from section 3 *is* sufficient to provide a unified framework for examining these results, and we present several characterizations. These characterizations shed light on the elusive issue of what are the implications of common knowledge and certainty of rationality in extensive-form games. We feel that the most natural assumption is common certainty of rationality; this assumption characterizes the solution obtained by applying one round of deletion of weakly dominated strategies and then iterated deletion of strongly dominated strategies, which we call rationalizability with caution (see Ben Porath (1994) and Gul (1995b)).

Section 6 examines what happens if common certainty is weakened to various notions of almost common certainty. Not only does this allow us to investigate the robustness of different solution concepts and characterizations when replacing common certainty with these various notions, but it also enables us to characterize some refinements. In section 4 we observe that refinements and common certainty are inconsistent. In particular, this suggests that the idea that iterated deletion of weakly dominated strategies follows from some basic premise concerning caution and common knowledge (see, e.g., Kohlberg and Mertens (1985)) is flawed. In section 6.2 we show that the closest result one can get is that almost common certainty of caution and rationality characterizes rationalizability with caution – the same solution concept as results from common certainty of rationality in extensive-form games.

Section 6.3 uses the notion of almost common knowledge to raise concerns about refinements of Nash equilibrium, and to obtain new "refinements." We consider two notions of robustness for solution concepts. In the spirit of Fudenberg, Kreps, and Levine (1988), we first consider the following requirement. A solution concept is robust if, given a game G, the solution of G does not exclude any outcomes that it would accept if applied to *some* game in which G is almost common certainty. Rationalizability with caution is the tightest refinement of iterated deletion of strongly dominated strategies that is robust in this sense. Kajii and Morris (1995) and Monderer and Samet (1989) investigate a related notion of robustness: a solution concept is robust in their sense if any predicted outcome of G is a prediction in *all* games where G is almost common certainty. Different notions of almost common certainty lead to different conclusions concerning which solution concepts are robust. Monderer and Samet (1989) show that ε-Nash equilibrium is robust using a strong notion of almost common certainty; Kajii and Morris (1995) use a weaker notion and show that the only standard solution concept that is robust in their sense is that of a unique correlated equilibrium.

Section 7 considers models of asymmetric information where the information structure need not take the form of a partition. The connection between this and weakening the notion of knowledge is discussed, and the implications of these weakenings are explored. The section concludes with a discussion of the problems of this literature.

We need to make one final organizational point. The discussion of various interesting issues, that are related to our presentation, would be disruptive if included within the main body of the text. In addition to simply ignoring many issues, we adopt a non-standard use of footnotes to deal with this problem: we include formal statements and proof sketches within some footnotes.

Many disclaimers are appropriate; the following three are necessary. First, we describe ourselves as presenting and showing various results, but it should be understood that most of the chapter reviews existing work and these terms do not imply any originality. Second, while we make sure to reference the source of all results, and attempt to mention and cite most related research, for brevity we tend to cite the relevant work once rather than on every occasion. Finally, studying a large number of concepts and theorems formulated in different settings within a single framework, as we do here, has its costs. We cannot expect to do full justice to original arguments or hope to convey the full strength of the authors' insights. Thus, we do not expect to provide a perfect substitute for the authors' original treatment of the issues discussed below. However, a unified treatment and the comparisons it enables has benefits that hopefully will offset the inevitable loss such a treatment entails in the analysis of each individual theorem.

2   A RATIONAL VIEW OF SOME PARADOXES OF RATIONALITY

The purpose of this section is to provide a single "explanation" of some familiar and some new paradoxes of rationality. We begin with an informal review of the paradoxes, and then offer our resolution.

2.1   The paradoxes

2.1.1   The Prisoners' Dilemma

The term paradox refers either to a logical inconsistency or a counter-intuitive conclusion. For most game theorists and economists the Prisoners' Dilemma poses neither of these. Instead, it offers a simple and valid insight, perhaps the most basic insight of game theory; the conflict between individual and group incentives and the resulting inefficiency. For non-game theorists, the Prisoners' Dilemma is apparently much more problematic (see Campbell and Sowden (1985)) and thus it serves as the ideal starting point for our analysis. The argument is the following. The obvious symmetry of the problem faced by the two agents is sufficient for anyone analyzing the problem (including the players themselves) to conclude that both agents will take the same action. Hence, player 1 knows that the outcome will be either cooperate–cooperate or defect–defect. It follows that if player 1 cooperates then cooperate–cooperate will be the outcome whereas if he defects then defect–defect will be the outcome. Since the former yields a higher payoff than the latter, rationality should lead player 1 to cooperate. This conflicts with the obvious dominance argument in favor of defecting. Most economists not working on epistemic foundations of rationality will probably dismiss the above argument for cooperating by saying that the assertion that both agents will take the "same" action is true only in *equilibrium* which according to the dominance argument specifies that both agents will defect. If player one chooses to cooperate (or contemplates cooperation) this is a deviation and hence the equilibrium hypothesis, that both agents will take the "same" action, is no longer valid.[4]

2.1.2   Newcombe's Paradox

Closely related to the preceding discussion is the well-known Newcombe's Paradox. Suppose that a person is faced with two boxes: box A contains $1,000 and box B contains either zero or one million dollars. The person can choose either box B or both boxes. The prizes are placed by a genie who has profound insight into the psyche of the person and thus knows whether the person will choose both boxes or just one. If the person is to choose both boxes than the genie will put zero dollars into box B. If the person is to choose only box B, then the genie will put one million dollars into box B. By the time the person makes a choice he knows the genie has already made his decision as to how much money should go into box B. Thus, as in the above analysis of the Prisoners' Dilemma, a simple dominance argument suggests that the person should take both boxes. However, the infallibility of the genie suggests that the decision to choose box B alone yields one million dollars while the decision to choose both yields $1,000. Hence the person should choose box B alone.[5]

2.1.3   The paradox of backward induction

In the three stage take-it-or-leave-it game (see figure 5.1), the finitely repeated Prisoners' Dilemma, and other similar games, the apparently

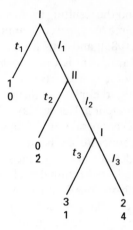

Figure 5.1 The three-stage take-it-or-leave-it game

compelling logic of backward induction suggests a solution that appears unintuitive. Yet, until recently, the strategy of always defecting in the repeated Prisoners' Dilemma was viewed to be the only "correct" solution that intuitively satisfies common knowledge of rationality. The issue of extensive-form games is discussed in more depth in section 5, where we show that a formal model of common knowledge of rationality does not yield the backward-induction outcome.

2.1.4   Bonanno's Paradox

In a recent paper (discussed further in section 5 below), Bonanno (1991) provides a more precise statement of the following paradox: Let R be the set of all propositions of the form

$$\{((P_a) \rightarrow (\pi \geq x)) \text{ and } ((P_\beta) \rightarrow (\pi \leq y)) \text{ and } (x > y)\} \rightarrow \neg(P_\beta),$$

where objects in parenthesis correspond to propositions as follows: (P_a) is the proposition that "the agent chooses α"; $(\pi \geq x)$ is, "the agent receives utility no less than x;" (P_β) and $(\pi \leq y)$ are defined in an analogous manner; and, finally, $(x > y)$ is the proposition "x is strictly greater than y." Thus R is the proposition that an agent faced with these choice of α or β is rational. Suppose, for instance, that the agent faces a choice between a and b where a will yield 100 dollars and b will yield zero dollars. Thus, we have $(P_a \text{ or } P_b)$ and $\neg(P_a \text{ and } P_b)$. Suppose we postulate R to capture the hypothesis that the agent is rational. Then we conclude from the parameters above and the assumption of rationality that the agent does not choose b. It follows that

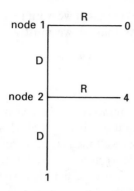

Figure 5.2 The game of the absent-minded driver

the proposition $(P_b \rightarrow (\pi \geq 1000))$ is true by virtue of the fact that (P_b) is false. Then applying R again to $(P_b \rightarrow (\pi \geq 1000))$ and $(P_a \rightarrow (\pi \leq 100))$ yields $\neg (P_a)$ which, together with $\neg (P_b)$, contradicts the fact that the agent had to choose either a or b. Thus rationality is impossible in this formulation.

2.1.5   Piccione and Rubinstein's Paradox

Consider the problem described in figure 5.2. A person with imperfect recall is faced with the choice of choosing R or D. If he turns out to be in node 1, R will have very unpleasant consequences. Choosing D at node 1 leads to node 2 which, owing to imperfect recall, is a situation that the decisionmaker considers indistinguishable from node 1. Choosing R at node 2 yields the most desirable outcome while choosing D a second time yields an intermediate outcome. The optimization problem faced by the decisionmaker is the following. He must choose a probability p with which to play the action D (and hence R is played with probability $1 - p$). By imperfect recall, the same p must be used at each information set. Hence the decisionmaker must maximize $4p(1 - p) + p^2$, yielding $p = 2/3$. The first observation here is that the optimal strategy is unique but not a pure strategy. Second, and this is what Piccione and Rubinstein (1995) consider paradoxical, if the decisionmaker were Bayesian and assign a probability α to the event of being at node 1, then his decision problem would be to maximize $\alpha[4p(1 - p) + p^2] + (1 - \alpha)[p + 4(1 - p)]$. It is easy to verify that, for any value of α other than 1, the solution of the second optimization yields an answer different from 2/3. Thus, we are either forced to insist that a Bayesian agent facing this problem must always assign probability 1 to being at node 1, or we must accept that the *ex ante* solution differs from the Bayesian solution. That is, if we want to allow the probability of being at node 1 to be less than 1, we must accept the dynamic inconsistency.

2.2   The resolution

The purpose of this section is to isolate a "common cause" for each of these paradoxes. Whether this counts as a "resolution" is not at all clear. If by paradox we mean unexpected or surprising result then we may continue to believe that the results are surprising even if we agree as to what the main cause of the paradox is. On the other hand, if by a paradox we mean a logical inconsistency then understanding the cause certainly does not remove the original inconsistency. Of course, we hope that the reader will agree that the same "cause" underlies all of these paradoxes and, having identified this cause, will find the paradox less surprising or the inconsistency less troublesome as a comment on rationality.

Let us start with the Prisoners' Dilemma which is likely to be the least controversial for game theorists and economists. Most game theorists would agree that the rational course of action in the Prisoners' Dilemma is to defect. But then what happens to the claim that the two agents will choose the same action? This is still satisfied if both agents defect and will be satisfied only if agents behave as they are supposed to, i.e., in equilibrium. That is, we are investigating what outcomes are consistent with the given assumptions: that the players are rational and the outcome is symmetric. The reason that economists and game theorists are not puzzled by the paradox of the Prisoners' Dilemma as perceived by philosophers is that this kind of reasoning is very familiar from (Nash and competitive) equilibrium analysis. Whenever we investigate the implications of a set of assumptions including the assumption that each agent is rational, we are forced to justify the rationality of a given agent by comparing what he expects to receive if he behaves as we predict with what he expects to receive if he behaves otherwise. But when he contemplates behaving otherwise he cannot expect that assumptions made about his own behavior will continue to hold, even if these were very reasonable assumptions to begin with. If we insist that the rational agent will expect assumptions about his own behavior to continue to hold even as he deviates, then we will be confronted with paradoxes.

The application of this idea to the Prisoners' Dilemma is clear. The defense of the cooperate–cooperate outcome relies on showing than defect–defect cannot be the answer since by deviating an agent can conclude (by using the assertion that he and his opponent will take the same course of action) that cooperating leads to cooperate–cooperate which is better that defect–defect. But clearly, in this argument we are using the fact that player

1 knows that player 2 will choose the same course of action even as 1 contemplates deviating. Hence the contradiction.

The analysis of Newcombe's paradox is similar. If we were confronting this genie, then we would surely take both boxes. So, if the genie is as knowledgeable as claimed, he will put nothing in box B. If we were to deviate, then the genie would be wrong (but of course we would not gain from this deviation). If we hypothesize the existence of a genie that is always right, even when somebody deviates, then we will get a contradiction.

The fact that the same factor is behind the backward induction paradox is more difficult to see for three reasons. First, the dynamic nature of the strategic interaction forces us, the analysts, to discuss not only the possibility that a player may contemplate deviating, but also the fact that if he does deviate, then some other player will get a chance to observe this deviation. Hence, we are forced to analyze the deviating player's analysis of some other player's reactions to the deviation. Second, in the backward-induction paradox, unlike the remaining paradoxes discussed in this section, identifying the cause does not immediately suggest an alternative model that is immune to the problem identified. This can be seen from the fact that a number of other game-theoretic solution concepts, such as Nash equilibrium or iterative removal of weakly dominated strategies, yield the same backward-induction outcomes in the well-known examples such as the take-it-or-leave-it game or the repeated chain store paradox or the repeated Prisoners' Dilemma. Nevertheless, identifying the cause is the first step to the more sophisticated non-backward induction theories and the more elaborate arguments for backward induction that will be discussed in section 5. The task of evaluating other concepts, such as Nash equilibrium or iterative weak dominance, need not concern us here. As we will discuss in section 5, the cause of the backward-induction paradox is by now well understood. Implicit in the backward-induction argument is the assumption that, if the second information set were reached in the game depicted in figure 5.1, then player 2 continues to be certain that player 1 is rational even though this is precisely the assumption utilized in concluding that the second information set will not be reached.

Once again, the difficulty stems from insisting on apparently plausible assumptions regarding the behavior of some player even in the face of deviations. (In particular, the assumption that rationality is common knowledge and the conjecture that this implies the backwards-induction solution are upheld in the face of behavior that conflicts with the combination of these two statements.) The added difficulty of the paradox comes into play at this stage: we know where the difficulty is but the resolution – unlike those discussed above – is not agreed upon by game theorists. Some authors have concluded at this stage, that we must give up on backward induction while others have suggested stronger notions of rationality for extensive-form games. Yet others have argued that, while we must give up on backward induction as a consequence of common knowledge of rationality, alternative plausible assumptions about behavior may (in certain games) yield backward induction. Some of the work along these lines will be discussed in section 5. Our current objective is only to note that the origin of the paradox is the same in all the cases studied in this section.

In Bonanno's Paradox we can see the same effect coming in through the fact that rationality is postulated throughout the model, and not used as a test of outcomes. Thus, even as the agent contemplates (or chooses) the irrational b, the proposition "the agent is rational" is maintained. Hence, by making the irrational choice the agent can create a falsehood. But a false proposition can imply anything, in particular it can imply that the agent receives an infeasible level of utility. Which makes the irrational action very rewarding and yields the contradiction.[6]

The Piccione–Rubinstein Paradox is more subtle but also similar. Consider the calculation that the Bayesian rational person is to undertake: choose p so as to maximize $\alpha[4p(1-p) + p^2] + (1-\alpha)[p + 4(1-p)]$. Implicit in this calculation is the assumption that whatever p is chosen today will be implemented tomorrow as well, even if the choice of p reflects some sort of deviation or irrationality. Setting aside the question of whether giving a memoryless agent this implicit ability to recall past actions is a good modeling choice, we note that the absence of perfect recall presumably means that the agent cannot systematically implement different plans at the two nodes. It does not mean that the actions chosen at the two nodes are by *logical* necessity the same. To see this note that if the actions are by logical necessity the same then the agent's decision to change his mind, and choose $p \neq 2/3$, would have no meaning were he, in fact, at the second node. Alternatively put, when the agent makes a choice, since he does not know at which node he is located, his deviation must assume that whatever he planned to do originally – in this case $p = 2/3$ – stills holds elsewhere. As in the other paradoxes above, the analysis of the agent's rationality requires the analyst to assume that everything else that the agent cannot change is held constant.

This resolution, based on dropping the logical equivalence between the agent's choices at both nodes, is discussed by Piccione and Rubinstein (1995) in the section entitled "Multi-selves approaches." The analysis there proceeds as follows. First, they fix p and compute $\alpha(p)$, the long-run relative frequency of visiting the first node for an agent that exits with probability p at each node. Next, they ask what should p be so that $p' = p$ maximizes $p'[\alpha(p)p + 4(1-p) + (1-\alpha(p))] + (1-p')4(1-\alpha(p))$. They show that for

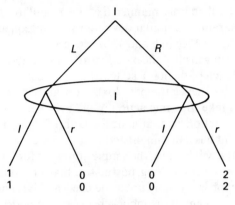

Figure 5.3

$p = 2/3$ – which is the value of p that maximizes expected utility when *ex ante* commitment is possible – any p', in particular $p' = p = 2/3$, is a maximizer. Thus, they observe that having the decisionmaker view his "other" self as a distinct agent resolves the paradox. They find this resolution unconvincing, however, noting that treating a rational decision-maker as a collection of agents allows for the possibility that (l, L) is a solution to the single-person decision problem described in figure 5.3. They state that this way of dealing with imperfect recall ignores the fundamental difference between single-person and multi-person situations. They argue that it should be possible for a rational decisionmaker to change his strategy, not just at the current information set but also in the future. By contrast, we think that this resolution of their paradox does not require that agents are stuck with arbitrary and inefficient behavior in the future. It is only required that the agent should not assume that changing his mind now (i.e., deviating) will generate a corresponding change later in the *same* information set. To get back to the theme of this section, if at node 2, the agent cannot remember whether he has been to node 1 or not and hence what he has done at node 1, then the requirement that he take the same action at both nodes can hold only if he does what he is supposed to do; not if he deviates. This is not an endorsement of a full-blown, non-cooperative (multi-agent) equilibrium approach to the problem of imperfect recall. We may rule out (l, L) as a possible solution to the problem described in figure 5.3 because we find this to be an unacceptable plan for the agent given that $r, R)$ is also a feasible plan. It does not follow from this that a decisionmaker implementing the plan $p = 2/3$ in figure 5.2, when faced with the actual implementation, can assume that if he were to choose to go down without randomizing, he would end up with a payoff of 1 for sure. Modeling the problem of imperfect recall in this manner (i.e., by postulating that a deviation at one node guarantees a similar deviation at a subsequent node) causes the paradox noted by Piccione and Rubinstein.

What is worth emphasizing in all of the paradoxes discussed above is that the driving force behind each of them is a statement that most of us would find a priori quite plausible (hence the paradox): it certainly makes sense that both players should take the same action in the Prisoners' Dilemma, especially since the same action is dominant for both of them; in New-combe's Paradox the agent has a dominant action so it makes sense that a genie would know how she will behave, the simple argument for backward induction is very intuitive and compelling, postulating that a rational agent will choose the higher payoff is certainly not far-fetched, and it is almost by definition that an agent who cannot distinguish between two nodes should not be able to implement different actions at these two nodes. The purpose of this section has been to use an idea very familiar to economists to suggest a way of resolving all of these paradoxes. We certainly do not wish to claim that all logical inconsistencies can be removed in this manner. We only suggest an informal modeling idea that might help in avoiding these and other paradoxes of rationality. We feel that our resolution is implicit in the epistemic models that we discuss in sections 4, 5, and 6.[7]

3   WHAT IS A STATE OF THE WORLD AND IS THE MODEL COMMON KNOWLEDGE?

We outline here the topics of the subsections to follow. In subsection 3.1 we briefly review the basic model of asymmetric information used in economics and game theory, and discuss the connection with a model commonly used in other fields, called a Kripke model. We formally define a knowledge operator, discuss its relation with the partition model of information, and review the formal definition of common knowledge.[8] The main conclusion is that the standard interpretation of the definition of common knowledge implicitly assumes that the model itself is common "knowledge." In some contexts, where knowledge or information arises through a physical process, prior to which agents have identical information, the meaning of this assumption is clear. Moreover, in such contexts it is conceivable that the model (i.e., the description of the information-acquisition process) is commonly "known." In subsection 3.2 we take as a starting point a situation of incomplete information, where players' knowledge and beliefs are already formed and a real *ex ante* situation does not exist. In this case the choice of model to represent these beliefs and knowledge is not clear. Moreover, it is not clear a priori that a model chosen to represent these beliefs can be assumed to be common "knowledge." So in this case such an assumption needs justification. We provide such a justification by presenting two ways to *construct* a commonly known model, using first a syntactic approach for modeling knowledge, and then Harsanyi's (1967) Bayesian approach, which is based on a probabilistic notion of knowledge that we call certainty. Subsection 3.3 discusses the relationship between knowledge and certainty. Finally, subsection 3.4 discusses the limitations of these two solutions to the problem. While they both construct a commonly known *ex ante* model, the construction does not generate a prior. Hence we argue that *ex ante* notions of efficiency and assumptions such as the common prior assumption, are not sensible in contexts where a real physical *ex ante* stage does not exist, that is, in all situations where Harsanyi's justification of the model of incomplete information is needed.

3.1   The issue

In order to understand the first issue that we will discuss, it is necessary to review the basic definition of knowledge and common knowledge in an environment of asymmetric information. An information structure is a collection $\mathscr{I} \equiv (\Omega, (\mathscr{F}_i, p_i)_{i \in N})$. The finite set Ω is the set of states of the world. Each player $i \in N$, where N is the finite set of players, has a possibility correspondence $\mathscr{F}_i: \Omega \to 2^\Omega$, where $\mathscr{F}_i(\omega)$ is the set of states i considers possible when the true state is ω. We abuse notation and also denote by $\mathscr{F}_i$ the set of possible information cells $\{F_i \subset \Omega: F_i = \mathscr{F}_i(\omega) \text{ for some } \omega\}$. The standard interpretation in economics is that when the true state is ω, i is informed that one of the states in $\mathscr{F}_i(\omega)$ occurred. For now $\mathscr{F}_i$ is assumed to be a partition of Ω; justifications for this assumption will be presented below, and weakenings will be presented in section 7. Finally, $p_i \in \Delta(\Omega)$ is a prior over Ω. We will usually assume that each cell in $\mathscr{F}_i$ has strictly positive probability, so that conditional probabilities $p_i(\cdot \mid \mathscr{F}_i(\omega))$ are well defined. In cases where $p_i(\mathscr{F}_i(\omega)) = 0$ for some state ω, we (implicitly) assume that the model is extended to some specification of all the conditional probabilities, $\mathscr{I} = (\Omega, (\mathscr{F}_i, p_i, p_i(\cdot \mid \mathscr{F}_i))_{i \in N})$.

In most economic models, a state ω describes something about the real world, for example, the different states might correspond to different preferences for one of the players. Thus, a model will specify, for each state, the value of the relevant parameters of the real world. For example, i's utility function at ω can be denoted by $\mathbf{u}_i(\omega)$; the event that i's utility function is some particular u_i is denoted by $[u_i] \equiv \{\omega \in \Omega: \mathbf{u}_i(\omega) = u_i\}$. This is clarified further and formalized in subsection 3.2.1 below. A model of asymmetric information, $\mathscr{I}$, combined with such a specification, will be called a Kripke model (see, e.g., Fagin *et al.* (1995, chapter 2.5)). Throughout section 3 the term model refers to a model of asymmetric information, $\mathscr{I}$, either on its own, or appended with such a specification, i.e., a Kripke model. (The context will clarify the appropriate notion.)

We say that agent i *knows an event* $A \in \Omega$ *at state* ω, if i's information in state ω implies that some state in A must be true: $\mathcal{F}_i(\omega) \subset A$. Therefore, the set of states in which, say, 2 knows A is $K_2(A) \equiv \{\omega: \mathcal{F}_2(\omega) \subset A\}$; similarly the set of states at which 2 knows that i's utility function is u_i is $K_2([u_i])$. So, at state ω, 1 knows that 2 knows A if $\mathcal{F}_1(\omega) \subset K_2(A)$. Continuing in this way Aumann (1976) showed that at a state ω the event A is common knowledge – in the sense that all players know it, know they know it, etc. – if and only if there is an event F in the meet of the partitions with $\mathcal{F}_i(\omega) \subset F \subset A$. The meet of a collection of partitions is the finest partition that is a coarsening of all partitions in the collection, denoted by $\wedge_{i \in N} \mathcal{F}_i$. It is easy to see that the meet is a partition that includes all the smallest events that are self evident, where self-evident events are those that are known to have occurred whenever they occur: F is self evident if for all i and all $\omega \in F, \mathcal{F}_i(\omega) \subset F$. (Clearly the union of disjoint self-evident sets is self evident and will not be in the meet; hence the qualification to smallest events.)

To summarize and further develop the above argument, given the possibility correspondences $\mathcal{F}_i$ we have derived operators $K_i: 2^\Omega \to 2^\Omega$ which tell us the set of states at which i knows an event A; $K_i(A) \equiv \{\omega: \mathcal{F}_i(\omega) \subset A\}$. This construction then tells us, for each state of the world ω, what each player knows, what each player knows about what each player knows, etc. This operator satisfies the properties below.

T $K_i(A) \subset A$: if i knows A then A is true;

MC $K_i(A) \cap K_i(B) = K_i(A \cap B)$: knowing A and B is equivalent to knowing A and knowing B;

N $K_i(\Omega) = \Omega$: player i always knows anything that is true in all states of the world;

4 $K_i(A) \subset K_i(K_i(A))$: if i knows A then i knows that i knows A;

5 $\neg K_i(A) \subset K_i(\neg K_i(A))$, where $\neg$ denotes complements: not knowing A implies knowing that A is not known.

These properties can be used to axiomatically characterize knowledge and partitions. That is, instead of starting with partitions $\mathcal{F}_i$, and deriving a knowledge operator K_i which satisfies these properties, we could have started with such an operator K_i and derived the partitions. Formally, given any operator K_i satisfying these properties, one can define a possibility correspondence $\mathcal{F}_i: \Omega \to 2^\Omega$ by $\mathcal{F}_i(\omega) = \cap \{A \subset \Omega: \omega \in K_i(A)\}$, and such a possibility correspondence in turn would generate the same K_i according to the definition above. In fact, the only properties needed for this result are [MC] and [N]. (We allow $\mathcal{F}_i = \emptyset$; if we wanted to rule this out we would need to add the axiom $K_i(\emptyset) = \emptyset$.) It is straightforward to check that properties [T], [4], and [5] imply that $\mathscr{F}_i$ will be a partition. We can now define $K_M(A)$ to be the event that all i in $M \subset N$ know $A, K_M(A) \equiv \cap_{i \in M} K_i(A)$, and then the event that A is common knowledge is simply $CK(A) \equiv \cap_{n=1}^{\infty} K_N^n(A)$, where K_N^n denotes n iterations of the K_N operator. In his discussion of reachability, Aumann (1976) shows that $CK(A) = \cup \{F : F \in \wedge_{i \in N} \mathscr{F}_i, F \subset A\}$; the interpretation of this result is that A is common knowledge at ω if the member of the meet of the partitions at ω is contained in A.

But, as Aumann (1976) pointed out, for this *interpretation* we must assume that 1 "knows" 2's information partition, since this is needed to interpret the set of states $K_1(K_2(A))$ as the set in which 1 knows that 2 knows A. Moreover, we will need to assume that the partitions are common "knowledge" among the players. We use quotes around the words know and knowledge since it is not the formal term defined earlier; it is a meta notion of knowledge that lies outside our formal model. But the fact that this knowledge is not formally within the model is not the main issue. Our concern is whether it is reasonable to assume that the information structure is common "knowledge," informally or otherwise.

The assumption that the information structure is common "knowledge" is easy to interpret if there is an actual *ex ante* situation and "physical" procedure that leads to asymmetric information. For example, this is the case if the underlying uncertainty Ω is the amount of oil in some tract, and each of two firms is entitled to take one soil sample, and there is a thorough understanding based on published experiments of both the prior likelihood of oil and of the distribution of possible soil samples as a function of the oil in the tract. In contrast, consider the case where the agents already have their perceptions (i.e., knowledge or beliefs) about the world, and there was no *ex ante* commonly known physical environment which generated their perceptions. Following Harsanyi (1967), we call this a situation of incomplete information. Can we model this situation of incomplete information as one that arises from a commonly "known" starting point (i.e., *as if* we are at the interim stage of a commonly "known" physical procedure such as the oil-tract story above)?[9]

Before discussing the way this issue has been addressed, it is worth clarifying why it is an issue at all. Clearly, if the model that we write down is not common "knowledge," then it is not a complete description of the players' views of the world. So, in a basic sense the model is incomplete. While this is a concern, there is a more disturbing issue. If the model is not commonly "known," we can no longer justify solution concepts, or any other conclusions that rely on the hypothesis that some event is common knowledge, such as the no-trade results. How can one interpret an assumption that rationality, or anything else, is commonly known when there is no commonly "known" model within which to define common knowledge?[10]

Thus, our objective in the next subsection is to start with a description of an arbitrary situation of incomplete information, and develop a model and a state $\omega^* \in \Omega$, such that if the model is commonly "known," the knowledge (according to the K_i operators) of the agents at ω^* coincides with the knowledge contained in the original description of the incomplete-information situation.

3.2   Constructing a model that is commonly "known"

Aumann (1976) argued that, if the model is complete, in that each state ω is a complete description of the state of the world, then the model is common "knowledge" (at least so long as Ω is common knowledge). This is because a complete specification of a state should determine the partitions and beliefs of all the players in that state, so if the set of states is common "knowledge" then the partition cell (and beliefs corresponding to that cell) for each state will be common "knowledge."

While this seems compelling, it does not say, for example, that a complete model exists, nor does it say how, from a complete description of a situation which is not common knowledge, a commonly "known" model can be constructed. Understanding the construction is important, since, if we are going to impose assumptions on the constructed space, we need to know how to interpret these assumptions in terms of our starting point, which is a situation of incomplete information and not a commonly "known" model.

Thus, the first question that we will consider is what is a state of the world; what constitutes a complete description. Naturally, it will include two aspects: what is true about the physical world, and what is true about the epistemic world, i.e., what players know.

A preliminary example Assume that a description of the state of the world included the following: (1) a description of the true physical world, which can be either p or $\neg p$, and (2) what each player knows about p and $\neg p$. In particular, say, a state could be the specification p, player 1 knows p holds, and knows that it is not the case that $\neg p$ holds, and player 2 does not know whether it is p or $\neg p$ that holds, but 2 knows that either p or $\neg p$ holds. If we do not say anything further there are many models which would generate this knowledge. For example, consider figure 5.4, where ovals are 1's partition and rectangles are 2's partition, and ω^* indicates the true state of the world. In model (a), $\Omega = \{\omega^*, \omega\}$, $\mathscr{F}_1 = \{\{\omega^*\}, \{\omega\}\}$, $\mathscr{F}_2 = \{\{\omega^*, \omega\}\}$. In the second model ($b$), $\Omega = \{\omega^*, \omega, \omega', \omega''\}$, $\mathscr{F}_1 = \{\{\omega^*, \omega'\}, \{\omega, \omega''\}\}$,

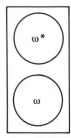
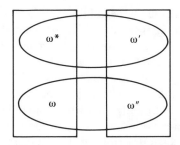

Figure 5.4 Two information structures, which at ω^*, coincide insofar as our partial description of a situation can determine, but differ in terms of the knowledge they imply if they are assumed to be common "knowledge"

$\mathscr{F}_2 = \{\{\omega^*, \omega\}, \{\omega'\}, \{\omega''\}\}$. In both cases to complete the (Kripke) model we need to specify what aspects of the real world are true in the different states: in (a), a property p is true in state ω^* and $\neg p$ is true otherwise, while in (b), p is true in states ω^* and ω', and $\neg p$ is true otherwise. We can immediately verify that in both of these models $\omega^* \in K_1([p])$ and $\omega^* \notin K_2([p])$, where $[p]$ is the set of states where p is true. Therefore, if we assume only that the players "know" the model then the state ω^* does incorporate the description above.

However, if we assume that these models are common "knowledge," then they would generate many more statements about the players' knowledge than our original description – in particular they clearly model different epistemic situations. In (a), in state ω^* player 1 knows that 2 does not know that p is true, while in (b) player 1 does not know this. So the assumption that the model is common "knowledge" would be substantive, and we could not use either model to say that given our description of a situation of incomplete information, we can construct a commonly "known" model with a state such that knowledge at that state coincides with the description. How then can we construct an information structure that may be assumed to be common "knowledge" w.l.o.g.?

It is clear what goes wrong in the example: a description needs to be complete and should specify everything possible about the physical state of the world and about the state of mind of the agents – including how they perceive the state of mind of the other agents. Thus a description will be a list of what is true of the physical world and all relevant perceptions of the agents, including perceptions about perceptions. There will also be some natural consistency conditions on states, for example, the description of a state should not say that the physical world has some property and that it does not have that property. More interesting consistency conditions arise concerning the perceptions of the agents, for example, it seems natural to assume that the agent knows what she knows.

Thus, we are looking for a description of a situation of incomplete information that is a "complete" list of "internally consistent" statements about the agents, perceptions and the physical world. The next step is to show that this description coincides with the knowledge at a state ω^* in some commonly "known" model. This step is accomplished as follows. With the notion of a complete description in hand, we will consider the set of all such descriptions as a universal set of possible states, Ω. Then, we would like to find an information structure on Ω which, if we assume it to be common "knowledge," will generate in the state ω^* the same perceptions as we used in describing the situation of incomplete information.[11] (By generate we mean calculate the agents' perceptions using the information structure as if the structure is common "knowledge" – just like the knowledge operators K_i were derived from the possibility correspondences $\mathcal{F}_i$ above.) Then we can say that taking this information structure to be common knowledge yields nothing more nor less than our description. So, we can work with models that are commonly "known," instead of with complete descriptions.

3.2.1   The syntactic approach

The syntactic approach takes the view that a description of the world should involve a specification of the true state, each person's knowledge about the true state, each person's knowledge about the players' knowledge about the true state, etc.[12] Thus the syntactic approach starts with a countable set of symbols representing the following objects: a set of basic propositions, $X \equiv p, q, \ldots$; a set of players, $i = 1, 2, \ldots n$; conjunction $\wedge$; negation $\neg$; a constant representing truth $\top$; and knowledge of i, k_i.[13]

The set of basic propositions, X, includes, for example, "it is raining," "it is snowing," etc. Thus elements of X are not complete descriptions of the physical world. A complete description of the physical world would be $\{True, False\}^X$ – a specification for each basic proposition whether it is true or false.

The language of sentences, L, is the smallest collection of sequences of these symbols containing X that is closed under negation, conjunction, and knowledge (i.e., if $\phi, \psi \in L$ then $\neg \phi \in L$, $\phi \wedge \psi \in L$, and $k_i \phi \in L$). For example, if $X = \{p\}$ then $\neg p \in L$, as is $k_i \neg k_j p$, where the latter is interpreted as i knows that j does not know p. Since L is the *smallest* such collection, all sentences have finitely many symbols. There is an alternative approach that mirrors our construction in the next subsection; this approach builds up longer and longer sentences starting from the basic propositions, X.

Roughly speaking, the first step has two ingredients: (i) extending the set of sentences from X to the set of all sentences that is closed under conjunction and negation; and (ii) allowing knowledge to operate *once* on elements of this closure of X. Then, inductively, consider the closure under conjunction and negation of the just constructed set of sentences, and add one more level of knowledge. In this way the language would be indexed by the depth of knowledge one wants to consider. (For a precise development, see, for example, Fagin, Halpern, and Vardi (1991).) This approach has the obvious additional advantage of allowing sentences with infinitely many symbols (by extending the depth of knowledge in the sentences transfinitely). However, the notational complexity does not warrant an explicit development, and we will informally discuss sentences with infinitely many symbols where relevant.

The following axioms will be used to impose consistency in the definition of a state.

T $k_i(A) \to A$, where the symbol $\phi \to \psi$ stands for $\neg(\phi \wedge \neg \psi)$: if i knows A then A is true;

MC $k_i(A) \wedge k_i(B) \leftrightarrow k_i(A \wedge B)$: knowing A and B is equivalent to knowing A and knowing B;

N $k_i\mathsf{T}$: agent i knows the truth constant;

4 $k_i(A) \to k_i(k_i(A))$: if i knows A then i knows that i knows A;

5 $\neg k_i(A) \to k_i(\neg k_i(A))$: not knowing A implies knowing that A is not known.

Note the similarity to the assumptions on K_i above. We will see that these assumptions on k_i generate partitions over states, just like the same assumptions on K_i generated partitions $\mathscr{F}_i$ in subsection 3.1. The difference is that K_i is an operator on exogenously given states, *assuming* that there is some commonly "known" model. On the other hand, k_i is a primitive symbol for describing the players' knowledge in some situation of incomplete information; we will now show how it is used to *construct* a commonly "known" model of a set of states and partitions.

In constructing the commonly "known" model the first step is to define the set of states as all complete and consistent descriptions within our language. To formalize this, a useful notion is that of a theorem: these are all sentences that are true in every state. Formally, these include T and all sentences that can be derived from the five axioms above using two rules of inference: [MP] if ϕ and $\phi \to \psi$ are theorems then so is ψ; and [RE] if $\phi \leftrightarrow \psi$ is a theorem then so is $k_i\phi \leftrightarrow k_i\psi$. A complete and consistent description of a state of the world is a subset of sentences in L that includes all theorems, includes ϕ if and only if it does not include $\neg \phi$, and is closed under the usual rule of logic, [MP], namely if the formulas ϕ and $\phi \to \psi$ are in the state then so is ψ. A state of the world is thus a list of sentences that are interpreted as true in that state, where the sentences fall into two categories: sentences concerning only basic propositions in X and epistemic sentences concerning knowledge (i.e., involving k_i). Such states are artificial constructs describing imaginable situations of incomplete information.[14] How then do we construct a commonly "known" model? Consider the set of all states of the world as just constructed. In each state ω we can identify the set of sentences that each individual knows: $\mathbf{k}_i(\omega) = \{\phi : k_i \phi \in \omega\}$. The natural information structure is that at each state ω, i cannot distinguish between states where his knowledge is the same, so $\mathcal{F}_i(\omega') = \{\omega : \mathbf{k}_i(\omega') = \mathbf{k}_i(\omega)\}$. Thus far, we have constructed a standard model of asymmetric information: we have a state space Ω and partitions $\mathcal{F}_i$.[15] Finally, we associate with each state in the model the basic propositions which are true in that state. Thus, in addition to a standard model of asymmetric information, this construction yields a function specifying for each state which propositions in X are true.[16] In this constructed Kripke model we ignore the specification of which epistemic sentences are true.

There is a formal equivalence between the Kripke models that we have just constructed, and the complete description of states in our language. The main point is that we can forget about the complete description of the state and derive from the model – which includes only a set of points Ω, partitions of Ω, and a list of those *basic propositions in X* that are true at each $\omega \in \Omega$ – what each player knows, what each player knows about what each one knows, etc., at a particular state of the world, using the assumption that the model is common "knowledge." The sentences we derive in this way will be exactly those in the complete description of the state. Formally, let $[\psi]$ be the set of states at which ψ is true, $[\psi] = \{\omega : \psi \in \omega\}$; the result is that ψ is known according to the language – i.e., the sentence $k_i(\psi)$ is part of the description of ω, $k_i(\psi) \in \omega$ – if and only if ψ is known according to the model – $\omega \in K_i([\psi])$.[17] Hence we have constructed a commonly "known" model from a complete description of a situation of incomplete information.[18]

The construction and results above suggest that one can work with standard partition models, define knowledge in the standard way – i knows A at ω if $\mathcal{F}_i(\omega) \subset A$ – and assume the partition and state space is informally common "knowledge" w.l.o.g. However, this is not precisely the case. There are two issues concerning the richness of the language L. Our original model was based on this language, so only sentences ϕ could be known according to k_i. So only events of the form $[\phi]$ could be known.[19] But in a standard model of asymmetric information any event $A \subset \Omega$ can be known. So assuming the model is common "knowledge" will enable us to say more then we could using our language. For instance, if the model of figure 5.4b, is commonly "known" then we could deduce the following:

$\omega^* \in K_1(\neg CK_N(p))$, 1 knows that p is not common knowledge. But there is no sentence expressing this in our language, as our language only had finite sentences (and common knowledge requires infinitely many conjunctions).[20] Nevertheless, there is no other model that agrees with the model of figure 5.4b on all finite sentences.[21] Thus the finite language uniquely determines the model here. So, while there are statements that the Kripke model can imply that the language cannot even express, there is no doubt that this model is "correct" and, assuming it is common "knowledge" w.l.o.g., in that if we were to extend the language to infinite sentences we would get exactly the same conclusions as arise from the model.

There is, however, a second, more worrisome, problem. In general the model is *not* uniquely determined by what we called a complete description. Moreover, there is no way to a priori bound the depth of statements about knowledge that is needed to obtain a complete description.

Consider the two models in figure 5.5.[22] Player 1's partitions are ovals, 2's are rectangles, and 3's are diamonds. Assume the true state is any state of the world ω except ω^* and that p is a proposition that is true, say, only in state $\omega_{0,0}$. Then, formally, in the model of figure 5.5a, $\omega \in K_3(\neg CK_{1,2}(p))$, while, in figure 5.5b, this is not true. If we assume, informally, that the model is common "knowledge," then clearly all three players' knowledge coincide in both models except that in 5.5b player 3 does not know that p is not common knowledge among 1 and 2, and, in 5.5a, 3 does know this. However, such a sentence would not be included in ω since such sentences were not part of our finite syntactic framework.

Thus, the syntactic framework cannot distinguish between these two models while our informal common "knowledge" assumption does enable a distinction. So we have not fully achieved our objective of constructing a model that is common "knowledge" w.l.o.g. If we take as a complete description all sentences about finite levels of knowledge, then in the example of figure 5.5, assuming common "knowledge" of the information structure *is* a substantive assumption providing more information than originally contained in the, so-called, "complete" description.

One might think that the problem can be solved by allowing for a richer language, namely one in which not only finite conjunctions are permitted, but also conjunctions of sets of formulas of higher cardinality. Similarly, perhaps the problem can be addressed by introducing a syntactic symbol c_M analogous to CK_M for $M \subset N$.[23] However, there is no conjunction, and no collection of symbols, which would be large enough – Heifetz (1995c (see also 1995b)) shows that an example with the properties of figure 5.5 can be derived no matter how many conjunctions and symbols are introduced.[24]

This shows that the sense in which the constructed model can be assumed to be common "knowledge" w.l.o.g., depends crucially on the epistemic

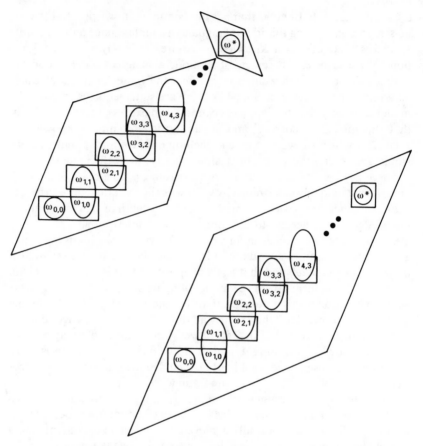

Figure 5.5 Two information structures, which, at any $\omega_{k,k-1}$, coincide insofar as our, so-called, complete description of a situation of incomplete information can determine, but differ in terms of the knowledge they imply if they are assumed to be common "knowledge." Thus a "complete" description does not distinguish between these two models, hence is not truly complete.

sentences which we want the model to incorporate. It is impossible to construct a model which allows us to interpret *all* conclusions that can be made with the model using the assumption that the model is common "knowledge." Only those conclusions that are meaningful in our original syntax are permitted. Alternatively put, while in figure 5.5a we could derive a statement about $K_3(\neg C K_{1,2}(p))$, we are not justified in interpreting this as player 3 knowing that p is not common knowledge among 1 and 2. Moreover, however large a language we start with, the model we construct will still have conclusions of this form – i.e., using K_is and CK_Ms, etc. – that seem to have an intuitive interpretation, but whose interpretation is not valid since they are not expressible in the syntax.

On the other hand, it *might* be that we do not care about results where, say, CK_Ms appear transfinitely many times.[25] If this is the case, i.e., if we can a priori place a bound on the depth of knowledge about knowledge that is of interest to us, then we can construct a model such that all the "interesting" conclusions derived using the assumption that the model is commonly "known" will be correctly interpreted. To do this we would simply use the syntax that includes as deep an iteration as we are interested in for our results.

In conclusion, the syntactic approach does construct a commonly "known" partition model. Each state of the world is constructed from a "complete" and consistent list of sentences, and the derived model specifies only an abstract set of states, a specification of which elements in X are true in each state, and partitions. Consider any sentence about the knowledge of the individuals, that lies in some state of the world, say $k_i(\phi) \in \omega$. Using the K_i operators, we can derive an analogous result from the constructed commonly "known" partition model: $\omega \in K_i([\phi])$. Assuming the constructed model is common "knowledge" we thus obtain the same conclusions from the partition model as from the syntactic sentence. The problem we saw was that the converse is false: in the constructed model there are statements about players' knowledge that could not arise in the sentences of the syntactic framework. (That means that there may be formal results which can be proven using models, and which can be interpreted using the assumption that the model is common "knowledge," that could not be derived in the given syntactic framework.) No particular syntactic language enables a construction of a model which can be assumed to be common "knowledge" in this stronger sense. The extent to which this problem should concern us is not clear. First, instead of asking whether there is a language that provides complete descriptions for all possible models, we could reverse the order of the question. In fact, given any model that is assumed to be common "knowledge," there is some syntactic language, possibly a language that allows for "very many" conjunctions, that justifies and provides a complete description of that model.[26] For example, a language which would distinguish between the models of figure 5.5 would require either infinitely many conjunctions and/or a symbol for common knowledge among a subset of players, c_M. Second, as a pragmatic matter, if there exists a sufficiently rich language, in the sense that it incorporates every sentence that we might ever care about, then again there is no problem as we could just construct the models generated by that language.

3.2.2   The Bayesian approach

Harsanyi (1967) argued that a complete description of a situation of incomplete information would involve a specification of each person's beliefs, beliefs about beliefs, etc., and that the constructed *ex ante* state space is one where Ω is equal to the set of all such infinite hierarchies of beliefs. Mertens and Zamir (1985) explicitly constructed such an Ω, as did Ambruster and Böge (1978) and Böge and Eisele (1979), using a less familiar framework; these authors focused on Harsanyi's concern with games of incomplete information. Basically, they have shown that any situation of incomplete information that is completely described by a hierarchy of beliefs is equivalent to a state of the world in a standard, commonly "known," model of asymmetric information. Thus, in the context of a Bayesian model, the problem we ran into above with a syntactic model seems to be solved.[27]

Consider a basic space of uncertainty, S, which is commonly known to be the basic set of physical uncertainties of interest for agents 1 and 2.[28] Let $X_0 = S$, and for any $n > 0$, let $X_n = [\Delta(X_{n-1})]^N \times X_{n-1}$. Player i's (first-order) beliefs over S are an element of $\Delta(X_0)$, denoted by t_1^i; i's (second-order) beliefs about S and about j's beliefs over S are an element t_2^i of $\Delta(X_1)$, and so on.[29] Thus, a complete specification of i's beliefs is an element of i's type space, $T_0^i = \Pi_{n=1}^{\infty} \Delta(X_n)$. This generates an expanded space of uncertainty that appears to include all uncertainties: an element of $\Omega \equiv S \times T_0^1 \times T_0^2$ specifies the true physical state as well as all of i's beliefs and all of j's beliefs.

However, there are two related problems. First, this construction just begs the question of what are i's beliefs over j's types, i.e., over T_0^j. Second, the beliefs just constructed may be incoherent; for example i may fail to know his own beliefs (we have allowed him to have non-degenerate beliefs over his own beliefs), and i's beliefs may fail to uniquely specify his own beliefs, for example, i's belief about S calculated from i's second-order beliefs t_2^i, $\text{marg}_{X^0} t_2^i \in \Delta(S)$ may differ from i's first-order beliefs, $t_1^i \in \Delta(X_0)$. Since we want to assume that i's beliefs are coherent we make two assumptions: i's beliefs over his own beliefs are his actual beliefs, i.e., i knows his own beliefs (see [4] and [5] above), and i's beliefs on any set calculated using any order belief coincide. Thus, it is assumed that i's beliefs are an element of $T_1^i \subset T_0^i$ which denote those beliefs which are coherent.[30] It turns out that restricting attention to coherent beliefs also solves the first problem. This follows from Kolmogorov's theorem which implies that a complete specification of beliefs for i, $\tau_0^i = (t_1^i, t_2^i, \ldots) \in T_0^i$ is coherent, i.e., is in T_1^i if and only if there is a corresponding belief for i over S and over all of j's possible types, namely a $\mu \in \Delta(S \times T_0^j)$ such that the beliefs given by μ on any measurable set A in X_n

coincide with the beliefs given by τ_0^i (equivalently, the beliefs given by t_n^i) on A. That is, a coherent belief for i, which is a belief over S and over j's beliefs, and j's beliefs over S etc., also determines a belief over j's possible types. But i's beliefs, even if coherent, are not guaranteed to determine a belief for i over j's beliefs over i's types. This will happen if and only if i assigns probability zero to types of j that are incoherent. If we define knowledge as probability 1 – this will be discussed further in section 3.3 below – then we can say that if i knows that j is coherent then i can derive beliefs over j's beliefs over Ω. Note the similarity with partitions: if i "knows" j's partition and that j knows i's partition, then i can calculate j's belief over i's beliefs; while here, if i knows j is coherent then i can calculate j's beliefs over i's beliefs. More generally, there is a similar correspondence between i knowing that j knows that . . . i is coherent and i knowing that j knows . . . i's partition. Thus, common knowledge of coherency is a formalization within the model of the informal assumption that the partitions and beliefs are common knowledge; however it seems less controversial.

Thus, by assuming common knowledge of coherency we will generate spaces $T^i \subset T_0^i$ which have the property that each type in T^i is a complete and consistent description: each type is a belief over S, and over the other players' belief over S, etc., moreover each such type generates a belief over $\Omega \equiv S \times T^1 \times T^2$. So we have created an *ex ante* space Ω, and a possibility correspondence where each player i is informed only of his type in T^i, i.e., for $\bar{\omega} = (\bar{x}, \bar{t}^1, \bar{t}^2)$, we have $\mathscr{F}_i(\bar{\omega}) \equiv \{\omega \in \Omega : \omega = (x, t^1, t^2) \text{ s.t. } t^i = \bar{t}^i\}$. This information structure generates a belief over the space that coincides with the belief described by the state of the world. So, this structure can be taken to be common "knowledge" w.l.o.g.

How have we achieved this result which was unattainable before? The richer and continuous structure of countably additive beliefs is crucial here. Consider the example in figure 5.5 again. As before, for any strictly positive probability measure, at any state other than ω^*, 3 does not know $\cap_{m=1}^n K_{1,2}^m(p)$ for any n. In the syntactic approach we say no more, so we cannot specify whether 3 knows $\neg CK_{1,2}(p)$ or not. In the Bayesian approach, if, say 3 does not know $\cap_{m=1}^n K_{1,2}^m(p)$, for all m, then there exists a decreasing sequence, $p_n < 1$, of the probabilities which 3 assigns to this sequence of events. The countable intersection of these events is exactly $CK_{1,2}(p)$. So the probability of this limit event is given by the limit of the sequence. If the limit is 0, then 3 knows that p is not common knowledge among 1 and 2, while if it is positive 3 does not know that p is not common knowledge among 1 and 2. And this conclusion is true regardless of 3's partition, i.e., for both models in figure 5.5, since knowledge here is defined as belief with probability 1.[31]

3.3   Belief with probability 1 or knowledge?

The usual notion of knowledge requires that when a player knows something it is true. This is property [T], which in the partition model of section 3.1 results from the assumption that ω is an element of $\mathscr{F}_i(\omega)$, and which is assumed directly in the syntactic framework of section 3.2.1 and built into the construction in section 3.2.2. However, the probabilistic notion of certainty used in the Bayesian model need not have such an implication. This subsection discusses the relationship between knowledge and certainty and briefly shows how to adapt the presentations above to a notion of certainty. The distinction between certainty and knowledge, and the combined development of both notions within one model in subsection 3.3.3 below, turn out to be very useful in discussing extensive-form games (see section 5).

3.3.1   A certainty operator

Given an information structure $(\Omega, \mathscr{F}_i, p_i)$, we can derive, in addition to K_i, a belief-with-probability-one operator $B_i: 2^\Omega \to 2^\Omega$ given by $B_i(A) = \{\omega: p_i(A \mid \mathscr{F}_i(\omega)) = 1\}$. Recall that we use the term certainty as an abbreviation for belief with probability one. This certainty operator is equivalent to the following: at any state ω you are certain of (any superset of) the intersection between your information at that state $\mathscr{F}_i(\omega)$ and the support of your beliefs (denoted by S). The operator B_i satisfies the properties below.

  D $B_i(A) \subset \neg B_i \neg A$: if i is certain of A then i is not certain of the complement of A;
  MC^B $B_i(A) \cap B_i(C) = B_i(A \cap C)$: being certain of A and C is equivalent to being certain of A and of C;
  N^B $B_i(\Omega) = \Omega$: i is always certain of anything that is true in all states of the world;
  4^B $B_i(A) \subset B_i(B_i(A))$: if i is certain of A then i is certain that i is certain of A;
  5^B $\neg B_i(A) \subset B_i(\neg B_i(A))$, being uncertain of A implies being certain that one is uncertain of A.

As in subsection 3.1, given such a certainty operator B_i we can define an information structure on Ω: let p_i be any probability on Ω with support $S \equiv \cap \{E: B_i(E) = \Omega$ and E is closed$\}$, and let $\mathscr{F}_i(\omega) = \{\omega': \forall E, \omega' \in B_i(E) \Leftrightarrow \omega \in B_i(E)\}$.[32] Moreover, this information structure will generate (in the way defined above) the same B_i as we started with.

3.3.2 A syntactic symbol for certainty

How is the syntactic notion of knowledge weakened to certainty? Start with a language as in subsection 3.2.1, and introduce a symbol b_i for certainty instead of k_i for knowledge. Consider modifying the axioms [D, MC^B, N^B, 4^B, and 5^B] as we did in going from the operator K_i to the language symbol k_i. That is, replace B_i with b_i, $\supset$ with $\to$, sets A with propositions ϕ, etc., and add [RE] and [MP]. We can then create a consistent and "complete" description of situations of incomplete information, which will generate a state space and an operator B_i satisfying the axioms. Since we have just seen that such a B_i is equivalent to an information structure we again have an equivalence between the syntactic approach and the asymmetric information model.

3.3.3 Knowledge and certainty combined

For characterizing solution concepts in games we will want a model that allows for both knowledge and certainty: for example, a player should know what her own strategy is, but can at most be certain, but not know, what her opponent's strategy is. Therefore, we now present a unified treatment of K_i and B_i.[33] Given an information structure we can generate K_i and B_i as above. In addition to the properties derived above, these will satisfy the following.

BK $K_i(A) \subset B_i(A)$: you are certain of anything that you know;
4^{BK} $B_i(A) \subset K_i(B_i(A))$: you know when you are certain of something;
5^{BK} $\neg K_i(E) = B_i(\neg K_i(E))$.

Similar to the equivalencies in subsections 3.1 and 3.3.1, given a B_i and a K_i satisfying [T, BK, 4^{BK}, 5^{BK}, MC, MC^B] we can construct a partition and a non-unique prior which in turn generate K_i and B_i.[34] In the future we will need a notion analogous to common knowledge for the case of beliefs. We say that an event E is common certainty at ω if everyone assigns probability 1 to E, and to everyone assigning probability 1 to E, etc.

3.4 The implications of constructing a commonly "known" model

We have discussed the constructions of Harsanyi's and Aumann's expanded state spaces. These constructions show that it is without loss of generality to work with models where we assume (informally) that the information structure is common "knowledge." Alternatively put, we *can* take any situation of incomplete information that is completely specified and consistent, and view it as a state in a model that is commonly "known."

This will be useful in formalizing assumptions such as common knowledge or rationality, and in solving games where we are given some situation of incomplete information. The main purpose of this subsection is to argue that these constructions do *not* justify acting as if all circumstances derive from a commonly known *ex ante* model. The most obvious reason for this is that the constructed models of subsection 3.2 do not contain a prior: only probabilities conditional on a players' information are constructed.[35] Moreover, it seems problematic to argue that, say, Savage's (1954) framework justifies assuming that players have a prior on the constructed state space. This state space includes states that the individual views as impossible. So forming preferences over acts would require contemplating preferences conditional on knowledge that conflicts with knowledge that the player actually has, which seems conceptually problematic (and in violation of the behavioral objectives of Savage (1954)). We have a second type of concern with assumptions that are based on an *ex ante* model; these concerns follow from the difference between justifying assumptions and solution concepts for the artificially constructed model and justifying them for a true physical *ex ante* model.

The argument that no prior was constructed immediately leads to the conclusion that we ought to be cautious in using concepts that must be defined in terms of priors. So, for example, *ex ante* efficiency and the CPA are both questionable notions in true situations of incomplete information. Naturally, in contexts where a real physical *ex ante* stage does exist, there is no problem: then a Savage (1954) approach would justify assuming priors on the space at the *ex ante* stage.[36] But here we focus on situations of incomplete information where the commonly "known" information structures, as constructed in section 3.2, are needed.

In the remainder of this subsection we elaborate further on the limitations of these constructions. First we highlight the artificial nature of the construction. Then we suggest that this raises doubts about other notions, such as interim and *ex post* efficiency, as well as raising additional concerns with justifications for the CPA. To clarify the artificial nature of the state space constructed in subsection 3.2, we consider a simple version of this construction, one which does not yield a space of all possible situations of incomplete information, but does have a particular infinite hierarchy of beliefs that is captured by a standard model. First, assume that there is some fact about the world and the agents are concerned as to whether it is true or false. Denote this fact by p, and assume that we are in a situation where for $i = 1, 2$, and $j \neq i, i$ knows p but does not know if j knows it, and believes that j does not know if i knows it, and more generally i's hierarchy of beliefs is that there is common knowledge that i does not know if j knows it and j does not know if i knows it. This can be captured by the following Kripke

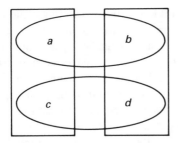

Figure 5.6

model: $\Omega = \{a, b, c, d\}$; p is true in states a, b, and c, and false in state d; $\mathcal{F}_1 = \{\{a, b\}, \{c, d,\}\}$; $\mathcal{F}_2 = \{\{a, c\}, \{b, d\}\}$ (figure 5.6).

The true situation is described by state a. All the states other than a are artificial constructs. While they represent situations the agents can imagine, they do not represent reality in any way. Recall that we are assuming that we are given the situation of incomplete information described above, which did not arise from any particular commonly known *ex ante* physical situation. In particular both agents as well as the analyst know that state d is false, and that it is an artificial construct.

What does this artificiality imply? First, we think it raises doubts about the use of other efficiency notions, such as interim and *ex post* efficiency. These notions seem to us to be based on giving the artificially constructed states more meaning then they have. However, we have not been able to develop this argument. Therefore, we should emphasize that our concerns with interim and *ex post* efficiency notions are on less solid grounds than the clear-cut argument – based on the lack of a prior – against *ex ante* efficiency.

A second consequence of the artificial nature of the *ex ante* state space can be found in Bhattacharyya and Lipman (1995). They provide an example of trade with a common prior, despite the no-trade theorem. Trade occurs because *ex ante* utilities are not well defined, since the *ex ante* utility functions are unbounded. But the interim utility functions can be bounded without changing the essence of the example. While it seems plausible to argue that utility functions are bounded, does this argument apply to an *ex ante* artificial construct? We would say no, raising doubts about no-trade theorems in such contexts, over and above any concerns about the common prior assumption.[37]

The final problem that results from the artificial nature of the state space concerns the main argument in favor of the CPA. This problem is of interest because justifications for standard equilibrium concepts require a common prior on such an artificial state space. (We say that an artificial state space is necessary, because in the model that justifies solution concepts, the *ex ante* stage is one where the player does not know his own strategy, and may not even know whether or not he is rational. The assumption that there actually exists such a stage for decisionmakers seems very questionable.) The problem focuses on Aumann's (1987) argument that a common prior is plausible because players with identical information would have the same beliefs. But how could player 1 receive the information that corresponds to 2's artificial information set $\{a, c\}$, which is constructed as the set where player 1 both knows p and does not know p? (see also Gul (1995a)).

While we have said this several times, it is probably worth repeating here. If we set aside the question of justifying solution concepts, then for some economic applications the discussion of this subsection is not of direct interest. If there is a real *ex ante* situation, then the notions are meaningful since they do not rely on tradeoffs over artificial constructs. For example, auction theory, while often citing Harsanyi's work as a justification for the incomplete-information model, could be based on·an oil-sample story such as was described in subsection 3.1, where intuitively there is a real physical *ex ante* commonly known framework. Alternatively, in auctions with private values, an *ex ante* foundation exists by arguing that bidders are drawn from a population with a commonly known distribution of preferences. On the other hand, while a private-values with correlated beliefs model could be imagined, it does not seem to correspond to any plausible *ex ante* story, in which case any research examining *ex ante* efficiency of various mechanisms in such a context needs to be motivated much more carefully.

Having argued that both the notion of efficiency in games of incomplete information, and the assumptions underlying standard solution concepts, are not plausible in the artificially constructed space, one might think that the whole exercise was vacuous: can any sensible assumptions be made on the constructed model? Assumptions that do not refer to the constructed state space, but rather are assumed to hold in the true state are on a solid footing. For example, the assumption that at the actual state rationality is common knowledge, is sensible. Such a statement only uses the artificially constructed states the way they originated – namely as elements in a hierarchy of beliefs. This obviously contrasts with assumptions that essentially require the artificial constructs in order to be interpreted, such as the CPA.

3.5   Conclusion

When there is a real commonly known *ex ante* stage then clearly it is appropriate to model the situation with an asymmetric information model that is commonly "known." The constructions in subsection 3.2 justify the assumption of a commonly known asymmetric information model in all contexts where the players' views of the world are complete. These two justifications of (almost) the same model differ in that only the former has a well-defined notion of a prior and only in the former are all the states truly feasible. This distinction argues against using *ex ante* notions in cases where the second model is deemed necessary.

However, these notions are used heavily in information economics and – in the case of the CPA – in the characterizations of solution concepts and the analysis of their robustness. For these reasons we will emphasize results that avoid the CPA, but we will still review other results, such as Aumann's provocative characterization of correlated equilibrium, as well. Moreover, we will use both the real *ex ante* stage and the artificially constructed commonly known model interchangeably with the hope that by now the reader understands the important differences between them. In particular, we will continue to describe a model as $(\Omega, \mathcal{F}_i, p_i)$, rather than $(\Omega, \mathcal{F}_i, p_i(\cdot \mid \mathcal{F}_i))$, even though the latter, rather than the former, is what we justified in this section. We will leave it to the reader to decide on the usefulness of the various results, and we try to minimize repetition of our concerns in the remainder of the chapter.

4 A STATE-SPACE MODEL FOR KNOWLEDGE, CERTAINTY, AND RATIONALITY – CHARACTERIZING NORMAL-FORM SOLUTION CONCEPTS

We now introduce the notion of a model for characterizing solution concepts, which specifies an information structure and a function from states to normal-form games and to strategy profiles of the game in that state.[38] (A model is the same as the interactive belief systems used by Aumann and Brandenburger (1995)), and closely related to the framework used in Aumann (1987) to characterize correlated equilibrium (see also Stalnaker (1994)). For simplicity we assume that strategy spaces of the games are the same in every state; Σ_i denotes i's strategy set, and $\Sigma \equiv \Pi_i \Sigma_i$ is the set of strategy profiles. Thus, for the remainder of the chapter, a model is a collection $\{\Omega, \mathcal{F}_i, p_i, \Sigma_i, \mathbf{u}, s_i\}$, where, $s_i : \Omega \to \Sigma_i$ specifies i's actions in each state ω, $\mathbf{s}(\omega) = (\mathbf{s}_1(\omega), \dots, \mathbf{s}_n(\omega))$, and $\mathbf{u} : \Omega \to \{(u_i)_{i \in N} \mid \forall i, u_i : \Sigma \to \mathfrak{R}\}$ specifies the payoff functions. Thus $\mathbf{u}_i(\omega')(\sigma)$ is the payoff to i in state ω' if the strategy profile σ is played. We also assume that the partitions of i have the property that in each cell a common strategy of i is specified at all states: i knows his own action, $\forall F \in \mathcal{F}_i, \forall \omega, \omega' \in F, \mathbf{s}_i(\omega) = \mathbf{s}_i(\omega')$. Finally, we assume that each player knows his own payoff function (u_i is the same in each cell of i's partition). This last assumption is substantive, see, e.g., footnote 4. Note that if we ignore the function s specifying the strategy profile in each state, then a model is just a game with a move by Nature: it specifies an information structure, and, for each state of the world, a game. Under this interpretation s is a strategy profile for the game with a move by Nature. This interpretation will be useful later.

We denote by $[u]$ the event in Ω that the payoff functions are $u = (u_1, \ldots, u_n)$, $[u] \equiv \{\omega \in \Omega : \mathbf{u}(\omega) = u\}$ by $[\sigma]$ the set of states where the strategy profile is σ, $[\sigma] \equiv \{\omega \in \Omega : \mathbf{s}(\omega) = \sigma\}$, and similarly for $[\sigma_i], [\sigma_{-i}]$, etc. This notation simplifies our assumptions above: i knows his own action is simply $\forall \sigma_i, K_i[\sigma_i] = [\sigma_i]$; and i knows his payoff becomes $\forall u_i, K_i[u_i] = [u_i]$. At each state ω, each player has an induced belief over the opponents, which we denote by $\text{marg}_{\Sigma_{-i}} p_i(\cdot \mid \mathscr{F}_i(\omega))$; the event that these beliefs equal some particular distribution $\phi_{-i} \in \Delta(\Sigma_{-i})$ is denoted by $[\phi_{-i}]$. Following Aumann and Brandenburger (1995) we use the term conjectures of i as an abbreviation for i's induced beliefs over Σ_{-i}. Finally, we denote by $\mathscr{S}$ the operator on games of deleting one round of strongly dominated strategies for all players; similarly $\mathscr{W}$ denotes deletion of weakly dominated strategies. Since the strategy spaces are held constant we abuse notation and write $\mathscr{S}^{\infty}(u)$ to denote the operation of infinite deletion of strongly dominated strategies in the game $G = (\Sigma, u)$.

Definition Player i is rational in state ω if given i's beliefs at ω, his action maximizes his expected utility

$$\sum_{\omega' \in \mathscr{F}_i(\omega)} p_i(\omega') \mathbf{u}_i(\omega')(\mathbf{s}_i(\omega), \mathbf{s}_{-i}(\omega')) \geq \sum_{\omega' \in \mathscr{F}_i(\omega)} p_i(\omega') \mathbf{u}_i(\omega)(\sigma_i, \mathbf{s}_{-i}(\omega'))$$

for all $\sigma_i \in \Sigma_i$.

The set of states at which all players are rational is the even [rationality].

Proposition 1 (Bernheim (1984), Pearce (1984))[39] $CB([u] \cap [rationality]) \subset [S^{\infty}(u)]$. Moreover, there exists a model such that $CB([u] \cap [rationality]) = [S^{\infty}(u)]$.

If at a state ω, rationality and the game is common certainty, then at ω each player is choosing an action that survives iterative deletion of strongly dominated strategies. The idea of the proof is well known – rationality is equivalent to players choosing only strategies in $\mathscr{S}^1(u)$; the fact that rationality is known implies that they only choose best replies to $\mathscr{S}^1(u)$, so only strategies in $\mathscr{S}^2(u)$ are chosen, etc.

What is the relationship between equilibrium concepts and $\mathscr{S}^{\infty}$? Brandenburger and Dekel (1987a) show that the strategies and payoffs resulting from $\mathscr{S}^{\infty}(G)$ are the same as the strategies and payoffs in the interim stage of an a posteriori subjective correlated equilibrium of G.[40] An a posteriori subjective correlated equilibrium of a game G is essentially a Nash equilibrium of the game where an information structure, interpreted as a correlating device about which players may have different priors, is observed before G is played. (Aumann (1974) introduced this solution concept.) The interim stage of such an equilibrium is the stage after receiving the information of the correlating device. A correlated equilibrium is the same as an a posteriori equilibrium except that there is a common prior over the correlating device. A correlated equilibrium distribution is the probability distribution over Σ induced by the correlated equilibrium.

Proposition 2 *Fix an information structure $(\Omega, \mathscr{F}_i, p_i)$ and a game $G = (\Sigma, u)$. Consider a game G', where before G is played, the players observe their private information concerning Ω. Strategies for i in G' are functions $s:\Omega \rightarrow \Sigma_i$ that are constant on an information cell for i. Consider a Nash equilibrium $\bar{s}$ of G', where $\bar{s}_i(F_i)$ is optimal for all F_i (even those with zero prior probability). The interim strategy choices (and expected utilities) are rationalizable: $\bar{s}(\omega) \in \mathscr{S}^{\infty}(G)$ for any F_i in $\mathscr{F}_i$.*

Conversely, given any strategy $\sigma \in \mathscr{S}^{\infty}(G)$ there is an information structure and a Nash equilibrium as above where σ is played in some state of the world.[41]

Thus, common certainty of rationality justifies equilibrium analysis so long as the equilibrium allows for differing priors. To get more traditional equilibrium concepts one typically needs to assume a common prior on Ω.[42] Aumann's characterization of correlated equilibrium was the first characterization of an equilibrium concept within a formal state-space model describing common knowledge of players' rationality.

Proposition 3 (Aumann (1987)) *If there is a common prior p in a model, and the support of p is a subset of $[rationality] \cap [u]$, then the distribution over actions induced by the prior p is a correlated equilibrium distribution of $G = (\Sigma, u)$.*

Intuitively, this follows from propositions 1 and 2: common certainty of rationality is the same as $\mathscr{S}^{\infty}(G)$ which is the same as subjective correlated equilibrium; imposing a common prior in addition to common certainty of rationality should then be the same as objective correlated equilibrium. This is not precise because propositions 1 and 2 focused on the players' actual beliefs at a state of the world, not on the *ex ante* constructed model and an overall distribution of actions.[43]

Proposition 4 (Aumann and Brandenburger (1995)) *In a two-person game if the events* [*rationality*], [*u*] *and* [ϕ_{-i}] *for* $i = 1, 2$, *are mutually certain at* ω (*i.e., each player assigns conditional probability* 1 *to these events*), *then* (ϕ_1, ϕ_2) *is a Nash equilibrium of* $G = (\Sigma, \mathbf{u}(\omega)) \equiv (\Sigma, u)$.

The idea of the proof is as follows. First add the assumption that the players are mutually certain that they are mutually certain that the payoffs are *u*. If *i* is certain that *j*'s conjecture is $\phi_{-j} \in \Delta(S_i)$, and that *j* is rational and that *j* is certain his payoffs are u_j, and *i* assigns positive probability to σ_j, then σ_j must be a best reply for *j* given *j*'s conjecture about *i*'s actions, ϕ_{-j}, and given u_j. So, under the additional assumption the result that (ϕ_1, ϕ_2) is a Nash equilibrium is obtained. In fact, since we assume that players know their own payoffs, Aumann and Brandenburger show that one only needs to assume that the payoffs are mutually known. This is because if *i* assigns probability 1 at ω to [u_j], [*rationality*] and [ϕ_{-j}], and positive probability to σ_j, then there must be a state $\omega' \in [u_j] \cap [rationality] \cap [\phi_{-j}] \cap [\sigma_j]$. At ω', *j* is rational, *j*'s conjecture is [ϕ_{-j}], *j*'s payoffs are [u_j] and *j* knows this by our assumption, and *j* is choosing σ_j. This completes the proof.[44]

It is worth emphasizing that the statement that [ϕ_i] are mutually certain is significantly stronger than saying that *i* is certain *j*'s conjecture is [ϕ_j]. Since players have beliefs about their own conjecture, and naturally their beliefs about their own conjecture are correct, assuming that conjectures are mutually certain implies that the beliefs about the conjectures are correct (see Aumann and Brandenburger (1995, lemma 4.2)). By contrast, for an arbitrary event *E*, players 1 and 2 could be mutually certain of *E* but be wrong.

Aumann and Brandenburger (1995) also characterize Nash equilibrium in games with $n > 2$ players, using the CPA, common knowledge of the conjectures, and mutual knowledge of payoffs and rationality. They also provide a series of examples to show the necessity of these assumptions. They discuss a second characterization of Nash equilibrium, where the CPA and common certainty of the conjectures are replaced with independence, which they find less attractive (see also Brandenburger and Dekel (1987a) and Tan and Werlang (1988)). Given our concerns with the CPA we find the characterization using independence no less palatable.

In conclusion, we have concerns with applications of game theory whose conclusions rely on Nash or correlated equilibrium. The role of the CPA raises doubts about the use of correlated equilibrium; the necessity of mutually certain conjectures raises some doubts about Nash equilibrium in two-person games; and the peculiar combination of the CPA and common certainty of conjectures, or independence and mutual certainty of conjectures, raises serious doubts about the interpretation of Nash equilibrium in games with more than two players. Naturally, other foundations for these solution concepts may exist, and some are currently being developed in the context of evolutionary and learning models. However, until such foundations are obtained we must be cautious in interpreting applications that rely on Nash equilibrium.

We now discuss the application of the ideas above to games with moves by Nature and games of incomplete information. As we know from section 3 there is a difference between these two environments. In one, there is a real *ex ante* stage at which an analysis can be carried out, at the other *ex ante* stage is an artificial construct used to think about the situation of incomplete information. Obviously, the way we would analyze the case of a real *ex ante* stage is by embodying the whole game with a move by Nature into a state. To clarify this, recall that in the analysis above the state ω determined the game by specifying the strategies and the payoffs. In the case of a game with a move by Nature these strategies are functions from the players' private information into their choices, and the payoffs are the *ex ante* payoffs. Carrying out the analysis at a state ω will mean providing an *ex ante* solution of this game, i.e., specifying what functions from private information about Nature into Σ will be played. So, in the case of a game with a move by Nature, i.e., with a real *ex ante* stage, the model is unchanged and the results above can be meaningfully applied to the *ex ante* stage of the game. In the case of a game of incomplete information, the space Ω will capture all the incomplete information, and carrying out the analysis at a state ω will mean specifying a strategy in Σ (not a function from private information about Nature into Σ). The model for this case will be the same as the one used throughout this section, except that now $[u]$ is no longer mutual or common certainty, so the results obtained earlier are not meaningful. We now examine the implications of this in the context of the characterizations of $\mathcal{S}^{\infty}$ and of Nash equilibrium.[45]

First consider proposition 1: in this case common certainty of rationality implies that players will choose actions that are iteratively undominated in the interim sense in the game of incomplete information. (The distinction between *ex ante* and interim dominance can be seen, e.g., in the example in Fudenberg and Tirole (1991, p. 229).) On the other hand, if a game with a move by Nature is played at ω then the *ex ante* payoff function is commonly known and iterated deletion of *ex ante* dominated strategies will be the consequence of common certainty of rationality.

Next consider proposition 4. If we consider the case of a game with a move by Nature there are no problems: if we assume that the game and rationality are mutually certain at ω, as are the players' conjectures – which are over functions from private information into Σ – then we have characterized Nash equilibria of the game with a move by Nature.

However, for the case of true games of incomplete information, where there is no *ex ante* model, there seems to be no obvious characterization of "Bayesian Nash equilibrium at ω." That is, we are not aware of an equilibrium analog to iterated deletion of interim-dominated strategies.

The solution concepts above do not include any refinements. One might want to see the extent to which concepts from the refinements literature can be characterized using assumptions about knowledge, certainty, and rationality. In particular, one might want to add an assumption of *caution* as a requirement, namely that player i is never certain about j's strategy; the event where this holds, [*caution*], is formally $\cap_i \cap_{\sigma_{-i}} \neg B_i \neg [\sigma_{-i}]$. On this event i's conjecture over his opponents has full support on Σ_{-i}. Clearly this is inconsistent with common knowledge or common certainty of rationality since these full support beliefs do not allow a player to know or be certain about anything concerning their opponents' strategies. Thus there is no way to assume common certainty of rationality and that players are cautious, since caution conflicts with certainty.[46] We return to this issue in section 6 below.

5   CHARACTERIZING SOLUTION CONCEPTS IN EXTENSIVE-FORM GAMES AND COMMON KNOWLEDGE/CERTAINTY OF RATIONALITY

5.1   The model

Much of the research on rationality in the extensive form falls in one or more of the following categories: criticisms of backward induction and analysis of the problematic nature of common knowledge of the rationality assumption for extensive-form games, identification of weaker, non-backward induction theories as the consequence of rationality, and, finally, alternative axioms or formulations of common knowledge of rationality that yield backward induction. Below we will utilize the knowledge and belief structure described in section 3 to discuss and summarize these results.

Let $\Gamma = \{Y, Z, \prec, N, I, A, (u_i)_{i=1}^n\}$ be an extensive-form game of perfect information. The set $X \equiv Y \cup Z$ denotes the set of nodes and Z is the set of terminal nodes. The binary relation $\prec$ on X is transitive and irreflexive and hence has a minimal element. Furthermore, $\prec$ satisfies arborescence: $x \prec v, y \prec v$ implies $x \prec y$ or $y \prec x$ or $x = y$. The function I determines for each non-terminal node in Y the player $i \in N$ who moves at that node. The mapping A associates with each non-terminal node in Y, a non-empty set of nodes (the set of actions for player $I(v)$), $A(v) = \{y \mid v \prec y \text{ and } v \prec y' \text{ implies } (y = y' \text{ or } y \prec y')\}$. A strategy s_i for player i is a collection actions, one from each node that is not precluded by and earlier action of player i. The set S_i is the set of all strategies for player i, s denotes a strategy profile, and S is the set of all strategy profiles. Each u_i associates with every terminal node a payoff for agent i.

As in section 4, a model specifies an information structure and for each state the game to be played at that state and the strategies chosen at that state. Here we assume for simplicity that the game is the same, Γ, in every state. A model is then $\mathbf{M} = (\Omega, \mathbf{s}, \mathscr{F}_i, p_i, \Gamma)$. As in section 3.3.3 the model generates knowledge and certainty operators K_i and B_i satisfying Axioms $[BK, T, 4^{BK}, 5^{BK}, MC, MC^{BK}]$. Much of the following will be stated using these operators, rather then using the partitions, $\mathscr{F}_i$, and conditional probabilities $p_i(\cdot \mid \mathscr{F}_i)$. In order to identify the implications of common knowledge of rationality or common certainty of rationality in various settings, we need to identify nodes with subsets of Ω: $[\Lambda] = \bigcup_{x \in \Lambda}[x]$ for $\Lambda \subset S, S_i,$ or S_{-i}.

It is often said that in discussing rationality in the extensive form there is a need to incorporate counterfactuals or nearby worlds or hypotheticals or at least a different kind of implication than the standard material implication of propositional logic into the analysis (see Binmore (1987–8), Samet (1993) and Aumann (1995b)). There are two separate issues that necessitate counterfactuals. The first arises even in normal-form games. To justify the rationality of action α for a given player, the other players and the modeler have to argue that, given what he knows and believes, choosing α is a good as any other action the agent might have undertaken. But this requires discussing what would happen if this player were to choose β at some state in which he is specified to choose α. To be sure, this is a counterfactual of some sort but not one that requires an elaborate theory of nearby worlds. As in section 4, such counterfactuals will play a role only in the definition of rationality and only implicitly. The second source of need for counterfactuals or hypotheticals is present only in extensive-form games. The rationality of a particular action α may rest on the predicted reaction of the opponent to the alternative course of action β which itself may or may not be consistent with rationality. Furthermore, the prescribed rational course of action α or the contemplated alternative β may or may not be anticipated by the opponent of the player. Thus, the modeler is forced to discuss not only contemplated deviations by a rational player but also predicted responses to deviations or surprises. In our approach to rationality in the extensive form we will utilize the distinction between knowledge and certainty to do away with this second source of need for counterfactuals. Specifically, an event E will be considered a surprise by player i at any state in $\neg K_i \neg E \cap B_i \neg E$. Moreover, we will often require that agents are, at most, certain about their opponents' strategies and cannot know the strategies their opponents are using. Thus we will not need to consider what players do when faced with situations they *know* to be impossible (i.e., counterfactuals). Therefore, the only counterfactuals will be those implicit in the definition of rationality; strategy β will be irrational in some state at which the agent is to choose α since had he chosen β he would receive a lower payoff.

Definition (extensive-form rationality): For any model **M** let (*a*) $D(s_i) = \{E \subset \Omega \mid \exists \beta \in S_i \, s.t. \, u_i(\beta, s_{-i}(\omega)) > u_i(s_i, s_{-i}(\omega)) \forall \omega \in E\};$ (*b*) $\neg R^v(s_i) = \neg K \neg [v] \cap \bigcup_{E \in D(s_i)} K_i([v] \to E) \bigcup \neg B \neg [v] \cap \bigcup_{E \in D(s_i)} B_i([v]$ $\to E);$ (*c*) $R^v = \{\omega \mid s_{I(v)}(\omega) \in R^v(s_{I(v)}(\omega))\}, \, R_i = \bigcap_{I(v) = i} R^v, R = \bigcap_i R_i.$

The first item of the definition above identifies the collection of events in which the strategy s_i is strictly dominated. The second item defines the set of states of the world in which the strategy s_i is irrational at a particular node v. The strategy s_i is irrational at $[v]$ if $[v]$ is possible ($\neg K_i \neg [v]$) and i knows that s_i is dominated at v or v is plausible ($\neg B \neg [v]$) and i believes s_i is dominated at v. Note that, if i knows that v will not be reached, then he is rational at v regardless of what he plans to do there. The final part of the definition states that i is rational at v in state ω if and only if the prescribed strategy for i is not irrational at $[v]$. The event "i is rational" corresponds to all states at which i is rational at every v.

5.2   Common knowledge of rationality

Since knowledge implies truth (Axiom T of section 3), a standard model of knowledge may fail to incorporate even the most basic requirement of extensive form rationality. Consider the game Γ_1 in figure 5.7.

Player 2's knowledge that player 1 will not choose β renders any analysis of what *might* happen *if* Player 1 chooses β irrelevant for the analysis of Γ_1 given our definition of rationality. Various ways of dealing with this issue have been studied in the literature. Following the lead of the refinements literature and extensive-form rationalizability (see Pearce (1984)), Ben-Porath (1994), Reny (1993), Gul (1995b) require rationality in the extensive form to imply that a player at an information set chooses a best response to some conjecture that reaches that information set. Hence common knowledge of rationality rules out player 1 choosing α in Γ_1. By contrast Samet's (1993) formalism does not yield the result that common knowledge of rationality implies player 1 chooses α. Without further assumptions, any Nash equilibrium outcome is consistent with common knowledge of rationality in his model. The same is true of the standard model defined above. If player 2 knows that player 1 will not choose β then any analysis of

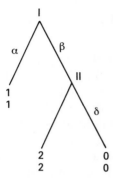

Figure 5.7

what 2 would do when faced with a surprise is moot. This suggests that an additional assumption is needed if the standard model is to incorporate surprises: in an epistemic model of extensive-form rationality, convictions regarding opponents should be limited to beliefs if this model is to adequately deal with surprises and the issue of credibility. This is a weakening of the assumption of caution introduced at the end of section 4, which required that a player not be certain about an opponent's action, here we allow for certainty but rule out knowledge of an opponent's action. This idea is formalized in the definition below. Proposition 5 summarizes the implications of common knowledge of rationality for the standard model when no such axiom is imposed.

Proposition 5 *Let s be a Nash equilibrium of the perfect information extensive-form game Γ. Then, there exists a model $\mathbf{M}$ such that $CK[R] = [s]$. Moreover, if Γ is generic, then for any model $\mathbf{M}$, $CK[R] \subset \bigcup_{s \in NE}[s]$ where* **NE** *is the set of Nash equilibrium profiles of Γ.*

It can be verified that the set of outcomes consistent with common knowledge of rationality in Samet's model is identical to the set of outcomes corresponding to strategies associated with common knowledge of rationality in the standard model of proposition 5 above. Samet's model incorporates a theory of hypotheticals that enables him to impose additional restrictions regarding the "beliefs" at unreached information sets. In our setting the distinction between knowledge and belief was developed to handle just such concerns. As noted above, an additional principle is needed in the current setting to rule out incredible threats as in the imperfect equilibrium of Γ_1. We will call this principle the Weak Caution (WC). We view WC to be an essential element of extensive-form rationality.

Definition (WC) $WC = \bigcap_i \bigcap_{s_{-i}} \neg K_i[\neg [s_{-i}]]$.

5.3   The problematic nature of extensive-form rationality

Consider the game in figure 1 from section 2. This game, or a closely related alternative, is studied by Basu (1990), Ben-Porath (1994), Bicchieri (1989), Binmore (1987–8), Rosenthal (1981), Reny (1993), (1992), and Gul (1995b). The standard argument of backward-induction is as follows: if 2 is rational then he will choose t_3 at his final information set if given a chance. Therefore if 2 is given a chance then he knowing that 1 is rational and being rational himself will choose t_2. Hence, being rational, knowing that 2 knows he is rational and that 2 is rational, 1 should choose t_1 at his first information set. This is the well-known argument of backward induction. All of the authors listed above note the following flaw in this argument: the claim that 2 knows that 1 is rational when she has a chance to move is legitimate only if 2 has no reason to doubt the rationality of 1 when she is reached. The backward induction argument outlined above, shows that when reached, 2 can no longer maintain all the assumptions that yield the backward induction prediction. Basu (1990) and Reny (1993) provide two rather different ways of formalizing this criticism of backward induction. Reny (1993) defines formally what it means for rationality to be common certainty at every relevant information set and proves that except for a rare class of games, rationality cannot be common certainty at every relevant information set. In particular, he shows that rationality cannot be common certainty at player 2's information set in Γ_2. In related work, Basu (1990) shows that there cannot be any solution concept for extensive-form games that satisfy the following apparently plausible restrictions. (1) Rational agents take, at each information set, actions that maximize their payoff. (2) Agents start off certain of the rationality of their opponents and remain certain until actions that are inconsistent with *any* rational strategy are observed. (3) If rational agents observe their opponents take an irrational action then they can no longer rule out any possible action of the irrational opponents. (4) Finally, any course of action which can lead to a payoff at least as high as a possible payoff according to the theory, must be an allowed action for the theory. To see the inconsistency, note that in Γ_2 backward induction cannot be the theory, since if it were and 1 were to choose l_1 then 2 would have to believe that 1 is irrational and hence by (3) might choose l_3 if given a chance. Hence 2 might choose to give him this chance. But this means that 1 might do better by choosing l_1 then t_1. But this contradicts (4) since t_1 is prescribed by the theory and l_1 is not. Thus, any theory satisfying Basu's requirements must allow for player 2's information set to be reached by some rational strategy. But, then (1) and (2) imply that player 2 must choose t_2 which contradicts the rationality of l_1.

Proposition 6 *If v is not on the unique backward induction path of a generic extensive-form game and $[v] \cap CB[R] \neq \emptyset$ in some standard model of this game* **M**, *then there exists $[v']$ such that $[v'] \cap CB[R] \cap \bigcup_i B_i \neg [v'] \neq \emptyset$.*

Proposition 6 is related to Reny (1993). If there is an information set not on the unique backward induction path then it is either common certainty that this information set will not be reached (hence rationality cannot be common certainty once the information set is reached) or there is some other state consistent with the common certainty of rationality where some player is being surprised. That is, one player is choosing a strategy that another player believes will not be chosen. The possibility of this type of surprise is ruled out by Basu (1990) since his axiom (4) implicitly rules out the possibility that the opponent may believe that the information set $[v']$ will not be reached even though reaching it is not inconsistent with $CB[R]$ (i.e., the theory). Note that proposition 6 above is not vacuous. We can construct standard models for generic games in which $[v] \cap CB[R]$ is non-empty even when v is off the backward induction path.

5.4 The resolution: weak caution and common certainty of rationality

Gul (1995b) proposed the solution concept described next as the weakest solution consistent with extensive-form rationality. For any extensive-form game Γ, let $\mathscr{S}_i^e \subset S_i$ be the set of strategies of i that are not strongly dominated at any information set that they reach against conjectures that also reach that information set, and let $\mathscr{S}^e = \Pi_{i \in N} \mathscr{S}_i^e$. Gul's solution concept is $R^e = \mathscr{S}^\infty \mathscr{S}^e$. For generic extensive-form games, the set of strategies $\mathscr{S}_i^e$ corresponds to the set of weakly undominated strategies in the normal-form representation, G, of Γ, and hence $R_i^e = \mathscr{S}^\infty \mathscr{W}(G)$, the strategies that are left after one round of removal of weakly dominated strategies and then iterative removal of strongly dominated strategies. The main result of Ben-Porath (1994) establishes in an axiomatic framework, that in generic perfect information games a strategy profile s is consistent with common certainty of rationality at the beginning of the game if and only if it is in $\mathscr{S}^\infty \mathscr{W}(G)$.

Proposition 7 below is closely related to the ideas of Ben-Porath (1994) and Gul (1995b):

Proposition 7 *In any standard model* **M**, $WC \cap CB[R] \subset [R^e]$. *Moreover, for every extensive game of perfect information there exists some standard model* **M** *such that $CB[R] = [R^e]$.*

5.5   Backward induction revisited

Three recent papers Aumann (1995a), Bonanno (1991), and Samet (1993) have provided formal logical systems for backward induction in perfect information games. Aumann identifies, with each state a behavioral strategy and defines rationality as not knowing that the behavioral strategy is dominated at any information set. He proves that common knowledge of rationality implies and is consistent with backward induction. Bonanno augments the standard model of propositional logic with a description of the given extensive-form game (as a collection of propositions) and a rule of inference that states that if it can be shown that an i permissible hypothesis implies that the choice α is sure to yield a payoff greater than the payoff associated with the choice β, then choosing β is irrational for agent i. (An i permissible hypothesis is one that does not utilize any reference to player i's rationality or utilize in its proof any propositions that invokes i's rationality.) Bonanno proves that adding the axiom "all agents are rational" to this extended propositional logic, yields backward induction as a theorem in certain games, Bonanno also shows that without restriction to i permissible hypothesis, the new system of logic yields a contradiction (i.e., is inconsistent). Samet proves that an assumption that he calls common hypothesis of node rationality yields backward induction. The significant difference between these three formulations and the models discussed above is the fact that the key assumption of rationality in these models has an "ignore the past" feature. To see this note that in Aumann's formulation the relevant objects of analysis are behavioral strategy profiles; rationality of i at node v has force even at a node v that is inconsistent with the rationality of i. Similarly, in Bonanno (1991), the restriction to i permissible hypotheses ensures that when making deductions about the behavior of agent i at a node v only the behavior of agents at successor nodes are relevant since deductions about the behavior of predecessors will typically involve conclusions about i's own behavior. The same effect is achieved by Samet's common hypothesis of the node rationality assumption. In the reasoning of each agent or the reasoning of an agent about the reasoning of any future agents, observed past deviations are assumed to be irrelevant for future expectations. As suggested by Selten (1975), implicit in the idea of backward induction is this notion that past deviations are "mistakes" that are unlikely to be repeated in the future. Such a flavor is present in all three of the results mentioned above. In our setting, we can utilize the distinction between knowledge and belief to achieve this effect. Specifically, we will characterize backward induction by the requirement that agents have doubts about behavior at predecessor nodes and hence are (weakly) cautious. On the other hand, we will assume that rationality of successors is common knowledge. Our aim is not to strengthen the case for backward induction but to provide a unified framework for evaluating both the criticisms of backward induction and its axiomatizations.

We need the following notation. Let s_M denote a subprofile of strategies, one for each $i \in M \subset N$, and let S_M and s_M be defined in a similar fashion. Finally, let $R_M = \cap_{i \in M} R_i$.

Definition (CK of rationality of non-predecessors) $CK[R_{np}] = \cap_{E \in \Psi} E$ where $\Psi = \{CK_M[R_{M'}]$ for all $M, M' \subset N$ such that M' contains no player who moves at a successor node to some node owned by a player in $M\}$.

Definition (Weak caution regarding predecessors) $WC_p^i = \cap_{s_M} \neg K_i \neg [s_M]$ where M is the subset of players that own an information set preceding an information set owned by i; $WC_p = \cap_i WC_p^i$.

Proposition 8 *If* **M** *is a standard model for a generic extensive-form game in which each player moves once, then* $WC_p \cap CK[R_{np}] \subset [s^o]$, *where* s^o *is the unique backward induction strategy profile. Moreover, for any such game there exists some standard model such that* $WC_p \cap CK[R_{np}] = [s^o]$.

6   WEAKENING THE NOTION OF CERTAINTY: THE BAYESIAN APPROACH

Rubinstein (1989) provides a provocative example of a game with a move by Nature, similar to the information structure and payoffs in figure 5.8 below. Rubinstein's story for this information structure is that either game a or b is played, and it is a with probability greater than $1/2$. If it is b, 1 is so informed and a signal is sent from 1 to 2, and a confirmation from 2 to 1, and a (re)confirmation from 1 to 2, etc. Confirmations are lost with probability ε, and once a confirmation is lost the process ends. Players observe how many signals they have sent (which for player 1 equals the number received plus one, and for player 2 is equal to the number received). One can readily verify Rubinstein's result that with $\varepsilon > 0$ the only Nash equilibrium in which (U, L) is played when the game is a, has (U, L) played when the game is b as well. (More precisely, the only Nash equilibrium in which player 1 plays U when not informed that the game is b, has the players choosing (U, L) in every state of Nature except a state that has zero probability when $\varepsilon > 0$, namely $\omega = (\infty, \infty)$.) By contrast consider the case where there are no doubts about which game is being played, e.g., if $\varepsilon = 0$ there are no doubts in the only two states that have positive probability: $(0, 0)$ and (∞, ∞). In this case there is an equilibrium where (U, L) is played when the game is b, and (D, R) if it is a.

Clearly, it is common certainty at state (∞, ∞) that the game is b; similarly, when $\varepsilon = 0$ the probability that the game will be commonly certain is 1. Moreover, $(n, n + 1) \in B_N^n([b])$, i.e., at $(n, n + 1)$ the players are certain that . . . [n times] . . . that they are certain the game is b. Therefore, it might appear that when ε is small and/or at states $\omega = (n, n + 1)$ for n large, there is "almost" common certainty of the game.[47]

This suggests that when there is "almost" common certainty that the game is G, the equilibria may be very different from the case when it is commonly certain that the game is G.

The example above generated a literature examining the robustness of solution concepts to weakening common-certainty assumptions.[48] In the current section we review this literature and relate it to the characterizations in the preceding sections. While previously we assumed Ω is finite, clearly we now need to allow Ω to be infinite; however, we restrict attention to countably infinite Ω.

In subsection 6.1 we define various notions of almost common certainty, and in subsection 6.2 we provide characterizations results. First, we examine the robustness of the normal-form characterizations of section 4. The main message here is that for results to be robust, common certainty can be weakened to "almost common 1 belief" (defined below), which is not satisfied by the example of figure 5.8. Next we use a notion of almost common certainty – which avoids the conflict between certainty and caution discussed at the end of section 4 – to characterize refinements. The main result here is that almost common certainty of caution, rationality, and of the game yield the same solution concept we saw in section 5: $\mathscr{S}^{\infty}\mathscr{W}$. Subsection 6.3 examines refinements from a different perspective from the rest of this chapter. Instead of axiomatically characterizing solution concepts, we examine directly the robustness of solution concepts to a particular perturbation of the game. Given a game G, we consider applying the solution concept to a game with a move by Nature, $\tilde{G}$; we focus on those games $\tilde{G}$ in which it is almost common certainty that the game is in fact G. For example, $\tilde{G}$ could be the game of figure 5.8, G could be the game b, and we could look at states in $\tilde{G}$ where G is "almost" common certainty. We then ask what is the relationship between the solution of G and the solution of $\tilde{G}$ in those states. That is, we are asking whether the solution concept is robust to assuming the game is almost common certainty, instead of common certainty as is typically assumed. Our interest in these refinements issues is enhanced by the fact that both the methods and the results are closely related to the characterizations in section 6.2. There are two types of questions we consider when examining solution concepts. First, in subsection 6.3.1, we ask whether, for a given solution concept, an outcome that is excluded by that solution concept in game G would still be excluded by the

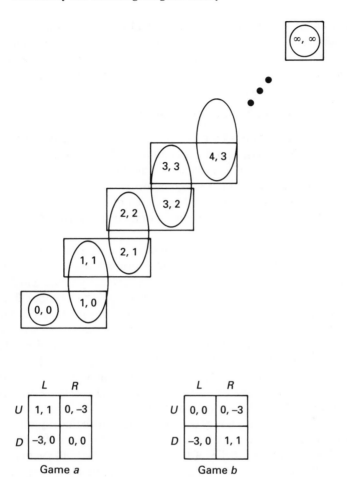

Figure 5.8 Rubinstein's e-mail game. In state $(0,0)$ game a is played, in all other states game b is played

same concept in $\tilde{G}$ when the game is almost common certainty. The main conclusion here is that rationalizability with caution is the tightest refinement of rationalizability that is robust in this sense.[49] In subsection 6.3.2 we ask the converse. Will an outcome that is accepted by a solution concept for a particular game, continue to be accepted by the same solution concept if the game is only almost common certainty? Here we show first that strict Nash equilibrium (and ε Nash equilibrium) are robust in this sense, but, as in subsection 6.2, only with the notion of "almost common 1 belief"; and, second, other solution concepts are robust to weaker notions of almost common certainty. Thus there will be several notions of almost common certainty, and various questions which can be asked using each of these notions. We restrict attention to a few of the most interesting results rather than provide an exhaustive analysis of each notion and question.

6.1   Notions of almost common certainty

One possible definition is based on the number of levels for which mutual certainty holds. That is, E is nth order mutual certainty at ω if $\omega \in B_N^n(E)$, and E is almost ∞ certain if n is large. One might well expect that almost ∞ certainty is quite different from common certainty, since no finite n is similar to ∞. As Rubinstein (1989) observed this is familiar from repeated games where large finite repetitions is quite distinct from infinite repetitions.

All the other notions we use weaken the certainty aspect of the notion of common certainty. Instead of requiring probability 1, we require only probability close to 1. For example, common certainty of an event E is when everyone assigns probability 1 to . . . everyone assigning probability 1 to E. So Monderer and Samet (1989) (see also Stinchcombe (1988)), consider common q belief of E – everyone assigns probability at lest q to . . . everyone assigning probability at least q to E. To formalize this let $B_i^q(E) = \{\omega : p_i(E \mid \mathcal{F}_i(\omega)) \geq q\}$ denote the set of states in which i assigns probability at least q to E.[50] Then E is common q belief at ω if $\omega \in \cap_{n=1}^{\infty}(B_N^q)^n(E)$.[51] The event that E is common q belief is denoted $C^q(E)$.[52] We will say that E is almost common 1 belief at ω, if E is common q belief at ω, for q close to 1. This is a very demanding notion: in the example of figure 5.8 for no state $\omega \neq (\infty, \infty)$ and not event E that is a strict subset of Ω is there almost common 1 belief of E at ω. However, we will see that it is the appropriate notion for obtaining robustness of our characterizations.

Both preceding notions directly weaken the definition of an event being common certainty at a state ω; the former weakens the number of iterations, the latter the degree of certainty. Thus they do not require a prior, only conditional probabilities, as we argued for in section 3. Therefore, they will not be useful for examining solution concepts that are based on common prior, or more generally, for considering solution concepts from an *ex ante* perspective. One possible *ex ante* notion involves a strengthening of the notions above. In particular, continuing with our approach of assuming probability close to 1 instead of equal to 1, we may want to assume that almost surely an event, say E, is almost common certainty. Formally, consider the assumption that everyone assigns probability at least q to the event that E is common q belief: $p_i(C^q(E)) > q$. When this is true for q close to 1 we say that E is almost certainly almost common 1 belief.

An *ex ante* notion that is weaker is used by Kajii and Morris (1995). If there is a common prior, then $p(E) = 1$ implies that $p(C(E)) = 1$: if E is certain then it is certain that E is common certainty. Then one could say that E is almost certain if $p(E)$ is close to 1, and one could explore this as an alternative notion of being close to common certainty (since it is close to a sufficient condition for common certainty). However, this is not a notion of "almost common certainty" when there is no common prior, since without a common prior even the extreme case of $p_i(E) = 1$ for all i does not imply that E is commonly certain (so naturally $p_i(E)$ close to 1 for all i need not look at all like common certainty). To see the problem consider the following information structure; $\Omega = \{a, b, c, d\}$, $\mathscr{F}_1 = \{\{a\}, \{b\}, \{c, d\}\}$, $\mathscr{F}_2 = \{\{a, b\}, \{c\}, \{d\}\}$, $p_1^n = (0, 1 - 1/n, 0, 1/n)$, $p_2^n = (1/n, 0, 1 - 1/n, 0)$, and let $E = \{b, c\}$. While 1 and 2 are both almost certain that E occurs, each is almost certain that the other is almost certain that E does not occur. So, in the limit (using the conditional probabilities given by the limit of the conditionals), E is subjectively certain but not common certainty. Nevertheless, for examining robustness of conclusions, one might be interested in the notion of (subjective) almost certainty. This is because there may be occasions where we think our assumptions (about the payoffs, rationality, etc. of the players) are almost certainly correct, but we may not be sure that they are almost common 1 belief.[53]

The relationship among the last two, *ex ante*, notions is worth clarifying. Clearly if E is almost certainly almost common 1 belief then E is almost certain, and in general the reverse implication is false. However, if there is a common full support prior and Ω is finite, then the reverse implication does hold; see Fudenberg and Tirole (1991, theorem 14.5) and Kajii and Morris (1995, equation 7.1).[54]

6.2   Robustness of characterizations and introducing caution

We begin by examining the robustness of the characterizations in section 4. First we formally state that proposition 1 is robust to weakening common certainty to almost common 1 belief.[55]

Proposition 9 *Fix a game* $G = (S, u)$. *There is a* $\bar{q} \in (0, 1)$ *such that given a model* $\{\Omega, \mathscr{F}_i, p_i, s, u\}$ *if* $q > \bar{q}$ *then* $C^q([u] \cap [rationality]) \subset [\mathscr{S}^\infty(u)]$.

The proof of this result is the same as the iterative part of the proof of proposition 12.

Aumann's characterization of correlated equilibrium is also robust: a common prior and almost certainty of rationality and of the game characterize almost correlated equilibrium.[56]

Proposition 10 *Consider a sequence of models, which differ only in the common prior:* $\{\Omega, \mathscr{F}_i, p^n, \mathbf{s}, \mathbf{u}\}_{n=1}^{\infty}$. *Assume that* $\mathbf{u}$ *is bounded, i.e.,* $\mathbf{u}(\omega)(s) < b \in \mathfrak{R}$ *for any* ω *and all* s.[57] *Let* E^n *be the event that the payoffs are* u *and the players are rational in model* n.[58] *If* $p^n(E^n) \to 1$, *then the limit of any convergent subsequence of the distribution on actions induced by* p^n *and* $\mathbf{s}$ *is a correlated equilibrium distribution.*

This is an upper hemi continuity result which can be proven along lines similar to those used by Kajii and Morris (1995, theorem 3.2) (see also the end of subsection 6.3.2 below).[59]

It is interesting that the results suggest that the characterization of correlated equilibrium does not really rely on common certainty of rationality or of the game. In the context of section 4, the characterization can be stated using the assumption either that rationality and the game have prior probability 1, or, that at every non-null ω the event [*rationality*] $\cap$ [*u*] is common certainty; the two assumptions are equivalent with a common prior. However, here we saw that we can make do with almost certainty of rationality and of the game, and we do not need the assumption of almost certainty that [*rationality*] $\cap$ [*u*] is almost common 1 belief at each non-null ω. As we mentioned at the end of subsection 6.1, the latter assumption *is* stronger than almost certainty of [*rationality*] and of [*u*].[60]

We conclude our analysis of robustness of characterizations of solution concepts by considering Nash equilibrium. We show below that the characterization of Nash equilibrium for two-person games in proposition 4 is robust if mutual certainty at ω is weakened to conditional probability close to 1 at ω. The characterizations of Nash equilibrium for games with $n > 2$ players are similarly robust, if common certainty of the conjectures at ω is weakened to almost common 1 belief of the conjectures at ω.

Proposition 11 *Consider a sequence of models* $\{\Omega, \mathscr{F}_i, p_i^n, \mathbf{s}, \mathbf{u}\}_{n=1}^{\infty}$, *assume* $N = \{1, 2\}$, $\mathbf{u}$ *is bounded and fix an* ε. *There is a* δ *such that if the utility functions, rationality, and the conjectures are almost certain at* ω, *i.e.,* $p_i([u] \cap [\phi_1] \cap [\phi_2] \cap [rationality] \mid \mathscr{F}_i(\omega)) = 1 - \delta$, *then* (ϕ_1, ϕ_2) *is an* ε *Nash equilibrium in the game* $G = (S, \mathbf{u}(\omega))$.

The notion here of an ε-Nash equilibrium is the standard one; ϕ_i is within ε of a best reply to ϕ_j.[61] The idea of the proof is the same as for the case of common certainty, proposition 4.[62]

To summarize, all the characterization results are robust to weakening certainty to probability close to 1, e.g., weakening common certainty at ω to common almost 1 belief at ω.

We now introduce caution into the model. Recall that [*caution*]

$= \cap_i \cap_{s_{-i}} \neg B_i \neg [s_{-i}]$; thus if a player is cautious at ω then her conjectures assign strictly positive probability to every action of her opponents: ϕ_{-i} has support S_{-i}. The main result of this section is that, if rationality, the game G, and caution are almost common 1 belief, then players choose strategies in $\mathscr{S}^\infty \mathscr{W}(G)$; we called this solution concept rationalizability with caution. That is, to the extent that "admissibility" can be made common knowledge, it does not characterize iterated deletion of weakly dominated strategies, $\mathscr{W}^\infty$; rather it characterizes rationalizability with caution. Similarly, applying caution to Nash-equilibrium characterizations yields Nash equilibrium in strategies that are not weakly dominated, not any stronger refinement.[63]

Proposition 12 (Börgers (1994)) *Fix a game G. There is a $\bar{q} \in (0, 1)$ such that, given a model $\{\Omega, \mathscr{F}_i, p_i, \mathbf{s}, \mathbf{u}\}$, if $q > \bar{q}$ then $C^q([u] \cap [caution] \cap [rationality]) \subset [\mathscr{S}^\infty \mathscr{W}(u)]$.*

The idea of the proof is as follows. Each i's strategy is a specification of what to do conditional on each information cell. We consider two types of cells – the cell including ω, denoted by F_i and the other cells. At ω each player i knows her payoffs are u. Caution then implies that everyone chooses a strategy that, conditional on F_i, specifies something that is not weakly dominated in $G = (u, S)$. If q is large enough, then i believes with high probability that player j is choosing a strategy that survives one round of deletion of weakly dominated strategies in G. Being rational at ω, we deduce that i chooses a strategy that is a best reply to such a belief. For q close enough to 1, conditional on F_i, $\mathbf{s}(\omega)$ cannot specify that i choose something that is strongly dominated in the restricted game $\mathscr{W}(G)$. (If it did then i is not rational at ω since i could do better by avoiding the dominated strategy.) Now iterate on the last step.[64]

6.3 Robustness of solution concepts

In this subsection we view a model as a game with a move by Nature, which we solve using various solution concepts. With this interpretation, the game is given by $(\Omega, \mathscr{F}_i, p_i, \mathbf{u})$, and s will be a strategy profile, of the players in this game, satisfying some solution concept. We assume for the remainder of this section that $\mathbf{u}$ is bounded. We consider sequences of games parametrized by probabilities, p_i^n, and we denote the solution of the nth game by $\mathbf{s}^n$. The question we ask is what solution concepts are robust to the game being almost common certainty, and for which notions of almost common certainty does this robustness hold?

How would the different notions of almost common certainty be used to examine this question? Let $\tilde{G}$ be a game with a move by Nature: $(\Omega, \mathscr{F}_i, \tilde{p}_i, \mathbf{u})$, and $G = (S, u)$. If $\omega \in C^q([u])$ for q close to 1, then in $\tilde{G}$ at ω there is almost common 1 belief that the game is G. Similarly, if $\tilde{p}_i(C^q([u])) > q$ for q close to 1, then in $\tilde{G}$ the game G is almost certainly almost common 1 belief. Finally, if $\tilde{p}_i([u]) > q$ for q close to 1, then we say that in $\tilde{G}$ the game G is almost certain.

Next we need to ask how we formally compare the solution of $\tilde{G}$ with the solution of G. Strategies for i in $\tilde{G}$ are not elements of S_i; they are functions from i's private information $\mathscr{F}_i$ into S_i. What we compare is, for example, the specification of the equilibrium strategy in $\tilde{G}$ *in state* ω, at which G is almost common 1 belief, with the equilibrium of G. More generally, we compare the distribution over S given by the equilibrium conditional on an event where u is almost common certainty. (More formal specifications will be given below.)

In addressing the question of this subsection, there is an issue concerning what one means by comparing the case of almost common certainty with the common certainty situation. Fixing a model where some event is common certainty, there are many "nearby" models in which that event is almost common certainty. Should we ask: What is the outcome that survives in all these "nearby" models, or in some? More specifically, one might ask whether strategy profiles that are excluded by a solution concept when the game G is common certainty are also excluded for all games $\tilde{G}$ within which G is almost common certainty. Alternatively one might wonder if strategy profiles that are accepted by our solution concept are also accepted in all possible games $\tilde{G}$ in which G is almost common certainty. The former perspective – which amounts to comparing the solution of G with the union of the solution concept over all possible games $\tilde{G}$ in which G is almost common certainty – is appropriate for questioning refinements: we should not exclude an outcome in a given, commonly certain, game G if that outcome is plausible in some "nearby" game when G is almost common certainty. This is the motivation underlying the research initiated by Fudenberg, Kreps, and Levine (1988).[65] The second perspective – which amounts to comparing the solution of G with the intersection of the solutions of all games $\tilde{G}$ in which G is almost common certainty – is more in the spirit of obtaining new solution concepts. We should not feel comfortable accepting a prediction of an outcome in a particular environment if there is some "nearby" environment where the game is almost common certainty and all the assumptions underlying our solution concept are satisfied, but the prediction in this "nearby" environment is very different from the original prediction. This is closer to the motivation of Monderer and Samet (1989) and Kajii and Morris (1995).

We will be applying the solution concepts explicitly here, rather than axiomatically. This gives us greater flexibility in considering solution concepts, but involves a different interpretation: we are not trying to justify the solution concepts, but are investigating whether outcomes are excluded or accepted in a robust manner. An example of the significance of this different interpretation of results will be discussed in subsection 6.3.2 below.[66]

6.3.1 Almost common certainty and excluding outcomes robustly

Following Fudenberg, Kreps, and Levine (1988), the first version of this robustness question argues that it is unreasonable to exclude particular outcomes if our solution concept when applied to G yields very different outcomes than when it is applied to a game with a move by Nature in which G is almost common certainty. For example, we might think that any strict Nash equilibrium is a reasonable prediction when a game is common certainty among the players. However, since we the analysts might only know that some game G is almost common certainty, it would be unreasonable to rule out any outcomes which are strict Nash equilibria in a game of incomplete information where G is almost common certainty (and the game of incomplete information is assumed to be common certainty among the players).

While the focus is different there is an obvious connection between this question and the characterization results of the previous section. There we also asked whether our axioms excluded behavior which would not be excluded if the game were almost common certainty, rather than common certainty. For example, a corollary to proposition 9 is that $\mathscr{S}^{\infty}$, applied to a game $\tilde{G}$ and evaluated at a state ω at which G is almost common 1 belief, yields a subset of $\mathscr{S}^{\infty}$ applied to G. (Moreover, taking the union over all such games $\tilde{G}$ yields all of $\mathscr{S}^{\infty}(G)$, since we can always take the game $\tilde{G}$ to be equal to G.) Thus the previous subsection showed that $\mathscr{S}^{\infty}$ is robust (to almost common 1 belief) in the first sense considered in this subsection.[67]

A similar connection to the previous section is via proposition 12. That result suggests that if we are given a game $\tilde{G}$, in which a particular game G is almost certainly almost common 1 belief, then applying the solution concept of rationalizability with caution to $\tilde{G}$, evaluated at those states where G is almost common 1 belief, yields a subset of the same concept applied to G; roughly speaking this says that $\mathscr{S}^{\infty}\mathscr{W}(\tilde{G}) \subset \mathscr{S}^{\infty}\mathscr{W}(G)$. Moreover, once again, it is trivial that there is a game $\tilde{G}$, in which G is almost certainly almost common 1 belief, such that, evaluated at those states where G is almost common 1 belief, $\mathscr{S}^{\infty}\mathscr{W}(\tilde{G})$ yields exactly $\mathscr{S}^{\infty}\mathscr{W}(G)$ – simply take $\tilde{G} = G$.

Thus, rationalizability with caution is robust in the sense that, when applied to a game G, it only excludes strategy profiles that would be excluded when applied to any game in which G is almost certainly almost common 1 belief. One might also ask if there are any tighter solution concepts that are robust in this sense. Dekel and Fudenberg (1990) show that this is essentially the tightest non-equilibrium solution concept. Formally they show that the union of solutions of all games in which G is almost certainly almost common 1 belief using iterated deletion of weakly dominated strategies yields rationalizability with caution. The proof is similar to the arguments already given.

Dekel and Fudenberg (1990) also show how this robustness test corresponds to issues that have come up in analyzing extensive-form games. The robustness question examines what happens if payoff are almost common 1 belief. Thus, in particular, in an extensive-form game, it allows players to change their beliefs about the payoffs in a game if they are surprised by an opponent's action. This formally corresponds to the issues raised in criticism of backwards induction: if a player is surprised and observes non-backward-induction play, what should she believe? The robustness test allows her to believe that the payoffs are different than she previously thought. (Or, equivalently, revise her view of the rationality of the opponents. These are equivalent since there is no way to distinguish irrationality as it is used here from different payoffs.) This explains why the solution concept $\mathscr{S}^{\infty}\mathscr{W}$, which was introduced when Dekel and Fudenberg (1990) analyzed the robustness of solution concepts, is the same as the one achieved using common certainty of rationality in extensive-form games (see section 5).

6.3.2   Almost common certainty and accepting outcomes robustly

We now turn to the second, and opposite, notion of robustness: an outcome should be accepted as a prediction for game G only if it would be accepted in all games $\tilde{G}$ in which G is almost common certainty. For brevity and simplicity, we restrict attention to strict Nash equilibria of G in this discussion. As before, consider a game G, and a sequence of games G^n in which G is, in one of the senses formally defined earlier, almost common certainty. Roughly speaking, we want to know if equilibria of G are also equilibria in all such sequences G^n.

We first consider the case in which G is common q^n belief at ω, where $q^n \to 1$. This is the case considered by Monderer and Samet (1989). Their results imply that a strict Nash equilibrium s of G is robust in that for any G^n there is always a Nash equilibrium which plays s on states where G is almost common 1 belief. Moreover, the interim payoffs are the same and if almost common 1 belief of G is almost certain then the *ex ante* payoffs converge as well.[68]

But are strict Nash equilibrium robust when all we know is that G is almost certain? This is the question asked by Kajii and Morris. They show that the answer is no – there exists a generic game G with a *unique* strict Nash equilibrium s, and a sequence G^n of games in which G is almost certain, $p^n([u]) \to 1$, with a unique rationalizable strategy profile s, s.t. the distribution of actions generated by s on the event $[u]$ is not s.[69] Kajii and Morris go on to examine sufficient conditions for a Nash equilibrium of a game G to be robust in this strong sense. They obtain two types of sufficient conditions. The first is that a unique correlated equilibrium is robust. This follows from an upper-hemi continuity argument related to the one we gave following proposition 10. The limit of the distribution of actions in the game G^n, conditional on the event $[u]$, where the game G^n is solved by Nash equilibrium, must be a correlated equilibrium distribution of G if G is almost certain in G^n. Then, if there is a unique correlated equilibrium of G, these limits must all be converging to that correlated equilibrium distribution, so it is robust.

The preceding paragraph may help clarify the relationship between this subsection, which takes solution concepts as given, and subsection 6.2, which looks at characterizations. Both the characterization of correlated equilibrium, and the solution concept itself are robust: this is the message of proposition 10 and the Kajii and Morris result discussed above. But proposition 11 suggests that the characterization of Nash equilibrium is robust, while the cited example of Kajii and Morris suggests that Nash equilibrium is not robust to allowing almost common certainty. Why is it that their example does not bear a similar relationship to proposition 11 as does the relationship of their robustness of unique correlated equilibrium to proposition 10? The answer is complex since the analysis of robustness of characterizations and of the equilibrium concept are different in many ways. However, by considering how one could modify the models to make them more similar, it appears that there is a basic incompatibility between the lack of robustness of Nash equilibrium as in Kajii and Morris on the one hand, and the robustness of characterizations of Nash equilibrium. This incompatibility may raise doubts about the robustness test used by Kajii and Morris for Nash equilibrium.[70]

Kajii and Morris have a second sufficiency condition for robustness of Nash equilibrium. While the general version requires too much setup for this survey, a very special case of their second result is useful for drawing connections to the literature and to examples above. The restriction of their results to two-person two-strategy games with two strict Nash equilibrium, implies that the robust outcome is the risk-dominant one. This is exactly what happens in the Rubinstein example at the beginning of the section, and a similar result of this kind was obtained by Carlsson and van Damme (1993) for 2×2 games when players observe their payoffs with noise.[71]

6.4   Necessity of almost common 1 belief for robustness

The final issue we consider in this subsection is the question of necessity. We saw that almost common 1 belief is sufficient for robustness of strict Nash equilibrium, while almost certainty is sufficient for robustness of a unique correlated equilibrium. Is almost common 1 belief necessary for the former result? Monderer and Samet (1990), and subsequently, Kajii and Morris (1994a), show that one cannot in general weaken the hypothesis of almost common 1 belief.[72] As noted, the interest in this result is that it shows that the sufficiency of almost common 1 belief for robustness presented throughout this section is, in some sense, necessary for lower hemi continuity of the equilibrium strategies and payoffs.

7   WEAKENING THE NOTION OF KNOWLEDGE: THE SYNTACTIC APPROACH

7.1   Generalized knowledge operators and possibility correspondences

In section 3 we observed that any knowledge operator $K_i: 2^\Omega \to 2^\Omega$ satisfying [MC, N] generates a possibility correspondence $\mathscr{F}_i: \Omega \to 2^\Omega$, and conversely. More precisely, using the definitions in section 3.1, starting from either K_i (or $\mathscr{F}_i$), going to $\mathscr{F}_i$ (or K_i), and then going back, one ends up with the same operator as one started with. Moreover, we saw that if the knowledge operator satisfies [T], [4], and [5] as well, then $\mathscr{F}_i$ is a partition.

Many authors have questioned the appropriateness of [T] and of [5] for modeling knowledge and decision making.[73] As we discussed in subsection 3.3 above, [T] is often weakened to [D] to model belief rather than knowledge, and the importance of this weakening for modeling weak caution in extensive-form games is explained in section 5.[74] In this section we focus on dropping [5].

Alternatively, some authors have directly questioned the appropriateness of partition for modeling information. They consider various properties of the possibility correspondence, all of which are satisfied by partitions, and examine the effect of weakening them and the relationship between these properties and the axioms on K_i. In this section we will be discussing these two approaches; in the current subsection we present the basics. In subsection 7.2, as a first view of these models, we show the implication of

weakening the knowledge axioms, and the partition structure of information, in single-person decision theory. We consider games in subsection 7.3;
we show that without a common prior there is a sense in which these
weakenings have no effect, therefore the only insights these weakenings may
yield are in the context of assuming the CPA. In subsection 7.4 we present
the most widespread application of these weakenings, namely to no-trade
results. (Readers for whom the no-trade results are new may want to look at
the appendix, where we review the analogous results for the case where
partitions are used.) We conclude in subsection 7.5, where we discuss severe
problems with the motivation for most of these results, especially applications such as those in subsection 7.4.

The remainder of this subsection presents the relationship between
weakening axioms on a knowledge operator and weakening the partition
structure of information. The following are some properties of possibility
correspondences, $\mathcal{F}_i$, which have appeared in the literature.

P1 (reflexive) $\omega \in \mathcal{F}_i(\omega)$

P2 (nested)   For F and F' in $\mathcal{F}_i$, if $F \cap F' \neq \phi$ then either $F \subset F'$ or $F' \subset F$.

P3 (balanced)   For every self-evident E, i.e., E s.t. $\omega \in E \Rightarrow \mathcal{F}_i(\omega) \subset E$, there exists $\lambda_E: \mathcal{F}_i \to \mathfrak{R}$ s.t. $\forall \omega \in \Omega, \Sigma_{F:\omega \in F \in \mathcal{F}_i} \lambda(F) = 1$ if $\omega \in E$ and 0 otherwise. We say that $\mathcal{F}_i$ is positively balanced and satisfies $[P3^+]$ if λ_E can be taken to be non-negative.

P4 (transitive) $\omega'' \in \mathcal{F}_i(\omega')$ and $\omega' \in \mathcal{F}_i(\omega) \Rightarrow \omega'' \in \mathcal{F}_i(\omega)$.

P5 (Euclidean) $\omega' \in \mathcal{F}_i(\omega)$ and $\omega'' \in \mathcal{F}_i(\omega) \Rightarrow \omega'' \in \mathcal{F}_i(\omega')$.

Possibility correspondences satisfying several of these properties can be
seen in figure 5.9. The connection among the axioms on K_i and properties of
$\mathcal{F}_i$, where K_i and $\mathcal{F}_i$ are related as discussed above, are presented in
proposition 13 below. The most interesting parts are (i)–(iii), which relate K_i
to $\mathcal{F}_i$; the rest are useful properties for understanding the results below.

Proposition 13
   (i) K_i satisfies $[T]$ if and only if $\mathcal{F}_i$ satisfies $[P1]$.
   (ii) K_i satisfies $[4]$ if and only if $\mathcal{F}_i$ satisfies $[P4]$.
   (iii) K_i satisfies $[5]$ if and only if $\mathcal{F}_i$ satisfies $[P5]$.
   (iv) If $\mathcal{F}_i$ satisfies $[P1]$ and $[P2]$ or $[P1]$ then it satisfies $[P3]$.
   (v) If $\mathcal{F}_i$ satisfies $[P1, P2,$ and $P4]$ then it satisfies $[P3^+]$.
   (vi) If $\mathcal{F}_i$ satisfies $[P1]$ and $[P5]$ then it satisfies $[P4]$.
   (vii) $\mathcal{F}_i$ satisfies $[P4]$ if and only if $\omega' \in \mathcal{F}_i(\omega) \Rightarrow \mathcal{F}_i(\omega') \subset \mathcal{F}_i(\omega)$.

For proofs see Chellas (1980) and Geanakoplos (1989).

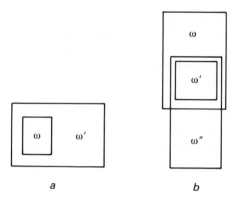

Figure 5.9 Examples of possibility correspondences that are not partitions.

(a) $\mathscr{F}(\omega) = \{\omega\}$, $\mathscr{F}(\omega') = \{\omega, \omega'\}$. [P1]–[P4] are all satisfied, [P5} is not.

(b) $\mathscr{F}(\omega) = \{\omega, \omega'\}$, $\mathscr{F}(\omega') = \{\omega'\}$, $\mathscr{F}(\omega'') = \{\omega', \omega''\}$. [P1], [P3], and [P4] are satisfied, [P2} and [P5] are not.

7.2   An application to single-person decision theory: When is "information" valuable?

A single-person decision problem with information is determined by an information structure $\{\Omega, p_i, \mathscr{F}_i\}$, a strategy space S_i, and utilities $u_i: S_i \times \Omega \to \mathfrak{R}$. Given any information $F \in \mathscr{F}_i$ the player can choose any element of S_i, so a decision rule is a function $\mathbf{s}_i: \mathscr{F}_i \to S$, which determines a function from Ω into S_i that we also (with abuse of notation) denote by $\mathbf{s}_i$, where $\mathbf{s}_i(\omega) \equiv \mathbf{s}_i(\mathscr{F}_i(\omega))$. Given any $F \in \mathscr{F}_i$, the player's interim expected utility is naturally defined as $Eu(\mathbf{s}_i \mid F) \equiv \Sigma_{\omega' \in F} u(\mathbf{s}_i(\omega), \omega') p_i(\omega')/p_i(F)$. However, if $\mathscr{F}_i$ is not a partition then it is not clear how to define *ex ante* utility. The *true ex ante* utility is $Eu(\mathbf{s}_i \parallel \mathscr{F}_i) \equiv \Sigma_{\omega \in \Omega} p_i(\omega) Eu(\mathbf{s}_i \mid \mathscr{F}_i(\omega))$. On the other hand, the expectation of the interim utilities, $\Sigma_{F \in \mathscr{F}_i} p_i(F) Eu(\mathbf{s}_i \mid F)$, may be different. But this latter notion does not make sense: if a person thought she had a non-partitional $\mathscr{F}_i$, then she would refine it to a partition. For example, if she thought that in state $\omega' \in \mathscr{F}_i(\omega)$ the information received were different from $\mathscr{F}_i(\omega)$, which must happen for some ω and ω' if $\mathscr{F}_i$ is not a partition, then she would not think that ω' is possible when ω happened. So $\mathscr{F}_i(\omega)$ would not be the possibility set for ω. For this reason, when working with non-partitional possibility correspondences, $\mathscr{F}_i$, it is often said that the players do not know their information structure. Therefore, the notion of *ex ante* expected utility should be thought of as something the analyst considers and not the player, and as such we focus on the true *ex ante* utility $Eu(\mathbf{s}_i \parallel \mathscr{F}_i)$.

A partition $\mathscr{F}_i$ is more informative than $\mathscr{F}'_i$ if the former is a refinement of the latter, i.e., if for all $\omega, \mathscr{F}_i(\omega) \subset \mathscr{F}'_i(\omega)$. It is well known that the *ex ante* expected utility increases when a partition becomes more informative: if $\mathscr{F}_i$ is a more informative partition than partition $\mathscr{F}'_i$, then $Eu(s \parallel \mathscr{F}_i) \geq Eu(s \parallel \mathscr{F}'_i)$. Does this result hold if information is not given by a partition? Equivalently, does this result hold if some of the axioms of knowledge are dropped?

Proposition 14 (Geanakoplos (1989)) *If a possibility correspondence $\mathscr{F}_i$ satisfying [P1, P2, and P4] is a refinement of a partition $\mathscr{F}'_i$ then $Eu(s \parallel \mathscr{F}_i) \geq Eu(s \parallel \mathscr{F}'_i)$. Moreover, if $\mathscr{F}_i$ fails [P1, P2, or P4] then there is a partition $\mathscr{F}'_i$ that is less informative but yields higher ex ante expected utility.*

Thus [P1, P2, P4] are necessary and sufficient for information to be valuable.[75]

7.3   Solution concepts with general possibility correspondences

In order to examine the effect of allowing for non-partitions in multi-person environments, we need to extend and re-examine our definitions of common knowledge and of equilibrium. As before, the basic definition of common knowledge of E at ω is that all players know E, know that they know E, etc., and a person knows E at ω if $\mathscr{F}_i(\omega) \subset E$.[76] A (Bayesian) Nash equilibrium in a game with a non-partitional information structure, will also be defined as in the usual case.

Definition Given an information structure $(\Omega, (\mathscr{F}_i, p_i)_{i \in N})$ and a game $G = (S_i, u_i)_{i \in N}$, where $u_i: \Omega \times S \to \mathfrak{R}$, a decision rule for each player is, as above, a function $s_i: \mathscr{F}_i \to S_i$. A profile $\mathbf{s} = (s_i)_{i \in N}$ is a Nash equilibrium if for all i, and for all ω, i prefers $s_i(\omega)$ to any other s_i: for all i, $F \in \mathscr{F}_i$, and s_i.

$$\sum_{\omega' \in F} u(\mathbf{s}(\omega), \omega') p_i(\omega')/p_i(F) \geq \sum_{\omega' \in F} u(s_i, \mathbf{s}_{-i}(\omega), \omega') p_i(\omega')/p_i(F).$$

What are the implications of these weakenings of knowledge for solution concepts? This line of research has only been explored to a limited extent; the main result is that a posteriori equilibria continue to correspond to $\mathscr{S}^\infty$, even when the information structures of the correlating devices violate all of the properties above, so long as each player has a well-defined "conditional" probability given each information she can receive.

Proposition 15 (Brandenburger, Dekel, and Geanakoplos (1992)) *Consider a Nash equilibrium, $\mathbf{s}: \Omega \to S$, as defined above, of a game $G = (S, u)$ with* *possibility correspondences $\mathscr{F}_i$ and priors p_i on Ω, where $u: S \to \mathfrak{R}$. (Note that u is not a function of Ω.) For all i and all $\omega, \mathsf{s}(\omega) \in \mathscr{S}^\infty(G)$.*

Why is it that weakening the assumption that $\mathscr{F}_i$ is a partition has no effect on the set of strategies and payoffs that can arise in a posteriori equilibria? The definition of Nash equilibrium requires that for every i and each $F_i \in \mathscr{F}_i, \mathsf{s}(F_i)$ is a best reply to beliefs over the set $\{s_{-i} \in S_{-i} : \exists F_{-i} \in \mathscr{F}_{-i} \text{ s.t. } \mathsf{s}(F_{-i}) = s_{-i}\}$. Therefore, the product of the sets $\{s_i \in S_i : \exists F_i \in \mathscr{F}_i \text{ s.t. } \mathsf{s}(F_i) = s_i\}$ are best-response closed sets (cf. Pearce (1984)) and hence in $\mathscr{S}^\infty$. Thus, weakening the assumptions does not enlarge the set of a posteriori equilibrium. We saw in proposition 2 that $\mathscr{S}^\infty$ corresponds to a posteriori equilibrium with partitions. Therefore, allowing for non-partitions has no effect on this solution concept. On the other hand, this equivalence between a posteriori equilibria with and without partitions breaks down if a common prior is imposed. That is, the set of correlated equilibria without partitions but with a common prior, allows for strategies and payoffs that cannot arise in any correlated equilibrium with a common prior and with partitions. This is demonstrated by the betting example below. Thus one can interpret weakening the partition structure as weakening the CPA. The relation between propositions 1 and 2, suggests that there ought to be a reformulation of proposition 15 that directly states that common knowledge of rationality and the game, even when knowledge violates [T, 4, and 5], will also continue to characterize $\mathscr{S}^\infty$.

Proposition 16 *If at ω both $[u]$ and $[rationality]$ are common knowledge, where for all i, K_i satisfy $[MC]$ and $[N]$, then $\mathsf{s}(\omega) \in \mathscr{S}^\infty(u)$.*

7.4   No-trade theorems and general possibility correspondences

In the appendix we review the no-trade results used in this subsection for the case where $\mathscr{F}_i$ are partitions. The propositions below show that results, which in the context of partitions seem quite similar, are no longer similar when non-partitions are considered. The results differ in the extent to which partition properties, equivalently the axioms on knowledge, can be weakened. For example, Aumann's (1976) agreeing-to-disagree result is more robust than the no-bets-in-equilibrium and no-common-knowledge-of-bets results. (Moreover, the last two also differ in their requirements on knowledge.)

Proposition 17 (Geanakoplos (1989)) *(see also Rubinstein and Wolinsky (1989) and Samet (1990)). Consider two agents, $i = 1, 2$, who share a common* *prior p, on a state space Ω, and each has a possibility correspondence $\mathcal{F}_i$ that satisfies [P1] and [P3] (a fortiori [P1] and [P4]).*

If in some state of the world ω, the agents' posterior beliefs concerning an event $A \subset \Omega$, namely the values $\bar{p}(A \mid \mathcal{F}_i(\omega))$, for $i = 1, 2$, are common knowledge, then these posteriors are equal.

Conversely, if for some i, $\mathcal{F}_i$ violates [P3], then there exists a space Ω, partitions $\mathcal{F}_j$ for all $j \neq i$, a common prior p and an event A such that the value of the posteriors are common knowledge but they differ.

For simplicity we present a sketch of the proof for the first part of the proposition only, and assuming [P1, P4]. There are two main aspects to the proof. First, posterior probabilities have a "difference" property: if $F'' \subset F$ and $p(A \mid F) = p(A \mid F'') = \bar{p}$, then $p(A \mid [F - F'']) = \bar{p}$ also. Second, using (vii) of proposition 13, [P1] and [P4] imply that $\mathcal{F}_i$ also has a "difference" property described below. The rest follows from the definitions and the two difference properties just mentioned. Since it is common knowledge that i's posterior probability of A is $\bar{p}_i$, there is a self-evident event G such that, for all ω in $G, p(A \mid \mathcal{F}_i(\omega)) = \bar{p}_i$. The difference property of $\mathcal{F}_i$ alluded to above implies that G is the union of disjoint sets F_i such that each F_i is either in $\mathcal{F}_i$ or is the difference of two sets in $\mathcal{F}_i$. Using the difference property of posterior probabilities, for each such $F_i, p(A \mid F_i) = \bar{p}_i$. But this implies $p(A \mid G) = \bar{p}_i$.

Proposition 18 (Geanakoplos (1989)) *Consider two agents, $i = 1, 2$, who share a common prior p, on a state space Ω, and each has a possibility correspondence $\mathcal{F}_i$ that satisfies [P1, P2, and P4]. Assume in addition that these two agents are considering saying yes or no to a bet $X: \Omega \to \mathfrak{R}$ and the agents' utility is their expected gain.*

In any Nash equilibrium the expected payoffs of the agents are zero. Conversely, if a players' possibility correspondence violates one of the assumptions, there is a betting environment with all other players having partitions, and with a Nash equilibrium where the expected utilities would not be zero.

There is also an analog to the no-common-knowledge-of-bets result.

Proposition 19 (Geanakoplos (1989)) *Consider two agents, $i = 1, 2$, who share a common prior p, on a state space Ω, and each has a possibility correspondence $\mathcal{F}_i$ that satisfies [P1] and [P3$^+$]. Assume in addition that these two agents are considering saying yes or no to a bet $X: \Omega \to \mathfrak{R}$, and an agent says yes if and only if her expected utility is non-negative.*

If it is common knowledge at ω that the agents are saying yes to the bet, then their expected payoffs equal zero.

Conversely, if a player's possibility correspondence violates one of the assumptions, there is a bet against players with partitions and a state of the world at which it would be common knowledge that all the players accept the bet, but their expected utilities would not be zero.

To understand why the agreeing-to-disagree result requires fewer assumptions than the two no-betting results, recall the proof of the agreeing-to-disagree result (see the appendix for a review). The "difference" property does not hold for inequalities: $F'' \subset F$ and $p(A \mid F) \geq 0$ and $p(A \mid F'') \geq 0$ do not imply $p(A \mid [F - F'']) \geq 0$. For example, let $\Omega = \{a, b, c\}$, $p(\omega) = 1/3$, $\mathcal{F}_1(\omega) = \Omega$ for all ω, $\mathcal{F}_2(a) = \{a, b\}$, $\mathcal{F}_2(b) = \{b\}$, $\mathcal{F}_2(c) = \{b, c\}$, and 1's payments to 2 are $X(a) = X(c) = -\$5.00$, $X(b) = \$7.00$. Clearly in every information cell both players will say yes if they expect their opponent to always say yes to the bet, and this is a Nash equilibrium, but their conditional expected utilities are strictly positive. Note that 2's *ex ante* utility is negative despite her interim expected utility always being strictly positive.[77]

7.5   Motivation

Weakening the assumptions on knowledge and on information seems appealing. People are not perfect reasoners and an axiomatic approach to weakening knowledge should clarify which aspects of their reasoning ability we are weakening. In fact, in contrast to the almost common certainty approach of the previous section, the syntactic approach seems to address more fundamental problems with our assumptions on knowledge. Similarly, partitions do not seem appropriate with agents who are boundedly rational, if our notion of bounded rationality allows for errors in processing information.

In this subsection we review the motivations for the weakenings of K_i and $\mathcal{F}_i$ discussed earlier, and argue that, while these weakenings might seem a priori interesting, the framework to which they are applied and the results obtained are problematic. Our concerns are based on three related issues.

> The ideas of bounded rationality and reasoning ability used to motivate non-partitions do suggest, in some *examples*, that we drop the assumptions needed to get the partition structure. However, there are very few results explaining why we should be willing to assume, say, [P1]–[P4] but not [P5] or be interested in possibility correspondences that satisfy [P1–P3], etc. The examples no more imply that we should drop [P5] in a general

analysis of games and of trade, than does the fact that juries are supposed to ignore a defendant's decision not to testify on his own behalf. Perhaps the decision making by such jurors in court may be fruitfully modeled using a particular non-partition (which violates [P5]). However, these people ought not be modeled using non-partitions in other aspects of their lives. Moreover, even if people carry this mistake outside the courtroom, it is not clear why it generalizes to other contexts as a failure of [P5]: while the non-partition that captures the ignoring of someone's decision not to provide information does violate [P5], there are many non-partitions where [P5] is violated that do not have the same easy interpretation.

The most compelling motivations for particular weakenings often argue strongly for making other modifications in the framework; but the analysis typically relies heavily on keeping the rest of the framework (e.g., the CPA and Nash equilibrium) that underlies most applications.

1 For example, the use of priors and of Bayesian updating seems to be questioned by the very same arguments used to motivate dropping [P5]. As we said at the beginning of this section, *ex ante* analysis without partitions is questionable. On the one hand, players are assumed not to know what they know; on the other hand, they are assumed to have a prior and use it in Bayesian updating based on information cells. There are essentially no *results* that justify stapling traditional frameworks together with non-partitions.

2 The motivations for non-partitions make the use of equilibrium especially questionable: if people are that boundedly rational, what justifications are there for standard equilibrium notions? Moreover, if one is inclined to use a solution concept that has stronger, albeit in this context not very strong, foundations, namely $\mathscr{S}^\infty$, then propositions 15 and 16 show that allowing for non-partitions has no effect. Clearly, as Geanakoplos (1989) observes, justifications of Nash equilibrium that are based on introspection and assumptions about knowledge of rationality and strategies seem in conflict with an environment where players do not know their own information structure. Drew Fudenberg (personal communication) has argued that it will be hard to obtain a learning environment in which players will learn enough to play a Nash equilibrium but not enough to

learn their own information structure, so that learning-based justifications of equilibrium with non-partitions are also questionable.

3 In an analysis using equilibrium and common knowledge, when non-partitions are involved, each player is assumed to correctly know the opponents' possibility correspondences, but not her own. Moreover, each player i knows what each opponent j thinks i's possibility correspondence is, but i thinks j is wrong despite j being correct. This seems like an odd assumption. There seems to be no reason to restrict their mistakes to their own information, and moreover to take the form of weakening [5].[78]

To clarify our concerns we will review the motivations for this research that appear in the literature. These arguments fall into two categories: explanations for why $\mathcal{F}_i$ need not be a partition when players are boundedly rational; and motivations for why K_i need not satisfy all the axioms [T, MC, N, 4, 5] when players have limited reasoning ability.

Provability and complexity *Modeling knowledge as something that agents deduce satisfies* [4] *and violates* [5].

Geanakoplos (1989) informally proposed, and independently Shin (1993) formally considered, the case where knowledge comes from proofs; we call such knowledge *provable knowledge* in this paragraph. Clearly, not having a proof for something, say fact p, implies that p is not provably known. On the other hand, not having a proof does not imply that one has a proof that a proof does not exist, so one would not provably know that p is not provably known. We find this motivation for results along the lines of subsection 7.4, questionable. Why is provable knowledge a useful notion for decision theory? The mathematician who has not proven Fermat's last theorem, and who certainly does not have a proof that such a proof is impossible, would not say that he does not know that he does not have a proof of the theorem. So, while Shin (1993) demonstrates that provable knowledge satisfies [P1] and [P4] and may violate [P5], we do not view this as a compelling motivation for considering knowledge and information that violates [P5].

Similarly, Samet (1990) motivates keeping [T] and [4], while dropping [5] by proposing axioms on the complexity of sentences that a person can use or "produce." He considers a sentence, say p, that has complexity greater than the bound on the person's ability, and argues that the person will not know that she does not know this sentence. (The axioms imply that, not knowing p, and knowing that one does not know p, should have greater complexity than p.) Nevertheless, it is possible, even with these complexity bounds, for a person to know whatever they do know; so [4] can be satisfied. Here again, it is not clear that the violation of [5] is relevant.

Forgetfulness *Since people often forget information, the representation of what they ultimately remember may fail to be a partition.*

Geanakoplos (1989) formalizes this idea and proves that nestedness corresponds to a condition on memory. Assume that each state is a list of n statements concerning the truth or falsity of an ordered list of n facts. That is, $\Omega = \{T, F\}^n$, where the kth element of ω, denoted $\omega(k)$ says whether the kth fact is true or false.[79] Assume that information satisfies [P1] and that information about facts is remembered in the ordered sequence. That is, given any possibility cell $\mathscr{F}_i(\omega)$ there is an l s.t. $\mathscr{F}_i(\omega) = \{\omega': \omega(j) = \omega'(j), j = 1, \ldots l\}$. This could happen if people remember the truth and falsehood only of recent facts, or of important facts. If, in addition, $l < n$ is possible, then $\mathscr{F}_i$ need not be a partition but it will satisfy [P3]. Moreover, given any nested $\mathscr{F}_i$ there is a memory-based justification of this sort.

Forgetfulness is an important limitation to incorporate into decision making. However this form of forgetfulness implies that whether or not you forget depends on the sequence of truths and falsehoods and not on the facts which are true or false. So, to get a non-partition it is necessary to forget, say, whether statements $2, \ldots, n$ are true when statement 1 is false but to remember differently when statement 1 is true. It would be interesting to see what other conditions can be motivated by more realistic models of forgetfulness. In this light it is worth noting that if people forget things in a less orderly manner, then any $\mathscr{F}_i$ satisfying [T] can be obtained. That is, if what causes people to forget can depend on particulars of the precise state of the world, then it would be equally plausible to assume that in each state ω you remember only the information received corresponding to $\mathscr{F}_i(\omega)$. This would then justify looking at any non-partition (satisfying [P1]).

Moreover, to the extent that forgetfulness provides a motivation for nestedness, it is worth noting that none of the results in the literature rely on nestedness alone. So, the sufficiency results are of limited interest unless the other conditions can be motivated as well. The necessity results fare better – they imply that bets can arise so long as there is one person with a memory problem of this ordered type, and that information may be "bad" for anyone with this memory problem.

Dynamic models *The information provided by a dynamic process may be best summarized by a non-partition.*

Shin (1989) shows that [P1, P3, P4] are necessary and sufficient for information to come from a particular dynamic model. This motivation for an interesting class of non-partitions is then as compelling as is this dynamic model. The reader is referred to the paper for details, but we do not think the decision problem portrayed by this dynamic model is a common situation. However, in contrast to Geanakoplos' forgetfulness result, Shin (1989) characterizes exactly those information structures for which information is valuable. So, to the extent that the dynamic representation is compelling, it succeeds in motivating both the sufficiency and necessity results concerning bets and valuable information.

Preferences and axioms *Different axioms on preference relations may yield behavior that is equivalent to that arising from non-partitions.*

Morris (1996) proposes a Savage-like model of preferences, where in each state the player's preferences over acts may differ. (This is not state-dependent utility; the whole preference relation on acts may depend on the state.) Knowledge is defined subjectively – similar to certainty, where a person knows if she (subjectively) assigns probability 1 – and may depend on preferences at each state. Naturally one can assume that preferences at each state correspond to expected utility preferences conditional on information received at that state, where information is given by some partition; this will correspond to a partition model. Instead Morris considers axioms on preferences that do not assume any particular information structure and shows how different axioms correspond to different information structures. For example, some of the axioms have natural interpretations concerning the value of information. The problem is that the basic axiom tying together the preferences at different states is hard to interpret, and in fact highlights the problem with non-partition models: there is no sensible way for the individual to have an *ex ante* view of the world that corresponds to a non-partition model.

This just reinforces a general problem raised earlier: if there is no *ex ante* view corresponding to a non-partition model, then there is no justification for modeling the decisionmaker as having a prior which is updated in a Bayesian like manner on non-partition information cells. But in that case, why look at *ex ante* equilibrium notions and the value of information?

Imperfect information processing *Mistakes in processing information may be modeled by non-partitions.*

These motivations do not have formal results relating them to non-partitions. Nevertheless, they do seem to justify the use of certain non-partitions. For example, Geanakoplos (1989) discusses a situation where *selection bias* – a situation where individuals select which information to use, e.g., ignoring bad news but taking good news into account – will lead to non-partitional $\mathscr{F}_i$s. However, no connection is developed between selection bias and the properties used in results on non-partitions. So, while this might motivate dropping the partition structure of information, it does not motivate results based on the particular weakenings discussed in the previous sections.

The argument in the previous paragraph seems to apply also to *implicit information*, a related cause for non-partitional information. It is argued that when reading the newspaper few people make deductions based on what is not there. But it remains to be seen that this motivates dropping [P5] in general.

Unawareness: an example and a reappearance of syntax *Axiom* [5] *implicitly requires awareness of all states and hence should be dropped.*

The most commonly cited argument for dropping [5] is unawareness. The argument that only partitions make sense starts by assuming that a person believes $\mathscr{F}(\omega)$ is the set of possible states, and that for $\omega' \in \mathscr{F}(\omega), \mathscr{F}(\omega') \neq \mathscr{F}(\omega)$. Then the person would conclude that when the state is ω' she would think the possible states are $\mathscr{F}_i(\omega')$, and differ from what she actually thinks at ω, so it cannot be that ω' is possible. But, the counterargument says that if the individual is unaware of ω', she could not "know" the set $\mathscr{F}(\omega')$.[80] Non-partition possibility correspondences may be plausible for this reason.

But this raises another question: What does it mean to say that, since $\omega' \in \mathscr{F}(\omega)$, when ω occurs the person thinks ω' is possible, even though ω' is not conceivable. The following example of unawareness, from Geanakoplos (1989), suggests a potential answer. A scientist, who is unaware of γ rays, and a fortiori is unaware of the fact that γ rays indicate that the ozone layer is disintegrating, is interested in knowing whether or not the ozone layer is disintegrating. When it is not disintegrating, the scientist can not use the non-existence of γ rays to deduce that it is not disintegrating (since she is unaware of γ rays she can not use their absense to update); when it is disintegrating she discovers γ rays and then deduces the connection with ozone, concluding that the ozone layer is disintegrating. If we describe the state space as $\{d, \neg d\}$, where d denotes disintegrating, the scientist information is non-partitional: $\mathscr{F}(d) = \{d\}, \mathscr{F}(\neg d) = \{d, \neg d\}$. The answer this suggests to our question concerning ω' above seems to be that the scientist does not have a complete description of the state. Thus what the scientist thinks is possible in state $\neg d$ has nothing to do with the γ rays of which she is unaware; rather she only thinks about the payoff – relevant events and views *disintegration* and *not disintegration* as possible.[81]

But this introduces another concern: we have not provided a correct description of the model, neither from the scientist's limited perspective nor from ours. In the state corresponding to d the scientist is aware of γ rays. Could the model then have $\{d, \gamma\}, \neg d$ as the two states? Not if we want a model of the world as the scientist perceives it, since then in state $\neg d$ the scientist's perception is no longer that either of those two states are possible. Could this be a model of the world from the analyst's perspective? The non-partitional model is an incomplete shorthand for a more complete model with *partitions* and a prior for the person that differs from the "actual" prior. The true state space is $\{\gamma, \neg d\} \times \{d, \neg d\}$, the information *is* partitional: the scientist observes either $\{\gamma\} \times \{d, \neg d\}$ or $\{\neg \gamma\} \times \{d, \neg d\}$, and the "correct" prior on this state space has probability zero on $\neg \gamma, d$ while the scientist behaves as if this state had positive probability. (Once again, this may clarify why allowing for non-partitions is like allowing for different priors in a game.)

So what of our unawareness motivation for non-partitions satisfying [P4] but violating [P5]? It seems to be having a hard time. At best, it is a shorthand for a partitional model and it does not really justify weakening [P5]. It suggests that certain "wrong" priors can be modeled as one very special form of non-partitions; it fails to motivate general results along the lines in the previous subsection. Like our discussion of jurors' decision making earlier, the model of the scientist can at most suggest using particular non-partitions in particular examples, not exploring the general implications of non-partitions that violate [P5].

We conclude that the intuitive example of unawareness fails to motivate results where [P5] is dropped and other axioms retained. The main remaining argument for dropping [P5] in general is based on the syntactic interpretation of [5] (which we saw is equivalent to [P5]). Assumption [5] states that if an individual does not know something, then she knows she does not know it. If she does not know it because she is not aware of it, then presumably we should not insist that she knows that she does not know it. But if one is adopting the syntactic approach, one should do so with care. Modica and Rustichini (1993, 1994) argue that to model unawareness, the notion should be introduced into the language and examined. They then accept the definition that a person is unaware of ϕ if she does not know ϕ

and she does not know that she does not know ϕ, formally they introduce the symbol $\mathcal{U}$ and define it by $\mathcal{U}(\phi) \leftrightarrow \neg k(\phi) \wedge \neg k(\neg k(\phi))$. But, they argue that in a state in which you are aware of γ rays then you should also be aware of *no* γ rays; that is, they impose the symmetry axiom, [S], $\neg \mathcal{U}(\phi) \leftrightarrow \neg \mathcal{U}(\neg \phi)$. They develop various interesting results on the relationship of this symmetry axiom with [T, N, MC, 4, 5]. In particular they show that [T, N, MC, 4, S] characterizes partitions: symmetry of awareness is equivalent to [5] so leads to no real unawareness in this context.[82] Dekel, Lipman, and Rustichini (1996) make a related point. They say that to be unaware of ϕ at ω the person should not know that (she does not know)^n ϕ for all n (since if there is a sentence where there is positive knowledge of ϕ she must be aware of ϕ). They prove that requiring this for all integers n allows for unawareness, but extending it (as one should) transfinitely, results in the impossibility of real unawareness. In conclusion, these papers show that non-partitions are not an appropriate way to model unawareness because [N] and [MC] must be dropped, so a knowledge operator that allows for unawareness cannot come from a partition.[83]

APPENDIX

No-trade results

We review here three simple and basic "no-trade theorems."[84] The earliest explicit result of this kind is in Aumann (1976).[85]

Result 1 (Aumann (1976)) *Consider two agents, $i = 1, 2$, who share a common prior p, on a state space Ω, and each has information given by a partition $\mathcal{F}_i$.*

If in some state of the world ω, the agents' posterior beliefs concerning an event $A \subset \Omega$, namely the values $\bar{p}_i$ of $P_i(A \mid \mathcal{F}_i(\omega))$, for $i = 1, 2$, are common knowledge, then these posteriors are equal.

The basic property used in the proof is a version of the sure-thing principle:
If $p_i(A \mid F) = p_i(A \mid F') = \bar{p}_i$ for $F, F' \in \mathcal{F}_i, F \cap F' = \phi$, then $p_i(A \mid F \cup F') = \bar{p}_i$. This property and the formal definition (see below) that at ω the events $\{\omega': p_i(A \mid \mathcal{F}_i(\omega')) = \bar{p}_i\}$ for $i = 1, 2$, are common knowledge, immediately imply the result. More directly interesting for economics is the version of this result that speculation and trade cannot be a consequence of private information alone. If private information cannot explain speculation, other reasons must be the driving force in trade and speculation.

Result 2 (Sebenius and Geanakoplos (1983)) *Consider the framework in the result above. Assume in addition that these two agents are considering saying* *yes or no to a bet, which is a specification of how much agent 1 will pay agent 2 if a certain state occurs. That is, the bet is a random variable* $X:\Omega \to \Re$. *(Negative amounts indicate payments from 2 to 1.) Assume also that, at some state of the world* ω, *both agents are willing to accept the bet if and only if in such a state of the world each agent has a non-negative expected payoff:* $E(X \mid \mathscr{F}_i(\omega)) \geq 0$.

If it is common knowledge that the agents are willing to bet, then their expected payoffs are equal to zero.

Given the first result, at a formal level this second result is not surprising: the first result says that if it is common knowledge that a particular conditional expectation for both players – namely their conditional probabilities of an event A – equal $\bar{p}$, then these conditional expectations are equal. The second says that for any conditional expectation for both agents, if it is common knowledge that they lie in the intervals $[0, \bar{p}_1]$ and $[-\bar{p}_2, 0]$ then both conditional expectations equal 0. However, the second result is, in a sense that is made precise in section 7, less robust than the first.

The final preliminary result is an equilibrium version of no-speculation. This result shows that the conclusion obtained above, by assuming a common prior and common knowledge that players are optimizing, is also obtained when we use a common prior and solve the game using correlated equilibrium. This foreshadows Aumann's (1987) characterization result, see proposition 3, that correlated equilibrium is equivalent to the assumptions of common knowledge of rationality and a common prior.

Result 3 *Consider the betting framework of the result above. In any correlated equilibrium (a fortiori any Nash equilibrium) of the game where players say YES or NO to the bet as a function of their private information and the bet is in effect if both say yes, the expected payoffs of the agents are zero.*

It is worth noting that a solution concept based solely on common knowledge of rationality – namely rationalizability – does not yield the same no-trade result: even if there is a common prior on Ω, rationalizability implicitly introduces non-common priors since it is equivalent to subjective correlated equilibrium (see proposition 2).

Notes

We are grateful to the NSF and Alfred P. Sloan for financial support, to Aviad Heifetz, Bart Lipman, Giacomo Bonanno, Steve Morris, and Aldo Rustichini for very helpful and insightful comments and conversations, and to our colleagues for their patience while we agonized over this chapter.

1 Some additional sources that include an overview or a more complete presentation of material related to this survey are Aumann (1995b), Bacharach and Mongin (1994), Binmore and Brandenburger (1990), Bonanno (1993), Brandenburger (1992), Brandenburger and Dekel (1993), Chellas (1980), Fagin et al. (1995), Fudenberg and Tirole (1991), Geanakoplos (1992), Lipman (1995b), Lismont and Mongin (1994a), Morris (1995a), Myerson (1991), Osborne and Rubinstein (1994), Reny (1992), Rubinstein and Wolinsky (1989), and Tan and Werlang (1984).

2 Stephen Morris has suggested that an equivalent way to view our argument is that the paradoxes arise from confusing the (exogenous) states and the (endogenous) choice of actions. This interpretation fits in better with the topic of the next section, which is concerned with constructing the state space.

3 Alternatively, in accordance with the view of footnote 1, the player is confusing the opponent's action which from her perspective is exogenous, with her own choice.

4 A game theorist reading this analysis might be inclined to dismiss it entirely as absurd and the resolution offered below as obvious. A survey of the philosophy literature on the analysis of the Prisoners' Dilemma will offer ample evidence that to many the analysis is not absurd and the resolution is not trivial. Consider the following passage from Campbell and Sowden (1985) regarding the first two paradoxes discussed in this section: "Quite simply, these paradoxes cast in doubt our understanding of rationality and, in the case of the Prisoners' Dilemma, suggest that it is impossible for rational creatures to cooperate. Thus, they bear directly on fundamental issues in ethics and political philosophy and threaten the foundations of social science." For our purposes, the most important thing to note is that the "resolution" is the same as those offered for the less obvious paradoxes below.

5 We suspect that most economists would dismiss Newcombe's Paradox as uninteresting since the source of the difficulty appears to be arising from the infallibility of the genie which in itself would appear to be problematic and perhaps not a relevant modeling hypothesis. However, as is often noted, the paradox persists even if the genie is correct with high probability, since expected-utility calculations would still yield that it is better to take box B alone rather than both. Thus, it is argued that the problem is not one postulating an all-knowing genie and hence is genuine. The "resolution" that we will offer is equally applicable to this probabilistic version.

6 Bonanno's resolution to the paradox is instructive. As discussed in section 5, he replaces the rationality axiom above with a rule of inference that allows inferences about agent i's behavior only if the hypothesis does not involve any reference to i's behavior or to any proposition that utilizes a hypothesis involving i's behavior in its proof. This "solves" the paradox since, effectively, the new rationality hypothesis overcomes the problematic feature of maintaining the truth of a player's rationality while he contemplates deviating. However, the solution goes too far by not allowing i to use deductions made about the behavior of j which relied on j's belief of i's rationality. As a consequence, Bonanno's modified model

of rationality will fail to eliminate even those strategies that require two rounds of deletion of strategies that are strictly dominated by pure strategies, in a two-person simultaneous-move game.

7 The paradoxes discussed in this section are of a different nature than the discussions of Anderlini (1990), Binmore (1987–8), and Canning (1992). These authors model players as machines and obtain impossibility and inconsistency results, closely related to, and following from, Gödel's famous work, concluding that rationality is a problematic assumption.

8 The review and some of the development below is rather terse, one source for a more thorough presentation of the material in 3.1 and 3.2.1 is Fagin *et al.* (1995, chapters 2 and 3); Chellas (1980) is a very comprehensive reference.

9 Thus Aumann's (1976) discussion of the assumption that the information structure is commonly "known" is closely related to Harsanyi's (1967) development of a commonly "known" game for situations of incomplete information.

10 Of course justifications of solution concepts that do not impose common-knowledge assumptions – such as those using an evolutionary approach, or Aumann and Brandenburger's (1995) characterization of Nash equilibrium in two-person games, see proposition 4 below – do not require a commonly "known" model.

11 In fact, we will find an information structure that, if it is assumed to be common "knowledge," generates in every state ω' the perceptions that are described by state ω'.

12 Bacharach (1985, 1988) and Samet (1990) present different, but related, approaches. As in most of the literature, the models that we will construct from this framework will involve partitions only, and no probabilities.

13 The symbol for conjunction should not be confused with the same symbol used earlier for the meet of partitions. Since in both cases ∧ is the standard symbol, we abuse notation in this way. Similarly, ¬ will represent both set complements and syntactic negation as will be clear from the context.

14 Excepting, of course, our original description of the actual situation of incomplete information which is not a construct, but a given primitive of our analysis.

   Aumann (1995b) and Hart *et al.* (1995) show that the constructed state space has the cardinality of the continuum.

15 The fact that the $\mathcal{F}_i$s constructed in this way are partitions is a result; see, e.g., Aumann (1995b), Chellas (1980), and Fagin *et al.* (1995), for proofs of such results.

16 This is a more formal version of the Kripke models described in the preceding subsection. Kripke models are usually defined using binary relations, e.g., ω *is considered possible at* ω', rather than possibility correspondences $\mathcal{F}_i$. The two methods are easily seen to be equivalent so we use the one more familiar to economists.

17 For proofs of this type of result, and more general connections between results in the language, called syntax in the literature, and those in the model, called semantics in the literature, see references cited at the beginning of this section.

18 There is an issue here which requires some caution. We have just constructed a set Ω where each ω is a list of true sentences in L. Our main claim is that this construct is equivalent to the following: view Ω as a set of states, with each state specifying only what sentences in X are true; append to Ω a partition (which we derived) for each player and using this commonly "known" information structure derive which epistemic sentences are true (just as we constructed K_i from the partitions). However, we could imagine a slightly different question. Start with a set Ω and functions $\mathscr{F}_i : \Omega \to 2^{\Omega}$, and a function from Ω into 2^X representing the subset of X that is true in each ω. Use this to determine which epistemic sentences are true. (Where $k_i(\phi)$ is true at ω if $[\phi] \in \mathscr{F}_i(\omega)$.) Check if the epistemic sentences satisfy [T, MC, N, 4, and 5]. If so, is it necessary that $\mathscr{F}_i$ is a partition? *No.* Consider the following example: $X = \{p\}$, $\Omega = \{\omega, \omega'\}$, $\mathscr{F}_i(\omega) = \mathscr{F}_i(\omega') = \{\omega\}$, and the unique basic sentence in X is p, and p is true at both ω and ω'. It is easy to see that all the axioms are satisfied concerning knowledge about p, but $\mathscr{F}_i$ is not a partition. To conclude that any Kripke structure that satisfies [T, MC, N, 4, and 5] must be partition we either need to verify the axioms on $K_i : 2^{\Omega} \to 2^{\Omega}$ or, if we want to verify it on sentences $k_i(\phi)$, then we must allow for all possible assignments of truth valuations from Ω into X. For more on this see, e.g., Fagin *et al.* (1995).

19 Maruta (1994) develops the notion of events that are *expressible* in the syntax, and, among other results, characterizes partitions using a weaker axiomatic structure but assuming that many events are expressible.

20 Actually, common knowledge can be defined without infinitely many conjunctions, by adding symbols to the language and providing a fixed-point definition of common knowledge. Even then, one might be concerned with the notion of common knowledge in a syntactic framework, since it seems to require working with sentences that involve infinitely many conjunctions. Thus, it might seem questionable to model decisionmakers who, in some vague sense, need to conceptualize, let alone verify, infinitely many sentences to know whether a sentence in their language is true.

Aumann's (1976) state-space characterization of common knowledge suggests that this should not be a concern. While common knowledge can be defined as everyone knowing that everyone knows, it is equivalent to define common knowledge in terms of the meet of the information partitions, which are simple to construct and have a simple interpretation as self-evident events. This is often called the fixed-point characterization of common knowledge. Since it seems obvious that certain events, e.g., publicly announced events, are common knowledge, it seems natural that we can verify common knowledge without getting into "infinities" (see, e.g., Milgrom (1981)).

A related issue has been addressed in syntactic models by asking whether common knowledge can be characterized with finitely many finite axioms. That is, add a symbol c_M for common knowledge among $M \subset N$ to the language of subsection 3.2.1. The question is whether there are assumptions that can be added to [T, MC, N, 4, and 5] which define c_M and have the property that, when we construct the state space and partitions (analogously to the construction above), we get an equivalence not only between k_i and K_i, as in subsection 3.2.1, but also between c_M and CK_M? Intuitively, the answer is yes if we allow for infinitely many conjunctions and define c_M that way. But it can also be done with finite axioms using the fixed-point approach, allaying any concerns of this type. (See, Bonanno (1995), Bonanno and Nehring (1995), Fagin et al. (1995), Halpern and Moses (1992), and Lismont and Mongin (1993, 1994a, b). See also Barwise (1988) for a different perspective.)

21 To be more precise, there is no other model without redundant states, or put differently, any other model that agrees with that of figure 5.4b on finite levels also agrees with it on all levels.

22 This is related to Fagin, Halpern, and Vardi (1991), Fagin et al. (1995) and Rubinstein (1989). Carlsson and van Damme (1993) describe a realistic environment which generates an information structure with similar properties, see footnote 6.

23 The relationship between the approach of allowing more conjunctions and that of adding symbols is discussed briefly in subsection 3.2.1.

24 Heifetz (1995c) constructed a more general two-person example which has two advantages: first all the models have the property that in every state the players' knowledge coincide except concerning sentences outside the original syntax – this is not true at state ω^* in the example above, and, second, he shows that there are as many such models as partitions of Ω. See also the second part of subsection 3.2.2.

25 By contrast we definitely should care about the model of figure 5.5: A straightforward extension of Rubinstein (1989), by adding a third player, yields those types of models; and, as pointed out in footnote 6, Carlsson and van Damme (1993) provide an economically interesting model with the same properties as Rubinstein's model. The point here is that examples with even greater transfinite depth of knowledge may not have similar motivations.

26 See theorem 3.1 in Heifetz and Samet (1995).

27 Tan and Werlang (1984) are concerned with the reverse implication: they show how any standard model of asymmetric information can be mapped into (a subspace of) the Mertens and Zamir (1984) model. Brandenburger and Dekel (1993) re-examine the Mertens and Zamir formalization, focusing on Aumann's concern with common knowledge of the information structure, in particular showing which assumption in Mertens and Zamir plays the role of the assumption that the information structure is common "knowledge."

28 We present the case where there are only two players; the extension to more players is straightforward. In this discussion S is assumed to be complete, separable, and metric. Heifetz (1993) generalizes the result to the case where S is Hausdorf.

29 It is necessary to allow i to have joint beliefs over S and over j's beliefs over S since the true state in S may naturally influence j's beliefs, e.g., if i thinks j has private information about S.

30 Formally, $T_1^i \equiv \{(t_1^i, t_2^i, \ldots) \in T_0^i :: \mathrm{marg}_{X_{n-1}} t_{n+1}^i = t_n^i$ and the marginal of t_{n+1}^i on the ith copy of $\Delta(X_{n-1})$ assigns probability 1 to $t_n^i \in \Delta(X_{n-1})\}$.

31 Heifetz (1995a) shows that there is an additional implicit assumption of countable additivity: not only are we assuming that the beliefs τ_k are countably additive, but also the meta assumption is adopted that the beliefs generated by the sequence τ_k, over types of the opponent, are countably additive. This is a meta assumption because it concerns how we extend beliefs from the hierarchy to the state space, and it turns out that many finitely additive beliefs over T exist which yield the correct marginals, and only one of these is countably additive. So the uniqueness, as in subsection 3.2.1, is not completely w.l.o.g. On the other hand, Heifetz also shows that there is an alternative way to generate a Bayesian model, using non-well founded sets, which does not require this meta assumption.

There is a mathematical feature that might be helpful in understanding the difference between constructions in subsection 3.2.1 and 3.2.2. The cardinality of the set of beliefs over a set can be the same as the cardinality of the set itself. Therefore, it is feasible to construct a model where every possible belief over the state space is represented by some state. On the other hand, the cardinality of the set of partitions of a set is always bigger than the set itself. Therefore, one cannot construct a state space in which each state incorporates every possible partition of the set. So, we should expect that it will not be the case that each state can express every possible sentence about the players' knowledge (see also the discussion following figure 5.5, and Gilboa (1988) and Heifetz and Samet (1995)).

32 The extension of this subsection to infinite Ω is delicate as it requires attention to various topological and measure-theoretic details, such as why E must be closed. We maintain the finiteness assumption for simplicity.

33 Battigalli and Bonanno (1995), Brandenburger and Dekel (1987b), Lamarre and Shoham (1994), and Nielson (1984) also consider the relationship between knowledge and certainty.

34 Note that property [N] follows from the other assumptions, and that any prior with the same support, S, will generate the same B_i and K_i.

35 However, the model of certainty and knowledge at the end of subsection 3.3 does create a support, even though it does not create a unique prior. This suggests that perhaps a weaker assumption, such as common supports, can be justified. There is very little exploration of this issue. Assumptions like this have been used, together with additional assumptions, to characterize Nash equilibrium in generic games of perfect information (Ben Porath (1994)). Stuart (1995) shows that common support and common certainty of rationality yields Nash equilibrium in the finitely repeated Prisoners' Dilemma.

36 Morris (1995a) compellingly argues in favor of dropping the CPA even when an *ex ante* stage does exist.

37 The reader will note that in section 6 some results rely on the uniform boundedness of the utility functions and should therefore be treated with similar scepticism.

38 The reader might wonder why we care about characterizations of solution concepts. The common view of characterization results such as those in this chapter is that they explain how introspection alone can lead agents to play in

accordance with various solution concepts. We would like to emphasize two closely related roles: characterizations provide negative results and they suggest which solution concepts are more appropriate in different environments. For example, there may be results which provide very strong sufficient conditions for a particular equilibrium notion, such as Nash equilibrium. This cannot constitute a proof that the equilibrium notion is unreasonable, since it is possible that an alternative model with appealing sufficient conditions exist (such as, for example, recent evolutionary models). Nevertheless, most results are tight in that if assumptions are weakened then play could be different from the characterized solution concept. Thus, these results do suggest that various solution concepts, in particular Nash equilibrium and backwards induction, are implausible in various contexts. An example of the second type is the following: for some solution concepts it is shown that common certainty of rationality rather than common certainty of beliefs is sufficient. Such a result may be important in a learning or evolutionary environment where common certainty of rationality is more plausible than common certainty of beliefs. Similar insights can be obtained by examining the robustness of characterizations to weakenings of the common-certainty assumptions. For example, different characterizations are robust to replacing common certainty with different notions of "almost" common certainty. Therefore, since common certainty assumptions are unlikely to be satisfied in any real context, the appropriate concept should depend on which form of "almost" common certainty is most likely to be satisfied in that context.

39 See also Stalnaker (1994) and Tan and Werlang (1988).

40 That $\mathscr{S}^\infty$ is equivalent to an interim solution concept is natural: it is characterized by an assumption that is made about a particular state of the world, not an *ex ante* assumption about the constructed states of the world.

41 That any such equilibrium uses strategies that survive $\mathscr{S}^\infty$ follows from arguments similar to Bernheim's and Pearce's characterization of rationalizability: each strategy used in such an equilibrium is a best reply to a belief over the set of those opponents' strategies that are used; therefore these sets of strategies are best reply sets, hence survive iterative deletion. To construct an a posteriori subjective correlated equilibrium that uses any strategy that survives iterative deletion we simply construct an information structure where the state space is the set of strategy profiles, each player is informed of a recommendation for her own strategy, and the players' conditional probabilities on the state space are, for each possible recommendation to i, say σ_i, the belief – which is over the opponents' strategies that survive iterative deletion – which makes σ_i a best reply. (Such a belief exists since the strategies are rationalizable.) For more detail see Brandenburger and Dekel (1987a).

42 For two-person games the CPA is not needed.

43 Clearly the hypothesis that each ω in the support of p is also in [*rationality*] $\cap$ [*u*] is equivalent to the assumption that at each such ω there is common certainty of [*rationality*] and of [*u*]. Thus it might appear that common certainty of rationality is necessary for correlated equilibrium. However, in

subsection 6.2 we will see that the appropriate statement of this *ex ante* result is as in proposition 3 and not with common certainty; see the text preceding footnote 6.2.

44 It is important that *j knows* the payoffs are u_j; if *j* were only certain of the payoffs then *j* could be wrong, and then the players would not necessarily be playing a Nash equilibrium of the game $(\Sigma, \mathbf{u}(\omega))$. Moreover, they would not even necessarily be playing a Nash equilibrium of the game they believe they are certain they are playing, as each player *i* could believe that *j* has wrong beliefs about *j*'s own payoffs. Thus, while we agree that certainty "of one's own payoff is tautological" (Aumann and Brandenburger (1995, section (7c)), knowledge of one's own payoff is not tautological, and seems necessary for proposition 4.

45 Applying this analysis to the case of correlated equilibrium may shed light on which of the various definitions of correlated equilibrium, see, e.g., Cotter (1991) and Forges (1992), are appropriate and in which contexts.

46 These and related concerns with characterizing refinements are discussed, e.g., by Börgers and Samuelson (1992) and Pearce (1982), see also Cubitt (1989) and Samuelson (1992).

47 Throughout this section we use the term almost common certainty for the general idea only – each particular notion will go by a different label. Thus, while the term common certainty is formally equivalent to the term common 1 belief (defined below), almost common certainty is not a formal precise term, and is not equivalent to almost common 1 belief, formally defined below.

There are other models of noise, which may appear more natural, that lead to similar information structures; for example, Carlsson and van Damme (1993) use a generalization of an information structure where players are interested in the value of a parameter *x*, but each player is informed of the true value of *x* plus some i.i.d. noise with support $(-\varepsilon, \varepsilon)$. Then a player may believe that the true value is close to zero, and that the other believes the true value is close to zero, but given any value *y* as far from zero as you want, there is a chain that one believes 2 believes . . . 1 believes *y* is possible. Formally, neither Carlsson and van Damme's (1993) model, nor Rubinstein's (1989) model, have a non-empty strict subset which is common *q* belief at any state for *q* close to 1. See below for a definition of common *q* belief.

48 A related question would be to ask what notions of convergence of probabilities yield (lower hemi) continuity results. For example, consider a coin tossed infinitely often (including infinity) and let *p* be the probability of heads. Consider the game where a player can choose to play and get 2 if the coin never falls on heads, 0 otherwise, or not to play and get 1 for sure. Clearly she should choose to play for $p = 1$ and not to play for $p < 1$. Consider $p_n \to 1$. The induced probability distributions on the state space of the first time the coin falls on heads, $\Omega = \{1, 2, \ldots\} \cup \{never\}$, converge weakly but the *ex ante* expected payoffs are 1 along the sequence and 2 in the limit, and the strategy choice is not to play in the sequence and to play in the limit. Clearly, the standard notion of weak convergence is not sufficient. The notions of convergence of probability that yield lower hemi continuity in this context are developed in Engl (1994).

Kajii and Morris (1994a) develop other notions of convergence more closely related to almost common certainty. Both these papers discuss the relationship among these notions of convergence and almost common certainty.

49 Fudenberg, Kreps, and Levine (1988) obtained the analogous result for refinements of Nash equilibrium, essentially that the only robust refinement is that of Nash equilibrium in strategies that are not weakly dominated (see also remark 4.4 in Dekel and Fudenberg (1990)).

50 In the case that $\mathscr{F}_i(\omega)$ has zero probability, choose any version of a conditional probability.

51 Here again the subscript N denotes the intersection of B_i^q over all i in N, and the superscript n denotes n iterations of the operator B_i^q.

52 There is a useful characterization of common q belief similar to that of common knowledge, simplifying the iterative definition to a fixed point definition. It is analogous to the result that A is common knowledge at ω if there exists a self-evident event that contains ω and is in A. Say that an event E is *evident q belief* if for all $\omega \in E$, it is true that $p_i(E \mid \mathscr{F}_i(\omega)) \geq q$, i.e., whenever E happens everyone assigns probability at least q that E happened. Monderer and Samet show that E is common q belief at ω if and only if there is an evident q belief set F, with $\omega \in F \subset B_N^q(E)$. (An extension of common q belief to uncountable Ω is in Kajii and Morris (1994b).)

53 It is worth emphasizing that this motivation is based on the *analyst's* prior and doubts about her own assumptions.

54 The rough idea for this fact can be seen as follows. If *ex ante i* thinks E is likely then it is *ex ante* likely to be the case that after receiving her private information i still thinks E is likely. (After all, i's *ex ante* belief in E is the weighted average, using the prior, of her conditional beliefs [which are bounded]. So if *ex ante E* is likely, "most" conditional beliefs are that E is likely.) Using the common prior, this implies that everyone thinks it is likely to be the case that everyone's conditional beliefs are that E is likely. But this is just the statement that E is likely to be evident q belief for q large, i.e., E is almost certainly almost common 1 belief.

55 As one might expect, since subjective certainty of an event is not at all like common knowledge, weakening our common knowledge requirement to the assumption that the game and rationality is almost subjectively certainty does affect our conclusions. In particular this would only characterize $\mathscr{S}^2(\pi, S)$. Moreover, here the assumption that it is common knowledge that everyone knows their own payoffs is important; in its absence the characterization is weakened to $\mathscr{S}^1(\pi, S)$.

Perhaps surprisingly, it turns out that almost certainty of the game and rationality is nevertheless sufficient to characterize iterated dominance. However, since almost certainty requires a common prior it does not make sense in this context where we are not assuming a common prior. We state this result when we discuss the incomplete-information-game interpretation below; see subsection 6.3.1.

It is also easy to see that for any finite game, weakening common certainty to almost ∞ certainty, i.e., requiring iteration to arbitrarily high (but finite) levels, also does not effect the conclusion of the results on $\mathcal{S}^\infty$ because only finitely many iterations are necessary in any finite game. Lipman (1994) examines infinite games, and this robustness does not extend to discontinuous infinite games.

As we should expect, proposition 9 above does not have anything to say about the *ex ante* payoffs in the model: it could be that while [*rationality*] is almost common certainty at ω, the state ω can be unlikely (*ex ante*). Nevertheless, it is an immediate corollary to proposition 9, and proposition 2, that if [*rationality*] and [*u*] are almost certainly almost common 1 belief, then the *ex ante* payoffs are also close to expected payoffs that survive $\mathcal{S}^\infty$.

56 An advantage of introducing the CPA as an event, [CPA], is that one can use it to evaluate the implications of assuming that it is almost common certainty that there is a common prior. Thus, one could examine the robustness of various results, including a local version of proposition 3 that holds at a state of the world ω instead of globally, but we have not done so.

57 This is a substantive assumption – see also section 3.4.

58 The event [u] is the same in each model, but, since the probabilities are changing, the optimal strategies may be changing, hence the event [rationality] may change in the sequence.

59 We introduce some simplifying assumptions that will make it possible to present a brief sketch of a proof. Consider a particular convergent subsequence of distributions on actions, say, $\{\phi^n\}_{n=1}^\infty$, where $\phi^n \in \Delta(S)$ is defined by $\phi^n(s) \equiv \Sigma_{\{\omega : s(\omega) = s\}} p^n(\omega)$. (We will denote the subsequence by n rather than the more precise n_k to simplify notation.) Our first simplifying assumption is that p^n converges; we denote its limit by p. We argue that $s : \Omega \to S$ is a correlated equilibrium with the information structure $(\Omega, \mathcal{F}_i, p)$. If not then some player i has a profitable deviation. Our second simplifying assumption is that this implies that there is a state ω, with $p(\omega) > 0$, at which playing something other than $s_i(\omega)$, say $\tilde{s}$, is a better reply against i conjecture at ω, $\phi_{-i}(\omega) \in \Delta(S_{-i})$, where $\phi_{-i}(\omega)(s_{-i}) \equiv \Sigma_{\{\omega' : s_{-i}(\omega') = s_{-i}\}} p(\omega' \mid \mathcal{F}_i(\omega))$. (This is simplifying since for infinite Ω we should consider the case where each ω is null, and look at deviations on measurable sets with positive probability.) But then, since $p(\omega) > 0, \phi_{-i}(\omega) = \lim \phi_{-i}^n(\omega)$, where $\phi_{-i}^n(\omega)(s_{-i}) \equiv \Sigma_{\{\omega' : s_{-i}(\omega') = s_{-i}\}} p^n(\omega' \mid \mathcal{F}_i(\omega))$. So, $\tilde{s}$ must be better than $s_i(\omega)$ against ϕ_{-i}^n for n large, i.e., $s_i(\omega)$ is not optimal for i in the nth model. On the other hand, since $p(\omega) > 0, \omega \in E^n$ for n large enough, which means that $s_i(\omega)$ should be optimal, leading to a contradiction.

60 See also footnote 4.

61 Proposition 10 could also be stated in this way; we chose not to do so because the notion of an ε-correlated equilibrium is not standard.

62 There we noted that if i assigned positive probability to j playing s_j, and probability 1 to $[u] \cap [rationality] \cap [\phi_j]$ then there is a state $\omega' \in [u] \cap [rationality] \cap [\phi_j] \cap [s_j]$ which implies that s_j is a best reply against ϕ_j given payoffs u_j. Now we simply note that the total probability that i assigns to strategies s_j that are not best replies is bounded by $1 - \varepsilon$, since at any

$\omega' \in [u] \cap [rationality] \cap [\phi_j]$, $s_j(\omega')$ is a best reply to $[\phi_i]$ given payoffs u_j. Also, as in the discussion after proposition 4, one could drop the assumption that players know their own payoffs, but this seems to require strengthening the hypothesis by adding the assumption that at ω there is almost mutual certainty that $[u]$ is almost mutually certain, i.e., $p_i([u] \mid \mathcal{F}_i(\omega)) \geq 1 - \delta$ and $p_i(\{\omega'': p_j([u] \mid \mathcal{F}_j(\omega'')) \geq 1 - \delta, j \neq i\} \mid \mathcal{F}_i(\omega)) \geq 1 - \delta$.

63 This result follows the same arguments as in preceding results, so will not be repeated. The result does imply that the only standard refinement with a somewhat appealing epistemic characterization is that of trembling-hand perfection, and then only for two-person games.

64 Because the strategy spaces are finite, there is a $\bar{q}$ that works uniformly throughout the iteration.

65 This is also the approach implicit in subsection 6.2. Fudenberg, Kreps, and Levine focus on the case where almost certainly there is almost common certainty that the payoffs are *almost as in G*. Formally, for a sequence $u^n \to u$ and $q^n \to 1$ they assume that with probability at least q^n, u^n is common q^n belief. By contrast we assume here $u^n = u$. For examining robustness of solution concepts theirs is a very sensible weakening of the assumption that the analyst is almost certain that the game G is almost common certainty, by adding the adjective *almost* before the game G as well. Since it turns out that this change only complicates the statement of the results, without contributing significantly to understanding the issues with which we are concerned here, we do not consider this additional weakening in this chapter. Dekel and Fudenberg (1990) precisely analyze the role of allowing for this additional "almost."

66 To be precise, it appears in the fourth paragraph of that section.

67 Not only is $\mathscr{S}^\infty$ robust in this first sense to weakening common certainty to almost common 1 belief; it is also robust to weakening it to almost certainty. Formally, assume that $s^n \in \mathscr{S}^\infty(G^n)$. This implies that if $\lim p^n([s]) > 0$ then $s \in \mathscr{S}^\infty(G)$. If the analyst believes that any uncertainties about the payoffs are reflected by a common prior of the players, but that strategic uncertainty is not captured by a common prior, the analyst will want to know if $\mathscr{S}^\infty$ is robust to weakening common certainty to almost certainty. This makes sense if the uncertainties about the payoffs arise from some physical structure about which players have asymmetric information (e.g., the success of player i's firm); but the uncertainties concerning opponents strategies are subjective.

On the other hand, if the uncertainties over payoffs do not come from a common prior, the appropriate question is whether $\mathscr{S}^\infty$ is robust to weakening common certainty to almost subjective certainty. As we noted above – see that text preceding section 6.2 – it is *not*. So, even though $\mathscr{S}^\infty$ is a very coarse solution concept, it is not robust in this very demanding sense.

68 To see all this fix a strict Nash equilibrium of G, denoted by s. Let C^n be the event in Ω on which G is common p^n belief, and let $[u]$ be the event in which the game is actually G. Finally, let $\Omega_i^n = B_i^{q^n}(C^n)$ – the event on which i believes with probability at least q^n that there is common q^n belief that the game is G; and $\Omega_*^n = C^n \cap [u]$. Note that for ω in Ω_i^n, i is almost certain that the event Ω_*^n

occurred: $\omega \in \Omega_i^n \Rightarrow p_i^n(\Omega_N | \mathcal{F}_i(\omega)) \to 1$. (This is because for such ω, i is almost certain that the game is G and that G is almost common 1 belief, so he is almost certain that both these events obtain.) Consider the following strategies s^n in G^n. (α) Play s_i on Ω_i^n. (β) Find a Nash equilibrium where i is choosing strategies only for other states assuming everyone is playing as given in (α). (That is, consider the restricted game where every i is required to play s_i on Ω_i^n and free to choose anything at all other states. Of course strategies must still only depend on a player's information.) Since s is a strict Nash equilibrium, all players are happy with (α) when n is large. (This is because on Ω_i^n player i is almost certain that everyone else is playing s and that the game is G.) Since in (β) we constructed a Nash equilibrium, everyone is happy with (β) as well. Clearly the interim payoffs of the equilibria we have constructed on G^n converge to those of G; the *ex ante* payoffs converge as well if it is almost certain that G is almost common 1 belief.

If s were not a strict Nash equilibrium, but just a Nash equilibrium, then the construction would yield an interim ε Nash equilibrium in G^n, i.e., strategies that are ε optimal at every information set. Thus, the notion of interim ε Nash equilibrium is robust in that given any $\tilde{G}$, every interim ε Nash equilibrium of G is played in some interim ε Nash equilibrium of $\tilde{G}$ in those states where G is almost common 1 belief.

69 The distribution of actions generated by s on $[u]$ is formally defined as the element $\phi|_u$ of $\Delta(S)$ given by $\phi|_u(s) = \Sigma_{\{\omega \in [u] : s(\omega) = s\}} p_n(\omega)/p_n([u])$.

70 See also the discussion of the characterization of Nash equilibria in games of incomplete information and games with moves by Nature at the end of section 4.

71 Kajii and Morris (1995) is not, strictly speaking, a generalization of Carlsson and van Damme (1993), because the latter allow for continuous noise, and do not assume that players know their own payoffs, but it seems that the methods of Kajii and Morris (1995) could be used to generalize Carlsson and van Damme (1993).

72 Monderer and Samet consider perturbations of $\mathcal{F}_i$s, whereas Kajii and Morris focus on changing only the probabilities as we do in this section. Formally, Kajii and Morris (1994a) show that given a Nash equilibrium s for G^∞ there is an ε-Nash equilibrium s^n for a sequence of games G^n, where the expected payoffs of s^n in G^n converge to those of s in G^∞ if an only if p^n converges to p in the sense that it is almost certain that it is almost common 1 belief that the difference in the conditional probabilities are uniformly almost zero. More precisely, the only if result is that when the sequence fails to converge there exists games where the expected payoffs fail to converge.

73 Assumption [N], that you always know Ω, is also strong – it implicitly rules out some forms of unawareness, in that the complete list of states is always known. Similarly, [MC] is strong since it implies monotonicity, $A \subset B \Rightarrow K_i(A) \subset K_i(B)$, which in turn implies that at any state at which you know anything, you also know the complete state space Ω. For now [N] and [MC], which are necessary and sufficient for the translation between possibility correspondences and knowledge operators, are maintained.

74 While some authors have briefly considered the effect of just dropping [T], without imposing [D], (Geanakoplos (1989), Samet (1990), Brandenburger, Dekel, and Geanakoplos (1992)), we feel that [D] is a basic property of belief and knowledge. Thus, since weakening [T] to [D] has already been analyzed and shown to correspond to weakening knowledge to belief, we will not focus on weakening [T] in this section. Nevertheless, we will present a result where both [D] and [T] are dropped – Brandenburger, Dekel, and Geanakoplos show that this is w.l.o.g. for some purposes, and the extra generality comes at no cost in the presentation. Naturally, one can ask many of the other questions that follows in the context of assuming [D] and not [T]. We leave such exercises to the interested reader.

75 Morris (1992, 1996) extends this in several directions. He provides a multi-stage dynamic decision-making context, and derives additional properties that the possibility correspondence must satisfy if it will meet some additional requirements concerning dynamic consistency and the value of information in these richer contexts; he allows for non-Bayesian updating of probabilities; and he considers non-expected utility preferences. The latter is an attempt to motivate non-partitional structures from an axiomatic perspective, and will be mentioned again below when we turn to the motivation for these structures.

76 As with partitions and common q belief, there exists a non-iterative characterization of common knowledge in this more general context as well: E is common knowledge at ω' if there is a self-evident F, (i.e., $\mathscr{F}_i(\omega) \subset F$ given any $\omega \in F$), that contains ω' and that is perceived to be a subset of E, i.e., given any ω in F, $\mathscr{F}_i(\omega) \subset E$. If $\mathscr{F}_i$ satisfies [P1] (equivalently, if K_i satisfies [T]), then this reduces to the following: E is common knowledge at ω if there exists a self-evident F with $\omega \in F \subset E$.

77 The hypothesis in proposition 19 may appear weaker than those in proposition 18, but this is not the case: the proposition 19 assumes that it is common knowledge that players say yes whereas in 18 the assumption is that we are considering a Nash equilibrium.

78 This clarifies why non-partitions with common priors leads to the same behavior as do non-partitions and partitions without common priors. The lack of a common prior corresponds to the disagreement about i's information structure.

79 This is similar to the syntactic construction of Ω; the difference is that the order of the elementary facts in X is now important.

80 See, e.g., Binmore and Brandenburger (1990).

81 A more common version of this story is Watson's deductions concerning the guilt of a person based on a dog not barking – he fails to use the lack of barking as an indication that the dog knew the individual, while he would (we presume) deduce from any barking that the person was not known to the dog.

82 What happens in the non-partition model of the scientist is instructive. The typical model has $\Omega = \{d, \neg d\}$: a state d which is characterized by the ozone layer disintegrating and γ rays appearing, and a state $\neg d$ which is characterized by no γ rays appearing and no disintegration. As before we specify

$\mathscr{F}(d) = \{d\}, \mathscr{F}(\neg d) = \{d, \neg d\}$. So at d, the scientist knows there are γ rays and the ozone layer is disintegrating, so is aware of everything including γ rays. At $\neg d$ she does not know d. Moreover, at $\neg d$, she does not know that she does not know d, since the set of states at which she does not know d is $\neg d$, and at $\neg d$ she does not know $\neg d$. So she is unaware of γ rays. So far so good. But consider the person's awareness of *no* γ rays. While it is true that at $\neg d$ she does not know there are no γ rays, she does know that she does not know it. This is because she knows Ω, and at both states she will not know that there are no γ rays, so she always knows that she does not know there are no γ rays. Thus, at state d she is aware of the sentence "there are no γ rays," so Modica and Rustichini argue she should be aware of the possibility of γ rays.

83 Dropping [N] and [MC] is related to dropping logical omniscience, the requirement that an individual can deduce all the logical implications of his knowledge. Dekel, Lipman, and Rustichini (1996) argue that, in fact, the state-space model is inappropriate for modeling unawareness as it imposes a form of logical omniscience by identifying events with all sentences that are true in that event, so that knowledge of any sentence implies knowledge of any other sentence that is logically equivalent. Various aspects of logical omniscience are weakened (in very different models) by Fagin and Halpern (1988), Lipman (1995a), and Modica and Rustichini (1993, 1994).

84 In order to focus on the foundations of knowledge and rationality we will not present the extensions to more interesting economic environments, such as Milgrom and Stokey (1982).

85 Actually, there is a precursor in Aumann (1974). The result stated there, that in a zero-sum game allowing correlations without differing priors will not change the value of the game, can be shown to imply result 3 below.

References

Anderlini, L. (1990). "Some notes on church's thesis and the theory of games." *Theory and Decision*, 29: 19–52.

Armbruster, W. and Böge, W. (1978). "Bayesian game theory." In Moeschlin, O. and Pallaschke, D. (eds.), *Game Theory and Related Topics*. Amsterdam: North-Holland.

Aumann, R. J. (1974). "Subjectivity and correlation in randomized strategies." *Journal of Mathematical Economics*, 1: 67–96.

(1976). "Agreeing to disagree." *The Annals of Statistics*, 4(6): 1236–9.

(1987). "Correlated equilibrium as an expression of Bayesian rationality." *Econometrica*, 55: 1–18.

(1995a). "Backward induction and common knowledge of rationality." *Games and Economic Behavior*, 8: 6–19.

(1995b). "Interactive epistemology." Working Paper No. 67, The Hebrew University of Jerusalem.

Aumann, R. J. and Brandenburger, A. (1995). "Epistemic conditions for Nash equilibrium." *Econometrica*, 63: 1161–80.

Bacharach, M. (1985). "Some extensions of a claim of Aumann in an axiomatic model of knowledge." *Journal of Economic Theory*, 37: 167–90.

(1988). "When do we have information partitions?" Mimeo, Oxford University.

Bacharach, M. and Mongin, P. (1994). "Epistemic logic and the foundations of game theory." *Theory and Decision*, 37: 1–6.

Barwise, J. (1988). "Three views of common knowledge." In Vardi, M. Y. (ed.), *Theoretical Aspects of Reasoning about Knowledge*. Los Altos, CA: Morgan Kaufman.

Basu, K. (1990). "On the non-existence of a rationality definition for extensive games." *International Journal of Game Theory*, 19: 33–44.

(1995). "A paradox of knowledge and some related observations." Mimeo, Cornell University.

Battigalli, P. and Bonanno, G. (1995). "The logic of belief persistency." Mimeo, University of California, Davis.

Ben-Porath, E. (1994). "Rationality, Nash equilibrium and backwards induction in perfect information games." Mimeo, Tel Aviv University.

Bernheim, D. B. (1984). "Rationalizable strategic behavior." *Econometrica*, 52: 1007–28.

Bhattacharyya, S. and Lipman, B. L. (1995). "Ex ante versus interim rationality and the existence of bubbles." *Economic Theory*, 6: 469–94.

Bicchieri, C. (1988). "Strategic behavior and counterfactuals." *Synthese*, 76: 135–69.

(1989). "Self-refuting theories of strategic interaction: a paradox of common knowledge." *Erkenntnis*, 30: 69–85.

Binmore, K. G. (1984). "Equilibria in extensive games." *Economic Journal*, 95: 51–9.

(1987–8). "Modeling rational players I and II." *Economics and Philosophy*, 3 and 4: 179–214 and 9–55.

Binmore, K.G. and Brandenburger, A. (1990). "Common knowledge and game theory." In Binmore, K. G. (ed.), *Essays on the Foundations of Game Theory*. Cambridge, MA: Blackwell, chapter 4.

Blume, L., Brandenburger, A., and Dekel, E. (1986). "Lexicographic probabilities and choice under uncertainty." *Econometrica*, 59: 61–79.

(1986). "Lexicographic probabilities and equilibrium refinements." *Econometrica*, 59: 81–98.

Böge, W. and Eisele, Th. (1979). "On solutions of Bayesian games." *International Journal of Game Theory*, 8: 193–215.

Bonanno, G. (1991). "The logic of rational play in games of perfect information." *Economics and Philosophy*, 7: 37–65.

(1993). "Information partitions and the logic of knowledge and common knowledge." Mimeo, University of California, Davis.

(1995). "On the logic of common belief." Mimeo, University of California, Davis.

Bonnano, G. and Nehring, K. (1995). "Intersubjective consistency of beliefs and the logic of common belief." Mimeo, University of California, Davis.

(1994). "Weak dominance and approximate-common knowledge." *Journal of Economic Theory*, 4: 265–76.

Börges, T. and Samuelson, L. (1992). "Cautious utility maximization and iterated weak dominance." *International Journal of Game Theory*, 21: 13–25.

Brandenburger, A. (1992). "Knowledge and equilibrium in games." *Journal of Economic Perspectives*, 6: 83–101.

Brandenburger, A. and Dekel, E. (1987a). "Rationalizability and correlated equilibria." *Econometrica*, 55: 1391–402.

(1987b). "Common knowledge with probability 1." *Journal of Mathematical Economics*, 16: 237–45.

(1989). "The role of common knowledge assumptions in game theory." In. Hahn, R. (ed.), *The Economics of Missing Marketes, Information and Games*. Oxford: Oxford University Press.

(1993). "Hierarchies of beliefs and common knowledge." *Journal of Economic Theory*, 59: 189–98.

Brandenburger, A., Dekel, E., and Geanakoplos, J. (1992). "Correlated equilibrium with generalized information structures." *Games and Economic Behavior*, 4: 182–201.

Campbell, R. and Sowden, L. (1985). *Paradoxes of Rationality and Cooperation: Prisoner's Dilemma and Newcombe's Problem*. Vancouver, British Columbia: University of British Columbia Press.

Canning, D. (1992). "Rationality, computability, and Nash equilibrium." *Econometrica*, 60: 877–88.

Carlsson, H. and van Damme, E. (1993). "Global games and equilibrium selections." *Econometrica*, 61: 989–1018.

Chellas, B. F. (1980). *Modal Logic: An Introduction*. Cambridge: Cambridge University Press.

Cotter, K. (1991). "Correlated equilibrium with type-dependent strategies." *Journal of Economic Theory*, 54: 48–68.

Cubitt, R. (1989). "Refinements of Nash equilibrium: a critique." *Theory and Decision*, 26: 107–31.

Dekel, E. and Fudenberg, D. (1990). "Rational behavior with payoff uncertainty." *Journal of Economic Theory*, 52: 243–67.

Dekel, E., Lipman, B., and Rustichini, A. (1996). "Possibility correspondences preclude unawareness." Mimeo, Northwestern University.

Engl, G. (1994). "Lower hemicontinuity of the Nash equilibrium correspondence." Mimeo, University of California, Irvine.

Fagin, R., Geanakoplos, J., Halpern, J., and Vardi, M. (1993). "The expressive power of the hierarchical approach to modeling knowledge and common knowledge." Mimeo, IBM Almaden Research Center.

Fagin, R. and Halpern, J. (1988). "Belief, awareness, and limited reasoning." *Artificial Intelligence*, 34: 39–76.

Fagin, R., Halpern, J. Y., Moses, Y., and Vardi, M. Y. (1995). *Reasoning About Knowledge*. Cambridge, MA: MIT Press.

Fagin, R., Halpern, J., and Vardi, M. (1991). "A model-theoretic analysis of knowledge." *Journal of the Association for Computing Machinery*, 38: 382–428.

Forges, F. (1992). "Five legitimate definitions of correlated equilibrium in games with incomplete information." Working Paper No. 383, Ecole Polytechnique.

Fudenberg, D., Kreps, D. M., and Levine, D. (1988). "On the robustness of equilibrium refinements." *Journal of Economic Theory*, 44: 354–80.

Fudenberg, D. and Tirole, J. (1991). *Game Theory*. Cambridge, MA: MIT Press.

Geanakoplos, J. (1989). "Game theory without partitions, and applications to speculation and consensus." Mimeo, Cowles Foundation for Research in Economics at Yale University.

(1993). "Common knowledge." *Journal of Economic Perspectives*, 6: 53–82.

Gilboa, I. (1988). "Information and meta information." In Halpern, J. Y. (ed.), pp. 227–43.

Gul, F. (1995a). "A comment on Aumann's Bayesian view." Forthcoming *Econometrica*.

(1995b). "Rationality and coherent theories of strategic behavior." Forthcoming *Journal of Economic Theory*.

Halpern, J. Y. (ed.) (1988). *Theoretical Aspects of Reasoning about Knowledge*. Los Altos, CA: Morgan Kaufman Publishers.

Halpern, J. Y. and Moses, Y. M. (1990). "Knowledge and common knowledge in a distributed environment." *Journal of the Association of Computing Machinery*, 51: 549–87.

(1992). "A guide to completeness and complexity for modal logics of knowledge and belief." *Artificial Intelligence*, 54: 319–79.

Harsanyi, J. (1967). "Games with incomplete information played by 'Bayesian' players, parts I–III." *Management Science*, 14: 159–82, 320–34, 486–502.

Hart, S., Heifetz, A. and Samet, D. (1995). " 'Knowing whether', 'knowing that', and the cardinality of state spaces." Forthcoming *Journal of Economic Theory*.

Heifetz, A. (1993). "The Bayesian formulations of incomplete information – the non-compact case." *International Journal of Game Theory*, 21: 329–38.

(1995a). "Non-well-founded type spaces." Mimeo, Tel Aviv University.

(1995b). "Infinitary S5-epistemic logic." Mimeo, Tel Aviv University.

(1995c). "How canonical is the canonical model? A comment on Aumann's interactive epistemology." Discussion Paper No. 9528, CORE.

Heifetz, A. and Samet, D. (1995). "Universal partition spaces." Mimeo, Tel Aviv University.

Kajii, A. and Morris, S. (1994a). "Payoff continuity in incomplete information games." CARESS Working Paper No. 94-17, University of Pennsylvania.

(1994b). "Common p-belief: the general case." CARESS Working Paper No. 94-15.

(1995). "The robustness of equilibria to incomplete information." CARESS Working Paper No. 95-18.

Kaneko, M. (1987). "Structural common knowledge and factual common knowledge." RUEE Working Paper No. 87-27.

Kohlberg, E. and Mertens, J.-F. (1985). "On the strategic stability of equilibria." *Econometrica*, 54: 1003–38.

Lamarre, P. and Shoham, Y. (1994). "Knowledge, certainty, belief and conditionalisation." Mimeo, IRIN, Université de Nantes.

Lipman, B. L. (1994). "A note on the implications of common knowledge of rationality." *Games and Economic Behavior*, 6: 114–29.

(1995a). "Decision theory with logical omniscience: toward an axiomatic framework for bounded rationality." Mimeo, University of Western Ontario.

(1995b). "Information processing and bounded rationality: a survey." *Canadian Journal of Economics*, 28: 42–67.

Lismont, L. and Mongin, P. (1993). "Belief closure: a semantics for modal propositional logic." CORE Discussion Paper No. 9339.

(1994a). "On the logic of common belief and common knowledge." *Theory and Decision*, 37: 75–106.

(1994b). "A non-minimal but very weak axiomatization of common belief." *Artificial Intelligence*, 70: 363–74.

Maruta, T. (1994). "Information structures on maximal consistent sets." Discussion Paper No. 1090, Northwestern University.

Mertens, J.-F. and Zamir, S. (1985). "Formulation of Bayesian analysis for games with incomplete information." *International Journal of Game Theory*, 14: 1–29.

Milgrom, P. (1981). "An axiomatic characterization of common knowledge." *Econometrica*, 49: 219–22.

Milgrom, P. and Stokey, N. (1982). "Information trade and common knowledge." *Journal of Economic Theory*, 26: 17–27.

Modica, S. and Rustichini, A. (1993). "Unawareness: a formal theory of unforeseen contingencies. Part II." Discussion Paper No. 9404, CORE.

(1994). "Awareness and partitional information structures." *Theory and Decision*, 37: 107–24.

Monderer, D. and Samet, D. (1989). "Approximating common knowledge with common beliefs." *Games and Economic Behavior*, 1: 170–90.

(1990). "Proximity of information in games with incomplete information." Forthcoming *Mathematics of Operations Research*.

Morris, S. (1992). "Dynamic consistency and the value of information." Mimeo, University of Pennsylvania.

(1995). "The common prior assumption in economic theory." *Economics and Philosophy*, 11: 1–27.

(1996). "The logic of belief change: a decision theoretic approach." *Journal of Economic Theory*, 60: 1–23.

Myerson, R. B. (1991). *Game Theory: Analysis of Conflict*. Cambridge, MA: Harvard University Press.

Nielson, L. T. (1984). "Common knowledge, communication and convergence of beliefs." *Mathematical Social Sciences*, 8: 1–14.

Osborne, M. J. and Rubinstein, A. (1994). *A Course in Game Theory*. Cambridge, MA: MIT Press.

Pearce, D. G. (1982). "*Ex ante* equilibrium; strategic behavior and the problem of perfection." Working Paper, Princeton University.

(1984). "Rationalizable strategic behavior and the problem of perfection." *Econometrica*, 52: 1029–50.

Piccione, M. and Rubinstein, A. (1995). "On the interpretation of decision problems with imperfect recall." Forthcoming *Games and Economic Behavior*.

Reny, P. (1985). "Rationality, common knowledge, and the theory of games." Mimeo, Princeton University.

(1992). "Rationality in extensive-form games." *Journal of Economic Perspectives*, 6: 103–18.

(1993). "Rationality in extensive-form games." *Journal of Economic Theory*, 59: 627–49.

Rosenthal, R. W. (1981). "Games of perfect information, predatory pricing and the chain-store paradox." *Journal of Economic Theory*, 25: 92–100.

Rubinstein, A. (1989). "The electronic mail game: strategic behavior under almost common knowledge." *American Economic Review*, 79: 385–91.

Rubinstein, A. and Wolinsky, A. (1989). "On the logic of 'agreeing to disagree' type results." *Journal of Economic Theory*, 51: 184–93.

Samet, D. (1990). "Ignoring ignorance and agreeing to disagree." *Journal of Economic Theory*, 52: 190–207.

(1993). "Hypothetical knowledge and games with perfect information." Mimeo, Tel Aviv University.

Samuelson, L. (1992). "Dominated strategies and common knowledge." *Games and Economic Behavior*, 4: 284–313.

Savage, L. J. (1954). *The Foundations of Statistics*. New York: Wiley.

Sebenius, J. and Geanakoplos, J. (1983). "Don't bet on it: contingent agreements with asymmetric information." *Journal of the American Statistical Association*, 18: 424–6.

Selten, R. (1975). "Re-examination of the perfectness concept for equilibrium points in extensive games." *International Journal of Game Theory*, 4: 25–55.

Shin, H. S. (1989). "Non-partitional information on dynamic state spaces and the possibility of speculation." Mimeo, University of Michigan.

(1993). "Logical structure of common knowledge." *Journal of Economic Theory*, 60: 1–13.

Stalnaker, R. (1994). "On the evaluation of solution concepts." *Theory and Decision*, 37: 49–73.

Stinchcombe, M. (1988). "Approximate common knowledge." Mimeo, University of California, San Diego.

Stuart, H. (1995). "Common belief of rationality in the finitely repeated prisoners dilemma." Mimeo, Harvard Business School.

Tan, T. C. C. and Werlang, S. R. C. (1984). "On Aumann's notion of common knowledge: an alternative approach." Mimeo, Princeton University.

(1988). "The Bayesian Foundations of solution concepts of games." *Journal of Economic Theory*, 45: 370–91.

Werlang, S. R. C. (1989). "Common knowledge." In Eatwell, J., Murrey, M., and Newman, P. (eds.), *The New Palgrave: A Dictionary of Economics*. New York, NY: W. W. Norton.

CHAPTER 6

Experiments and the economics of individual decision making under risk and uncertainty

John D. Hey

1   INTRODUCTION

Of all the areas of economics into which the experimental approach has spread its increasingly numerous tentacles, that of the economics of individual decision making under risk and uncertainty can probably claim the most productive (and possibly most successful) interaction between theorists and experimentalists. Here, over many years, we have seen a truly scientific approach to the production of economic knowledge. In this chapter I want to rather single mindedly concentrate on this interaction, emphasizing what has been achieved as a consequence, and what remains to be achieved. This single mindedness has its costs in that I will be pursuing my objective in a rather direct fashion, ignoring the many detours and *divertissements* that could be explored *en route*. Fortunately, I can refer those readers who would prefer the scenic route to the splendid survey by Colin Camerer (1995), "Individual decision making," in the recently published and invaluable *Handbook of Experimental Economics* edited by John Kagel and Al Roth. My direct approach will probably also wreak great damage to certain historical facts and figures; for this I can only apologize.

I adopt an historical approach, partly to set things in perspective, but also to emphasize that where we are now depends very heavily on the route we have followed in the past; it is not necessarily a place where we intended to be nor want to be; nor is it necessarily the best place from which to start our future research.

My interpretation of the historical facts, and the basis for the structure of the chapter, is the identification of three phases of theoretical work each followed by experimental investigations of that theoretical work. The first phase relates to *expected value maximization* as the theoretical decision rule;

the publication of Bernoulli (1738) could be regarded as where the "theoretical" phase ended and the "experimental" phase began – this latter ending with the publication von Neuman and Morgenstern (1947) and later Savage (1954) and Anscombe and Aumann (1963). These three publications define the beginning of the second phase of theoretical work, that relating to (*subjective*) *expected utility maximization* as the theoretical decision rule, and the consequent clarification of the treatment of both *risk* and *uncertainty*. The second phase of experimental work was primarily motivated by Allais (1952) and Ellsberg (1961), related to the theories of decision making under *risk* and under *uncertainty* respectively. The third phase of theoretical work began with a trickle (Kahneman and Tversky (1979)) which later (in the 1980s) turned into a torrent too voluminous to detail here, and rather too diverse to capture under the title of *generalized expected utility maximization*. The third phase of experimental work, investigating these "generalizations" of expected utility theory, began in the early 1990s; this will be my main concern. But first I must briefly set the scene by describing the earlier phases.

2   THE FIRST PHASE: EXPECTED VALUE MAXIMIZATION

The start of this phase is lost in historical mists, though Samuelson (1977, p. 38) remarks that "Pascal [1623–62] can be taken as a convenient name for those mathematicians who seem to base behavior decisions on the 'expected value of money (wealth or income).'" The end of this phase can be marked by Bernoulli's (1738) discussion of the "thought experiment" now known as the St Petersburg Paradox. Like the famous Ellsberg "thought experiment," to which we shall shortly turn, this experiment was not actually carried out (indeed there may well be difficulties in so doing) but there seems to be widespread agreement about what would happen if the experiment were to be carried out. Essentially the experiment asks the maximum buying price for a given risky gamble (one which yields £2^i with probability 1/2, for $i = 1, 2, \ldots$), and the generally accepted response is that most (all?) individuals would specify a finite rather than an infinite (which is the expected value of the risky gamble) amount of money as their maximum. If the maximum buying price had been induced appropriately (perhaps by the Becker–Degroot–Marschak mechanism? – see Becker *et al.* (1964)) this would appear to spell the death-knell of expected value maximization. Indeed, in Bernoulli (1738) it spelt also the onset of the labour pains preceding the formal birth of (subjective) expected utility theory.

3 THE SECOND THEORY PHASE: (SUBJECTIVE) EXPECTED UTILITY MAXIMIZATION

Eventually twins were born, their final arrival separated by several years. First on the scene was (von Neuman–Morgenstern) expected utility theory, for decision problems under risk, followed a few years later by (Savage/Anscombe–Aumann) subjective expected utility theory, for decision problems under uncertainty.

3.1 Expected utility theory: decision under risk

I now need some notation. Consider a one-off decision problem in which the decisionmaker is to choose from a set of risky choices, characterized as follows. The generic choice C will lead (after Nature has chosen) to *one* of the final outcomes or consequences $x_1, x_2, \ldots, x_n$. The actual final outcome will be determined stochastically, with x_i being the final outcome with probability $p_i (i = 1, 2, \ldots, n)$. The xs are complete descriptions of all aspects of the final outcomes relevant to the decisionmaker, and, of course, $\sum_{i=1}^{n} p_i = 1$. I will write

$$C \equiv [x_1, p_1; x_2, p_2; \ldots; x_n, p_n]. \tag{1}$$

This decision problem is described as one *under risk* since it is presumed that the probabilities are known and given and understood as such by the decisionmaker. Expected utility theory characterizes the solution to the decision problem as the choice of C which maximizes $U(C)$, given by

$$U(C) = \sum_{i=1}^{i=n} p_i u(x_i), \tag{2}$$

where $u(.)$ is the individual's (von Neuman–Morgenstern) utility function (unique up to a linear transformation). If we number the n outcomes so that x_n is the individual's most preferred outcome and x_1 the least preferred, and if we normalize the utility function so that $u(x_n) = 1$ and $u(x_1) = 0$, then intermediate values of $u(.)$ are determined by ascertaining from our individual the values of the probabilities u_i for which our individual is indifferent between $[x_i, 1]$ and $[x_1, (1 - u_i); x_n, u_i]$. Clearly, from (2), $u(x_i) = u_i$. One key axiom of this theory is that such a (unique) u_i exists for all x_i. Note carefully that there is no presumption, in the case where the x's are monetary amounts, that $u_i = (x_i - x_1)/(x_n - x_1)$, which would need to be the case if decisions were guided by expected value maximization. In this sense then one can say that the theoretical underpinnings of expected utility theory are guided by the "experimental evidence" originating from the St Petersburg Paradox and elsewhere.

A further crucial axiom of expected utility theory, but *not* one suggested by the "experimental evidence" originating from the St Petersburg Paradox, is the *Independence Axiom* (IA)

$$C_1 \sim C_2 \Rightarrow [C_1, p; C_3, (1 - p)] \sim [C_2 p; C_3, (1 - p)]$$
for all p and C_3.

Here $\sim$ denotes indifference. What this axiom asserts is that if an individual is indifferent between two risky choices C_1 and C_2, then that individual should also be indifferent between two mixtures: one that leads to C_1 with probability p and some third choice C_3 with probability $1 - p$, and another which leads to C_2 with probability p and the same third alternative C_3 with probability $1 - p$.

This axiom allows us to argue that the individual is indifferent between C (as described in (1)) and the (compound) lottery

$$[[x_1, (1 - u_1); x_n, u_1], p_1; [x_1, (1 - u_2); x_n, u_2], p_2;$$
$$\ldots; [x_1, (1 - u_n); x_n, u_n]; p_n]$$

and, in turn, the individual is indifferent (using the reduction of compound lotteries axiom, RCLA) between this and the equivalent single stage lottery

$$[x_1, \{p_1(1 - u_1) + p_2(1 - u_2) + \ldots + p_n(1 - u_n)\};$$
$$x_n, \{p_1 u_1 + p_2 u_2 + \ldots + p_n u_n\}]$$

the attractiveness of which amongst all such gambles involving just the worst and best outcomes is determined by the probability of gaining the best outcome

$$p_1 u_1 + p_2 u_2 + \ldots + p_n u_n \equiv p_1 u(x_1) + p_2 u(x_2) + \ldots + p_n u(x_n).$$

Hence the theory. Note crucially where experimental evidence influenced it, and where it did not.

3.2   Subjective expected utility theory: decision under uncertainty

Now consider a decision problem in which probabilities are *not* given. Instead, suppose that outcome x_i results when "state of the world" S_i occurs $(i = 1, 2, \ldots, n)$. Suppose further that the description of the final outcomes (the xs) are complete in themselves and are *not* conditional on which state of the world occurs. If we continue to assume (as we have implicitly done so far) that our decisionmaker has a complete transitive preference ordering over all such uncertain choices, which I now denote by

$$C \equiv [x_1, S_1; x_2, S_2; \ldots; x_n, S_n] \tag{3}$$

then, by adding to our set of axioms, we can infer not only the existence of a (subjective) utility function $u(.)$ over the xs, but also the existence of a subjective probability measure $p(.)$ over the Ss. Denote by $p_i \equiv p(S_i)$ the subjective probability implicitly attached by our decisionmaker to state of the world S_i.

In essence (see Anscombe and Aumann (1963, p. 202)) p_i is such that

$$[u^{-1}(p_i), 1] \sim [u^{-1}(1), S_i; u^{-1}(0), S_i^c], \tag{4}$$

where S_i^c denotes the complement of S_i (that is, if S_i^c happens, S_i does not, and *vice-versa*). In (4) the left-hand choice leads to an outcome which yields utility p_i with certainty, whilst the right-hand choice is our uncertain choice which leads to an outcome which yields utility 1 if state of the world S_i occurs and to an outcome which yields utility 0 if S_i does *not* occur. Applying (1) to (4) (and Anscombe and Aumann extend the axiom set so that one can) immediately gives $p_i = p(S_i)$. Representation (2) continues to specify preference over the set of all C.

Intuitively the crucial axioms are those that lead to a unique (up to a linear transformation) specification of the utility function $u(.)$ over outcomes, *independent of the states of the world*, and the unique specification of the probability measure $p(.)$ over states of the world, *independent of the outcomes*. If such "independence axioms" are violated then (subjective) expected utility theory breaks down, as indeed it does if the other axioms are violated.

4   THE SECOND EXPERIMENTAL PHASE: THE ALLAIS AND ELLSBERG PARADOXES

Fairly soon after the respective birth of the new conventional wisdom, experimental investigations of that wisdom began to appear – motivated by two paradoxes: that of Allais (for decision under risk) and that of Ellsberg (1961) (for decision under uncertainty).

4.1   Allais Paradox and subsequent experimental work

This relates to expected utility theory for decision under risk. The experimental work proceeded on two fronts – the first connected with *testing* and the second with *estimation*. I shall concentrate here on the methods, leaving a detailed survey to Camerer (1995, pp. 620ff.).

4.1.1   Testing

A simple expositional device – the Marschak–Machina triangle (see Machina (1982), for example) – will prove useful in explaining how certain tests were constructed and why. Consider choice problems involving just $(n =)3$ final outcomes: x_1, x_2, and x_3, where outcomes are numbered, as before, so that x_1 is the worst outcome (the least preferred by our decisionmaker), x_2 is in-between in terms of preferences, and x_3 is the best outcome (the most preferred by our decisionmaker). Risky choices yielding one or other of these three outcomes can be completely described by the respective probabilities p_1, p_2, and p_3, or indeed, since these three must sum to unity, by any two of them. Take p_1 and p_3, then the set of all possible risky choices (over x_1, x_2, and x_3) can be represented by the triangle drawn in figure 6.1: each point in this triangle represents some such risky choice. (For example, the point A represents a 50:50 gamble between x_2 and x_3.) An individual's preferences over these risky choices can be represented by his or her indifference map in the triangle. Consider the case when the individual obeys the axioms of expected utility (EU) theory; preferences are represented by (1), and hence indifference curves are given by

$$p_1 u_1 + p_2 u_2 + p_3 u_3 = \text{constant},$$

where $u_i \equiv u(x_i)$. Since $p_1 + p_2 + p_3 = 1$ we can eliminate p_2 from this expression, and, hence, after some manipulation, derive the following expression for an expected utility indifference curve

$$p_3 = \text{constant} + \frac{(u_2 - u_1)}{(u_3 - u_2)} p_1. \tag{5}$$

Three things are immediate from this: first EU indifference curves are *upward sloping* (since $u_3 > u_2 > u_1$ since x_3 is preferred to x_2 which is preferred to x_1); second EU indifference curves are *straight lines*, since (5) is linear in the ps; third, EU indifference curves are *parallel* straight lines, since the slope $(u_2 - u_1)/(u_3 - u_2)$ is constant (recall that x – and hence u – are given and fixed).[1] The last two of these are the implication of the independence axiom, though the second can be derived from a weaker axiom, the *betweenness axiom* (BA)

$$C_1 \sim C_2 \Rightarrow C_1 \sim C_2 \sim [C_1, p; C_2, (1 - p)] \text{ for all } p.$$

Note that the independence axiom implies, but is not implied by, the betweenness axiom. In words, the betweenness axiom states that if an individual does not mind which of two risky choices he or she gets, then equally well the individual does not mind if some random device chooses for him or her.

The importance property that EU indifference curves are parallel straight lines formed the basis for most of the early tests of expected utility theory. Consider figure 6.1: choose any two points C_1 and C_2 (such that the

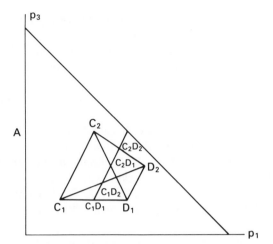

Figure 6.1 The Marschak-Machina triangle

line $C_1 C_2$ is upward sloping);[2] then choose any other two points D_1 and D_2 such that the line $D_1 D_2$ is *parallel* to the line $C_1 C_2$, (and where D_1 is lower than D_2 – as C_1 is lower than C_2). Now ask our individual whether he or she prefers C_1 or C_2; and then whether he or she prefers D_1 or D_2. If our individual behaves in accordance with expected utility theory then either (1) he or she strictly prefers C_1 to C_2 *and* D_1 to D_2; or (2) he or she is indifferent between C_1 and C_2 *and* between D_1 and D_2; or (3) he or she strictly prefers C_2 to C_1 *and* D_2 to D_1.

Most of the early tests took a stated preference of C_1 over C_2 combined with a preference for D_2 over D_1 (or of C_2 over C_1 and of D_1 over D_2) as being inconsistent with (the implications of) EU – though there is a potential problem with possible indifference. Suppose the experimenter allows the individual to express indifference, and *suppose the individual answers honestly*, then there is no problem. But this second supposition raises the hackles of most economists who would rather rely on *providing an incentive* for honest reporting rather than hoping for the best.[3] Consider then the following incentive mechanism (which is the type of mechanism increasingly used in economics experiments, but which was not used in many of the earlier ones): the experimenter tells the individual that *after* expressing a preference over C_1 and C_2, and over D_1 and D_2, the experimenter will pick one of the two pairs (C_1 and C_2) or (D_1 and D_2) at random and play out that choice of that pair which the individual had earlier stated was his or her preferred one. Moreover, if the indifference option is available and is stated by the individual, then the experimenter will choose (by some random mechanism) which of the two will be played out. Suppose our individual is EU and has strict preferences; then he or she will express them accurately for it is in his or her interests so to do.[4] But suppose our individual is EU and is indifferent between C_1 and C_2, and between D_1 and D_2. Then any possible configuration of responses is consistent with the individual acting in his or her own interests – it makes no difference what the answers are. In this case, C_1 with D_2 and C_2 with D_1 is *not* inconsistent with EU.

The argument must now proceed as follows: in such a case of indifference, unless there is some other reason, the individual will choose answers at random, and so the observance of $C_1 D_2$ or $C_2 D_1$ (and indeed $C_1 D_1$ or $C_2 D_2$) will be *equally likely*. Contrariwise, observing either $C_1 D_2$ or $C_2 D_1$ *significantly* more often than the other would be evidence of inconsistency with EU. This kind of argument formed the basis for the early statistical tests of EU.

Of course, if any one individual is asked such a pair of questions on just one occasion, there will be hardly enough observations to provide *any* statistical significance. So typically such pairs of questions were asked of large numbers of individuals and the number answering $C_1 D_2$ was tested against the number answering $C_2 D_1$, at some appropriate level of statistical significance, against the obvious null that the expected numbers were the same. In many experiments, significance was indeed found, with typically $C_1 D_2$ (when configured as in figure 6.1) being observed significantly more often than $C_2 D_1$. The inference drawn from these results was that indifference curves were not parallel, but instead *fanned out* across the triangle. This became known as the *fanning-out hypothesis* – and motivated many of the subsequent generalizations of EU.

Two comments should be made. The first relates to Holt (1986) who argues that subjects might consider the implications of their answers to the *whole* experiment, rather than to individual questions. In the context of the two-pairwise-choice-questions experiment described above, the subject could be regarded as choosing one of the four possible responses (I ignore indifference for the moment to keep things simple)

$$C_1 D_1, C_1 D_2, C_2 D_1, C_2 D_2.$$

The location of these four choices is indicated in figure 6.1. Elementary geometry shows that these four points lie on a straight line (parallel to $C_1 C_2$ and $D_1 D_2$). If the individual's preferences satisfy *betweenness* then *either* $C_1 D_1$ is the most preferred of these four *or* $C_2 D_2$ is the most preferred. Observation of either $C_1 D_2$ or $C_2 D_1$ (subject to the proviso concerning indifference expressed above) is a violation of betweenness and hence (*a fortiori* since independence implies betweenness) of independence and EU.[5] Reintroducing indifference and rerunning the argument above leads us to the same conclusion: significantly greater observations of either $C_1 D_2$ or $C_2 D_1$ implies violation of EU, *but we can no longer conclude anything about fanning out.*

Of course in many experiments, subjects are presented with a reasonably large number of pairwise choice questions (usually in "parallel pairs" as described above). If payment is related to the answers as described above, usually just one pairwise choice is selected for playing out for real. This is partly to save the experimenter money, but mainly so that the experimenter can infer the subjects' preferences over the *individual* questions – as long as the Holt objective described above is not valid. But this remains an empirical question: if confronted with a pairwise choice question, do subjects consider their preferences on each of these individually and in isolation, or do they consider the experiment as a whole and answer accordingly? Of course, if they are EU maximizers their answers will be the same whichever way they think about the experiment, but, if they are not, not. The implication of this is that if their responses are inconsistent with EU, then they cannot be EU subjects; whilst if their answers are consistent with EU, *they may or may not be EU subjects.*

Second, I return to the statistical tests discussed above: EU is deemed violated if, amongst a group of subjects presented with the (C_1, C_2) and (D_1, D_2) pairs, significantly more choose $C_1 D_2$ than $C_2 D_1$, or vice versa. Suppose n_1 subjects choose $C_1 D_2$ and n_2 choose $C_2 D_1$. The null hypothesis is that the $(n_1 + n_2)$ subjects select $C_1 D_2$ or $C_2 D_1$ at random: whether the observed n_1 and n_2 reject this null hypothesis is a standard test based on the binomial distribution. But recall the argument underlying this: it implies that all $(n_1 + n_2)$ subjects are really indifferent between C_1 and C_2 (and between D_1 and D_2) (and, of course, on average an equal number who responded $C_1 C_2$ or $D_1 D_2$). Typically (see, for example, Kahnemann and Tversky (1979)) $n_1 + n_2$ can be as high as 50 percent or more of the subjects (depending upon where in the triangle the pairs are chosen): are we really saying that up to 100 percent of the subjects are indifferent? Is this an amazing coincidence? Or just bad experimental design? Or perhaps it is a wrong interpretation of the subjects' behavior? We shall see.

4.1.2   *Estimation*

An alternative approach to that of experimentally *testing* (the axioms of) EU theory is that of *estimation*. Two routes have been followed – one valid and one invalid. The latter was followed by Allais and involved the elicitation/estimation of the (allegedly von Neuman–Morgenstern) utility function by two different procedures – and then demonstrating that these two functions were different. The first of these two procedures was the genuine procedure described above; the second was not. Let me be specific and let me restrict attention to the case where we wish to elicit the function over monetary outcomes in the range £0 to £1,000. Fix $u(£0) = 0$ and $u(£1,000) = 1$. The genuine procedure for finding the x such that our individual has $u(£x) = 0.5$ is to find the x such that our individual is indifferent between £x for sure and a 50:50 gamble between £0 and £1,000. This can be done in a number of ways: for example, by offering pairwise choices between

$$[£x, 1] \text{ and } [£0, 0.5; £1,000, 0.5]$$

and varying x until indifference is "observed"; or by using the BDM (Becker–Degroot–Marschak) mechanism (the individual is asked to specify a number x; then a number y between 0 and 1,000 is selected at random; if y is bigger than x the individual is paid £y; if y is smaller than x, the gamble [£0, 0.5; £1,000, 0.5] is played out and the subject paid accordingly – see Becker, Degroot, and Marschak (1964)).

The invalid procedure for finding the x such that $u(£x) = 0.5$ is by asking the individual to specify the value of x such that increasing his or her payment from £0 to £x increases his or her happiness by exactly the same amount as increasing it from £x to £1,000. I personally find this question meaningless (and certainly impossible to motivate correctly).

An alternative but valid way of eliciting two (potentially different) utility functions is to use different end-points or to use different chaining procedures; for example to elicit the x with a utility of 0.25 one can either elicit indifference between $[£x, 1]$ and $[£0, 0.75; £1,000, 0.25]$ or elicit indifference between $[£x, 1]$ and $[£0, 0.5; £y, 0.5]$ where y such that $u(£y) = 0.5$ has already been elicited. A number of studies (see Camerer (1995)) have suggested that differently elicited functions are different – which casts doubt on the assumptions of EU which imply that utilities exist *independent of the context*. However, many of these early experimental investigations were not motivated appropriately and statistical tests of significance (between differently induced functions) were not usually carried out – mainly because of the lack of consideration of the possible stochastic specification underlying such tests.

4.2   The Ellsberg Paradox and subsequential experimental work

This was virtually all to do with *testing* (the axioms of) *subjective* expected utility (SEU) theory – particularly those concerned with the existence of a well-defined probability measure over the various states of the world – and was largely motivated by Ellsberg's (1961) Paradox, of which there were two versions: the two-color and the three-color versions. Consider the former: in this the subject is confronted with two urns. Urn 1 contains 50 black and 50 white balls; urn 2 contains 100 balls each of which is either black or white, though the number of each is not known. A choice is defined by an urn and a color; a choice is played out by picking one ball at random from the specified urn; if it is of the specified color the subject gets outcome x_2; if it is not, the subject gets outcome x_1; as before x_1 and x_2 are picked by the experimenter so that x_2 is preferred by the subject to x_1. In financially motivated experiments x_2 is usually some money prize while x_1 is a consolation prize.

Ellsberg's conjecture was that many people would be indifferent between 1W and 1B, indifferent between 2W and 2B, but would *strictly* prefer either 1W or 1B to either of 2W and 2B. He did not actually carry out any experimental tests of this conjecture (though others subsequently have) so he did not indicate how such preferences could accurately be elicited, but his conjecture has commanded widespread approval (and was indeed confirmed by the subsequent experiments). It is rather damaging for subjective expected utility theory since it denies the existence of subjective probabilities (which sum to one) for urn 2. Examples of experiments replicating the Ellsberg Paradox can be found in Becker and Brownson (1964), Slovic and Tversky (1974), MacCrimmon and Larsson (1979), Einhorn and Hogarth (1986), Kahn and Sarin (1988), and Curley and Yates (1989). A more complete list can be found in Camerer and Weber (1992).

5   THE THIRD THEORY PHASE: GENERALIZED EXPECTED UTILITY MAXIMIZATION

This proceeded on two fronts: one responding to the Allais Paradox and subsequent experiments: the second responding to the Ellsberg Paradox and subsequent experiments. However, in some respects, these developments have overlapped and partially converged since many of the responses to the Ellsberg Paradox adopted a modeling stance in which uncertainty was characterized through risk. This is all rather odd – though perhaps the inevitable response to the practical problems involved with the experimental implementation of the Ellsberg Paradox.

5.1   On risk

The set of theories of decision making under risk provoked by the experimental evidence arising out of the Allais Paradox is large: a partial list, in alphabetical order, includes: Allais' 1952 theory (Allais (1952)), anticipated utility theory (Quiggin (1982)), cumulative prospect theory (Tversky and Kahneman (1992)), disappointment theory (Loomes and

Sugden (1986) and Bell (1985)), disappointment aversion theory (Gul (1991)), implicit expected (or linear) utility theory (Dekel (1986)), implicit rank-linear utility theory (Chew and Epstein (1989)), implicit weighted utility theory (Chew and Epstein (1989)), lottery dependent EU theory (Becker and Sarin (1987)), Machina's generalized EU theory (Machina (1982)), perspective theory (Ford (1987)), prospect theory (Kahneman and Tversky (1979)), prospective reference theory (Viscusi (1989)), quadratic utility theory (Chew, Epstein, and Segal (1991)), rank dependent expected (or linear) utility theory (Chew, Karni, and Safra (1987)), regret theory (Loomes and Sugden (1982) and (1987)), SSB theory (Fishburn (1984)), weighted EU theory (Chew (1983) and Dekel (1986)), Yaari's dual theory (Yaari (1987)). Some are special cases of others; most are generalizations of EU theory. Some (including others not mentioned here) are now forgotten – consigned to the waste paper basket of academia; others have yet to become known. Some were specifically designed to explain observed behaviors; others seem to have been merely designed for intellectual amusement; all display the great ingenuity of the economist's mind.

I shall confine myself to a subset of these theories, a subset I am tempted to call the *useful* theories amongst those listed. All try to explain the Allais Paradox and associated empirical evidence; some try to explain it as *parsimoniously* as possible – though what precisely this might mean is not clear; others try and explain it as reasonably as possible – perhaps using some psychological theory; others try and explain it as elegantly as possible.

Let me give some illustrations. I begin with axiomatically based theories, and with the apparent observation that the independence axiom is violated (since the experimental evidence does not seem consistent with parallel straight line indifference curves). An obvious response is either to weaken the independence axiom or to drop it entirely. If one follows the latter route, one gets implicit expected (or linear) utility theory in which only between-ness (in addition to completeness and transitivity) holds. In this theory, all that one can say is that the indifference curves in the Marschak–Machina triangles are straight lines; the only testable implication therefore, is that of betweenness (linearity). Somewhat stronger predictions are given by theories which weaken the independence axiom somewhat but do not completely drop it. Different weakenings are provided by weighted EU theory and by disappointment aversion theory; in the former, the indifference curves in the Marschak–Machina triangle fan out linearly from a point to the south-west of the origin of the triangle; in the latter, they fan out in the bottom right of the triangle and fan in in the upper left of the triangle. However, this description omits cross-triangle restrictions, which, in these cases, make substantial differences: weighted EU requires $(n - 2)$ extra parameters (where n is the number of outcomes) whereas disappointment aversion requires just one extra parameter. On the criterion[6] of the number of extra parameters needed, one could say that disappointment aversion theory is much more parsimonious than weighted EU theory.

An equally parsimonious generalization of EU theory, and again one motivated by (at least some of) the experimental evidence is that provided by perspective reference theory: this specifies that choice is determined by the maximization of a weighted average of the expected utility using the correct probability weights and the expected utility using equal probability weights for the non-null outcomes. The extra parameter is the weight parameter. The implication of this theory is that indifference curves in the triangle are linear *within the triangle,* but display discontinuities at the boundaries (where at least one of the outcomes becomes null).

A subset of theories start from an attempt at a psychological explanation of Allais Paradox phenomena; one of the earliest was prospect theory, which has been partially superseded by cumulative prospect theory, perhaps partly because it "is difficult to test because it has many more degrees of freedom . . . than any other theory" (Camerer (1989, p. 74)). This raises an important general issue, to which I shall return later. Two somewhat more parsimonious psychologically based theories are regret theory and disappointment theory (a precursor of, and generalization of disappointment aversion theory) – both out of the same stables. Both incorporate *ex ante* consideration of *ex post* psychological feelings: of regret, or rejoicing, concerning what has happened compared with what would have happened if the individual had chosen differently, in regret theory; and of disappointment, or delight, concerning what has happened compared with what the individual expected to happen, in disappointment theory. Whilst disappointment theory is like all the other theories listed above (except SSB theory) in that it is a *holistic* theory, regret theory (and SSB theory) is *not,* in that it is a theory of choice from a pair. It therefore does not necessarily lead to transitive choice patterns; nor indeed to the existence of indifference curves in the triangle (though they do exist when choices are played out independently – moreover, in this case, they look the same as in weighted EU theory, though the cross-triangle restrictions are not the same).

One very elegant theory which starts neither from axioms nor from psychological considerations is Machina's generalized EU theory. This simply starts from the assumption that there exists a complete transitive preference ordering $V(.)$ over the set of all C which is *differentiable* in a particular sense. (Whether differentiability is a desirable economic property is another issue.) Moreover, to add testability to the theory, that is to impose some structure on the indifference map in the Marschak–Machina triangle, the following restrictions on $V(.)$ are imposed – restrictions that are directly derived from the experimental evidence: first, that stochastically dominating choices are preferred to stochastically dominated choices; second, that the individual behaves in a more risk-averse fashion with respect to stochastically dominating choices than with respect to stochastically dominated gambles. The first of these restrictions implies that indifference curves in the triangle slope up; the second that they *fan out* (not necessarily linearly) across the triangle. There is an obvious testable implication here: indifference curves should get steeper as one moves to better parts of the triangle. Note, however, that it does not appear to be particularly strong (though Machina might claim otherwise).

One final very important class of theories comes under the heading of rank dependent EU theory (with generalization to implicit rank linear theory) of which special cases are anticipated utility and Yaari's dual model. This class of theories builds on an interpretation of the experimental evidence (perhaps first proposed by Kahnemann and Tversky (1979)) that subjects misperceive (or manipulate or transform in some way) supposedly objective probabilities. Early work in this area (including that of Kahnemann and Tversky (1979) and Handa (1977)) presumed that the raw probabilities themselves were transformed. It was soon pointed out that, in this case, violations of dominance should be observed – or, at least, observed much more frequently than appeared to be the case. This observation led to the new class of theories in which decumulative probabilities were transformed. Consider again (2) and rewrite it[7] as

$$U(C) = \sum_{i=1}^{i=n} \left(\sum_{j=i}^{j=n} p_j \right) [u(x_i) - u(x_{i-1})]. \tag{6}$$

Recall that x_1 is the worst outcome, x_2 the second worst, and so on.

Equation (6) expresses expected utility as $u(x_1)$, plus $[u(x_2) - u(x_1)]$ times the probability of getting at least x_2, plus $[u(x_3) - u(x_2)]$ times the probability of getting at least $x_3,\ldots$, plus $[u(x_n) - u(x_{n-1})]$ times the probability of getting (at least) x_n.

Now suppose the individuals distort the decumulative probabilities – the $\Sigma_{j=1}^n p_j$ – the probability of getting at least x_i. Instead of using the "correct" probabilities $\Sigma_{j=1}^n p_j$, they use $w(\Sigma_{j=i}^n p_j)$

$$U(C) = \sum_{i=1}^{i=n} w \left(\sum_{j=i}^{j=n} p_j \right) [u(x_i) - u(x_{i-1})], \tag{7}$$

where $w(.)$ is some *weighting function*. Impose the "natural restrictions": $w(0) = 0$, $w(1) = 1$ and $w(.)$ increasing, perhaps strictly, and we get rank dependent EU theory.

The immediate implication of this class of theories is that indifference curves in the triangle are no longer linear – since (7) is not linear in the p_i – and their precise shape depends upon the properties of $w(.)$. We can, however, show that, in general, the indifference curves are parallel along the hypotenuse ($p_2 = 0$), and get flatter as one moves *up* the vertical axis ($p_1 = 0$) and as one moves *rightwards* along the horizontal axis ($p_3 = 0$).

This completes my brief overview of the new theories. What is important for my story is that different theories have different implications for the shape (and perhaps the existence) of indifference curves in the Marschak–Machina triangle (and for cross-triangle restrictions) and that different theories differ in their degrees of parsimony. If we exclude Prospect theory,[8] we have a very simple structure: EU is a generalization of EV (expected value theory) and all the other theories are generalizations of EU. Being generalizations of EU they are bound to "explain" at least as much empirical evidence as EU. But explanatory power in itself is not particularly important – the "theory" which says that the individual chooses anything "explains" everything. Indeed predictive power, or what we might call parsimony, is also important. I will turn to that shortly.

5.2   On uncertainty

A fuller overview of recent work in this area can be found in Camerer and Weber (1992). What is particularly revealing is how recent theorizing has been informed by earlier experiments. One key branch starts from the experimental observation that subjective probabilities which are *additive* (in particular, adding to one over the entire set of states of the world) cannot exist. This branch responds by building a theory of expected utility behavior (called Choquet EU) which uses *non-additive probabilities*. This may seem perverse,[9] but becomes understandable when the expected utility formula (for a situation of risk) is written as in (6) above. Based on this write our rule for decision under uncertainty as

$$U(C) = \sum_{i=1}^{i=n} w\left(\bigcup_{j=i}^{j=n} S_j\right) [u(x_i) - u(x_{i-1})], \tag{8}$$

where $w(S)$ is the "weight" or "non-additive probability" attached to state of the world S. It is clear from (8) that there is no presumption that $\sum_{i=1}^{n} w(S_i) = 1$; moreover, since

$$w\left(\bigcup_{j=1}^{j=n} S_j\right) = 1$$

must be the case, it is immediate from (8) that if $C = [x, S_1; x, S_2; \dots; x, S_n]$ then

$$U(C) = u(x)$$

as one would hope. (That is, the utility of an "uncertain" choice which always leads to outcome x is simply the utility of x itself.)

A second branch of the theoretical literature responding to the Ellsberg Paradox begins with considerations of the actual implementation of the Ellsberg experiment: in particular, the practical construction of urn 2 (the urn of unknown composition). Suppose one were to try and carry out the Ellsberg experiment, and suppose you wanted your subjects to be fully informed as to the task they faced. Suppose further one subject were to ask you: "how was the composition of urn 2 determined?" or "how will the composition of urn 2 be determined?" How would you answer? Obviously there are a number of possible responses, but the most natural, and perhaps apparently fairest, would be to use some kind of randomizing device – for example to pick a number at random from a discrete uniform distribution over the range 0 to 100, and use that to determine the composition.

Such considerations lead naturally to the characterization of urn 2 in terms of a *second order probability distribution* (to use Camerer and Weber's (1992) phrase), and indeed many of the new "explanations" of the Ellsberg Paradox use such a characterization – which is, in a sense, odd, as it tries to characterize uncertainty through risk. Of course, if subjects are EU, this characterization does *not* lead to an explanation. More specifically, if subjects obey the RCLA (the reduction of compound lotteries axiom) again we do not get an explanation. We need an alternative view as to how subjects process multi-stage lotteries: one such view is Segal's *Certainty Equivalent* story (Segal (1990)). This, combined with some non-EU story at the single-stages, provides an explanation. In brief, it works as follows: consider how an individual processes (and hence compares) several different *multi-stage* risky choices. On way to process a multi-stage gamble is simply to reduce it to the equivalent single-stage gamble – and use one of the theories of decision making under risk to evaluate it. An alternative is to apply a form of backward induction: consider the final stage – of which there will be a number of alternatives depending on the resolution of the earlier stages. Take each of the various possible final stage gambles and reduce each to a *certainty equivalent* – by using the appropriate decision rule. Then replace each of the final-stage gambles by the respective certainty equivalent and carry out the same procedure on the penultimate stage – and continue working backwards until one reaches the first stage. Evaluate this in the same fashion. This gives a certainty equivalent for the entire multi-stage gamble. Of course, if the "appropriate decision rule" is EU, then the certainty equivalent of the multi-stage gamble obtained in this fashion will be *precisely the same* as the certainty equivalent of the single-stage gamble obtained by the usual rules of reduction from the multi-stage gamble. But if the decision rule is *not* EU, then these two certainty equivalents will (in general) *not* be the same – in which case we will get (in general) different decisions when gambles are presented in a multi-stage format rather than in their equivalent single-stage formulations.[10] This is the essence of Segal's explanation of the Ellsberg Paradox.

There are other formulations which also start from the presumption that individuals, when confronted with the Ellsberg urn problem, think of it as a multi-stage gamble: at the first stage the proportion of p of white balls is determined from some distribution of possible p values; at the second stage a ball is drawn from an urn in which a proportion p are white. Different theories differ in their description of the first-stage distribution of p and in the way that these two-stage gambles are evaluated and processed: for example, there is the maximin theory of Gilboa and Schmeidler (1989) which evaluates the two-stage gamble on the basis of the *least favorable* value of p and which ignores all the other possible values. I do not intend to go into detail here – what is really crucial for my argument is that these theories recast the "uncertain" world of the Ellsberg urn problem in a risky (albeit two-stage) world. After this recasting has been done, the previously discussed theories of decision under risk (as well as other theories) come into play. The "uncertainty" implicit in the Ellsberg urn problem has, once again, been theorized away.

6   THE THIRD EXPERIMENTAL PHASE

Most of the work has been done on the "risk" side; indeed, much of the experimental work on the "uncertainty" side has been done in the framework of a second-order probability characterization, and should therefore be more correctly considered as on the "risk" side.

6.1   On risk

As before, much of the work has been concerned with testing rather than with estimation, though, as we shall see, the two literatures are drawn together through their common concern with the appropriate stochastic specification.

6.1.1   Testing

The key papers are Battalio, Kagel, and Jiranyakul (1990), Camerer (1989 and 1992), Chew and Waller (1986), Conlisk (1989), Harless (1992), Prelec (1990), Sopher and Gigliotti (1990), and Starmer and Sugden (1989). In addition there is the very important paper by Harless and Camerer (1994) which gathers together the results from such earlier papers.

The basic testing procedure in all these papers is essentially the same: to present subjects with n pairwise choice questions in a Marschak–Machina triangle, of the form discussed earlier, with, almost invariably the n lines joining the two choices in each pair in a particular triangle all parallel. In some cases, each pair was constructed so as to have the same expected value – with, consequently, the one nearer the origin being the safer (less risky) one[11] and the one nearer the hypotenuse the riskier one; in such cases, the set of lines joining the two choices in each pair belong to the set of iso-expected-value lines. Very occasionally, for example Camerer (1989), one or more of the pairwise choice questions was repeated – to give some idea of consistency rates by subject; unfortunately, this feature has not been used as much as it might have been (this gives some idea about *error rates*).

Almost invariably the data on preferences generated by these experiments are analyzed *across all subjects*. Two basic procedures are employed. The first, a hangover from earlier work, takes pairs of pairwise choices and tests whether the proportion of subjects choosing the safer option in one of the pairs is significantly different from the proportion of subjects choosing the safer option in the second of the pairs. The underlying null hypothesis is that the proportions are the same, and the test employed is a standard test based on the binomial distribution. This type of test is then repeated for other pairs of pairwise choices – to check whether indifference curves in the triangle are parallel at all points within it. Usually it is concluded that they are not – hence discrediting EU – even though an obviously best generalization does not usually emerge (Camerer (1989), for example, concludes "there are substantial violations of EU, but no single theory can explain the patterns of violations").

A statistician may well object to the above procedure on the grounds that one should take into account that $n(n - 1)/2$ separate tests of significance between each 2 of n different proportions ignores a lot of information that should not be ignored: a better test would be a joint test of the null hypothesis that all n proportions are equal.

An economist would worry more fundamentally about the basis for such a test, which relies on each of the N observations (N being the number of subjects) for each of the two pairs independently being S or R (the Safer or the Riskier choice) with given probabilities (hypothesized to be equal under the null hypothesis). But this null is *not* what EU says: on the contrary EU states that if a subject chooses $S(R)$ in pair 1 he or she should also choose $S(R)$ in pair 2 (ignoring indifference for the moment); so the numbers choosing S and R should be the same if EU is true. Now admit indifference – let $N_S(N_R)$ denote the numbers strictly preferring $S(R)$

in each pair (recall our null is EU), so $N - N_S - N_R$ are the number who are indifferent. Suppose they (the indifferent subjects) answer SS, SR, RS, SS each with probability one quarter. Then the number who say S for the first pair is binomially distributed with mean $N_S + \frac{1}{2}(N_S - N_R)$ and variance $\frac{1}{4}(N - N_S - N_R)$ as is the number who say S for the second pair. Note these two distributions are independent (under the assumption that answers are truly randomly determined). Thus the *difference* in the *proportions* saying S in the two pairs is (approximately) normally distributed with mean 0 and standard deviation $[2(N - N_S - N_R)]^{-\frac{1}{2}}$ – *the value of which is unknown to the experimenter*. The test carried out in these papers is invalid as a test of EU as specified. Instead, the test carried out in these papers requires that the probability that a given subject chooses S in any given pair is constant across pairs. But EU is not a theory of stochastic choice.

The second test procedure is more systematic than the first in that it uses data on all n pairwise choices (within one given triangle) through it ignores cross-triangle restrictions. Given n pairwise choices, and excluding an indifference option, there are 2^n possible sets of answers that a particular subject may give. Typically n is a small number: three in Battalio, Kagel, and Jiranyakul (1990), four in Harless (1992) and Chew and Waller (1986), five in Sopher and Gigliotti (1993); so 2^n is a relatively manageable number – 8, 16, 32, respectively in these examples. Again the analysis is across subjects: data on the number of subjects responding in each of the 2^n possible ways are collated. Each theory permits some of these 2^n possible ways and denies others – though again there are problems with indifference. Consider the n pairwise choice design discussed above (with all n lines being parallel) and consider an EU subject. *Ignoring indifference*, there are just two possible responses out of the 2^n – all S and all R. Again ignoring indifference, different theories give different allowable responses; if they are generalizations of EU – as most theories are – these allowable responses include the EU-allowable responses (all S and all R) but include others as well. One could call a generalization of EU a *relatively parsimonious* generalization if the set of additional allowable responses was relatively small in some sense, though there are alternative characterizations: for example, one could use the number of additional parameters employed by the theory as an indicator of parsimony (the fewer the more parsimonious). On this latter criterion, disappointment aversion theory and prospective reference theory would appear as very parsimonious generalizations of EU – since each requires just one parameter extra to EU. But on the earlier criterion, they may not appear quite so parsimonious.

Indifference, unfortunately, remains a problem – for if indifference is admitted then all 2^n responses are consistent with EU and with all generalizations of EU. But the statistical tests using this approach necessarily ignore this problem – for otherwise we encounter the difficulty discussed earlier with respect to the first approach. The rationale, of course, is that this approach assumes a distribution of "types" across the subject pool – and, in particular, a distribution which has no mass points – so that the probability of encountering a subject who is indifferent is effectively zero (and such a possibility can therefore be ignored). But if indifference is implied by risk neutrality, for example, why should there not be a mass point?

Two tests are now employed: first a test as to whether the proportion of allowable responses (for a particular theory) is significantly higher than if subjects chose one of the 2^n responses at random. Usually, for example, EU passes this test well, with the proportion of subjects responding either all S or all R significantly higher than $1/2^{n-1}$ using, once again, a standard binomial test (as do most other theories). This seems legitimate as a test of the null hypothesis that subjects are choosing randomly against the alternative that they are "favoring" all S and all R.

The second test is one as to whether the distribution of the *non-allowable* responses is random across the set of all possible non-allowable responses. So, for EU, with two allowable responses, there are $2^n - 2$ non-allowable responses, and one can carry out a chi-squared test of the observed distribution of the subjects' responses across these $2^n - 2$ responses, against the null that the distribution is uniform. The chi-square test leads to a P-value (the probability of getting a chi-squared value at least as high as the observed value under the null hypothesis). This P-value is then used by some authors (for example, Harless (1992)) to rank theories (at least relative to the number of allowable responses).

The basis for this test appears obscure: for example, where does EU say that if a subject does not respond with all S or all R then he or she chooses from the remaining $2^n - 2$ *at random*? Perhaps because they are indifferent? But then an equal number (on average) must have responded all S or all R; so, for example, in Harless (1992, p. 403), around 87.6 percent were indifferent in the Gains triangle, 62.6 percent in the Mixed triangle, 66.6 percent in the Losses triangle, and 72.2 percent overall. Is this really what the data are saying?

The difficulty is that the theories, *a fortiori*, have nothing to say about *non-allowable* responses, while too many experimenters have routinely applied statistical tests without due thought for the underlying stochastic structure. All statistical tests require a stochastic specification: it is up to the experimenter to make that explicit. Where does the randomness (underlying the statistical tests) come from? Is it purely from the random behavior of indifferent subjects. Surely not – the magnitude appears too great. Is it from randomness across different subject groups? It cannot be if the subjects remain the same.[12] Then surely it must come from within individual subjects themselves.

This is the path pursued *par excellence* by Harless and Camerer (though it was used earlier by Starmer and Sugden (1989)). Harless and Camerer introduced the rather commonsense assumption that subjects sometimes make mistakes: even though their true preference is for $S(R)$ they sometimes choose $R(S)$ by mistake. More specifically, and in keeping with the notion that these are genuine mistakes, Harless and Camerer assume that such mistakes are made *probabilistically*. Even more specifically, and even more crucially, they assume that in any choice problem a subject expresses the wrong preference with a *constant probability* ε. Later they further assume that ε is constant also across subjects. Consider, for example, an experiment with $(n =)3$ pairwise choices. Again ignoring indifference, EU, for example, has two allowable responses: *SSS* and *RRR*. Harless and Camerer's formulation allows a subject with true preferences *SSS* to express not only the preference *SSS* (with probability $(1 - \varepsilon)^3$) but also the mistaken preferences *RSS, SRS, SSR* (each with probability $(1 - \varepsilon)^2\varepsilon$), *RRS, RSR, SRR* (each with probability $(1 - \varepsilon)\varepsilon^2$) and even *RRR* (with probability ε^3). Note that mistakes are assumed *independently* distributed across the n questions. Similarly, a subject with true preferences *RRR* can express not only the true preference (with probability $(1 - \varepsilon)^3$) but also the mistaken preferences *RRS, RSR, SRR* (each with probability $(1 - \varepsilon)^2\varepsilon$), *RSS, SRS, SSR* (each with probability $(1 - \varepsilon)\varepsilon^2$) and even *SSS* (with probability ε^3). Harless and Camerer now use the observed distribution of subjects' responses (across all eight possible responses) to estimate (using maximum-likelihood techniques) the underlying proportion of subjects with true preferences *RRR*, the underlying proportion of subjects with true preferences *SSS*, and the error probability ε. The estimation procedure also produces a maximized log-likelihood which indicates how well the particular model (in this case EU plus mistakes as specified above) fits the observed data.

This procedure can be repeated for other preference functionals, in each case the estimation procedure produces a maximized log-likelihood showing how well that particular preference functional, *plus Harless and Camerer's model of mistakes*, fits the observed data. Of course, the procedure also produces an estimate of ε, the mistake probability associated with that particular preference functional: the estimate of ε might be used to rank theories.

But a more obvious way to rank theories is through their maximized log-likelihoods. However, it should be recalled that most of the theories being investigated are *generalizations* of EU – their set of allowable responses include the EU set as a proper subset – which means that their maximized log-likelihoods are bound to be at least as large as the maximized EU log-likelihood. One needs to find some way of adjusting the log-likelihoods to make them comparable. Harless and Camerer adopt the Bayesian posterior odds criterion. Let LL_i denote the maximized log-likelihood for model i, and let k_i denote the number of parameters involved in model i. Then the log of the Bayesian posterior odds criterion for model 1 against model 2 is

$$(LL_1 - LL_2) - [(k_1 - k_2)/2]\log(N/2), \tag{9}$$

where N is the sample size. Note that (9) reduces to

$$[LL_1 - (k_1/2)\log(N/2)] - [LL_2 - (k_2/2)\log(N/2)] \tag{10}$$

which indicates correcting the log-likelihood by subtracting $(k/2)\log(N/2)$ from it, thus relatively penalizing relatively unparsimonious theories (at least as judged by the number of parameters involved in its estimation).

An alternative way to proceed (discussed briefly in footnote 14 of Harless and Camerer (1994, p. 1264)), if model 2 is generalization of model 1, is to carry out a tested hypothesis test: model 1 is a special case of model 2 when $(k_2 - k_1)$ of model 2's parameters are restricted in some way. So one could carry out a formal test concerning the validity of these restrictions; under the usual assumptions this leads to the result that $(LL_2 - LL_1)/2$ is $\chi^2(k_2 - k_1)$ under the null hypothesis. Again, relatively unparsimonious models are "punished" for their extra parameters.

The great joy of this Harless and Camerer's method is that results can be aggregated across studies: Harless and Camerer achieve this by expressing the maximized log-likelihoods for particular functionals in the form of a chi-squared statistic of the above form – where model 2 is the particular functional and where "model 1" is the same preference function but with ε constrained to be zero. The resulting chi-squared statistics can be added across studies (if one assumes independence across studies); as indeed can the degrees of freedom.

There remains the problem of trading off goodness of fit (chi-squared) and parsimony. Harless and Camerer (1994, p. 1282) summarize the statistical literature as suggesting a tradeoff which leads to the best model being that for which $\chi^2 - m \times$ (degrees of freedom) is the smallest. However there is no unambiguous guidance as to how m should be chosen.

There may also be some disagreement about the measure of parsimony chosen by Harless and Camerer: this is the *number of patterns that a theory allows* (Harless and Camerer (1994, p. 1259)). This is exactly the same as the number of parameters that need to be estimated to fit that theory to the data (if there are m allowable responses then there are $(m - 1)$ proportions to estimate – the mth being determined from the condition that all m proportions must sum to one – and ε needs to be estimated as well). So in the $n = 3$ EU case discussed above there are two parameters estimated: the proportion of subjects with true preferences SSS (the proportion of subjects with true preferences RRR is one minus this, of course) and the error probability ε. Note well that these are *not* the parameters describing a particular EU functional, but rather the parameters describing the distribution of preferences over some given population. So this approach does not involve the estimation of particular preference functionals. To this I now turn.

6.1.2   Estimation

The literature discussed above, and in particular the Harless and Camerer paper, was effectively addressed to the question: "suppose one has a group of individuals, about which one knows nothing, and suppose one is asked to choose one and only one preference functional to predict the behavior of the group, what should that preference functional be?" Some preference functionals (such as EU and EV) make stronger predictions than more general theories but are wrong more often. The literature discussed above allows us to measure the strength of the predictions and the accuracy of them, and invites us to consider the appropriate tradeoff.

But there is an alternative way to proceed, which starts from the observation that different individuals behave differently, and, in particular, have different preference functionals with different parameters. Some individuals are straight down-the-line EU maximizers; others behave as in regret theory. What is the point in trying to pretend they are all alike?

This line of argument suggests that we consider each subject individually and attempt to identify for each subject that preference functional which "best" explains their behavior.[13] In other words, we take each preference functional in turn and estimate the best-fitting specification for that functional, and then determine which of them is best-fitting in some sense. Let me be specific: suppose we have an experiment involving n final outcomes $x_1, \ldots, x_n$, where, as before, x_1 is the worst and x_n is the best. If, say, we want to find the best-fitting EU functional for a particular subject, then, normalizing as usual with $u(x_1) = 0$ and $u(x_n) = 1$, we need to find the values $u(x_i)$ for $i = 2, \ldots, n-1$ which best explains the subject's behavior in that experiment. Notice that no functional restrictions need to be imposed.[14] Obviously if we wish to estimate $(n-2)$ parameters we need a reasonably large number of observations on the subject's preferences. Two approaches have been followed: first, to give the subject a large number (e.g., 100 in Hey and Orme (1994)) pairwise choice questions, and ask the subject to say which of the two he or she prefers in each pair (motivating the experiment as before); second, to give the subject a largish number (e.g., 44 in Carbone and Hey (1995a and b)) of risky choices and ask the subject to rank them in order from the most preferred to the least preferred (motivating the experiment by telling the subject that after completion of the ranking, two of the choices will be picked at random and the one highest in the subject's ranking will be played our for real).

Estimation of the relevant parameters is usually carried out using maximum-likelihood techniques. This requires some stochastic specification. What I and my collaborators have mostly assumed is that subjects make mistakes when performing tasks in experiments: in particular, we have generally[15] assumed that when evaluating a risky choice, the evaluation is subject to an additive error which is i.i.d. $N(0, \sigma^2)$. Note crucially we have assumed a zero mean (no bias in the evaluation) and a constant variance; this latter, as we shall see, is at odds with Harless and Camerer's assumption.

This stochastic specification gives us a further parameter to estimate – σ, which could be called the magnitude of the error process. In some respects it is analogous to the ε in Harless and Camerer. Note that if the subject makes no mistakes, σ will be estimated to be zero (in which case there may well be identification problems for the other parameters); however, we very rarely encounter such a case.

Maximum-likelihood estimation gives us a maximized likelihood for each preference functional. We can use these to compare the goodness-of-fit for the various functionals. As before, we encounter the problem that different functionals have different numbers of parameters, so again we need to "correct" the log-likelihood for the number of parameters involved in the estimation. We have used the Akaike criterion, but have explored the efficiency of a second in a Monte Carlo study (Carbone and Hey (1994)). Note there that the number of parameters involved in the estimation of a particular preference functional is a completely different concept from that employed by Harless and Camerer. For example, irrespective of the number of questions, there are $(n - 2)$ utility values plus σ to estimate for EU – giving a total of $(n - 1)$ parameters – while with each of disappointment aversion theory or prospective reference theory there is just one more (giving a total of n). So, on our interpretation, these two preference functionals are *very* parsimonious generalizations of EU.[16]

For theories that are *generalizations* of EU, we can use standard likelihood ratio tests to compute whether these generalizations are significantly better than EU (in the sense of testing whether the restrictions on the parameters that reduce the generalizations to EU are rejected at some appropriate significance level). We can also compute corrected log-likelihoods and rank the theories on that basis. The general message that emerges from a series of experiments (Hey and Orme (1994), Carbone and Hey (1995a and 1995b)) is that EU emerges as the "best" for a little under half of the subjects, whilst other theories are better for other subjects. Rank dependent EU theory emerges as a strong contender, along with perspective reference theory and, possibly, regret theory. What has also emerged from Monte Carlo studies (including Carbone and Hey (1994)) is that many of the generalizations of EU "look alike" in the sense that it is difficult to distinguish between them. Perhaps, if this is the case, one should select the theory which is easiest to work with?

7   APPRAISAL AND ASSESSMENT – WHAT ARE WE TRYING TO DO?

One very important finding that emerges from the work of both Harless and Camerer (1994) and Hey and Orme (1994) is the importance of "error": both studies show that errors can be sizable. (This observation should have been made earlier – and probably was in earlier literatures but subsequently ignored: it is often apparent in experiments where subjects are asked to perform the same task on several occasions.) Of course, there are other theories of "error": the stochastic choice with deterministic preferences (through concave indifference curves in the Marschak–Machina triangle) story of Machina (1985), and the stochastic utility theory (of Luce (1958) and others). I have investigated the first (Hey and Carbone (1995)) and found it empirically rather implausible; Loomes and Sugden (1995) are exploring the second, with initially promising results (note that it "explains" the non-violation of stochastic dominance frequently observed in experiments while other stories may not).

However the simple "error" hypothesis is appealing; the only problem is that we do not have a convincing theory of errors (though Smith and Walker (1993) have proposed such a theory). Moreover different economists are using different specifications: note how my (Hey and Orme (1994)) specification differs from that of Harless and Camerer: in particular, I predict a lower probability of making a mistake the further apart are the two choices in a particular pairwise choice. Harless and Camerer do not. But note instead that I assume a constant error variance: further work that I have done (Hey (1995a)) shows that this is clearly not the case. Indeed adopting a heteroscedastic specification improves the fits significantly, so much so that EU with such a specification is often considerably superior to most of the generalization theories combined with a homoscedastic specification. Sadly, this is not the end of the story, since this particular heteroscedastic specification relates the error variance to the time taken by the subject to answer the particular question – but this, in turn, is as yet unexplained.

I suppose I should admit to a prejudice for simple stories: "EU plus noise" is a simpler story than rank dependent EU, for example. Clearly EU has formidable advantages to a theorist: it is very easy to apply (compared with most of the other theories) and often comes up with powerful predictions. The first of these advantages is difficult to quantify, but the second is easier – indeed it has been the concern of much of this chapter.

Nevertheless we are left with a tradeoff between predictive power and explanatory ability. This chapter has shown how we might measure these two components, but it has rather shied away from a discussion of the tradeoff. A solution is proposed by Selten (1991) who suggests using $(r - a)$ as a "measure of the predictive success" of a theory, where r is the percentage of the observations consistent with the theory, and a is the proportion of the entire outcome space consistent with the theory. Harless and Camerer (1994, p. 1258) are not convinced. Note that this kind of measure is naturally suited to the *across subjects* context since one looks at the distribution of actual responses over all possible responses. It is also more naturally suited to the situation discussed at the beginning of section 6.1.2: when one must select one theory to apply to an apparently homogeneous group of individuals.

Unfortunately, and perhaps fatally, it ignores the whole issue of errors, and it counts equally all types of non-allowable responses, irrespective of how close they are to allowable responses. The Harless and Camerer approach allows this closeness to be taken into account, as does the Hey and Orme approach, even if in a somewhat different fashion. They differ fundamentally in other respects, however, with the former approach across all subjects, while the latter is subject specific. A further key difference is in their definitions of parsimony: Harless and Camerer measure this through the number (proportion) of allowable responses – effectively Selten's a; Hey and Orme measure this through the number of parameters involved in the preference functional's specification. It is not clear that either is obviously superior: but there is one key practical difficulty with the Harless and Camerer measure: if n (the number of questions) gets at all large, the number of possible responses grows increasingly quickly (32 for $n = 5$; 1,024 for $n = 10$; 32,768 for $n = 15$; 1,048,576 for $n = 20$; 33,554,432 for $n = 25$) and is of course infinite for a potential continuum of questions. Moreover the practical task of identifying and counting the number of allowable responses for particular preference functionals gets increasingly complex as n increases. Indeed the identification of the set of allowable responses is a non-trivial problem in itself. What I have done, and what I am now analyzing, are the data from two experiments which allow the Harless and

Camerer and the Hey and Orme approaches to be fitted to the same set of data. This involves experiments in which there are a sufficiently large number of subjects (so that estimates *across* subjects can be performed), a sufficiently small number of questions[17] (so that the number of allowable responses under each preference functional can be calculated), but a sufficiently large number of questions so that preference functionals can be estimated subject by subject. These are not easily reconcilable objectives – yet I think we have succeeded. Details are given in Hey (1995b). With the data from these experiments we can estimate the Harless and Camerer approach (including their story of error) and we can estimate the Hey and Orme approach (including their model of error) and see which fits best when due allowance is made for the number of parameters to be estimated under each approach. This will give us some idea of which approach is superior.

Nevertheless, it begs an important question: what exactly is it that we are trying to do? Much of the literature seems to be concerned with the question: "what is the best theory of decision making under risk or under uncertainty?" but it is not clear what this question means. There are several different interpretations, but let me concentrate on those that have been implicit (and occasionally explicit) in my discussion above. It really all depends on what you think that economics is trying to do. Sometimes we seem to want to come up with predictions that will apply to an unspecified group of individuals about which we know nothing or very little. This often is the concern of the comparative static exercises that are found in the theoretical literature. So, for example, we have a literature which examines the effect of increases in risk on the behavior of price-taking firms. If the firms can be assumed to be EU-maximizers then we have some strong results. Clearly, it is useful to know whether these results might be applicable to the real world. In this case the Harless and Camerer question is undoubtedly the correct one; if EU emerges strongly then that theoretical literature becomes relevant and useful.

In contrast, we have situations in which one is trying to predict the behavior of a set of individuals about which one knows something. In such cases, we need to discover which is the best model of decision making for that group of individuals – in which case the Hey and Orme question becomes the relevant one. Perhaps it is all a question of "horses for courses"? But we need to be clear on what course we are running.

8   CONCLUSIONS

One fact that emerges from this chapter is that progress in the area of individual decision making under risk and uncertainty has been significant

– mainly because of the strong interaction between theoretical and empirical (essentially experimental) work in this area. Now is possibly the time to take stock and to ask where might we go next.

Perhaps it might be simplest to start from the generally acknowledged fact that not all people behave exactly in accordance with (subjective) expected utility theory all of the time. Moreover it is clear that there is variability in behavior – across subject pools, across individuals, and across time. Does it mean that *some* people do behave in accordance with (S)EU *some of the time*? Or that *no-one* behaves in accordance with (S)EU any of the time?

And why do we want a theory of decision making that is descriptively accurate in some sense? Presumably so we can predict behavior in some contexts. Is that the behavior of some (named) individual? – or of some group of individuals? And might we know anything about such individuals?

It normally seems to be the case that economists like to make fairly general (usually of a comparative static nature) predictions of behavior of an individual or a group of individuals represented by a representative individual. Typically, the economist likes to make some assumption about the objective function of the individual: such as that they are risk neutral, or constant absolute risk averse, or constant relative risk averse, or that they are expected utility maximizers. Normally there is a tradeoff: the more general the assumption made about preferences the less sharply defined will be the predictions. What the literature I have surveyed in this chapter seems to be telling us is that there is another kind of tradeoff: the more general are the assumptions made about the individual's preferences, the more likely we are to be correct in describing their choices. As I have remarked before, the most general assumption (that individuals do anything) describes all behavior. But it is singularly useless – as it has no predictive power.

So we must trade off goodness of fit against parsimony. I have discussed two ways that this might be done. But note the two different contexts. Harless and Camerer are positing: suppose we have a set of individuals and we wish to predict their behavior. We can employ one and only one preference functional to make that prediction. What should that be? Note that this approach does not require estimation of any parameters of any of the preference functionals; what is estimated is the proportions of the subjects having particular true preferences (and their error probability). In contrast what Hey and Orme are positing is the following: suppose we have one (or more) individuals and we can ask a number of preference questions of some form in order to learn something about the individual's tastes; we can then use those answers to try and discover what that individual's true preference functional is. What should that be?

In each instance, we are interested in the answer to the question "what should that be?" and this takes us right back to the issue of the "correct" model of decision making under risk. But note once again the difference of context: Harless and Camerer want one "best model for a whole set of subjects; in contrast, Hey and Orme want a "best" model for each subject. The choice of context must depend on what you think that the theory of *individual* decision making under risk and uncertainty is meant to provide.

Notes

I am grateful to Graham Loomes, Enrica Carbone and Vince Crawford for helpful comments.

1 Note that the more concave is the utility function – that is, the more risk averse is our individual – the steeper are the parallel indifference lines.

2 Tests of the upward-slopingness of EU indifference curves were generally not carried out – it being felt self-evident. But see later.

3 I should remark that there are strong differences of opinion (mainly between psychologists and economists) concerning the necessity for providing appropriate incentives.

4 Abstracting from any consideration of complexity or of decision costs.

5 Note that this argument extends to an experiment (of a type normally used) where subjects are asked *several* pairs of questions of the type just described.

6 But this may not be the appropriate criterion – see later.

7 Where, by convention, $u(x_0) = 0$.

8 And Yaari's dual model, which is the special case of the rank dependent EU theory when the utility function is the identity function ($u(x) = x$ in (7)), but which does not appear to be a particularly good explanation of observed behavior.

9 The initial stumbling block – the apparent paradox that, if probabilities did not sum to 1, then the expected value of a constant was less than that constant – was avoided by the Choquet formulation, described below (see, for example, Gilboa (1987) or Schmeidler (1989)).

10 A further discussion of multi-stage gambles can be found in Machina (1989).

11 In the Rothschild and Stiglitz sense.

12 In some tests, comparisons are made between responses made by different groups of subjects. Here one needs to appeal to some notion of distributions around some *representative* individual.

13 Another "alternative" is to try to estimate the individual's indifference map directly – see, for example Abdellaoui and Munier (1995).

14 Though of course estimation of a particular functional form (for example, the constant absolute risk averse form) could be carried out – and a test could be carried out as to whether the restriction to this particular form significantly worsened the fit.

15 In the complete ranking experiments we have employed an assumption of logistically – rather than normally distributed errors. (They are very close but the former is computationally easier.)

16 In the content of our experiments, it is extremely difficult to apply the Harless and Camerer concept. With all pairwise choice questions there are $2^{100} = 1.2676506 \times 10^{30}$ possible responses, and it is computationally very difficult to compute how many of these are allowable under each theory.
17 Pairwise choice in one experiment and a complete ranking in the second (which was actually carried out at the World Congress in Tokyo).

References

Abdellaoui, M. and Munier, B. (1995). "On the fundamental risk-structure dependence of individual preferences under risk." GRID Working Paper.

Allais, M. (1952). "Fondemonts d'une theórie positive des choix comportant un risque et critique des postulats et axioms de l'ecole Americaine." *Econometrie*, 15: 257–332. (English translation in Allais and Hagen 1979).

Allais, M. Hagen, O. (1979). *Expected Utility Hypothesis and the Allais Paradox.* Reidel.

Anscombe, F. J. and Aumann, R. (1963). "A definition of subjective probability." *Annals of Mathematical Statistics*, 34: 199–205.

Ballinger, T. P. and Wilcox, N. T. (1995). "Decisions, error and heterogeneity." Working Paper, Department of Economics, University of Houston.

Battalio, R. C., Kagel, J. H., and Jiranyakul, K. (1990). "Testing between alternative models of choice under uncertainity: some initial results." *Journal of Risk and Uncertainty*, 3: 25–50.

Becker, G. M., DeGroot, M. H., and Marschak, J. (1964). "Measuring utility by a single-response sequential method." *Behavioral Science*, 9: 226–32.

Becker, J. L. and Sarin, R. (1987). "Lottery dependent utility." *Management Science*, 33: 1367–82.

Becker, S. W. and Brownson, F. O. (1964). "What price ambiguity? Or the role of ambiguity in decision-making." *Journal of Political Economy*, 72: 62–73.

Bell, D. (1985). "Disappointment in decision making under uncertainty." *Operations Research*, 33: 1–27.

Bernasconi, M. and Loomes, G. C. (1992). "Failures of the reduction principle in an Ellsberg-type problem." *Theory and Decision*, 32: 77–100.

Bernoulli, D. (1738). "Specimen theoriae novae de mensura sortis." *Commentarii Academiae Scientiarum Imperialis Petropolitane*, Vol. VII. (English translation by L. Sommer, "Exposition of a new theory on the measurement of risk." *Econometrica*, 1954, 22: 23–36.)

Camerer, C. F. (1989). "An experimental test of several generalized utility theories." *Journal of Risk and Uncertainty*, 2: 61–104.

(1992). "Recent tests of generalizations of EU theories." In Edwards, W. (ed.), *Utility: Theories, Measurement and Applications.* Kluwer.

(1995). "Individual decision making." In Kagel and Roth (1995).

Camerer, C. F. and Weber, M. (1992). "Recent developments in modeling preferences: uncertainty and ambiguity." *Journal of Risk and Uncertainty*, 5: 325–70.

Carbone, E. and Hey, J. D. (1994). "Discriminating between preference functionals:

a preliminary Monte Carlo study." *Journal of Risk and Uncertainty*, 8: 223–42.

(1995a). "Estimation of expected utility and non-expected utility preferences using complete ranking data." In Munier, B. and Machina, M. J. (eds.), *Models and Experiments on Risk and Rationality*. Kluwer.

(1995b). "An investigation into the determination of the error: a comparison of estimates of EU and non-EU preference functionals arising from pairwise choice experiments and complete ranking experiments." *Geneva Papers on Risk and Insurance*, 20: 111–33.

Chew, S. H. (1983). "A generalization of the quasilinear mean with applications to the measurement of income inequality and decision theory resolving the Allais Paradox." *Econometrica*, 51: 1065–92.

Chew, S. H. and Epstein, L. G. (1989). "A unifying approach to axiomatic non-expected utility theories." *Journal of Economic Theory*, 49: 207–40.

Chew, S. H., Epstein, L. G., and Segal, U. (1991). "Mixture symmetry and quadratic utility." *Econometrica*, 59: 139–63.

Chew, S. H., Karni, E., and Safra, Z. (1987). "Risk aversion in the theory of expected utility with rank dependent probabilities." *Journal of Economic Theory*, 42: 370–81.

Chew, S. H. and Waller, W. (1986). "Empirical tests of weighted utility theory." *Journal of Mathematical Psychology*, 30: 55–62.

Conlisk, J. (1989). "Three variants on the Allais example." *American Economic Review*, 70: 392–407.

Curley, S. P. and Yates, F. J. (1989). "An empirical evaluation of descriptive models of ambiguity reactions in choice situations." *Journal of Mathematical Psychology*, 33: 397–427.

Dekel, E. (1986). "An axiomatic characterization of preferences under uncertainty: weakening the independence axiom." *Journal of Economic Theory*, 40: 304–18.

Einhorn, H. J. and Hogarth, R. M. (1986). "Decision making under ambiguity." *Journal of Business*, 59: S225–S250.

Ellsberg, D. (1961). "Risk, ambiguity, and the Savage axioms." *Quarterly Journal of Economics*, 75: 643–69.

Fishburn, P. (1984). "SSB utility theory: an economic perspective." *Mathematical Social Science*, 8: 63–94.

Ford, J. L. (1987). *Economic Choice under Uncertainty: A Perspective Theory Approach*. Edward Elgar.

Gilboa, I. (1987). "Expected utility with purely subjective non-additive probabilities." *Journal of Mathematical Economics*, 16: 65–88.

Gilboa, I. and Schmeidler, D. (1989). "Maximin expected utility with a non-unique prior." *Journal of Mathematical Economics*, 18: 141–53.

Gul, F. (1991). "A theory of disappointment in decision making under uncertainty." *Econometrica*, 59: 667–86.

Handa, J. (1977). "Risk, probabilities and a new theory of cardinal utility." *Journal of Political Economy*, 85: 97–122.

Harless, D. W. (1992). "Predictions about indifference curves inside the unit triangle:

a test of variants of expected utility theory." *Journal of Economic Behavior and Organization*, 18: 391–414.

(1993). "Experimental tests of prospective reference theory." *Economics Letters*, 43: 71–6.

Harless, D. W. and Camerer, C. F. (1994). "The predictive utility of generalized expected utility theories." *Econometrica*, 62: 1251–90.

Hey, J. D. (1995a). "Experimental investigations of errors in decision making under risk." *European Economic Review*, 39: 633–40.

(1995b). "Reconciling Harless and Camerer and Hey and Orme." Paper presented to the AWEE95 Conference in Amsterdam, September 1995.

Hey, J. D. and Carbone, E. (1995). "Stochastic choice with deterministic preferences: an experimental investigation." *Economics Letters*, 47: 161–7.

Hey, J. D. and Orme, C. D. (1994). "Investigating generalisations of expected utility theory using experimental data." *Econometrica*, 62: 1291–326.

Holt, C. A. (1986). "Preference reversals and the independence axiom." *American Economic Review*, 76: 508–15.

Kagel, J. H. and Roth, A. E. (eds.) (1995). *Handbook of Experimental Economics*. Princeton University Press.

Kahn, B. E. and Sarin, R. K. (1988). "Modelling ambiguity in decisions under uncertainty." *Journal of Consumer Research*, 15: 265–72.

Kahneman, D. and Tversky, A. (1979). "Prospect theory: an analysis of decision under risk." *Econometrica*, 47: 263–91.

Loomes, G. C. and Sugden, R. (1982). "Regret theory: an alternative theory of rational choice under uncertainty." *Economic Journal*, 92: 805–24.

(1986). "Disappointment and dynamic consistency in choice under uncertainty." *Review of Economic Studies*, 53: 271–82.

(1987). "Some implications of a more general form of regret theory." *Journal of Economic Theory*, 41: 270–87.

(1995). "Incorporating a stochastic element into decision theory." *European Economic Review*, 39: 641–8.

Luce, R. D. (1958). "A probabilistic theory of utility." *Econometrica*, 26: 193–224.

MacCrimmon, K. R. and Larsson, S. (1979). "Utility theory: axioms versus 'paradoxes'." In Allais and Hagen (1979).

Machina, M. J. (1982). "'Expected utility' analysis without the independence axiom." *Econometrica*, 50: 277–323.

(1985). "Stochastic choice functions generated from deterministic preferences over lotteries." *Economic Journal*, 95: 575–94.

(1989). "Dynamic consistency and non-expected utility models of choice under uncertainty." *Journal of Economic Literature*, 27: 1622–68.

Maffioletti, A. (1995). "Theoretical and experimental investigation of explanations for the Ellsberg Paradox." D.Phil Thesis, University of York.

Prelec, J. (1990). "A 'pseudo-endowment effect and its implications for some recent non-EU models." *Journal of Risk and Uncertainty*, 3: 247–59.

Quiggin, J. (1982). "A theory of anticipated utility." *Journal of Economic Behavior and Organization*, 3: 323–43.

Samuelson, P. A. (1977). "St Petersburg paradoxes: defanged, dissected, and historically described." *Journal of Economic Literature*, 15: 24–55.

Savage, L. J. (1954). *The Foundations of Statistics*. New York: Wiley.

Schmeidler, D. (1989). "Subjective probability and expected utility without additivity." *Econometrica*, 57: 577–87.

Segal, U. (1990). "Two-stage lotteries without the reduction axiom." *Econometrica*, 58: 349–77.

Selten, R. (1991). "Properties of a measure of predictive success." *Mathematical Social Sciences*, 21: 153–200.

Slovic, P. and Tversky, A. (1974). "Who accepts Savage's axiom?" *Behavioral Science*, 19: 368–73.

Smith, V. E. and Walker, J. M. (1993). "Monetary rewards and decision cost in experimental economics." *Economic Inquiry*, 31: 235–61.

Sopher, B. and Gigliotti, G. (1993). "A test of generalized expected utility theory." *Theory and Decision*, 35: 75–106.

Starmer, C. and Sugden, R. (1989). "Probability and juxtaposition effects: an experimental investigation of the common ratio effect." *Journal of Risk and Uncertainty*, 2: 159–78.

Tversky, A. and Kahneman, D. (1992). "Advances in prospect theory: cumulative representation of uncertainty." *Journal of Risk and Uncertainty*, 5: 297–323.

Viscusi, W. K. (1989). "Prospective reference theory: towards a resolution of the paradoxes." *Journal of Risk and Uncertainty*, 2: 235–64.

Von Neuman, John and Morgenstern, Oskar (1947). *Theory of Games and Economic Behaviour*, 2nd edn. Princeton University Press.

Yaari, M. E. (1987). "The dual theory of choice under risk." *Econometerica*, 55; 95–115.

CHAPTER 7

Theory and experiment in the analysis of strategic interaction

Vincent P. Crawford

One cannot, without empirical evidence, deduce what understandings can be perceived in a nonzero-sum game of maneuver any more than one can prove, by purely formal deduction, that a particular joke is bound to be funny.

Thomas Schelling, *The Strategy of Conflict*

1   INTRODUCTION

Much of economics has to do with the coordination of independent decisions, and such questions – with some well-known exceptions – are inherently game theoretic. Yet when the Econometric Society held its First World Congress in 1965, economic theory was still almost entirely non-strategic and game theory remained largely a branch of mathematics, whose applications in economics were the work of a few pioneers. As recently as the early 1970s, the profession's view of game-theoretic modeling was typified by Paul Samuelson's customarily vivid phrase, "the swamp of *n*-person game theory"; and even students to whom the swamp seemed a fascinating place thought carefully before descending from the high ground of perfect competition and monopoly.

The game-theoretic revolution that ensued altered the landscape in ways that would have been difficult to imagine in 1965, adding so much to our understanding that many questions whose strategic aspects once made them seem intractable are now considered fit for textbook treatment. This process was driven by a fruitful dialogue between game theory and economics, in which game theory supplied a rich language for describing strategic interactions and a set of tools for predicting their outcomes, and economics contributed questions and intuitions about strategic behavior against which game theory's methods could be tested and honed. As game-theoretic formulations and analyses enriched economics, economic applications inspired extensions and refinements of game theory's methods, transforming game theory from a branch of mathematics with a primarily normative focus into a powerful tool for positive analysis.

To date this dialogue has consisted mostly of conversations among theorists, with introspection and casual empiricism the main sources of information about behavior. A typical exchange proceeds by modeling an economic environment as a non-cooperative game; identifying its equilibria; selecting among them as necessary using common sense, equilibrium refinements, dynamic arguments, or convenience; comparing the selected equilibrium with stylized facts and intuitions about outcomes; and eliminating discrepancies, as far as possible, by adjusting the model or proposing new selection criteria. The unstated goal of most such analyses has been to predict behavior entirely by theory.

Although this approach has plainly been productive, it has also revealed the limits of what can be learned by theory alone. Theoretical analyses (traditional or adaptive) usually yield definite predictions only under strong assumptions, which are reasonable for some applications but unrealistic and potentially misleading for many others. As a result, most strategic applications raise questions about the principles that govern behavior that are not convincingly resolved by theory, in addition to questions about preferences and the environment like those encountered in non-strategic applications. Further progress in understanding those principles now seems likely to depend as much on systematic observation and careful empirical work as on further advances in theory.

Experiments will play a leading role in this empirical work. Behavior in games is notoriously sensitive to the details of the environment, so that strategic models carry a heavy informational burden, which is often compounded in the field by an inability to observe all relevant variables. Important advances in experimental technique over the past three decades allow a control that often gives experiments a decisive advantage in identifying the relationship between behavior and the environment.[1] There is now a substantial body of experimental work that uses well-motivated subjects and careful designs to address central questions about strategic behavior. I believe this work deserves to be taken seriously. For many questions it is the most important source of empirical information we have, and it is unlikely to be less reliable than casual empiricism or introspection. More generally, I believe that there is much to be gained by supplementing conversations among theorists with a dialogue between theorists and experimentalists, in which theoretical ideas are confronted with observation as well as intuition.

This chapter considers the roles of theory and experiment in the analysis of strategic interaction, with the goal of encouraging and focusing the dialogue that has already begun.[2] I emphasize the benefits to theorists of thinking about experiments, which is both what I know best and the direction in which the dialogue seems most in need of encouragement. My principal goals are to identify the kinds of theory that are useful in interpreting experimental evidence and to draw out the conclusions about behavior the evidence suggests. Accordingly, the discussion is organized along strategic rather than economic lines, even though this cuts across conventional boundaries in the experimental literature; and I favor experiments that seek clear identification of general principles, even when this comes at the expense of realism.[3] This approach makes applications seem more remote, but it exploits the generality of game-theoretic formulations in a way that seems most likely to yield the depth of understanding the analysis of economic models requires.

The experimental evidence suggest that none of the leading theoretical frameworks for analyzing games – traditional non-cooperative game theory, cooperative game theory, evolutionary game theory, and adaptive learning models – gives a fully reliable account of behavior by itself, but that most behavior can be understood in terms of a synthesis of ideas from those frameworks, combined with empirical knowledge in proportions that depend in predictable ways on the environment. In this view theory and experiment have complementary roles, with theory providing a framework within which to gather and interpret the empirical information needed to close the model, in addition to developing its implications, and experiments mapping the boundaries of the environments and aspects of behavior for which theoretical ideas allow adequate predictions, and identifying and observing the aspects of behavior theory does not reliably determine.

The chapter is organized as follows. Section 2 reviews the leading theoretical frameworks and unresolved questions. Section 3 gives an overview of experimental designs. Sections 4–6 discuss experimental evidence, and section 7 is the conclusion.

2   THEORETICAL FRAMEWORKS AND UNRESOLVED QUESTIONS

The leading theoretical frameworks for analyzing behavior in games – traditional non-cooperative and cooperative game theory, evolutionary game theory, and adaptive learning models – reflect different views of how beliefs and/or strategies are determined, each of which has something to contribute to our understanding of experimental results. This section reviews them, emphasizing important aspects that may be unfamiliar and concluding with a discussion of unresolved questions.

In traditional game theory behavior in a game is determined entirely by its *structure*, which consists of its players, the decisions they face and the information they have when making them, how their decisions determine the outcome, and their preferences over outcomes. The structure incorporates any repetition, correlating devices, or opportunities for communication. Some theories allow behavior to be influenced by other factors, such as how the game is presented or the social setting; I call such factors the *context*.

A player's decisions are summarized by a complete contingent plan called a *strategy*, which specifies his decision as a function of his information at each point at which he might need to make one. Players' strategies should be thought of as chosen simultaneously, at the start of play; taken together they determine an outcome in the game.

Something is *mutual knowledge* if all players know it, and *common knowledge* if all players know it, all players know that all players know it, and so on ad infinitum.

The essential difficulty of game theory is that the consequences of players' decisions depend on decisions by others that they cannot observe, and must therefore predict. In all but the simplest games, players typically bear uncertainty about each other's strategies, which I shall call *strategic uncertainty*. To focus on the issues strategic uncertainty raises, I simplify the problem of characterizing individual decisions by adopting the standard assumption that it is mutual knowledge that players are *rational* in the sense that their expectations about each other's strategies can be summarized by probability distributions called *beliefs*, and their preferences over uncertain outcomes can be described by assigning numerical *payoffs* to outcomes so that they maximize expected payoffs, given their beliefs.[4]

Strategic sophistication refers to the extent to which a player's beliefs and behavior reflect his analysis of the environment as a game rather than a decision problem, taking other players' incentives and the structure into account.[5] Like strategic uncertainty it is a multi-dimensional concept, which must be adapted to specific settings as illustrated below.

2.1   Traditional non-cooperative game theory

Traditional non-cooperative game theory is distinguished by the use of Nash's notion of equilibrium to describe players' behavior throughout the analysis. An *equilibrium* is a combination of strategies such that each player's strategy maximizes his expected payoff, given the others'. It reflects self-confirming beliefs in that rational players will choose equilibrium strategies if – and in general only if – they correctly anticipate each other's choices. This result can be formalized as follows, taking a broader, beliefs-based interpretation of equilibrium that is useful. Assume that rationality and the structure are mutual knowledge; that players have a common prior, so that any differences in their beliefs can be traced to differences in information; and that their beliefs are common knowledge. Then any two players' beliefs about a third player's strategy must be the same and these common beliefs, viewed as mixed strategies, must be in equilibrium (Aumann and Brandenburger (1995)).[6] In this *equilibrium in beliefs*, a player's mixed strategy represents other players' beliefs about his realized pure strategy, about which he himself need not be uncertain, and players' beliefs determine their optimal strategies and expected payoffs. (Assuming that each player bears the same uncertainty about his realized pure strategy as other players yields the standard notion of equilibrium in strategies.)

The stated conditions are the weakest sufficient conditions available for games in general. Equilibrium normally requires, in addition to rationality, the assumption that players' beliefs are coordinated on the same outcome. In applications this is either assumed, with beliefs taken as given, or viewed as the result of independent predictions based on a common *coordinating principle*, such as a convention, norm, or focal point; an equilibrium refinement; or a complete theory of equilibrium selection (Harsanyi and Selten (1988)).[7] Thus, traditional equilibrium analysis assumes an extreme form of strategic sophistication, in that players must understand the structure and how their partners will respond well enough to make beliefs or strategies mutual knowledge, eliminating strategic uncertainty. This assumption is appropriate for settings simple or familiar enough that players can predict each other's responses, and it is often helpful in thinking about players' likely responses to entirely new environments. However, it is plainly too strong for many applications. Yet assuming only common knowledge of rationality and the structure, with no restrictions on beliefs, implies only the iterated elimination of strategies that are never weak best replies, which in many games yields no useful restrictions on behavior. To analyze such games one must impose restrictions on beliefs or behavior from other sources.

I call a coordinating principle *structural* if it depends entirely on the structure of the game, and *contextual* if it also depends on the context. A principle is *inductive* if it predicts behavior directly from behavior in analogous games, and *deductive* if it is defined on a more general class of games, and predicts behavior in the current game only indirectly.[8] Traditional game theory usually studies principles that are structural and deductive. However, this is a matter of custom rather than logic, and beliefs can be coordinated equally well by contextual or inductive principles. Such principles often play important roles in experiments because they place more realistic demands on subjects' information and subjects find direct analogies more convincing than abstract arguments.

2.2 Cooperative game theory

Cooperative game theory studies frictionless bargaining among rational players who can make binding agreements about how to play a game. Like non-cooperative game theory, it is structural and assumes an extreme form of strategic sophistication. It differs in three ways: (i) it summarizes the structure by the payoffs players can obtain acting alone or in coalitions, suppressing other aspects; (ii) instead of explicitly modeling players' decisions, it assumes that they reach an efficient agreement; and (iii) it uses simple symmetry or coalition rationality assumptions to characterize how players share the resulting surplus. These features give cooperative game theory a strong comparative advantage in analyzing behavior in environments whose structures cannot be observed or described precisely.

2.3 Evolutionary game theory

Evolutionary game theory studies environments in which games are played repeatedly in populations, analyzing the dynamics of the population strategy frequencies under simple assumptions about how they respond to current expected payoffs. Although evolution presumably has little direct influence on behavior in experiments, evolutionary models are good templates for models of learning dynamics because they have interaction patterns like most experimental designs, they provide a framework for analyzing the effects of how players' roles and strategies are distinguished, and they suggest useful characterizations of the effects of strategic uncertainty. An evolutionary analysis is usually the first step toward understanding the dynamics of subjects' behavior, and combining the appropriate "evolutionary" structure with a realistic characterization of individual learning often yields a model well suited to describing experimental results.

In the simplest evolutionary models, a large population of players repeatedly play a symmetric game. I call the game that is repeated the *stage game* and strategies in the stage game *actions*, reserving "game" and "strategy" for the repeated game. Players are identical but for their actions. Their roles in the stage game are not distinguished, but their actions have a fixed common labeling, which gives meaning to statements like "players *i* and j played the same action" or "player i played the same action in periods s and t." Individual players play only pure actions, with payoffs determined by their own actions and the population action frequencies. This specification allows many of the symmetric interaction patterns studied in economics, including the familiar case of random pairing to play a two-person game (in which the stage game describes the simultaneous interaction of the entire population, with payoffs evaluated before the uncertainty of pairing is resolved).

In biology the law of motion of the population action frequencies is derived, usually with a functional form known as the replicator dynamics, from the assumption that players inherit their actions unchanged from their parents, whose reproduction rates, or *fitnesses*, are proportional to their payoffs (Maynard Smith (1982)). In economics similar dynamics are derived from plausible assumptions about individual adjustment (Schelling (1978, pp. 213–43), Crawford (1989, 1991), Friedman (1991)). The usual goal is to identify the locally stable steady states of the dynamics. A remarkable conclusion emerges: if the dynamics converge, they converge to a steady state in which the actions that persist are optimal in the stage game, given the limiting action frequencies; thus, the limiting frequencies are in Nash equilibrium.[9] Even though players' actions are not rationally chosen – indeed, not even chosen – the population collectively "learns" the equilibrium as its frequencies evolve, with selection doing the work of rationality and strategic sophistication.

In the Intersection and Confrontation examples of Crawford (1991, section 3), a large population of identical players are randomly paired to play games with common action labelings but undistinguished roles. In Intersection two drivers meet on different roads at an intersection and choose simultaneously between actions labeled Go and Stop, with payoffs of 1 if they choose different actions and 0 if they choose the same actions. Evolutionary dynamics converge to a frequency of Go of 1/2 for any initial frequencies between 0 and 1, because Stop's expected payoff exceeds Go's if and only if the frequency of Go exceeds 1/2. This outcome corresponds to the inefficient symmetric mixed-strategy equilibrium. In Confrontation two drivers confront each other on the same road and choose between actions labeled Left and Right, with payoffs of 1 if they choose the same actions and 0 if they choose different actions. The dynamics then converge to one of the frequencies of Right, 0 or 1, that corresponds to an efficient pure-strategy equilibrium; and the frequency 1/2 that corresponds to the symmetric mixed-strategy equilibrium is unstable. In this case then the dynamics exhibit a simple form of history dependence in that the limiting equilibrium is determined by the initial frequencies. This and the more complex forms of history dependence in related models of learning dynamics play important roles in describing the results of some experiments, illustrated in sections 6.1 and 6.3.

An evolutionary analysis can yield different outcomes in these games, even though their structures are identical, because in Intersection, but not in Confrontation, efficient coordination requires that undistinguished players choose actions with different labels. Similar differences in labeling often have substantive consequences in experiments because the labels are the language in which subjects interpret their experience, and in which inductive coordinating principles must sometimes be expressed. As the examples illustrate, evolutionary game theory has a system for modeling the effects of such differences. In Intersection the frequencies of the two efficient pure-strategy equilibria cannot even be represented in the state space used to analyze the dynamics, because the theory models the impossibility of systematic differences in aggregate action frequencies across roles that players cannot distinguish by assuming that undistinguished roles are filled by independent random draws from the same population.[10] This device is easily extended to adaptive learning models with "evolutionary" structures, where it suggests a characterization of the effects of strategic uncertainty whose usefulness is illustrated in section 6.3.

Most discussions of evolutionary games in economics treat them as synonymous with random pairing, but many important applications are better modeled by assuming that the entire population plays a single n-person game. The same methods can be used to analyze the population dynamics in such games, known in biology as *games against the field*.[11] In the simplest such environments, a population of identical players repeatedly plays a symmetric stage game with undistinguished roles, one-dimensional action spaces, and common action labels. Each player's payoffs are determined by his own action and a summary statistic of all players' actions, such as the mean, minimum, or median.

In the Stag Hunt example of Crawford (1991, section 3), n players simultaneously choose between two efforts, 1 and 2. Their efforts yield a total output of $2n$ times the minimum effort, which they share equally; and the unit cost of effort is 1. Thus if all players choose the same effort their output shares more than repay the cost, but if anyone shirks the balance of the others' efforts is wasted. For any n, Stag Hunt has two symmetric pure-strategy equilibria, one in which all choose 2 and one in which all choose 1. Both of these equilibria are steady states. The same conclusions hold for the game in which players are randomly paired from a population of n to play two-person versions of Stag Hunt. Crawford (1991, figure 1) graphs the expected payoffs of efforts 1 and 2 against the population frequency of effort 1 for Stag Hunt with random pairing and against the field. With random pairing both equilibria are evolutionarily stable, and the sets of initial frequencies from which the population converges to them – their *basins of attraction* – are equally large. Against the field, only the "all-1" equilibrium is stable, and its basin of attraction is almost the entire state space; other order statistics make the all-2 equilibrium locally stable, but with a small basin of attraction for order statistics near the minimum.

2.4   Adaptive learning models

Adaptive learning models describe players' beliefs or strategies as the product of learning from experience with analogous games (Crawford (1989, 1991), Fudenberg and Kreps (1993), Marimon (1996)). The learning process is usually modeled as a repeated game, in which the analogies are transparent. The stage game is played either by a small all-inclusive group or in one or more populations, with "evolutionary" interaction patterns. Players' actions and/or roles are distinguished by labels as in evolutionary game theory.

Adaptive learning is "adaptive" in that it need not be consistent with equilibrium in the stage game or the repeated game that describes the entire learning process.[12] Thus it allows for strategic uncertainty, often in arbitrary amounts. Players view actions as the objects of choice, and the dynamics of their choices are described either directly, or indirectly in terms of their beliefs, with actions modeled as best replies.[13] Strategic sophistication is limited, with restrictions on behavior derived from simple, plausible assumptions about players' adjustments or how they model each other's behavior. These range from probabilistic responses to realized payoffs as in the psychological learning literature, which require no strategic sophistication at all (Andreoni and Miller (1995), Roth and Erev (1995)), to models like best-reply dynamics, fictitious play, and more general inertial dynamics, which require that players understand the structure but not other players' decisions (Crawford (1995a), Broseta (1993a), Fudenberg and Kreps (1993)), and, finally, to models in which players have detailed models of other players' decision processes, whose sophistication approaches that assumed in traditional analyses (Stahl and Wilson (1995)).

2.5   Unresolved questions

Well-informed experimental subjects usually exhibit some strategic sophistication, but often not enough to eliminate all strategic uncertainty before they begin to interact. Their beliefs are influenced by various kinds of coordinating principles, often contextual and inductive rather than structural and deductive. When beliefs are not perfectly coordinated at the start, learning typically yields rapid convergence to an equilibrium, in beliefs if not in actions. However, the learning process is frequently history dependent, and strategic uncertainty, strategic sophistication, and the structure of learning rules often exert persistent influences on the outcome. Evolutionary and adaptive learning models, for instance, usually assume no strategic sophistication, but their dynamics do not always eliminate weakly dominated actions (Samuelson (1993)). Thus their predictions may be permanently off if players are sophisticated enough to eliminate such actions at the start.

The extent of strategic sophistication and strategic uncertainty, the coordinating principles that influence subjects' beliefs, and the structure of learning rules all appear to vary with the environment in predictable ways. There is a large body of experimental evidence on these patterns of variation from ultimatum and alternating-offers bargaining games and other dominance-solvable games, in which strategic sophistication is naturally identified with how many rounds of iterated deletion of dominated strategies players' beliefs reflect. There is also a large body of evidence from coordination and simultaneous-offers bargaining games and other games with multiple equilibria that survive iterated deletion of dominated strategies, where equilibrium requires what I shall call *simultaneous* coordination of beliefs and strategic sophistication can take more subtle forms. Sections 4 and 5 discuss evidence from these two kinds of environment that is "static," in that it can be understood without considering how behavior varies with repeated play. Section 6 considers "dynamic" evidence of both kinds.[14]

3   EXPERIMENTAL DESIGNS

This section discusses the designs used in most game experiments in economics. Many studies consider groups of related environments because the variations in behavior across them are often informative (Roth (1995a)). I call each such environment a *treatment*, a session in a treatment a *run*, and a set of related treatments an *experiment* (Roth (1994)).

A successful design must control the environment so that the results can be interpreted as responses to a clearly identified game. A typical design has one or more subject populations repeatedly playing a stage game in an "evolutionary" pattern (section 2.3), with the goal of testing theories of behavior in the stage game. Accordingly, the effects of repeated interaction are minimized by having subjects interact in small groups drawn from "large" populations, with repeated encounters unlikely or impossible; or in "large" groups with small influences on each other's payoffs.[15] Subjects are usually told the outcome after each play, including their current partners' or all subjects' actions. To maintain control, communication and correlation are allowed only as the stage game permits them. The stage game is otherwise free to vary, and can even be a repeated game. This freedom allows a wide range of strategic questions to be posed in tractable ways.

Subjects' unfamiliarity with such environments is overcome by using simple stage games and interaction patterns; explaining them in written instructions and question and answer sessions; and providing enough experience via practice rounds or repeated play to assure meaningful responses and reveal the effects, if any, of learning.

Non-strategic uncertainty is usually kept to a minimum to focus on strategic issues. Control of information is achieved by publicly announcing the structure at the start. The resulting condition, called *public knowledge*, comes as close as possible to inducing common knowledge in the laboratory.

Control over preferences is achieved by paying subjects according to their payoffs. Non-pecuniary effects are usually suppressed by avoiding frames with psychological associations and face-to-face or non-anonymous interactions (Roth (1995a, pp. 79–86)).[16] Subjects' payments are normally linear functions of their game payoffs, with the results analyzed assuming risk neutrality. Sometimes, as in the "binary lottery" procedure of Roth and Malouf (1979), each subject is rewarded with a probability, again a linear function of his payoff, of winning a given amount of money (or the larger of two possible amounts). Under standard assumptions subjects then maximize the probability of winning the prize (or the larger prize), hence are risk neutral in a variable under experimental control.

Departures from these "consensus" designs are noted below only when they are important. Otherwise the designs can be assumed to involve one or more subject populations repeatedly playing a given stage game in an "evolutionary" pattern, with subjects motivated by one of the above methods, and with public knowledge.

4   DOMINANCE AND ITERATED DOMINANCE

This section discusses static evidence on dominance, iterated dominance, and closely related extensive-form refinements such as backward and forward induction. I begin with environments subjects seem to code as "abstract" rather than identifying them with games they are familiar with. I conclude with ultimatum and alternating-offers bargaining games.

4.1   Abstract games

Experiments with abstract games are well suited to studying strategic sophistication because they limit the effects of prior experience. Most work in this area uses variants of two-person games like Stag Hunt or Battle of the Sexes, sometimes with outside options, in normal and/or extensive form. The conclusions are easy to summarize. Subjects avoid weakly or strongly dominated strategies, with frequencies usually greater than 90 percent. However, they rule out the possibility that others play dominated strategies with much lower frequencies, ranging from 20 percent to just over 80 percent; still fewer subjects rely on more than one round of iterated dominance; and the presence of dominated strategies often affects equilibrium selection even though they are rarely played (Beard and Beil (1994), Brandts and Holt (1993b), Cooper et al. (1994), Nagel (1995), Stahl and Wilson (1995), Van Huyck, Battalio, and Beil (1990, 1993)). Overall, subjects display significantly more strategic sophistication than evolutionary and adaptive learning models assume, but much less than is needed to justify many applications of iterated dominance and related refinements in economics.[17]

Beard and Beil (1994) investigated these phenomena more deeply by studying how outcomes vary with payoffs in two-person extensive-form games in which one player has a dominated strategy. They found that subjects' reliance on dominance varies in coherent, plausible ways with changes in the benefits to subjects and their partners, and in the cost a subject imposes on his partner by following the resulting strategy. They also found that experience in different roles made subjects more likely to rely on dominance in predicting the behavior of others in those roles.

In the elegant design of Nagel (1995), subjects simultaneously "guessed" numbers from 0 to 100, with the guess closest to a given fraction, p, of the population mean winning a prize. When $0 < p < 1$ this game has a unique equilibrium, which can be computed by iterated dominance: guesses greater than $100p$ are dominated; when these are eliminated guesses greater than $100p^2$ are dominated; and so on until (in the limit) only 0 remains. On the assumption that subjects ascribe a uniform level of sophistication to others, their initial responses reveal their levels of sophistication: a subject who thinks others guess randomly will guess $50p$; one who thinks other avoid dominated strategies but otherwise guess randomly will guess $50p^2$; and so on. Subjects never played equilibrium strategies; and most made guesses associated with only 1–3 rounds of dominance (see also Stahl (1994)).

Camerer et al. (1993) studied subjects' cognitive processes in a three-period alternating-offers bargaining game with a unique subgame-perfect equilibrium (assuming purely pecuniary payoffs), which is easily computed by backward induction (section 4.2). They used an ingenious computer interface that conceals the total payoffs of agreements in the three periods but allows subjects to look them up costlessly and as often as desired, but only one at a time, while the computer automatically records their look-up patterns.[18] If different cognitive processes yield different look-up patterns, the observed patterns allow direct tests of theories of cognition, along with their behavioral implications. This is an exciting prospect, which should speed progress in understanding strategic behavior.

Camerer *et al.* (1993) argued that backward induction in their game has a characteristic pattern in which: (i) subjects first check the third-period payoff, then the second-period payoff (possibly re-checking the third-period payoff), and finally the first-period payoff; (ii) most transitions are from later to earlier periods; and (iii) the most time is spend checking the second-period payoff.[19] Aware that this is a larger (or at least different) leap of faith than most of us are used to, they remarked, "The reader may object to our characterization of the information search process that is inherent in equilibrium analysis. We are eager to hear alternative characterizations." They also showed that a separate group of subjects, trained in backward induction and rewarded only for correctly computing their subgame-perfect equilibrium offers, came to exhibit just such a pattern.

As in related studies (section 4.2), subjects' behavior was far from subgame-perfect equilibrium. Unlike with backward induction, subjects spent 60–75 percent of their time checking the first-period payoff, 20–30 percent checking the second-period payoff, and only 5–10 percent checking the third-period payoff, with most transitions from earlier to later periods. As expected, subjects who looked more often at the second- and third-period payoffs tended to make, or accept, initial offers closer to the subgame-perfect equilibrium; but there were no other clear correlations between look-up patterns and behavior. Despite Camerer *et al.*'s (1993) success in teaching subjects backward induction, repetition did not alter these patterns. Subjects' focus on the first-period payoff, which determines the set of efficient agreements, suggests a concern for "fairness" of which we will see further evidence below.

4.2   Ultimatum and alternating-offers bargaining

The experimental literature on ultimatum and alternating-offers bargaining games with complete information is perhaps the largest body of evidence on dominance and iterated dominance (Roth (1995b), Camerer and Thaler (1995)). In these games two players, 1 and 2, take turns making offers about how to share a given "pie," with player 1 going first. In the ultimatum game this process stops after player 1's first offer, which player 2 must either accept or reject. Acceptance yields a binding agreement and rejection yields disagreement. In the alternating-offers game the process continues, indefinitely in some variants, until an offer is accepted, which again yields a binding agreement. Rejection forces a delay of one period, which is costly because future agreements yield lower payoffs.

With purely pecuniary payoffs, the ultimatum game has a unique subgame-perfect equilibrium, in which player 1's first offer gives player 2 zero and player 2 accepts, yielding an efficient outcome.[20] The alternating-offers game also has a unique subgame-perfect equilibrium, in which player 1's first offer extracts all of player 2's surplus from accepting, given that player 2's best alternative is to make a counter offer one period later, chosen in the same way. In that equilibrium player 2 accepts, again yielding an efficient outcome.

The experimental results for both games are very different from these predictions. In ultimatum games first offers average 40 percent of the pie. In both games offers are rejected, with frequencies of 14–19 percent, and the frequency of inefficient delays and disagreements averages more than 25% (Forsythe, Kennan, and Sopher (1991, fn. 7, p. 261), Roth (1995b, table 4.5a, p. 293)). In alternating-offers games rejections are followed by "disadvantageous" counter offers that yield less than the rejected offer (and therefore violate dominance when payoffs are purely pecuniary), with frequencies of 65–88 percent (Roth (1995b, table 4.1, p. 265)).

Of particular interest are the parallel ultimatum experiments conducted in four countries by Roth et al. (1991). The results resemble the findings on offers and rejections just summarized, but with player 1s making systematically lower offers in two of the four countries. If the deviations from subgame-perfect equilibrium were due to lack of strategic sophistication, there would be no reason to expect the conditional rejection rates of player 2s to differ systematically across countries, so countries with lower offers should have more disagreements. Roth et al. (1991) found, instead, that rejection rates varied across countries in tandem with offers, so that countries with lower offers did not have more disagreements. In each country the modal offer in the tenth and final period maximized the expected payoffs of player 1s when their beliefs were estimated from that country's rejection rates.[21]

The frequency of rejections and disadvantageous counteroffers in ultimatum and alternating-offers experiments is often taken as evidence that subgame-perfect equilibrium requires too much sophistication to be descriptive, or that subjects' desire to be fair outweighs all strategic considerations. It is clear that subjects do not perceive their payoffs as purely pecuniary, even when these games are framed as abstractly as possible. Although there is some evidence that the required backward induction is too complex to describe behavior in alternating-offers games of more than two periods, the evidence from abstract games (section 4.1) suggests that behavior in ultimatum games is unlikely to be completely unsophisticated. The simplest explanation of the results for ultimatum games one might hope for, then, is one in which player 1s are rational, motivated entirely by pecuniary payoffs, and respond in a strategically sophisticated way to the risk of rejection; and player 2s are rational but trade off pecuniary payoffs against their privately observed costs of accepting "unfair" offers, at a rate that may vary across countries, contexts, and players.

Adding this one plausible "epicycle" to the traditional model yields a parsimonious explanation of much of the evidence from ultimatum games. The behavior of player 1s is approximately consistent with equilibrium in beliefs, when beliefs are estimated from observed rejection rates. And the extended traditional model has the potential to explain other findings in which framing an ultimatum game so that player 1s "earned" the right to their roles, or allowing player 1s to impose an outcome without player 2s consent, moved outcomes closer to the subgame-perfect equilibrium (Roth (1995b)).

In the extended model players' ideas about fairness are treated as exogenous non-pecuniary payoff parameters, whose distributions must be estimated empirically for each new environment, but which appear to vary across environments in stable, predictable ways. The resulting theory is a hybrid of traditional equilibrium analysis and standard econometric methods. Similar hybrids are important in environments discussed below.

5   SIMULTANEOUS COORDINATION

This section consider static evidence from games in which players make some decisions in ignorance of other players' decisions and unaided by dominance. In such games equilibrium requires simultaneous coordination of beliefs, which relies on more detailed mental models of others' decisions and more subtle forms of strategic sophistication.[22] I begin with equilibrium refinements in signaling games. I then consider refinements, norms, and focal points in coordination games and unstructured bargaining games.

5.1   Signaling games

There is a small amount of static evidence on refinements in signaling games. Banks, Camerer, and Porter (1994) used the fact that the leading refinements – sequential equilibrium, the intuitive criterion, divinity, universal divinity, the never-a-weak-best-response criterion, and strategic stability – are nested, in the listed order, to construct a design that allows detailed comparisons of their performance in several games. The results were consistent with some sequential equilibrium for 44–74 percent of the subject pairs in early periods and 46–100 percent in later periods. Each refinement predicted better than its coarser predecessor, up to and including divinity, but with success rates of at most 60 percent.

5.2   Coordination games

The only refinements that discriminate among the multiple strict equilibria in coordination games that have been tested experimentally are Harsanyi and Selten's (1988) notions of risk- and payoff-dominance and the "general theory of equilibrium selection" of which they are a part. Harsanyi and Selten's theory is of particular interest because, although they assume that players' beliefs and strategies converge to an equilibrium before play begins, the mental tâtonnements by which they model players' thought processes (the "tracing procedure" that underlies risk-dominance) are responsive to strategic uncertainty.

Perhaps the most informative tests of these notions to date are the experiments of Van Huyck, Battalio, and Beil (1990, 1991). They studied symmetric coordination games with structures like Stag Hunt, in which players without identified roles choose among seven "efforts," with payoffs determined by their own efforts and order statistics of all players' efforts. Here I focus on five leading treatments: one in which a game like Stag Hunt was played against the field by 14–16 subjects, with the order statistic the population minimum effort; one in which such games were played by 14–16 randomly paired subjects, with new partners each period and the order statistic the current pair's minimum effort; and three in which such a game was played against the field by nine subjects, with the order statistic the population median effort. In each case a player's payoff is highest, other things equal, when his effort equals the order statistic, so that any symmetric combination of efforts is an equilibrium. The equilibria are Pareto-ranked, with all preferring those with higher efforts; the highest-effort equilibrium is the best possible outcome for all.[23] This equilibrium is plainly the "correct" coordinating principle, but the tension between its high payoff and its greater riskiness due to strategic uncertainty kept most subjects from choosing the highest effort.

These designs are well suited to testing structural refinements because they involve actions naturally ordered by their payoff implications and labeled accordingly; and the large action spaces and variety of interaction patterns considered allow particularly powerful tests. Applying Harsanyi and Selten's (1988) theory to the stage games in these five treatments predicts 15–52 percent of subjects' initial efforts (Crawford (1991)). Eliminating the priority they give payoff-dominance, allowing risk-dominance (which embodies most of their ideas about the effects of strategic uncertainty) to determine the predictions in most treatments, yields success rates of 2–52 percent. These results cannot be attributed to the dispersion of subjects' efforts because the theory predicts the modal response in only three of the five treatments (two of five without payoff-dominance). Although there was rapid convergence to equilibrium in four of five treatments, the success rates are no better for last periods: 0–67 percent with and 0–72 percent without payoff-dominance (Crawford (1995a)). Van Huyck, Battalio, and Beil's results are reconsidered from a dynamic point of view in section 6.3.

Contextual principles are also of great importance in coordination.[24] In one of the first game experiments, Schelling (1960, pp. 53–67) solicited hypothetical responses to symmetric coordination games in which two players choose among n commonly labeled actions, receiving payoffs of 1 if they choose actions with the same label and 0 otherwise. He focused on contextual principles by combining these games, in which structural principles have no bite, with real action labels such as Heads or Tails, or locations in New York City. The expected payoff of a player who ignores contextual features is $1/n$, independent of his partner's behavior (Crawford and Haller (1990, p. 580)). If, however, players have privately observed personal predilections for labels, whose population frequencies are publicly known, they can normally do better than this by ignoring their own predilections and choosing the label with the highest frequency. If the population frequencies are not a clear guide, they may seek a salient principle that depends only on public knowledge about the labels – a "focal point," in Schelling's terminology.

Schelling's subjects often exploited their intuitions about how the labels would be used to obtain expected payoffs much greater than $1/n$. Mehta, Starmer, and Sugden (1994) studied this phenomenon in more detail by comparing subjects' action choices when their payoffs did not depend on their own or other subjects' actions with their choices among actions labeled in the same way in coordination games like Schelling's. They interpreted the former choices as personal predilections and the latter as attempts to use the labels to coordinate.

Mehta, Starmer, and Sugden's results for coordination treatments replicated Schelling's, with the frequency of identical choices often several times higher than in the corresponding "personal" treatments. For most sets of labels the population choice frequencies were similarly ordered in both cases, with the popularity of labels in the personal treatment magnified in the coordination treatment, as if subjects were choosing the label with the highest frequency. In some cases the importance of public knowledge was clearly visible. In the personal "Write down any day of the year" treatment, for instance, 88 subjects gave 75 different responses – presumably mostly "personal" days, but led by December 25 at 5.7 percent. In the corresponding coordination treatment 44.4 percent of the subjects chose December 25; 18.9 percent chose December 10, the day of the experiment; and 8.9 percent chose January 1, all days their public knowledge made more salient than any day their knowledge of predilection frequencies could suggest. Overall, the results provide clear evidence of simultaneous strategic sophistication and the importance of contextual coordinating principles.

5.3   Unstructured bargaining

Some of the most important evidence on simultaneous coordination was provided by a series of bargaining experiments by Roth and his collaborators during the late 1970s and early 1980s (Roth (1987b)). These experiments are of particular interest because they left the bargaining process largely unstructured. This comes closer to bargaining in the field, where rules like those in non-cooperative models of bargaining are seldom encountered. It also allows more informative tests of cooperative and non-cooperative theories of bargaining.

Roth's designs employed the binary lottery procedure of Roth and Malouf (1979), in which pairs of subjects bargain over a fixed total of 100 lottery tickets, with each subject's share determining his probability of winning the larger of two possible monetary prizes, specific to him. If subjects could agree on how to share the lottery tickets by an announced deadline the agreement was enforced; otherwise they got zero probabilities. Subjects could make any binding proposal they wished, or accept their partner's latest proposal, at any time. They could also send non-binding messages at any time, except that they could not identify themselves or, in some treatments, reveal their prizes. The environment was public knowledge, except subjects' prizes or information about prizes in some treatments.

The designs exploit invariances created by the binary lottery procedure to test both cooperative and non-cooperative theories of bargaining. Under standard assumptions a player maximizes the expected number of lottery tickets he obtains, so that the number of tickets can be taken as his payoff. Cooperative game theory summarizes the implications of a structure by the payoffs players can obtain acting alone or in coalitions. This makes bargaining over a fixed total of lottery tickets equivalent to a complete-information Divide the Dollar game with risk-neutral players, whose symmetry leads cooperative theories to predict equal division of the lottery tickets. These conclusions are independent of players' risk preferences, prizes, or information about prizes, so that cooperative theories can be tested by observing the effects of varying those factors. Although non-cooperative theories are harder to test this way because their predictions may depend on the details of the structure, the binary lottery procedure also makes it possible to create invariances that allow such tests, as explained below.

Each treatment paired a subject whose prize was low (typically $5) with one whose prize was high (typically $20). A subject always knew his own prize. The first experiment compared two information conditions: "full," in which a subject also knew his partner's prize; and "partial," in which a subject knew only his own prize. The second experiment created a richer set of information conditions using an intermediate commodity, chips, which subjects could later exchange for money in private. A subject always knew his own chip prize and its value in money. There were three information conditions: "high," in which a subject also knew his partner's chip prize and its value; "intermediate," in which a subject knew his partner's chip prize but not its value; and "low," in which a subject knew neither his partner's chip prize nor its value. Subjects were prevented from communicating the missing information, and the information condition was public knowledge.

Partial and low information induce games with identical structures, given that players cannot send messages about chip or money prizes, because their strategy spaces are isomorphic (with chips in the latter treatment playing the role of money in the former) and isomorphic strategy combinations yield identical payoffs (in lottery tickets). For the same reasons full and intermediate information also induce games with identical structures, given that players in the latter cannot send messages about money prizes. Any structural theory, cooperative or non-cooperative, predicts identical outcomes in these pairs of treatments.

A third experiment explored the strategic use of private information by giving subjects the option of communicating missing information about prizes. There were no chips, and a subject always knew his own money prize. There were four basic information conditions: (i) neither subject knew both prizes; (ii) only the subject whose prize was $20 knew both prizes; (iii) only the subject whose prize was $5 knew both prizes; and (iv) both subjects knew both prizes. Some treatments made the basic information condition public knowledge, while in others subjects were told only that their partners might or might not know what information they had. Thus there were eight information conditions in all.

I first describe the observed patterns of agreements, and then discuss disagreements. With partial information almost all subjects agreed on a 50–50 division of the lottery tickets. With full information, agreements averaged about halfway between 50–50 and equal expected money winnings, with much higher variance (Roth (1987b, table 2.2)). With low and high information, respectively, agreements averaged close to 50–50 and roughly halfway between 50–50 and equal expected money winnings, again with higher variance. With intermediate information, agreements averaged close to 50–50 (Roth (1987b, figure 2.1)). Thus partial and low information yielded similar outcomes; but with full and intermediate information, strategically equivalent information about money and chips affected the outcomes in very different ways, which are inconsistent with any structural theory.

The authors attributed the strong influence of subjects' prizes and information about prizes, which are irrelevant in traditional analyses, to the different meanings subjects assigned to chips and money outside the laboratory. Their agreements can be summarized by postulating a commonly understood hierarchy of contextual equal-sharing norms in which subjects implemented the most "relevant" norm their public knowledge allowed, with money most relevant, then lottery tickets, and then chips (Crawford (1990)).[25]

In the third experiment agreements were largely determined by whether the $5 subject knew both prizes, clustering around 50–50 when he did not, and shifting more than halfway toward equal expected money winnings when he did (Roth (1987b, table 2.4)). In effect these agreements were determined by the most relevant norm in the above hierarchy that subjects could implement, using their public knowledge plus whatever private information they had incentives to reveal, on the anticipation that it would be used this way. Subjects' revelation decisions were approximately in equilibrium in beliefs in a restricted game in which they could either reveal the truth or nothing at all, when their beliefs are estimated from the mean payoffs in related treatments (Roth (1987b, pp. 27–32)).

There was a subtle interplay between the use of norms and the revelation of private information. In the public-knowledge version of condition (ii) in the third experiment, for instance, the $5 subject knew that his partner knew which agreement gave them equal expected money winnings, but the $20 subject usually refused to reveal his prize. This left the 50–50 division the only norm that could be implemented using public knowledge. Although many $5 subjects voiced suspicions (in transcripts) that they were being treated unfairly, in the end most settled for the 50–50 division. The influence of public knowledge here foreshadowed Mehta, Starmer, and Sugden's (1994) results on contextual focal points.

In all three experiments disagreements occurred, with frequencies ranging from 8–33 percent. Disagreements were most common when both subjects knew enough to implement more than one norm, or when the information condition was not public knowledge.

As explained above, the set of feasible divisions of lottery tickets and subjects' preferences over them were public knowledge, under standard assumptions, so it is natural to assume complete information in modeling the bargaining game. The non-negligible frequency of disagreements is then incompatible with explanations based on Nash's (1950) bargaining solution or the subgame-perfect equilibrium of an alternating-offers model, as is the strong influence of context on the agreements subjects reached. The manipulation of norms by withholding private information is inconsistent with non-strategic explanations in which subjects "try to be fair." However, most of the results can be understood using a simple strategic model, with players' shared ideas about fairness as coordinating principles.

The model summarizes the strategic possibilities of unstructured bargaining using Nash's (1953) demand game, in which players make simultaneous demands, in this case for lottery tickets. If their demands are feasible they yield a binding agreement; if not there is disagreement. To see how this simple, static game can describe the complex dynamics of unstructured bargaining, assume that delay costs are negligible before the deadline, so that the timing of an agreement is irrelevant. (This is a good approximation for the experiments and many applications to bargaining in the field.) Then, if equilibrium is assumed, all that matters about a player's strategy is the lowest share it can be induced to accept by the deadline. These lowest shares determine the outcome like players' demands in the demand game (Schelling (1960, pp. 267–90), Harsanyi and Selten (1988, pp. 23–4)).

In the complete model, players first decide simultaneously how much private information to reveal. They then bargain, with the ultimate acceptance decisions described by the demand game, in which there is effectively complete information. The demand game has a continuum of efficient equilibria, in which players' demands are just feasible and no worse than disagreement for both. There is also a continuum of inefficient mixed-strategy equilibria with positive probabilities of disagreement. Thus, in this model bargaining is in essence a coordination problem, with players' beliefs the dominant influence on outcomes.

Players' beliefs are focused, if at all, by the most relevant norm their public knowledge (including any revealed private information) allows them to implement. Pure-strategy equilibria, selected this way, yield agreements that closely resemble those observed in the various treatments. From this point of view, it is the desire to avoid a risk of disagreement due to coordination failure that explains $5 subjects' willingness to settle on the "unfair" 50–50 division in condition (ii) of the third experiment, a phenomenon that is difficult to explain any other way. Finally, mixed-strategy equilibria in which players' beliefs in each treatment are focused on the norms subjects' public knowledge allowed them to implement yield disagreement frequencies close to those observed in the various treatments (Roth (1985)). However, a subsequent, more comprehensive experiment showed that this model does not fully explain how disagreement frequencies vary with the environment (Roth, Murnighan, and Schoumaker (1988), Roth (1995b, pp. 309–11)).

It is instructive to contrast the view of disagreements as coordination failures suggested by Roth's results with the widespread view that they are explained primarily by asymmetric information about reservation prices. The evidence from the field is equivocal: asymmetric-information bargaining models enjoy some success in explaining strike incidence (Kennan and Wilson (1989)), but there is little evidence that bargaining ceases to be a problem when informational asymmetries are unimportant.

Forsythe, Kennan, and Sopher (1991) conducted an experimental test of a private-information model in which players bargain over the allocation of a "pie" whose size can take two values. One player observes the size and the other knows only its probability distribution; it is common knowledge that disagreement is inefficient in both states; and players can identify some, but not all, of the efficient agreements using common knowledge. With unstructured bargaining there was a non-negligible frequency of disagreements (3–12 percent) even when they were inconsistent with incentive efficiency (Forsythe, Kennan, and Sopher (1991, table 2)). When the pie was small disagreements were more than twice as frequent in treatments in which the informed player could not afford to concede half of the large pie (12–39 percent) than when he could (5–17 percent). Although some of these results are consistent with the incentive-efficiency view of disagreements, they also have a strong flavor of coordination failure.

Once again we find that a complex body of experimental results can be understood by combining traditional equilibrium analysis with empirical knowledge of subjects' ideas about fairness, entering here as coordinating principles rather than payoff perturbations.

6   DYNAMIC EVIDENCE

This section considers evidence on strategic behavior that is dynamic, in that its interpretation depends on how behavior varies over time. Most such evidence has been gathered in environments involving repeated play of a stage game. The typical pattern is an initial period of strategic uncertainty, followed by convergence to an equilibrium in the stage game (in beliefs, if not in actions). Interest usually centers not on convergence, but on how the environment influences the outcome. This influence may depend on complex interactions between the learning dynamics, strategic uncertainty, and the environment, whose effects can persist long after the uncertainty has been eliminated by learning.

Despite this complexity it is often possible to make useful generalizations about how outcomes are determined. This section discusses the methods and evidence on which such generalizations are based. I begin with evidence from simple environments in which evolutionary game theory yields good predictions of limiting outcomes. I then reconsider some of the "static" evidence from sections 4.2 and 5.2 from a dynamic point of view.[26]

6.1   Population interactions in simple environments

In simple environments with "evolutionary" structures, the analogy between evolution and learning is often close enough that an evolutionary analysis makes it possible to predict the limiting outcome. Friedman (1996) and Van Huyck, Battalio, and Rankin (1995) studied this issue in abstract two-person 2×2 and 3×3 normal-form games, and Van Huyck et al. (1995) studied it in two 3×3 games with structures like Divide the Dollar, one symmetric and one asymmetric.[27] The space of aggregate action frequencies was one, two, or (in one case) three dimensional. Except for the restriction to random pairing (or mean matching) the designs address most of the issues about how outcomes are determined in evolutionary games (section 2.3). Friedman's and Van Huyck, and his collaborator's results suggest that the aggregate action frequencies often converge to the evolutionary stable outcome whose basin of attraction contains the initial state. This can happen even when that basin of attraction is not the largest one, and equilibrium selection can go against risk-dominance, and/or predictions based on analyses of "long-run equilibria" (section 6.3).

Crawford (1991) studied this issue for Van Huyck, Batallio, and Beil's (1990, 1991) coordination experiments, finding that the limiting outcomes are surprisingly close to predictions based on evolutionary stability. As discussed in section 6.3, however, because of the larger action spaces and more complex interaction patterns in those experiments a full explanation of the dynamics requires a detailed analysis of learning at the individual level.

6.2   Dominance and iterated dominance revisited

In conjunction with the ultimatum experiments discussed in section 4.2, Prasnikar and Roth (1992) and Roth et al. (1991) studied market games, in which nine buyers made offers simultaneously to a single seller, and public-goods games. Although all three games had similar subgame-perfect equilibria, there were large, persistent differences in behavior across treatments, with rapid convergence to the subgame-perfect equilibrium in the public-goods treatment; and nonconvergence, or very slow convergence to a possibly different outcome, in the ultimatum treatment. The authors suggested an informal explanation for these differences based on differences in out-of-equilibrium payoffs, but their arguments leave room for doubt about whether the payoff differences are large enough to explain the variation in outcomes, or whether the dynamics involve interactions too complex to be understood by "eyeballing" the payoffs.

Roth and Erev (1995) conducted a dynamic analysis of the same data, using a simple model of adaptive learning driven by pecuniary payoffs.[28] In their model players choose actions with probabilities determined by "propensities," which are updated over time according to a formula that yields larger increases for higher realized payoffs. Their adjustment rule satisfies two desiderata from the psychological learning literature, in that the probabilities of actions with higher expected payoffs tend to increase over time (the "law of effect"), but the rate of increase slows over time as players gain experience (the "power law of practice"). Because action choices are random they cannot be viewed as rational responses to beliefs, which are almost always pure for expected-payoff maximizers. However, in stationary environments (and many that are not highly non-stationary) Roth and Erev's learning rule converges with high probability to a best reply. In this respect it resembles the more sophisticated rules discussed in section 6.3, in which action choices are rational responses to inertial, stochastically convergent beliefs. This resemblance is surprising because Roth and Erev's rule requires minimal information and is strategically completely unsophisticated: players do not need to know the structure or even that they are playing a game, and they do not need to observe other players' choices or payoffs.

Roth and Erev investigated the implications of their model by simulation, with the parameters of the learning rule set at the same plausible values for all treatments and initial propensities chosen randomly or estimated from the data for each treatment. The model closely reproduces the dynamics in all three treatments, except that convergence is much slower than in the experiments. Even so, in each case it is the model's predictions in the intermediate term, not in the long run, that resemble the experimental results. The ultimatum game's out-of-equilibrium payoffs make the predicted frequencies of low offers by player 1s fall much more quickly than the frequencies of their acceptance by player 2s rises. In all but (possibly) the longest run, this keeps predicted behavior away from the subgame-perfect equilibrium, to an extent that varies with the initial conditions in different countries approximately as in the experiments. The model even reproduces the tendency Roth et al. observed for the offers of player 1s to differ increasingly across countries while they converged within each country. By contrast, the very different out-of-equilibrium payoffs in the market and public-goods treatments quickly drive predicted behavior toward the subgame-perfect equilibrium, as in the experiments.

Gale, Binmore, and Samuelson (1995) (inspired by Andreoni and Miller (1995)) conducted a complementary analysis of behavior in ultimatum games based on stochastic replicator dynamics, also driven by pecuniary payoffs. Their model postulates aggregate noise in the dynamics, which interacts with the out-of-equilibrium payoffs in the ultimatum game roughly like the randomness of individual adjustments in Roth and Erev's model. Using a combination of simulation and analytical methods, they showed that if the responses of player 2s near the subgame-perfect equilibrium are noisier than those of player 1s, for whom deviations are much more costly, then even small amounts of noise yield intermediate-term ("long-run" in their terminology) outcomes near an imperfect equilibrium in the ultimatum game that resembles behavior in the experiments.

Nagel (1995) and Stahl (1994) conducted dynamic analyses of the data from Nagel's "guessing game" experiment (section 4.1), in which a subject's sophistication is naturally associated with the number of rounds of iterated dominance implicit in his guesses. Nagel's analysis suggests that sophistication varied across subjects, but had no clear tendency to increase with experience. Stahl postulated more complex learning rules and found evidence of heterogeneity and increasing sophistication over time.

6.3   Simultaneous coordination revisited

Brandts and Holt (1992, 1993a) replicated the results of Banks, Camerer, and Porter's (1994) experiments with signaling games (section 5.1) and conducted new signaling experiments. They found some support for traditional refinements, but they also found considerable strategic uncertainty, which allowed them consistently to obtain convergence to "un-refined" equilibria by varying out-of-equilibrium payoffs. This suggests that outcomes in these games cannot be fully understood without analyzing the learning dynamics.

Van Huyck, Battalio, and Beil (1990, 1991), provide perhaps the clearest evidence on learning and ·history-dependent equilibrium selection. As explained in section 5.2, their subjects played simple coordination games with seven "efforts," in which payoffs were determined by their own efforts and an order statistic or their own and others' efforts. There were five leading treatments, which varied with the order statistic, the number of subjects playing the game, and their interaction pattern. In each case the stage game had seven symmetric, Pareto-ranked equilibria, and a subject's payoff was highest, other things being equal, when his effort equalled the order statistic. In each treatment the stage game was played repeatedly, usually ten times, with the order statistic publicly announced after each play. These environments are a natural setting in which to study the emergence of conventions to solve coordination problems. Their large action spaces allow rich dynamics, whose variations across treatments discriminate sharply among traditional and different adaptive learning models.

All five treatments had similar initial effort distributions, with high to moderate variances and inefficiently low means, but subjects' subsequent efforts varied across treatments, with persistent consequences for equilibrium selection. In the large-group minimum treatment efforts quickly approached the lowest equilibrium, despite its inefficiency. In the random-pairing minimum treatment efforts slowly approached a moderately inefficient equilibrium, with little or no trend; and in the three median treatments efforts invariably converged to the initial median, although it varied across runs and was usually inefficient. Thus the dynamics were highly sensitive to the size of the groups playing the game and the order statistic, with striking differences in drift, history-dependence, rate of convergence, and the efficiency of the limiting outcome.

Traditional methods do not help to explain these results. Rationality with unrestricted beliefs implies no restrictions on behavior. Equilibrium in the stage game or the repeated game implies some restrictions, but they are the same for every treatment. Predictions based on risk- or payoff-dominance do not reflect the dispersion of initial responses, and differ substantially from subjects' modal initial or final efforts (section 5.2).

Crawford (1995a) and Broseta (1993a and b) proposed adaptive learning models to explain Van Huyck, Battalio, and Beil's results. The models describe players' decisions as rational responses to beliefs, but do not impose equilibrium even in perturbed versions of the game. Instead they use the "evolutionary" structure of the experimental designs to give a flexible characterization of players' learning rules and strategic uncertainty. This permits an informative analysis of the history-dependent learning processes in the experiments, which suggests that the results were strongly influenced by interactions between strategic uncertainty and the learning dynamics. These interactions are not adequately modeled by the mental tâtonnements in Harsanyi and Selten's (1988) theory: although perfectly strategically sophisticated players may be able to mentally simulate each other's responses, with strategic uncertainty there is no substitute for analyzing the effects of real feedback.

The specification of learning rules takes advantage of the facts that subjects' payoffs are directly affected by others' efforts only through the order statistic, and that subjects appeared to treat their influences on the order statistic as negligible. On this assumption, their optimal efforts are determined by their beliefs about the current value of the order statistic, so that it suffices to describe the evolution of those beliefs. The model represents beliefs directly by the optimal efforts they imply, as in the adaptive control literature, rather than as probability distributions or their moments.[29] On average each player's beliefs are assumed to adjust linearly part of the way toward the latest observation of the order statistic, in a way that generalizes the fictitious-play and best-reply rules to allow different values of parameters that represent the initial levels, trends, and inertia in beliefs.

Because subjects were externally indistinguishable and had virtually the same information, it does not seem useful to try to explain the differences in their beliefs within the model. Instead the model uses the evolutionary structure of the environment to give a simple statistical characterization of beliefs, in which the average adjustments described above are perturbed each period by idiosyncratic random shocks, which are independently and identically distributed across players, with zero means and given variances.[30] These shocks represent strategic uncertainty, described in terms of the differences in players' learning rules. In effect each player has his own theory of coordination, which gives both his initial beliefs and his interpretations of new information an unpredictable component.

Under standard restrictions on the parameters, these learning rules satisfy the law of effect and the power law of practice. They assume less strategic sophistication than a traditional analysis because players ignore their own influences on the order statistic, but more than Roth and Erev's (1995) learning rules because they depend on the best-reply structure. Van Huyck, Battalio, and Beil's subjects seemed to understand the best-reply structure, and it is important to take this into account. Roth (1995a, p. 39, figure 1.2,) found that Roth and Erev's model tracks the dynamics in the large-group minimum treatment much better if it is modified to allow "common learning," in which players' propensities are updated as if they had played the most successful action in the entire population. Because subjects did not usually observe each other's payoffs or actions, the most sensible interpretation of common learning is that players' learning rules incorporated the best-reply structure, and the resulting model yields adjustments close to those of the Crawford and Broseta models.

Specifying the distributions of the shocks yields a Markov process with players' beliefs, represented by their optimal efforts, as the state vector. The transition probabilities may vary over time, as determined by the distributions of the shocks. The dynamics are driven by the dispersion of beliefs, as represented by the variances of the shocks. Different distributional assumptions have different implications for how outcomes are determined, which go a long way toward identifying the stochastic structure.

If the variances of the shocks fall to zero after the first period, so that players differ in their initial beliefs but not in their responses to new observations, the process converges to the equilibrium determined by the initial realization of the order statistic, independent of the behavioral parameters and the environment. This is consistent with the results in the median treatments, but not with the results in the large-group minimum treatment, where in nine out of nine runs subjects approached an equilibrium below the initial minimum.

If, instead, the variances are positive and remain constant over time, the model is ergodic and allows an analysis of "long-run equilibria" (Kandori (1996)) as in Robles (1997). In the long run the process cycles among the pure-strategy equilibria in the stage game, whose prior probabilities are given by the ergodic distribution. Allowing the variances to approach zero, remaining constant over time, makes the probability of the equilibrium with the lowest (highest) effort approach one for any order statistic below (above) the median. These limits are completely independent of the number of players and the order statistic, as long as the order statistic remains below, or above, the median. (When the order statistic is the median, every pure-strategy equilibrium has positive probability in the limit.) Thus, studying the limiting behavior of an ergodic process with small dispersion leaves most of the questions raised by Van Huyck, Battalio, and Beil's experiments unanswered.

The dynamics are closest to the experimental results when the variances decline steadily to zero as players learn to forecast the order statistic, as suggested by the power law of practice. If the variances do not decline too slowly the model converges, with probability one, to one of the pure-strategy equilibria of the stage game. Its implications can then be summarized by the prior probability distribution of the limiting equilibrium, which is normally non-degenerate owing to the persistent effects of strategic uncertainty.

The model makes it possible, whether or not the process is ergodic or the dispersion is small, to solve for the entire history of players' beliefs and efforts as functions of the behavioral parameters, the shocks, the number of players, and the order statistic. The outcome is built up period by period from the shocks, whose effects persist indefinitely. This persistence makes the process resemble a random walk, in the aggregate, but with possibly non-zero drift that depends on the behavioral parameters, the variances, and the environment; and declining variances that allow the process to converge to a particular equilibrium. This limiting equilibrium is normally sensitive to the entire history of players' interactions.

The model allows a comparative dynamics analysis, which shows both qualitatively and quantitatively how strategic uncertainty interacts with the environment (holding the behavioral parameters constant across treatments) to determine the outcome. The quantitative analysis is based in part on analytical approximations of the drift of the process. These reveal that in the median and random-pairing minimum treatments the drift is zero, and that in the large-group minimum treatment the drift is increasingly negative with larger numbers of players, and proportional to the standard deviation that represents the dispersion of beliefs. These results and analogous approximations of the variances suggest patterns of variation across treatments like those in the experiments.[31]

To develop the model's full implications, or to test it, the behavioral parameters and the variances that represent strategic uncertainty must be evaluated. The model makes it possible to estimate the parameters econometrically, using the data from each treatment. The estimated parameters satisfy the restrictions suggested by the theory. The variances that represent the dispersion of beliefs are initially large and decline gradually to zero, and the hypothesis that subjects had identical beliefs throughout is strongly rejected. Using repeated simulation to infer the estimated model's implications confirms the accuracy of the approximations, and shows that the model provides an adequate statistical summary of subjects' behavior while reproducing the dynamics of their interactions in all five treatments. In this sense, taking the effects of strategic uncertainty into account yields a simple, unified explanation of Van Huyck, Battalio, and Beil's results.

Crawford and Broseta (1995) proposed a similar model to explain the results of Van Huyck, Battalio, and Beil's (1993) experiment, which modified one of the nine-player median treatments from their 1991 experiment by auctioning the right to play the same nine-person median game each period in a group of 18. The winners were charged the same market-clearing price, which was publicly announced each period before they played the median game. The auctions can be expected to enhance efficiency because subjects' beliefs usually differ, auctions select the most optimistic subjects, and the game is one in which optimism favors efficiency. The subjects did much better than this argument suggests, quickly bidding the price up to a level that could be recouped only in the most efficient equilibrium and then converging to that equilibrium. The dynamics focused their beliefs as in the intuition for forward induction refinements, in which players infer from other players' willingness to pay to play a game that they expect payoffs that repay their costs, and will play accordingly. This suggests an important new way in which competition may foster efficiency.

Surprisingly, Crawford's (1995a) and Broseta's (1993a and b) methods can be adapted to analyze the dynamics in this more complex environment. The results show how the strength of the efficiency-enhancing effect of auctions is determined by the environment and the behavioral parameters, apportioning it among an order-statistic effect like the one that drives the dynamics in the earlier models, modified by the "optimistic subjects" effect just described and a "forward induction" effect like the one just described. The estimated model suggests that these effects contributed roughly equally to the efficiency-enhancing effect of auctions in Van Huyck, Battalio, and Beil's environment, and that auctions will have similar but possibly weaker effects in nearby environments with different numbers of players, different order statistics, and different degrees of competition for the right to play.

These analyses suggest that it will often be possible to analyze the history-dependent learning processes commonly observed in experiments. Once again the models suggested by the experimental results are hybrids, in these cases combining the "evolutionary" structure of the experimental designs with simple characterizations of individual learning, with empirical parameters that reflect the structure of learning rules, the initial level of strategic uncertainty, and the rate at which it is eliminated by learning.

7   CONCLUSION

This chapter has surveyed a large body of experimental work with well thought-out designs and the careful control needed to test strategic models, which addresses issues central to the analysis of strategic interaction. I hope that my discussion conveys some of the richness of the possibilities of experiments, and gives some indication of the extent to which thinking about their results can suggest fruitful new directions for theoretical work.

Although the laboratory is not the field, many experimental results are so robust and so coherent that it is difficult to dismiss them as unrepresentative of "real" behavior. The notion that behavior is a rational response to beliefs, in conjunction with ideas from traditional non-cooperative and cooperative game theory, evolutionary game theory, and adaptive learning models, is surprisingly helpful in organizing the data. In no way, however, do the results justify the traditional view that rationality is all that is needed to understand strategic behavior. Most subjects seem to have some strategic sophistication, but seldom enough to justify an analysis based exclusively on equilibrium, however refined. Moreover, what sophistication they have often takes non-traditional forms, and their beliefs are more likely to be coordinated by inductive and/or contextual principles than deductive and/or structural ones. When subjects' beliefs are not coordinated at the start, learning commonly yields convergence to an equilibrium in the stage game; but the outcome is frequently history-dependent, and the effects of strategic uncertainty may persist long after it has been eliminated by learning. In such cases both traditional refinements and overly simple models of adaptive learning or evolutionary dynamics may predict poorly.

Nonetheless, the results of experiments give good reason to hope that most strategic behavior can be understood via a synthesis that combines elements from each of the leading theoretical frameworks with a modicum of empirical information about behavior, in proportions that vary with the environment in predictable ways. In this synthesis theory will play a wider role than in most strategic analyses to date, providing a framework within which to learn which ideas are useful and which aspects of behavior cannot reliably be determined by theory, and to gather the empirical information needed to close the model.

The analysis of such models will require new static methods that combine rationality with empirically sensible restrictions on strategies, without imposing coordination of beliefs, as in Cho (1994), Rabin (1993, 1994), and Watson (1993, 1996). It will also require new dynamic methods that take the persistent effects of strategic uncertainty in history-dependent learning processes fully into account, and that go beyond random pairing to consider other interaction patterns that are important in economics, as in Roth and Erev (1995), Crawford (1995a), Broseta (1993a and b), and Crawford and Broseta (1995).

Notes

Invited Symposium on Experimental Economics, Econometric Society Seventh World Congress, Tokyo, August 1995. I owe thanks to John McMillan, Alvin Roth, Joel Sobel, and especially Mark Machina for helpful advice and to Miguel Costa Gomes for able research assistance. My debt to Thomas Schelling and the many experimentalists and theorists who have since studied behavior in games should be clear from the text.

1 There is nonetheless a history of valuable empirical work using field data from strategic environments, usually with well-specified, readily observable structures.
2 See also Plott (1991), Roth (1987a, 1991, 1995a), and Smith (1989).
3 This focus and space limitations have led me to exclude a great deal of important experimental work; see Kagel and Roth (1995) for a comprehensive survey.
4 Hey's (1996) companion chapter surveys experiments on individual decisions. Conlisk (1996) gives a good overview of bounded rationality in decisions and games.
5 Compare the notion of "theory of mind" in cognitive psychology, where it has been found experimentally that some aspects of what I call strategic sophistication develop in normal (but not autistic) children around age three (Leslie (1994)).
6 Dekel and Gul (1996) give a good overview of this approach. Common knowledge of beliefs can be relaxed to approximate common knowledge for strict equilibria, and to mutual knowledge for two-person games.
7 Beliefs could also be coordinated by preplay communication, but communication does not always yield equilibrium in the underlying game (Aumann (1990)).
8 Making this distinction precise is difficult and probably premature at this stage of our empirical knowledge. For instance, a game theorist might find the analogies

created by Nash's (1950) axioms so transparent that applying his bargaining solution is just copying behavior inductively from one problem to another, but others are likely to view the Nash solution as a deductive theory (Schelling (1960, pp. 113–14)).

9   With random pairing stable frequencies are also in equilibrium in the game played by pairs. Some qualifications apply for finite populations or extensive-form stage games.

10   Individual pairs can of course play asymmetric action combinations by chance, but asymmetric aggregate frequencies are statistically unplayable, even in the limit. Crawford and Haller (1990, p. 580) give a "traditional" analog of this argument. Evolutionary game theory also has a way to model the effects of distinguished roles, illustrated by the Stoplight example of Crawford (1991, section 3).

11   The founding analysis of evolutionary game theory, Fisher's (1930) explanation of the tendency of the ratio of male to female births to remain near 1, is a game against the field (Maynard Smith (1982, pp. 23–7)). This problem – one of the most beautiful in science – requires a game-theoretic explanation because a ratio of 1 equalizes the fitnesses of having male and female offspring, and does not maximize the growth rate of the entire population. The model is a game against the field because the fitnesses depend (nonlinearly) on the population frequencies of male and female offspring.

12   By contrast, "rational" learning models such as Bray and Kreps (1987) and Crawford and Haller (1990) assume equilibrium in the repeated game.

13   In models that describe action choices directly, without reference to beliefs, I use "strategic uncertainty" loosely to refer to systematic deviations from equilibrium.

14   Preplay communication and repeated-game strategies, which raise similar analytical issues but deserve separate treatment because of their economic importance, are discussed in Crawford (1995b, sections 7 and 8), omitted here due to space limitations.

15   "Large" populations are surprisingly small: subjects usually treat individual influences as negligible in groups of 10–15, and sometimes in groups as small as five.

16   There is also a large body of experiments on nonpecuniary effects (see, for example, Camerer and Thaler (1995) and Roth (1995b)).

17   A survey in progress should reveal if failure to rely on dominance is more prevalent among those who were taught to look both ways before crossing one-way streets.

18   Thus it gathers the same information as eye-movement studies of problem-solving in psychology, but more systematically. Subjects were not allowed to record their payoffs, and their look-up patterns suggest that they did not memorize them.

19   Less time is spent checking the first-period payoff because as long as it is higher than the second-period payoff it does not affect the subgame-perfect equilibrium offer.

20 If the pie is discrete, there is also a nearby subgame-perfect equilibrium in which player 1 offers player 2 the smallest feasible positive amount and player 2 accepts.

21 Thus the modal offers are consistent with equilibrium in beliefs. Equilibrium would also require optimality of the other offers and consistency of the rejections of player 2s with the hypothesized distribution of nonpecuniary payoffs discussed below.

22 In coordination, for instance, it can be just as disadvantageous to be "too clever" for one's partners as to be not clever enough – provided that one's cleverness does not include the ability to predict the effects of others' lack of cleverness.

23 If players are risk neutral these conclusions extend to the stage game that describes the entire population's interactions in the random-pairing minimum treatment, with its median effort as the order statistic (Crawford (1995a, fn. 10, p. 110)).

24 The nun who taught me in third grade that Jesus was *exactly* six feet tall had an intuitive grasp of the importance of contextual principles, if not of their transience.

25 The equal-chip and equal-money norms are contextual because they depend on things that do not affect the feasible divisions of lottery tickets or subjects' preferences over them. Bar-Hillel and Yaari (1993) surveyed students' views about some less abstract norms, in which needs and beliefs enter as well as preferences.

26 Crawford (1995b, section 6.2), discusses analyses that explain "cooperative" deviations from subgame-perfect or sequential equilibrium in experiments with multi-period extensive-form games like the Centipede Game and the finitely repeated Prisoners' Dilemma by hypothesizing idiosyncratic, privately observed payoff or action perturbations. Crawford (1995b, section 6.4), discusses the small body of evidence on the structure of learning rules. Both topics are omitted here owing to space limitations.

27 Friedman often speeded convergence using *mean matching*, in which the payoffs of random pairing are simulated without the uncertainty of matching in a game against the field, by replacing them by their expectations given the population frequencies.

28 The complexity of dynamic models makes it natural to start by considering only pecuniary payoffs. However, the inertia of Roth and Erev's (1995) adjustment process and their estimation of subjects' initial responses from the data yield player 2s behavior similar to the static model with nonpecuniary payoffs proposed in section 4.2.

29 Players' efforts are actually determined by a discrete-choice model, in which their beliefs are the continuous latent variables. I ignore this distinction in the text.

30 Broseta (1993a and b) obtains similar results for a stochastic structure with richer dynamics.

31 The analysis shows that it was no coincidence that the most interesting dynamics were found in a game against the field, the large-group minimum

treatment: random pairing eliminates the effects of strategic uncertainty that drove those results.

References

Andreoni, James and Miller, John (1995). "Auctions with artificial adaptive agents." *Games and Economic Behavior*, 10: 39–64.

Aumann, Robert (1990). "Nash equilibria are not self-enforcing." In Gabszewicz, J. J. Richard, J.-F. and Wolsey, L. A. (eds.), *Economic Decision-Making: Games, Econometrics and Optimization*. Lausanne: Elsevier Science Publishers, pp. 201–6.

Aumann, Robert and Brandenburger, Adam (1995). "Epistemic conditions for Nash equilibrium." *Econometrica*, 63: 1161–80.

Banks, Jeffrey, Camerer, Colin, and Porter, David (1994). "An experimental analysis of Nash refinements in signaling games." *Games and Economic Behavior*, 6: 1–31.

Bar-Hillel, Maya and Yaari, Menahem (1993). "Judgments of distributive justice." In Mellers, Barbara and Baron, Jonathan (eds.), *Psychological Perspectives on Justice: Theory and Applications*. New York: Cambridge University Press.

Beard, T. Randolph and Beil, Richard (1994). "Do people rely on the self-interested maximization of others?: an experimental text." *Management Science*, 40: 252–62.

Brandts, Jordi and Holt, Charles (1992). "An experimental test of equilibrium dominance in signaling games." *American Economic Review*, 82: 1350–65.

(1993a). "Adjustment patterns and equilibrium selection in experimental signaling games." *International Journal of Game Theory*, 22: 279–302.

(1993b). "Dominance and forward induction: experimental evidence." In Isaac R. Mark (ed.), *Research in Experimental Economics*, Vol. V. Greenwich, CT: JAI Press, pp. 119–36.

Bray, Margaret and Kreps, David (1987). "Rational learning and rational expectations." In Feiwel, George (ed.), *Arrow and the Ascent of Modern Economic Theory*. New York: New York University Press, pp. 597–625.

Broseta, Bruno (1993a). "Strategic uncertainty and learning in coordination games." UCSD Discussion Paper 93–34.

(1993b). "Estimation of a game-theoretic model of learning: an autoregressive conditional heteroskedasticity approach." UCSD Discussion Paper 93–35.

Camerer, Colin, Johnson, Eric, Rymon, Talia, and Sen, Sankar (1993). "Cognition and framing in sequential bargaining for gains and losses." In Binmore, Kenneth, Kirman, Alan, and Tani, Piero (eds.), *Frontiers of Game Theory*. Cambridge, MA: MIT Press, pp. 27–47.

Camerer, Colin and Thaler, Richard (1995). "Anomalies: ultimatums, dictators and manners." *Journal of Economic Perspective*, 9: 209–19.

Cho, In-Koo (1994). "Stationarity, rationalizability and bargaining." *Review of Economic Studies*, 61: 357–74.

Conlisk, John (1996). "Why bounded rationality?" *Journal of Economic Literature*, 34: 669–700.

Cooper, Russell, DeJong, Douglas, Forsythe, Robert, and Ross, Thomas (1994). "Alternative institutions for resolving coordination problems: experimental evidence on forward induction and preplay communication." In Friedman, James (ed.), *Problems of Coordination in Economic Activity*. Boston: Kluwer, pp. 129–46.

Crawford, Vincent (1989). "Learning and mixed-strategy equilibria in evolutionary games." *Journal of Theoretical Biology*, 140: 537–50. Reprinted in Bicchieri, Chrislina, Jeffrey, Richard, and Skyrms, Brian (eds.), *The Dynamics of Norms*. New York: Cambridge University Press.

(1990). "Explicit communication and bargaining outcomes." *American Economic Review Papers and Proceedings*, 80: 213–19.

(1991). "An 'evolutionary' interpretation of Van Huyck, Battalio, and Beil's experimental results on coordination." *Games and Economic Behavior*, 3: 25–59.

(1995a). "Adaptive dynamics in coordination games." *Econometrica*, 63: 103–43.

(1995b). "Theory and experiment in the analysis of strategic interaction." UCSD Discussion Paper 95–37.

Crawford, Vincent and Broseta, Bruno (1995). "What price coordination? Auctioning the right to play as a form of preplay communication." UCSD Discussion Paper 95–41.

Crawford, Vincent and Haller, Hans (1990). "Learning how to cooperate: optimal play in repeated coordination games." *Econometrica*, 58: 571–95.

Dekel, Eddie, and Gul, Faruk (1996). "Rationality and knowledge in game theory." Chapter 5 in this volume.

Fisher, R. A. (1930). *The Genetical Theory of Natural Selection*. Oxford: Clarendon Press.

Forsythe, Robert, Kennan, John and Sopher, Barry (1991). "An experimental analysis of strikes in bargaining games with one-sided private information." *American Economic Review*, 81: 253–70.

Friedman, Daniel (1991). "Evolutionary games in economics." *Econometrica*, 59: 637–66.

(1996). "Equilibrium in evolutionary games: some experimental results." *Economic Journal* 106: 1–25.

Fudenberg, Drew and Kreps, David (1993). "Learning mixed equilibria." *Games and Economic Behavior*, 5: 320–67.

Gale, John, Binmore, Kenneth, and Samuelson, Larry (1995). "Learning to be imperfect: the ultimatum game." *Games and Economic Behavior*, 8: 56–90.

Harsanyi, John and Selten, Reinhard (1988). *A General Theory of Equilibrium Selection in Games*. Cambridge, MA: MIT Press.

Hey, John (1996). "Experiments and the economics of individual decision making under risk and uncertainty." Chapter 6 in this volume.

Kagel, John and Roth, Alvin (eds.) (1995). *Handbook of Experimental Economics*. Princeton: Princeton University Press.

Kandori, Michihiro (1996). "Evolutionary game theory in economics." Chapter 8 in this volume.

Kennan, John and Wilson, Robert (1989). "Strategic bargaining models and interpretation of strike data." *Journal of Applied Econometrics*, 4 (Supplement): S87–S130.

Leslie, Alan M. (1994). "Pretending and believing – issues in the theory of TOMM." *Cognition*, 50: 211–38.

Marimon, Ramon (1996). "Learning from learning in economics." Chapter 8 in this volume.

Maynard Smith, John (1982). *Evolution and the Theory of Games*. New York: Cambridge University Press.

Mehta, Judith, Starmer, Chris, and Sugden, Robert (1994). "The nature of salience: an experimental investigation of pure coordination games." *American Economic Review*, 84: 658–73.

Nagel, Rosemarie (1995). "Unraveling in guessing games: an experimental study." *American Economic Review*, 85: 1313–26.

Nash, John (1950). "The bargaining problem." *Econometrica*, 18: 155–62.

(1953). "Two-person cooperative games." *Econometrica*, 21: 128–40.

Plott, Charles (1991). "Economics in 2090: the views of an experimentalist." *Economic Journal*, 101: 88–93.

Prasnikar, Vesna and Roth, Alvin (1992). "Considerations of fairness and strategy: experimental data from sequential games." *Quarterly Journal of Economics*, 107: 865–88.

Rabin, Matthew (1993). "Incorporating fairness into game theory and economics." *American Economic Review*, 83: 1281–302.

(1994). "Incorporating behavioral assumptions into game theory." In Friedman, James (ed.), *Problems of Coordination in Economic Activity*. Boston: Kluwer, pp. 69–86.

Robles, Jack (1997). "Evolution and long run equilibria in coordination games with summary statistic payoff technologies." *Journal of Economic Theory*, forthcoming.

Roth, Alvin (1985). "Toward a focal-point theory of bargaining." In Roth, Alvin (ed.), *Game-Theoretic Models of Bargaining*. New York: Cambridge University Press, pp. 259–68.

(1987a). "Laboratory experimentation in economics." In Bewley, Truman (ed.), *Advances in Economic Theory: Fifth World Congress*, Econometric Society Monograph No. 12. New York: Cambridge University Press, pp. 269–99.

(1987b). "Bargaining phenomena and bargaining theory." In Roth, Alvin (ed.), *Laboratory Experimentation in Economics: Six Points of View*. New York: Cambridge University Press. pp. 14–41.

(1991). "Game theory as a part of empirical economics." *Economic Journal*, 101: 107–14.

(1994). "Let's keep the con out of experimental econ." *Empirical Economics*, 19: 279–89.

(1995a). "Introduction to experimental economics." In Kagel, John and Roth, Alvin (eds.), pp. 3–109.

(1995b). "Bargaining experiments." In Kagel, John and Roth, Alvin (eds.), pp. 253–348.

Roth, Alvin and Erev, Ido (1995). "Learning in extensive-form games: experimental data and simple dynamic models in the intermediate term." *Games and Economic Behavior*, 8: 164–212.

Roth, Alvin and Malouf, Michael. (1979). "Game-theoretic models and the role of information in bargaining." *Psychological Review*, 86: 574–94.

Roth, Alvin, Murnighan, J. Keith and Schoumaker, Françoise (1988). "The deadline effect in bargaining: some experimental evidence." *American Economic Review*, 78: 806–23.

Roth, Alvin, Prasnikar, Vesna, Okuno-Fujiwara, Masahiro, and Zamir, Shmuel (1991). "Bargaining and market behavior in Jerusalem, Ljubljana, Pittsburgh, and Tokyo: an experimental study." *American Economic Review*, 81: 1068–95.

Samuelson, Larry (1993). "Does evolution eliminate dominated strategies?" In Binmore, Kenneth, Kirman, Alan, and Tani, Piero (eds.), *Frontiers of Game Theory*. Cambridge, MA: MIT Press, pp. 213–35.

Schelling, Thomas (1960). *The Strategy of Conflict*. Cambridge, MA: Harvard University Press.

(1978). *Micromotives and Macrobehavior*. New York: W.W. Norton.

Smith, Vernon (1989). "Theory, experiment and economics." *Journal of Economic Perspectives*, 3: 151–69.

Stahl, Dale (1994). "Rule learning in a guessing game." Working Paper 9415, University of Texas.

Stahl, Dale and Wilson, Paul (1995). "On players' models of other players: theory and experimental evidence." *Games and Economic Behavior*, 10: 218–54.

Van Huyck, John, Battalio, Raymond, and Beil, Richard (1990). "Tacit coordination games, strategic uncertainty, and coordination failure." *American Economic Review*, 80: 234–48.

(1991). "Strategic uncertainty, equilibrium selection, and coordination failure in average opinion games." *Quarterly Journal of Economics*, 106: 885–910.

(1993). "Asset markets as an equilibrium selection mechanism: coordination failure, game form auctions, and tacit communication." *Games and Economic Behavior*, 5: 485–504.

Van Huyck, John, Battalio, Raymond, Mathur, Sondip, Ortmann, Andreas, and Van Huyck, Patsy (1995). "On the origin of convention: evidence from symmetric bargaining games." *International Journal of Game Theory*, 24: 187–212.

Van Huyck, John, Battalio, Raymond and Rankin, Frederick (1995). "On the origin of convention: evidence from coordination games." Research Report 4, Texas A&M University Economics Laboratory.

Watson, Joel (1993). "A reputation refinement without equilibrium." *Econometrica*, 61: 199–205.

(1996). "Reputation in repeated games with no discounting." Forthcoming in *Games and Economic Behavior*.

CHAPTER 8

Evolutionary game theory in economics

Kandori Michihiro

1   INTRODUCTION

The success of game theory in the 1980s has revolutionized economics. In addition to optimization and competitive market equilibrium, the concept of Nash equilibrium became a basic analytical tool and a common language of economists in almost all fields. In his famed text book (1948), Paul Samuelson quoted an epigram: "You can make even a parrot into a learned economist; all it must learn are the two words, 'supply' and 'demand.'" But now the parrot needs two more words, "Nash equilibrium," to be academically correct.

As the game theoretic approach penetrated into many fields, however, some basic problems became apparent. First, it is not clear *how* players come to play a Nash equilibrium. Although Nash equilibrium was once perceived as the outcome of perfectly rational reasoning, active research in the past decade revealed that common knowledge of rationality only implies rationalizability, which is much weaker than Nash equilibrium. Second, game theoretic models quite often possess multiple equilibria *which have markedly different properties*. This is in contrast to the general equilibrium model where all equilibria are efficient. Hence in applications of game theory it is vital to pin down *which* equilibrium is selected. A host of refinements literature tried to solve this problem by defining a stronger notion of rationality than Nash equilibrium assumes, but it was not entirely successful. We are left with a number of new solution concepts, and there seems to be no clear consensus among economists as to which one is right.

Partly due to these difficulties in the rationality approach, the study of the boundedly rational adjustment process toward Nash equilibrium became an active field of research in the past few years. The literature is (vaguely) classified into two categories, *learning* and *evolution*. The learning literature typically assumes that players can calculate the best response and examines how players update their beliefs about their opponents' strategies in a *fixed match*. In contrast, the evolutionary approach does not necessarily assume the ability to optimize and analyzes the evolution of sophisticated behavior through trail and error and natural selection in a *population* of players.

The basic idea of the evolutionary approach is in line with the oral tradition in economics about the justification of rationality. This basic premise of neoclassical economics has often been justified in the following way. Economic agents may not consciously optimize but behave *as if* they were rational, because economic competition selects optimizing agents. This was articulated in particular by Alchian (1950) and Friedman (1953).[1]

A big impetus for the formal study of such a process came from biology. Following the pioneering work on sex ratio by Fisher (1930) and Hamilton (1967), Maynard Smith and Price (1973) introduced the notion of *evolutionary stable strategy* (*ESS*), and asserted that the observed traits of animals and plants can be explained by Nash equilibria of suitably defined games. The idea is that the combination of natural selection and mutation leads the population to a stable Nash equilibrium (ESS) in the long run. Since then, this view has been verified in a number of field studies. Here, the "as if" explanation is not just a plausible parable but rather a quite accurate description of reality. Animals and plants have little or no ability for rational reasoning, yet their behavior can be explained by Nash equilibrium!

Encouraged by the success in biology, a number of economic theorists recently became involved in active research in evolutionary game theory. For economists, this has a feeling of *dé já vu*, because the study of adjustment dynamics has a long history before evolutionary game theory. The *tâtonnement* stability of general equilibrium was extensively studied in the late 1950s, and the adjustment dynamics in oligopoly models goes back to the original work of Cournot in 1838. After extensive research, however, those theories have been criticized as being *ad hoc* and dismissed by some economists. Given this experience, why should we be interested in such an approach again? What differentiates evolutionary game theory from the previous literature on adjustment dynamics?

The answer may be found in the aforementioned two basic problems of game theory. Firstly, unlike previous literature, evolutionary game theory in economics clearly acknowledges that something *ad hoc* is *necessary*. Only after the extensive study of game theory, which clarifies what rationality means in strategic situations and what it implies, did the necessity become apparent. Rationality alone fails to justify Nash equilibrium, and the theory must search for some elements other than rationality (i.e., something which is necessarily *ad hoc*) to explain equilibrium behavior.

Secondly, the necessity of equilibrium selection, which became a pressing issue in the course of extensive applications of game theory to a variety of concrete economic problems, is something which the previous literature on adjustment dynamics did not encounter. In the highly abstract Arrow–Debreu model which equilibrium is selected is rarely discussed, and the traditional oligopoly theory did not enjoy a wide range of applications because it was plagued by a host of alternative "solution" concepts and deemed as unreliable.

The study of evolutionary game theory in economics has just started and it is rather early to judge how successful it is in achieving its goals. This chapter tries to review the present state of research,[2] and is organized as follows. Section 2 presents the basic concepts developed in biology, and its extensions are discussed in the next section. Section 4 reviews what evolutionary game theory has to say about the "as if" justification of rationality, and the emergence of efficiency is addressed in section 5. The next section examines the long-run implications of repeated random mutations, and concluding remarks are given in section 6. For convenience, major results are somewhat roughly summarized in the form of *Claims*.

2 BIOLOGICAL GAMES – ESS AND REPLICATOR DYNAMICS

In this section we review the basic concepts of evolutionary game theory developed in biology, namely, evolutionarily stable strategy and replicator dynamics. *Evolutionarily stable strategy (ESS)* was introduced by Maynard Smith and Price in their seminal paper (1973). This solution concept is meant to capture the stable outcome of the evolutionary process, which is driven by natural selection and mutation. Consider a large population of a single species. Individuals are randomly matched in pairs and play a two-person symmetric game $g: A \times A \to \mathbb{R}$. $A = \{1, \ldots, K\}$ is a finite set of pure strategies and $g(a, a')$ is a payoff of a player when he plays a and his opponent chooses a'. Let S be the set of mixed strategies, and the expected payoff from a mixed strategy profile (s, s') is denoted $g(s, s')$ with an abuse of notation.[3] A strategy may represent a mode of behavior (how aggressive one fights, for example), or a characteristic (such as sex or body size), and each individual is genetically programmed to choose a particular strategy. The payoff g is interpreted as the number of offspring, and called *fitness*. Reproduction is assumed to be asexual and offspring inherit the parent's strategy, unless mutations occur. The strategy distribution in the population can be represented by $s \in S$, and this admits alternative interpretations. When each individual is programmed to play a pure strategy, s represents the population frequencies of pure strategies. Alternatively, all players may be choosing exactly the same mixed strategy s. In general, when different (possibly mixed) strategies coexist, we say that the population is *polymorphic*: otherwise, we have a *monomorphic* population.

Definition 1 A strategy s of a symmetric two-person game is an *evolutionarily stable strategy (ESS)* if there is ε^0 such that for any $s' \neq s$ and any $\varepsilon \in (0, \varepsilon^0]$

$$g(s, (1 - \varepsilon)s + \varepsilon s') > g(s', (1 - \varepsilon)s + \varepsilon s'). \tag{1}$$

An ESS represents a stable state of population which is resistant to mutant invasion. When the incumbent strategy s is invaded by a small fraction ($\varepsilon\%$) of mutants playing s', equation (1) says that the incumbents do strictly better than the mutants. As the payoffs represent the number of offspring, this means that the population share of the mutants eventually vanishes.

Given $g(x, (1 - \varepsilon)y + \varepsilon z) = (1 - \varepsilon)g(x, y) + \varepsilon g(x, z)$, the above condition can be simplified: strategy s is an ESS if and only if

(E1) s constitutes a Nash equilibrium ($\forall s' g(s, s) \geq g(s', s)$), and
(E2) if $s' \neq s$ satisfies $g(s', s) = g(s, s)$, then $g(s, s') > g(s', s')$.

Condition (E2) highlights how an ESS refines Nash equilibrium. The unique feature of an ESS is to consider the possibility that a mutant encounters its copy (another mutant).

As an example, consider the infinitely repeated Prisoner's Dilemma game with no discounting, whose stage game is given in figure 8.1. Axelrod and Hamilton (1981) showed that the population of "always defect (D)" can be invaded by "tit-for-tat (TFT)."[4] When TFT meets D, it is cheated in the first stage but then reverts to defection. Since the loss in the first stage is negligible under no discounting, TFT fares as good as D against the incumbent strategy D (both yielding an average payoff of 2). However, when matched with TFT, TFT achieves cooperation (yielding a payoff of 4) and hence does strictly better than D, which yields a payoff of 2 against TFT. Hence, when the population of D is invaded by a small number of TFT, the TFT population grows faster than that of D and eventually takes over the whole population. The upshot is that D is not an ESS.

ESS has been quite successfully applied in biology, especially for a mixed strategy equilibrium. In typical applications, the actual population frequencies of strategies, such as body size, sex, or timing of emergence, are measured and compared with the evolutionarily stable mixed strategy equilibrium. In this regard, it should be stressed that one of the merits of ESS is its ability to differentiate stable versus unstable mixed strategy equilibria. Figure 8.2 may be helpful to understand this point. One can see, by checking (E2), that $s = (1/2, 1/2)$ is an ESS in figure 8.2 (a) but not in (b).

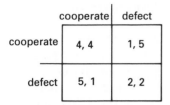

	cooperate	defect
cooperate	4, 4	1, 5
defect	5, 1	2, 2

Figure 8.1

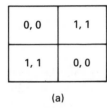 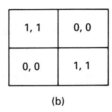

0, 0	1, 1
1, 1	0, 0

(a)

1, 1	0, 0
0, 0	1, 1

(b)

Figure 8.2

Note that the traditional refinements fail to capture the stability of completely mixed equilibria: the non-ESS $s = (1/2, 1/2)$ in figure 8.2 (b) passes all the tests of the traditional refinements in economics that are based on trembles (such as perfection, properness, or stability). The reason is that the mathematical definition of trembles fails to perturb completely mixed strategies.

While the definition of ESS does not formalize an explicit dynamic, it is meant to capture a locally stable point of a dynamic process of evolution. In biology, the following process, called the *replicator dynamic*, is widely used. First, we consider the case where each player plays a pure strategy. In this case, the replicator dynamic is given by

$$ds_k/dt = s_k[g(k, s) - g(s, s)], \quad k = 1, 2, \ldots, K. \tag{2}$$

This is derived as follows. Consider a large (continuum)[5] polymorphic population with pure strategies and suppose that $\alpha\Delta\%$ of players with each strategy breed according to the fitness function g within a small time interval Δ. Let M and κ be the total population and the population of strategy k at time t, and let M' and κ' denote those variables at $t + \Delta$. Similarly, we denote $s = s(t)$, $s' = s(t + \Delta)$ and let $g_k = g(k, s)$, $g = g(s, s)$. The we have

$$\frac{s'_k - s_k}{\Delta} = \frac{1}{\Delta}\left(\frac{\kappa'}{\kappa} - \frac{M'}{M}\right)\frac{\kappa}{M'} = \alpha(g_k - g)\frac{\kappa}{M'}. \tag{3}$$

As $\Delta \to 0$, we get $ds_k/dt = \alpha s_k(g_k - g)$, and aside from the speed of adjustment α this is the replicator equation (2).

According to the replicator dynamic, the population share of a strategy is increased (decreased) if it does better (worse) than the population average. If this is a reasonable description of an actual population dynamic, it is desirable that its asymptotically stable[6] rest points exactly correspond to the ESS's. This issue was studied by Taylor and Jonker (1978) under a certain restriction, followed by generalizations by Hofbauer, Schuster, and Sigmund (1979) and Zeeman (1981):

Claim 1 *ESS is always an asymptotically stable point of the pure strategy replicator dynamic* (2), *but the converse is not true.*

An example of an asymptotically stable point of (2) which fails to be an ESS is a mixed strategy equilibrium which works as follows (see van Damme (1987) for the details). Since it is not an ESS, an invading group of mutants can do better than the *average* incumbents. However, as the incumbent population is polymorphic, there can be a particular incumbent pure strategy which does strictly better than the mutants. Then it is possible that the mutants will die out.

The above explanation shows that the definition of ESS (1) is motivated by a *dimorphic* situation where a monomorphic population *s* is invaded by a small monomorphic group of mutants s'. In such a situation, selection pressure operates only among the two existing strategies, *s* and s', and clearly the system returns to *s* if and only if (1) holds. In particular, contrary to the polymorphic situation, *s* cannot be stable unless it is an ESS. Hence, we can expect that the converse in claim 1 is true when players can play mixed strategies. The replicator dynamics where each player chooses a mixed strategy are examined by Hines (1980), Zeeman (1981), Cressman (1990), Weissing (1990) and Bomze and van Damme (1992) and basically their works show:

Claim 2 *Under the mixed strategy replicator dynamics asymptotic stability and ESS exactly coincide.*[7]

3   EXTENSIONS OF THE BASIC CONCEPTS

Some modifications are necessary when one tries to apply the basic biological concepts to various economic problems. First, the original definition of an ESS applies only to *symmetric two-person* games. Clearly, extension to more general classes is necessary both in economics and in biology. Such modifications are possible but involve some subtle issues, as we will see. Secondly, the basic premises in biology, that strategy is genetically programmed and a payoff represents the number of offspring, do not literally apply in economics. Reinterpretations and alternative formulations are in order in economic applications.

Let us examine the second issue first. In economics, successful strategies may proliferate by means of imitation rather than reproduction. Consider a continuum of players each of whom is randomly matched with another player in each period. Suppose that in each period with probability α each player randomly and independently samples one player from the population and observes the sampled player's payoff with observation error ε. The observation error for each player is i.i.d. with uniform distribution on $[-c, c]$, where c is sufficiently large.[8] Assume that a player switches to the sampled strategy if and only if the observed payoff is better than her own payoff. When the current strategy distribution is s, the following fraction will use strategy k in the next round (within the α percent of the population who can potentially adjust):

$$z_k \equiv s_k \sum_{i,j,h} [\Pr(g(k,h) + \varepsilon > g(i,j)) + \Pr(g(i,j) + \varepsilon < g(k,h))]s_i s_j s_h.$$

The first term is the fraction of players who sample k and find the observed payoffs better, and the second term represents the original k-users whose observed payoffs are worse than their own. A simple calculation shows $z_k = s_k[g(k,s) - g(s,s)]/c + s_k$, and we have the replicator equation

$$s_k(t+1) - s_k(t) = (\alpha/c)s_k(t)[g(k, s(t)) - g(s(t), s(t))].$$

With a similar calculation one can derive the replicator dynamic if (1) there is no observation error, (2) a player switches to the sampled strategy only when the latter is better, and (3) the switching probability is proportional to the payoff difference (Cabrales (1994) and Schlag (1994)). Point (3) can be justified by a positive switching cost which is uniformly distributed. Schlag provides and axiomatic foundation for imitation behavior (2) and (3). Thus we conclude that the replicator dynamic can be justified by imitation, provided that imitation is done in plausible but rather specific ways.[9]

In economic application we may assume that players are more rational than are supposed in the above discussion. In particular, players may be aware of the payoff function and can optimize, while revising their expectations in an adaptive way. Gilboa and Matsui (1991) analyze such a case and propose *best-response dynamics*

$$d^+ s(t)/dt = \alpha(h(t) - s(t)),$$

$$h(t) \in BR(s(t)).$$

(4)

Here, d^+s/dt denotes the right-derivative $\lim_{\Delta \downarrow 0}(s(t + \Delta) - s(t))/\Delta$ and $BR(s)$ is the set of mixed strategy best responses against s. The best-response dynamics assume that $\alpha\Delta\%$ of the players switch to a best response against the current state within a small time interval Δ. Note that under the replicator dynamics a suboptimal strategy can grow if it does better than the average, while only the best response can grow under the best-response dynamics. Gilboa and Matsui propose a *cyclically stable set (CSS)* as the stable outcome of their process. We say that s' is reachable from s, if s' is an accumulation point of a trajectory of (4) with $s(0) = s$. If s'' is reachable from s', which in turn is reachable from s, we also say that s'' is reachable from s. A CSS is a set such that (i) its elements are mutually reachable and (ii) no point outside is reachable from it.[10] Intuitively a CSS includes stable equilibria and limit cycles (and more complicated objects), and its relationship to evolutionary stability will be discussed later.

The imitation and best-response dynamics may be too naive for economic application, because the players do not try to predict the rivals' future behavior change at all. Incorporating sophistication, however, leads us to a dilemma. Unless we treat the adjustment process itself as a dynamic game and look at the equilibrium path with rational expectations, the model can be criticized as being naive and *ad hoc*. However, such an approach is inadequate to examine how equilibrium is reached and which one is selected, because the dynamic game itself begs the same questions. Economists have not yet agreed on how adjustment processes should be formulated, and it is not clear if they will ever agree. This has been a major obstacle for evolutionary game theory in becoming a standard analytical tool in economics.

Now let us turn to the question of how to extend the notion of an ESS beyond symmetric two-person games. Let us introduce a general n-person game $g: A \rightarrow \mathbb{R}^n$, where $A = A_1 \times \cdots \times A_n$ is the finite set of pure strategy profiles. As before, the payoff function g is extended to the set of mixed strategy profiles $S = S_1 \times \cdots \times S_n$. First note that the extension to *symmetric n-person games* is straightforward, if we reinterpret $g(x, (1 - \varepsilon)s + \varepsilon s')$ in (1) as player 1's payoff when she plays x and each of her opponents plays pure strategy k with probability $(1 - \varepsilon)s_k + \varepsilon s'_k$.

For a general n-person game, which is not necessarily symmetric, Selten (1980) considers the case where groups of n players are randomly chosen from a single population, and then each player in a group is randomly assigned to one of the n players' roles in the stage game. Note that a strategy in this setting is a contingent action plan, specifying one action for each role. Then we can apply condition (1) for this symmetrized version to define an ESS in any game. However, this approach does not provide a new concept of equilibrium refinement, as Selten (1980) showed:

Claim 3 *ESS is equivalent to strict equilibrium under random role assignment.*[11]

To see this, take a stage game played by a buyer and a seller, and consider a non-strict equilibrium where the buyer has an alternative best reply. If some players' actions for the buyer's role mutate to the alternative best reply, while their actions in the seller's position remain unchanged, the mutants clearly fare equally well as the incumbents, and the condition (1) is violated (it is satisfied with equality). The essential feature underlying the definition of an ESS in a symmetric contest is that new actions are matched together, but under random role assignment this is not necessarily true.

A similar problem arises in extensive form games, where there is no selection pressure upon the actions off the path of play. For example, consider the repeated Prisoner's Dilemma discussed in section 2. While D can be invaded by TFT, TFT itself is not an ESS because it can be invaded by strategy C, which always cooperates (both sides of condition (1) are equal). In general, *an ESS in an extensive form game fails to exist if there are off-the-equilibrium actions*, because mutants whose actions differ only off the path of play fare equally well as the incumbents.

Let us say that mutants are *neutral* if they fare equally well as the incumbents do, and let us call invasion by neutral mutants *evolutionary drift*. As we have seen, when we go beyond symmetric two-person normal form games, quite often the possibility of evolutionary drifts causes the non-existence of an ESS. Hence how to treat evolutionary drifts is a crucial point in the extension of ESS to general games.

An easy way to deal with this problem is to simply allow for neutral mutations. Strategy s in a symmetric game is called a *weak ESS* or *neutrally stable strategy (NSS)* if (1) is satisfied with weak inequality.[12] The population share of neutral mutants remains unchanged until additional mutations happen, so NSS captures the stability in the short or medium run. However, this may not capture the stability in the long run, where the system can drift away from a NSS with enough accumulation of neutral mutations, leading to an unstable point as figure 8.3 (a) shows.

This observation motivates the following set-valued concept, introduced by Thomas (1985). First, when we have $g(x, x) = g(y, x)$ and $g(x, y) = g(y, y)$, we write xDy. This is similar to condition (E2), and it shows that y is a neutral mutant which can remain in the incumbent population of x. Note that the system can drift from x to y in the long run by the accumulation of such neutral mutations. Then we define the following.

Definition 2 A closed set $X \subset S$ is *evolutionary stable (ES)* in a symmetric two-person game if (i) each element of X is NSS and (ii) $x \in X$ and xDy implies $y \in X$.

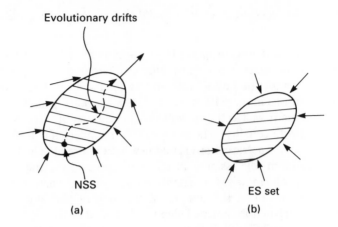

Figure 8.3

The state can drift within an ES set but cannot go outside; if a small fraction of mutants move the state outside the set, the mutants do strictly worse than the incumbents and the state moves back to the set, as figure 8.3 (b) shows. In fact, Thomas (1985) proves:

Claim 4 *An ES set is asymptotically stable under the replicator dynamic* (2).

We can see that tit-for-tat (TFT) in the repeated Prisoner's Dilemma is a NSS but it does not belong to an ES set, as TFT D C but C, which always cooperates, is not Nash (hence not a NSS).

The last point suggests that ES may be modified in economic applications to preclude such fragile mutations as C. Although the drift to C is possible in biological evolution, rational economic agents may hesitate to invade the population of TFT with such a fragile plan. Swinkels (1992a) proposed the following concept:

Definition 3 A set $X \subset S$ is *equilibrium evolutionarily stable (EES)* in an n-person game if it is a minimal closed non-empty set such that (i) each element of X is a Nash equilibrium and (ii) $\exists \varepsilon' > 0$ such that $\forall \varepsilon \in (0, \varepsilon')$, and $\forall x \in X$ and $\forall y \in S$, $y \in BR((1 - \varepsilon)x + \varepsilon y)$ implies $(1 - \varepsilon)x + \varepsilon y \in X$.

A motivation for this concept is to endow a certain amount of rationality for the mutants. If we have $y \in BR((1 - \varepsilon)x + \varepsilon y)$, $\varepsilon\%$ of the incumbent population x can be invaded by y, because such a plan is self-enforcing among the mutants. An EES set is robust to such *equilibrium entrants*; the population can never leave an ESS set by a series of small equilibrium entries. Swinkels goes on to show that for any extensive form all points in an ESS set generically differ only in off-the-equilibrium behavior and possess the same equilibrium path.[13]

Matsui (1992) provided another motivation for EES based on the best-response dynamics. First let us modify definition 3 (ii) to allow ε' to depend on x and y.[14] Also let us allow only piecewise linear trajectories of the best-response dynamics in the definition of CSS. Under these modified definitions, Matsui showed:

Claim 5 *A set of Nash equilibria is EES if and only if it is a CSS.*

In other words, an EES is a set of Nash equilibria which cannot be upset by the best-response dynamics. The basic reason for this result is the following. It can be shown that for any given $x \in X$ and y, if $y \in BR((1 - \varepsilon)x + \varepsilon y)$ holds for a small enough $\varepsilon = \varepsilon'$, it also holds *for all* $\forall \varepsilon \in (0, \varepsilon')$. Then, clearly there is a best-response path from x to $(1 - \varepsilon')x + \varepsilon'y$.

Selten (1983) proposes a different line of approach to deal with the evolutionary drifts in extensive-form games. We may expect that the information sets off the path of play are reached with small but strictly positive probabilities in reality by various reasons which are ignored in the formal model. If there are such "trembles," selection pressure is at work off the equilibrium path, and such effects provide a sharper prediction. Selten defines the notion of **limit ESS** to formulate this idea for a symmetric two-person extensive-form game.[15] Let Γ be a symmetric two-person extensive form game, and let b, h, and $C(h)$ denote a behavioral strategy for player 1, an information set for either player, and the set of available actions at h. We will consider symmetric "trembles," which they can be represented by a function δ from $\cup_h C(h)$ to $\mathbb{R}$ that satisfies (i) $\forall c \; \delta(c) \geq 0$, (ii) $\forall h \Sigma_{c \in C(h)} \delta(c) \leq 1$, and (iii) $\delta(c) = \delta(c')$ whenever player 1's action c corresponds to player 2's action c' under the given symmetry. A perturbed game (Γ, δ) is a game where each action c must be taken with a probability greater than or equal to $\delta(c)$. Suppose b_m and its symmetric counterpart for player 2 constitute an ESS (defined with respect to behavioral strategies) of (Γ, δ_m) for each m, where $\delta_m \to 0$ and $b_m \to b^*$ as $m \to \infty$. Then we say that b^* is a limit ESS. Note that an ESS is always a limit ESS because $\forall_m \delta_m \equiv 0$ is allowed.

Finally, we comment on the existence of various solution concepts:

Claim 6 *ESS, NSS, ES set, EES set, and limit ESS do not always exist, while CSS always exists.*

The reason is that those concepts try to capture the stable outcome of the evolutionary process but there is no guarantee that the process converges to a Nash equilibrium. In some cases, a limit cycle can be global attractor. Therefore, all those concepts which require the solution to be Nash equilibrium fail to have the existence property. To get existence, we must allow for other behavior patterns such as the limit cycle, as CSS does. In this respect it is interesting to note that limit cycles can provide a certain justification for Nash equilibria. Schuster, Sigmund, Hofbauer, and Wolff (1981) show that if all strategies appear on the limit cycle of the replicator dynamic (2), the time average on the limit cycle corresponds to a completely mixed strategy equilibrium.

4   EVOLUTION AND RATIONALITY

In this section we examine if the evolutionary models developed above actually support the Alchian–Friedman's thesis of "as if" rationality (Alchian (1950) and Friedman (1953)). In a strategic situation, various degrees of rationality can be defined, ranging from the use of undominated strategy, rationalizability, Nash equilibrium, sequential rationality and forward induction. We examine how they are justified by evolutionary processes, and also show that evolution can explain certain types of irrational behavior.

4.1   Optimization

Without strategic interaction (i.e., for a single person decision problem), the combination of selection pressure and mutation should lead to the optimal choice. This rather straightforward intuition can fail when we have uncertainty. Suppose that a choice s induces a probability distribution $q(s) = (q_1(s), \ldots, q_I(s))$ over the set of realized payoffs $\{R_1, \ldots, R_I\}$. The underlying shocks are *global*, such as weather, so that *in each period the players with the same strategy receive the same realization of R*, but the shocks are independent over time. After T periods, the number of offspring of a player is $W = R(1) \times \cdots \times R(T)$, where $R(t)$ is the realized payoff at time t. Since $E[W] = \Pi_t E[R(t)]$, the strategy that maximizes the *number* of offspring in the long run is equal to the expected payoff maximizer. However, it does not maximize the long-run *population share*. Suppose a player and its offspring adopt a strategy which induces distribution q. By the law of large numbers, if T is sufficiently long, R_i is realized approximately in $q_i T$ periods. Then, with a large probability the number of offspring after T is approximately

$$(R_1^{q_1} \cdots R_I^{q_I})^T \equiv L^T.$$

Hence if a strategy (uniquely) maximizes L, its expected population share is almost 1 for a large enough T. As maximizing L is equivalent to maximizing $\log L = \Sigma_i q_i \log R_i = E[\log R]$, we have:

Claim 7 *If payoff R is subject to common random shocks across players, the strategy which maximizes E[logR] dominates the populations share with probability one.*

As $R = e^{\log R}$, the log of payoff (fitness) is interpreted as the growth rate. Hence, biologists use expected growth rate, rather than expected fitness, under the kind of uncertainty described above (see Cohen (1996)). In economics, a strategy may be interpreted as an investment opportunity and R as the return for an asset. The above analysis shows that the market selects the optimal choice for von Neumann–Morgenstern utility $u(R) = \log R$. Hence, when the investors are risk neutral, economic natural selection leads to suboptimal, rather cautious behavior in the long run, and Alchian–Friedman's thesis fails for this important class of situations. See Blume and Easley (1992, 1993, 1995) for a systematic treatment.

4.2   Domination and rationalizability

If a game is played by rational players, and, if this fact is common knowledge, the outcome should be rationalizable as defined by Bernheim (1984) and Pearce (1984). Let us say that a player is first-order rational if she can calculate the best responses. A player is nth-order rational if she takes a best response given that the other players are $(n-1)$th-order rational. A rationalizable strategy is defined to be an ∞-order rational choice.[16] Suppose players are first-order rational and update their beliefs in an *adaptive* fashion, in the sense that a strategy which is never played after a finite period will asymptotically receive zero probability. Fictitious play in the learning literature and the best-response dynamics satisfy this property. Then, a player's rationality evolves toward a higher order over time, and in the long run players will end up choosing rationalizable strategies. See Milgrom and Roberts (1991) for a comprehensive treatment of this issue:

Claim 8 *If players take the best response against expectations which are revised adaptively, only iteratively strictly undominated strategies survive.*

The above argument needs to be modified when the players are not even first-order rational. Under natural selection or imitation where players switch to *better* strategies, a strategy doing sufficiently well may survive even if it is never a best response. The following example, due to Dekel and Scotchmer (1992) serves as such an example. Figure 8.4 is the column player's payoff matrix of a symmetric two-person game, which is basically a Rock–Paper–Scissors game with an additional strategy D. Assume that D is strictly dominated by the mixture of the first three strategies (i.e. $(a + b + c)/3 > a + \varepsilon$). Without D, the population share under a variety of

$$
\begin{array}{c}
\begin{array}{cccc} R & P & S & D \end{array} \\
\begin{array}{c} R \\ P \\ S \\ D \end{array}
\left(\begin{array}{cccc}
a & c & b & \delta \\
b & a & c & \delta \\
c & b & a & \delta \\
a+\varepsilon & a+\varepsilon & a+\varepsilon & 0
\end{array}\right)
\end{array}
$$

$c < a < b, \ 0 < \varepsilon < b - a, \ 0 < \delta$

Figure 8.4

better-response dynamics, including the discrete-time replicator dynamic (3) with simultaneous reproduction ($\alpha = \Delta = 1$), can approach the cycle of Rock (R) → Paper (P) → Scissors (S) → $\cdots$ as depicted in figure 8.5. Because $\varepsilon > 0$, D can proliferate when a majority of the population play a single strategy, and therefore can survive near this cycle. Hence we conclude that the strictly dominated strategy can survive under some better-response dynamics.

This example has the property that D is strictly dominated by a *mixed* strategy. In contrast, Nachbar (1990) and Samuelson and Zhang (1992) show:

Claim 9 *If a pure strategy is strictly dominated by another pure strategy (or, iteratively strictly dominated in pure strategies), it cannot survive under any monotonic dynamic, provided that all strategies exist initially.*

Monotone dynamic[17] is a class of selection processes over pure strategies

$$ds_i/dt = s_i F_i(g(1, s), \ldots, g(K, s), s) \tag{5}$$

whose "growth rate function" F_i satisfies

$$g(i, s) > g(j, s) \Rightarrow F_i > F_j. \tag{6}$$

Claim 9 holds because the relative share s_j/s_i under such a dynamic tends to zero, if j is strictly dominated by i.

A strengthening of (6),

$$g(x, s) > g(j, s) \Rightarrow \Sigma_i F_i x_i > F_j \tag{7}$$

is called *convex monotonicity*. Hofbauer and Weibull (1995) showed a sweeping result:

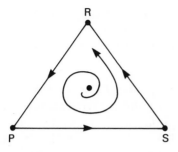

Figure 8.5

Claim 10 *Convex monotonicity is necessary*[18] and sufficient for a selection dynamic (5) to eliminate iteratively strictly dominated strategies, when all strategies are present initially.

Convex monotonicity admits a wide class of selection dynamics, including the replicator dynamic. Hence we conclude that players act as if rationality were common knowledge under a wide class of selection processes.

4.3   Refinements

Van Damme (1987) showed:

Claim 11 *An ESS is a proper equilibrium.*

Therefore ESS is also trembling-hand perfect. Van Damme also showed (1984) that a proper equilibrium in the normal form of an extensive form game induces a sequential equilibrium. Those two facts, taken together, have the remarkable implication that such sophisticated behavior as sequentiality can evolve from a minimal amount of rationality. However, this observation is in a sense vacuous, because an extensive form most often possesses no ESS because of the evolutionary drifts off the path of play. Swinkels (1992b) handles this problem by his set-theoretic notion of EES. With this concept, he provides an evolutionary justification not only for backwards induction (sequentiality), but also for forward induction (the "never a weak best response" property of Kohlberg and Mertens (1986)). He first modifies the definition 3 (ii) of EES as; (iia) $\exists$ a neighborhood of X, denoted U, such that $\forall \varepsilon \in (0, 1)$, $\forall x \in X$ and $\forall y \in S$, $z = (1 - \varepsilon)x + \varepsilon y \in U$ and $y \in BR(z)$ imply $z \in X$.[19] Then he shows the following.

Claim 12 *In a generic extensive form, if an EES set (defined with (iia)) is convex,*[20] then the set possesses a single outcome, and it satisfies both backwards induction (sequentiality) and forward induction (the never a weak best-response property).

This comes from the fact that, under the stated assumptions, the EES set contains a set that is both fully stable (implying sequentiality) and stable (implying forward induction).[21] Swinkels demonstrates that in the beer–quiche example (Cho and Kreps (1987)) only the "right" (beer drinking) equilibria correspond to an EES set.

4.4   Irrationality

Evolutionary game theory also has a potential to explain particular *irrational* behavior that we observe in reality. One prominent reason why irrational behavior may survive is that *commitment* to a suboptimal strategy pays in strategic situations. Rational people may give way to a crazy driver, and a stubborn player with a short temper may obtain better terms in negotiation than a sensible person does. Frank (1987, 1988), Banerjee and Weibull (1995), Biais and Shadur (1993), and Carmichael and MacLeod (1995) elaborate on this point. This idea is built on the assumption that there is a credible way to signal that a player is committed to a certain type of behavior. Frank argues that physical symptoms of emotional arousal, such as posture or facial expression, can serve as such signals. A weakness of this theory is that it ignores the possibility that mutants who are not committed but only mimic the signals can proliferate.

Casual observation suggests that people tend to put more emphasis on relative performance than is justified by rationality, ("peer pressure" or "jealously"). In a small population where a player's action has a great impact on others, a suboptimal behavior which harms one's opponents more than oneself may prosper. Evolution of such *spiteful behavior* has been studied by Hamilton (1970), Schaffer (1988), Crawford (1991), Rhode and Stegeman (1994), and Vega-Redondo (1995). There is also a large body of literature on evolution of altruism in biology. See, for example, Hamilton (1972). Given those observations, one may take a fundamentalist view that evolution is the first principle and rationality is only one of its many consequences.

5   EVOLUTION AND EFFICIENCY – SECRET HANDSHAKE

One of the most notable implications of evolutionary game theory is that efficient outcomes emerge in some important classes of games in econ-

	a	b
a	3, 3	0, 0
b	0, 0	2, 2

Figure 8.6

omics. This idea dates back to Axelrod and Hamilton's paper (1981) on the evolution of cooperation (see also Axelrod (1984)) in the repeated Prisoners' Dilemma, which has attracted much attention. As we have seen, "tit-for-tat" is evolutionarily stable (a NSS), while "always defect" is unstable. However, it turns out that some inefficient equilibria are also evolutionarily stable. For example, it is easy to check that the following strategy is a NSS: (i) it cooperates every other period and (ii) reverts to defection once the opponent deviates from the behavior pattern (i). Hence one cannot readily conclude that evolution always leads to cooperation. This problem was resolved by Fudenberg and Maskin (1990) and Binmore and Samuelson (1992), who found reasonable sets of assumptions under which the unique evolutionary outcome of the repeated Prisoners' Dilemma is efficient.

On the other hand, Matsui (1991), Wärneryd (1991), and Kim and Sobel (1995) discovered that the evolutionary process derives meaningful pre-play communication and leads to an efficient outcome in a class of games. These two sets of results, evolution of cooperation in repeated games and evolution of meaningful pre-play communication, share the same basic logic, which Robson (1990) calls "secret handshake." As we already have an excellent survey of the former issue (Fudenberg (1992)), we will focus on the latter. Sobel (1993) provides a general survey of those issues.

Consider the game in figure 8.6. If players can discuss before playing this game, our intuition strongly suggests that they agree to play the efficient equilibrium (a,a), However, explaining such "meaningful pre-play communication" had long been a notoriously difficult open problem before evolutionary game theory.

To see this, let us formally incorporate pre-play communication into the above game. In the first stage, each player simultaneously sends a costless message ("cheap talk") from a set M. After seeing the messages they choose actions in the above game. A strategy in this augmented game is a pair $s = (m, \sigma)$, where $m \in M$ and σ is a function from M^2 to $\{a, b\}$. Once this setup is made, it is easy to see that not all equilibria have meaningful pre-play communication. For example, strategy s^0 which sends a fixed message m^0 and always plays the inefficient action b constitutes a Nash equilibrium. Hence traditional equilibrium analysis fails to derive meaningful communication.

In contrast, evolution can explain how meaningful communication emerges. First we show that the population of s^0 can be invaded by s^1, which sends a different message m^1 and plays the efficient outcome a if and only if the exchanged message profile is (m^1, m^1). The mutant strategy takes the efficient action if and only if the opponent is another mutant, and otherwise it takes the same action as the incumbent does. Clearly, the mutant fares strictly better than the incumbent after invasion, and therefore s^0 is not an ESS (nor a NSS). In contrast, any strategy which plays the efficient action cannot be outperformed by mutants and therefore is a NSS.

Note that the following, which Robson (1990) calls "*secret handshake*," are the key to upsetting the inefficient equilibrium s^0.

(SH1) Mutants send a new message to identify themselves and achieve cooperation among themselves.

(SH2) Incumbents do not react to the new message.

To kill more complicated inefficient equilibria we need to apply the logic of the secret handshake in a more sophisticated manner. First, if the incumbent chooses all messages with positive probabilities and always plays b, mutants cannot identify themselves ((SH1) fails). Such a strategy is called the babbling equilibrium. Secondly, if the game is given by figure 8.7, the incumbent can react to the mutant and (SH2) fails. For example, consider strategy s^2, which sends m^0, and plays b if the opponent sends m^0, but otherwise plays c. Against this strategy, anyone sending a new message is punished, so mutants cannot directly invade.

One way to deal with these problems is to invoke evolutionary drifts. Since the choice of message is inconsequential in the babbling equilibrium, the probability distribution over messages can drift. When a particular message becomes sufficiently rare, mutants can invade by using that message. As for strategy s^2, the punishment is off the path of play in the incumbent population, so it can drift. When sufficiently many incumbents cease to choose c against unsent messages, mutants can invade. In either case, for any inefficient equilibrium s' there is a non-NSS s'' such that $s' \, D \, s''$. Hence the inefficient strategies do not belong to ES sets.[22] This observation can be generalized. Consider a two-person game, which has a unique weakly Pareto efficient strategy profile. Such a game is called a *common interest game*.

	a	b	c
a	3, 3	0, 0	0, 0
b	0, 0	2, 2	0, 0
c	0, 0	0, 0	1, 1

Figure 8.7

Claim 13 *Assume that a common interest game with pre-play communication is played with random role assignment. Then there is an unique ES set,*[23] *and* each of its elements supports the efficient outcome.

The above argument is based on substantial accumulation of evolutionary drifts and it may take a long time to kill inefficient equilibria. The availability of a new message may not be a fundamental problem because in reality there should always be some unsent messages. As for the drifts to derive (SH2), Bhaskar (1994) has shown that fast evolution is possible if there is a possibility of misperception of messages. If the receiver's perception is not known to the sender, it is not a Nash equilibrium to react to unsent messages, so without any drifts inefficient equilibria can be killed.

Finally, we briefly explain the evolution of efficiency in the repeated Prisoners' Dilemma. When we assume no discounting, actions in early stages of a repeated game, which do not affect the total payoff, can serve as costless messages to derive (SH1). For (SH2) to hold, players should not react harshly to such deviations, and Fudenberg and Maskin (1990) introduce trembling hands and Binmore and Samuelson (1992) employ cost of complexity to suppress harsh punishment.

6   STOCHASTIC EVOLUTION

The theories reviewed above rely on mutation, and most models treat mutation as a small one-shot perturbation of the underlying dynamical system. There are also some results relying on a substantial accumulation of neutral mutations, or evolutionary drift. In either case, random mutation is not explicitly incorporated in the formal models. In this section we will see that explicitly modeled dynamics with random mutations can provide sharper predictions in a specific sense. Such an approach was initiated by the seminal paper by Foster and Young (1990).

6.1   A motivating story

Let us begin with a simple story (taken form Kandori, Mailath, and Rob (1993), abbreviated KMR hereafter) to understand the basic logic and scope of potential applications. Imagine that there is a dormitory with ten graduate students. Each student is either using a Mac or IBM personal computer and the situation can be modeled as a random matching coordination game (figure 8.8). The stage game has two pure strategy equilibria, (Mac, Mac) and (IBM, IBM). The mixed strategy equilibrium assigns probability one third to Mac, and this means that Mac is the best response if more than one third of the fellow students are Mac users. The students buy new computers every once in a while, and, when they do, they switch to the current best response. We also assume that, with a small probability ε, the students "mutate" to a suboptimal choice. This may be caused by temporal shocks to the payoffs or mistakes. Or, each student sometimes exits from the dormitory and is replaced by a new comer, who brings his/her own computer.

Although the two pure strategy equilibria are locally stable (ESSs), each equilibrium can be upset *in the long run* where a large number of repeated mutations can happen. As the mutation rate ε tends to zero, it becomes harder to upset either equilibrium, but upsetting the IBM equilibrium becomes much harder. This is because upsetting the IBM equilibrium requires seven mutations, while upsetting the Mac equilibrium needs only four mutations. When the mutation rate is small, the former is much less likely to happen.[24]

Hence, if we look at the relative proportion of time spent on the Mac equilibrium in an *infinite* time horizon, it converges to one as ε tends to zero. In this sense in the (very) long run the Mac equilibrium is much more likely to appear under a small mutation rate.[25]

The above story is informal and will be made precise shortly. However, it illustrates both the strength and limitations of such an approach. First, note that stochastic evolution can select among strict equilibria, while this is impossible for virtually all existing equilibrium refinements, including ESS, based on the local stability of equilibria.

On the other hand, such a strong prediction is valid only under a specific class of situations. Whereas the crisp equilibrium selection requires a vanishing mutation rate, the same condition makes the waiting time to see the long-run effects indefinitely long. For example, assuming fast (instantaneous) adjustment, KMR report that the expected time to upset each equilibrium is about 78 periods for IBM and 100,00 for Mac, when the mutations rate is 0.1. When the analyst's time horizon is less than 100, the initial condition (or the "path dependence") is clearly more relevant than

	Mac	IBM
Mac	2, 2	0, 0
IBM	0, 0	1, 1

Figure 8.8

the long-run prediction. On the other hand, if the relevant horizon is more than 1,000, for example, the long-run effects cannot be ignored.

A similar caveat applies to the population size. If the dormitory in the above story had 1,000 students, upsetting the IBM equilibrium would require more than 333 mutations to Mac, and this is clearly very unlikely in any reasonable time horizon. Therefore stochastic evolution is most relevant for a small population.

6.2   The discrete model

Now we present formal models to capture the long-run effects of repeated random mutation. As the present approach is most relevant for a small population, we first consider the discrete model, which has a finite population and discrete time. Such a model was first introduced by KMR (1993), and generalized by Young (1993a) and Kandori and Rob (1995). Consider a general n-person game $g: A \rightarrow \mathbb{R}^n$. We consider the situation where a finite number of players play this game by random matching.[26] State z represents the current strategy distribution. We assume that each player chooses a pure strategy, so the state space is a finite set and denoted $Z = \{1, \ldots, J\}$. In each period, a certain set of players are selected (possibly randomly) and they adjust to myopic best responses. In addition, we assume that, at the end of each period, each player "mutates" with probability ε. When a player mutates, she randomizes with a fixed-probability distribution, which assigns a strictly positive probability for each action.

This defines a time-homogeneous Markov chain. The transition probability is denoted by $p_{ij} = \Pr(z(t + 1) = j \,|\, z(t) = i)$, and let P be the matrix whose ij element is p_{ij}. With this notation the law of motion is given by $q(t + 1) = q(t)P$, where $q(t)$ is the row vector representing the probability distribution over the state space Z at time t. The stationary point of this process μ ($\mu = \mu P$) is called a *stationary distribution*.

When the mutation rate ε is zero, the long-run outcome generally depends on the initial condition. A possible long-run outcome in the absence of mutation can be captured by a set $X \subset Z$ satisfying: (i) $\forall i, j \in X \exists t$ s.t. $Pr(z(t) = j \mid z(0) = i) > 0$, and (ii) $Pr(z(1) \in X \mid z(0) \in X) = 1$. Such a set is called a *recurrent communication class or limit set*, and it is similar to a CSS in the continuous framework. It may represent a Nash equilibrium or a cyclical behavior, and the system is eventually absorbed in one of such sets if mutations are absent.

In contrast, with a positive mutation rate the system fluctuates all over the state space, and the dependence on the initial condition vanishes in the long run.[27] More specifically, when $\varepsilon > 0$, there is a unique stationary distribution $\mu(\varepsilon)$, and it satisfies the following two properties for any initial condition $q(0)$: (i) $lim_{t \to \infty} q(t) = \mu(\varepsilon)$, and (ii) $\mu(\varepsilon)$ represents the relative proportion of time spent on each state (within infinite horizon). Such a system is called *ergodic*.[28]

When ε is small, the long-run behavior can be captured by the *limit distribution* $\mu^* = lim_{\varepsilon \to 0} \mu(\varepsilon)$. It can be shown that the limit distribution always exists and its support is a collection of limit sets.[29] A limit set in the support of μ^* is called a **long-run equilibrium**, and its element is called a **stochastically stable state** or **long-run state**. The Mac equilibrium in the above example is such a state, and it is most often observed in the long run when the mutation rate is small.

Long-run equilibria can be found by the following graph theoretic technique. First, given a finite path $f = (z(0), \ldots, z(T))$, the associated cost $c(f)$ is defined to be the minimum number of mutations to realize f with a positive probability. For a pair of limit sets X and Y, the cost of transition from X to Y is defined by $C(X, Y) = Min_f c(f)$, where the minimum is taken over the set of all paths from X to Y. Consider a tree whose set of nodes consists of all limits sets, and assume that it is directed into the root. Let us call such a graph a *transition tree*, and technically it is a collection of directed branches (X, Y) where X and Y are limit sets. We define the *cost of a transition tree* h by

$$\sum_{(X,Y) \in h} C(X, Y).$$

Then, we have the following "mutation counting" technique, originally due to Freidlin and Wentzell (1984). Their method was modified by KMR (1993) to analyze small population (discrete) models, followed by Young's (1993a) simplification to give the present form.

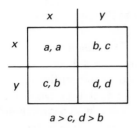

$a > c, d > b$

Figure 8.9

Claim 14 *A limit set is a long-run equilibrium if and only if it is the root of a minimum-cost transition tree.*

This procedure provides a selection among the limit sets, and some remarks are in order. First, in all existing results, the selection turns out to be unique for generic normal form games. Although the generic uniqueness of a long-run equilibrium is still a conjecture, it has been proved for a special class of games (see KMR (1993) for 2 × 2 games and Kandori and Rob (1994) for games with bandwagon effects). Second, for a class of games where the dynamic without mutation always converges to one of the Nash equilibria (Young (1993a) calls such a dynamic *acyclic*), stochastic evolution can provide a unique selection even among strict equilibria. Pure coordination games, supermodular games, and games with bandwagon effects fall in this category of games (Kandori and Rob (1992, 1995)).

6.3   Applications of the discrete model

The above technique has been applied to various games. KMR (1993) show:

Claim 15 *In a symmetric 2 × 2 game with two strict equilibria, the risk dominant equilibrium is the unique long-run equilibrium.*

According to Harsanyi and Selten (1988), equilibrium $X = (x, x)$ in figure 8.9 risk dominates $Y = (y, y)$ if and only if $a - c > d - b$. Calculation shows that x is the best response if and only if the opponent plays x with a probability more than

$$p = (d - b)/(a - c + d - b). \tag{8}$$

Since $p < 1/2$ if and only if $a - c > d - b$, the risk-dominant equilibrium is the one with the larger basin of attraction. The game has two limit sets, corresponding to the two strict equilibria, and (ignoring the integer problem) the cost of transition is pM for the transition from Y to X and

$(1 - p)M$ for the converse. Therefore, the root of the minimum cost tree is the risk dominant equilibrium.

An $m \times m$ symmetric game satisfies the *marginal bandwagon property* if for any a and b, $g(a,c) - g(b,c)$ is maximized when $c = a$. Kandori and Rob (1994) show that if an equilibrium pairwise risk dominates other equilibria in a game with a marginal bandwagon property, it becomes a unique long-run equilibrium.[30] In a pure coordination game, which is a symmetric two-person game with $g(a,a) > 0$ and $g(a,b) = 0$ for $a \neq b$, the Pareto efficient equilibrium is the unique long-run equilibrium (Kandori and Rob (1995)). Ellison (1995) and Maruta (1995) synthesize these results by showing that a 1/2-dominant equilibrium is the unique long-run equilibrium. In a symmetric game, strategy x constitutes a 1/2-dominant equilibrium if x is the unique best reply when more than 1/2 of the population is playing x.

Young (1993b) analyzes the Nash demand game and shows a striking result:

Claim 16 *For the Nash demand game (simultaneous offer bargaining game), the unique long-run equilibrium is the Nash bargaining solution.*

Consider two populations of players, such as buyers and sellers, who are going to bargain over a \$1 surplus. A seller and a buyer simultaneously announce their shares, α and β. If $\alpha + \beta \leq 1$, they get the announced shares, and enjoy payoffs $u(\alpha)$ and $v(\beta)$. Otherwise they get zero payoffs. Note that any exhaustive division $\alpha + \beta = 1$ is a Nash equilibrium, and, moreover, it is a strict equilibrium if both α and β are strictly positive. Young discretizes the strategy space by $S = \{0, 1/H, 2/H, \ldots, 1\}$, and shows that, for a sufficiently large integer H, the long-run equilibrium is the one that approximates the Nash bargaining solution $\text{Argmax}_{\alpha + \beta \leq 1} u(\alpha)v(\beta)$.

Nöldeke and Samuelson (1993) provide a useful characterization of the long-run equilibria and analyze extensive form games. Their result formalizes the idea that the set of long-run equilibria should be locally stable under dynamics without mutations. We say that a limit set X' is weakly reachable from a limit set X if $C(X, X') = 1$. If X'' is weakly reachable from X', which is in turn weakly reachable from X, we say that X'' is weakly reachable from X. A collection of limit sets constitutes a *locally stable component* if they are mutually weakly reachable and no other limit set is weakly reachable from them. This corresponds to a version of CSS (see endnote 10) and is similar in spirit to an ES set and an EES set. As we have seen, such a set-valued concept captures the effects of evolutionary drifts and is useful in analyzing extensive forms. Nöldeke and Samuelson show:

Claim 17 *The set of long-run equilibria corresponds to a collection of locally stable components.*

Using this, they show that a subgame perfect equilibrium emerges in the long run as a unique outcome only under a strong set of assumptions (1993). In the following paper (1995), they examine signaling games and show:

Claim 18 *In Spence's job market signaling game with two types, if the long-run equilibria possess a unique outcome, it must be an undefeated equilibrium.*[31]

Ellison (1993) shows that fast convergence to the stationary distribution holds true even in a large population, when the players interact locally. Suppose each player interacts with a small number of neighbors. If the neighborhoods have meager overlaps, the model is essentially a collection of isolated small populations and trivially fast convergence occurs. Ellison's contribution lies in the opposite, non-trivial case, where the overlap is substantial. Take the Mac versus IBM game (figure 8.8), and consider a large population covered by a number of small overlapping neighborhoods. Suppose more than one third of each neighborhood overlaps with an adjacent one. (Recall that one third is the critical mass of Mac users to make it a best response.) Even if all players are initially using IBM, if one neighborhood mutates into Mac, the adjacent neighborhoods may switch to Mac, thanks to the substantial overlap. Then, this "domino effect" continues until all players use Mac. Note that the opposite transition, from Mac to IBM, requires a substantial number of mutations in *each* neighborhood and therefore is very unlikely. Ellison also reports an example where different matching structures produce different long-run equilibria. Other models of local interaction include Blume (1993), An and Kiefer (1992), Goyal and Janssen (1993), and Anderlini and Ianni (1996). Durlauf (1991) and Aoki (1996) apply related techniques to macroeconomic problems.

6.4   The continuous model

The effects of perpetual randomness can be examined in a large (continuum) population in continuous time, using Brownian motion, and such a formulation provides somewhat different results. Foster and Young (1990) presented a continuous model, followed by Fudenberg and Harris (1992) and Vaughan (1993). Here we present Vaughan's approach, which provides a simple closed-form solution.

Consider the game in figure 8.9 and let $z \in [0, 1]$ represent the population of players adopting strategy x. The law of motion is given by the stochastic differential equation

$$dz = G(z)dt + \sigma(z)dW, \tag{9}$$

where dW represents the standard Brownian motion. The drift term $G(z)$ reflects selection pressure, and its graph is depicted in figure 8.10, where p corresponds to the mixed strategy equilibrium and is given by (8). Let $q(z,t)$ denote the probability density of state z at time t. It is known that the evolution of the system is described by the Fokker–Planck equation (or Kolmogorov's forward equation)[32]

$$\frac{\partial}{\partial t}q(z,t) = -\frac{\partial}{\partial z}[G(Z)q(z,t)] + \frac{1}{2}\frac{\partial^2}{\partial z^2}[\sigma^2(z)q(z,t)]. \tag{10}$$

Clearly this is satisfied if $\partial Pr(z(t) \leq z)/\partial t = \mathscr{F}q(z,t)$, where the operator $\mathscr{F}$ is defined by

$$\mathscr{F}q = -Gq + \frac{1}{2}\frac{\partial}{\partial z}\sigma^2 q.$$

We assume that (9) has reflecting boundaries, and this is formulated as the boundary conditions $\mathscr{F}q(0,t) = \mathscr{F}q(1,t) = 0$. Once the system reaches the stationary distribution $\mu(z)$, for any state z the probability mass below z does not change $(\partial Pr(z(t) \leq z)/\partial t = 0)$, so we must have

$$\mathscr{F}\mu(z) = 0, \tag{11}$$

not only at the boundaries $z = 0,1$ but everywhere. For simplicity, let us consider a special case where $\sigma^2(z) \equiv \sigma^2$. Solving the differential equation (11) with $\int_0^1 \mu(z) = 1$ yields

$$\mu(z) = \frac{e^{\psi(z)/\sigma^2}}{\displaystyle\int_0^1 e^{\psi(x)/\sigma^2}dx}, \tag{12}$$

where ψ/σ^2 is called the *potential* and given by

$$\psi(z) = 2\int_p^z G(x)dx.$$

As $\sigma^2 \to 0$, both the denominator and numerator of (12) diverge, so the stationary distribution places probability 1 at the state which maximizes ψ. Hence we have:

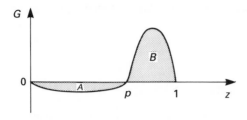

Figure 8.10

Claim 19 *Under the continuous dynamic* (9) *for a symmetric* 2 × 2 *game, the long-run equilibrium is the state with the maximum potential.*

Hence equilibrium (x, x) (corresponding to state $z = 1$) is the long-run equilibrium if area B is larger than area A in figure 8.10.

A couple of remarks are in order about the above result. First, the above model provides a simple closed form for all mutation rates (here measured by σ^2), whereas the discrete model in the previous section is intractable unless the mutation rate is vanishingly small. Second, the clean result depends on the assumption that the state space is one-dimensional (i.e., the underlying game is a 2 × 2 symmetric game). For a higher dimensional case, a closed-form solution can only be obtained under some restrictions on the drift terms.

Third, the nature of equilibrium selection is somewhat different between the discrete and continuous models. In the discrete model, the relative size of the basin of attraction determines the long-run equilibrium. In the continuous model, not only the size but also the strength of flow in each basin is important. For example, in figure 8.10, equilibrium (x, x) is risk dominated and has the smaller basin of attraction $(p < 1/2)$, but the flow of adjustment is much stronger there. As a result, area B is larger than area A, and the long-run equilibrium is the risk-dominated equilibrium (x, x).

Binmore, Samuelson, and Vaughan (1995) clarify the reason for the difference between the discrete and continuous models. If we examine the finite population case in continuous time with Poisson adjustment, the stationary distribution has a clean closed form when the state space is one-dimensional. Such a model is known as *the birth and death process*, and is employed by Amir and Berninghaus (1996) and Binmore and Samuelson (1993). Starting with the birth and death process, there are two ways to eliminate aggregate randomness. One method is to reduce the mutation rate for a fixed population size, which yields the prediction of the discrete model. The other way is to increase the population size with a fixed mutation rate. Binmore, Samuelson, and Vaughan show that increasing the population size for a fixed mutation rate and then reducing the mutation rate yields the prediction of the continuous model.

7   CONCLUDING REMARKS

How should we evaluate evolutionary game theory in economics? Mainstream economics, which only admits rational behavior, may criticize such an approach on the following grounds. First, allowing various behavioral assumptions provides too greater a degree of freedom and loses the prediction power of the theory. Second, the particular behavioral assumptions utilized so far in evolutionary game theory are too naive and implausible in economic applications. Third, the literature thus far is strictly theoretical and lacks convincing applications to concrete economic problems.

Evolutionary game theorists may admit these shortcomings but point to the necessity of a good theory of bounded rationality. Rationality itself is unable to explain how players come to play a Nash equilibrium or which equilibrium is selected. The long history of the rationality approach, which culminated in extensive research in non-cooperative game theory in the 1980s, finally revealed the necessity of another principle, and evolutionary game theory, although it is rather preliminary in its current form, hopefully provides a first step in this general direction.

Notes

Due to space constraints the choice of topics is far from exhaustive, and the references are limited to those directly discussed in the paper. Editing assistance by Antoine Bocquet is gratefully acknowledged.

1 Nelson and Winter (1982) also elaborate on natural selection in market competition.

2 A survey of evolutionary game theory can also be found in Banerjee and Weibull (1992), Bomze and Pötschner (1988), Fudenberg and Levine (1995), Hammerstein and Selten (1994), Hines (1987), Hofbauer and Sigmund (1988), Mailath (1992, 1993, 1995), Matsui (1995), Maynard Smith (1982), Samuelson (1993), Selten (1991), van Damme (1987, 1993), Vega-Redondo (1996), Weibull (1995) and Young (1995).

3 Also we do not distinguish pure strategy k and the mixed strategy which plays it with probability 1.

4 TFT starts with cooperation and then mimics the action taken by the opponent in the last period.

5 Boylan (1992, 1995) examines the relationship between the continuum, countable, and finite population cases.

6 We say s^* is *asymptotically stable* if for any $\varepsilon > 0$ there is $\delta > 0$ such that $\| s(0) - s^* \| < \delta$ implies (i) $\| s(t) - s^* \| < \varepsilon$ for all $t > 0$ and (ii) $\lim_{t \to \infty} s(t) = s^*$.

7 There can potentially be infinitely many mixed strategies and there is a question of how to reformulate (2) if a continuum of mixed strategies coexists (see Hines (1980) and Zeeman (1981)). Also, there are a variety of individual strategy distributions whose population average equals s, so the "stability of s" must be defined carefully. The cited works basically show that s is an ESS if and only if it is an asymptotically stable population average for *all* underlying individual strategy distributions.

8 More precisely, $c > \max_{i,j,k,h}[g(i,j) - g(k,h)]$.

9 Börgers and Sarin (1993) provides a learning model of a *fixed match* (N players playing an N-person game) based on the satisfying model of Busch and Mosteller (1955), and show that players' mixed strategies follow the replicator dynamics.

10 This is the definition employed by Matsui (1991) and (1992). The original definition by Gilboa and Matsui (1991) has a weaker notion of reachability. They say that z' is reachable from z if z' is reachable from all neighborhoods of z. This is the stability condition against small perturbations. They also propose similar definitions for general n-person games played by n populations of players.

11 A strict equilibrium is a Nash equilibrium with the unique best reply for each player.

12 Accordingly, the strict inequality in condition (E2) should be replaced with weak inequality to define NSS.

13 This is based on the Kohlberg and Mertens' result (1986) that a connected set of Nash equilibria has a single realized outcome for generic extensive-form games.

14 Formally, $\forall x \in X$ *and* $\forall y \in S$, $\exists \varepsilon' > 0$ such that for any $\varepsilon \in (0, \varepsilon')$, $y \in BR((1 - \varepsilon)x + \varepsilon y)$ implies $(1 - \varepsilon)x + \varepsilon y \in X$. Swinkels (1992a) conjectures that this is equivalent to the original definition 3 (ii).

15 As we have seen, an asymmetric extensive-form game can always be symmetrized by means of random role assignment. On the other hand, a given extensive form sometimes admits different ways to define symmetry. For the latter problem, see Selten (1983) or van Damme (1987) for details. The argument below presumes that a symmetry has already been defined for the game under consideration.

16 In a two-player game, iterative elimination of strictly dominated strategies, when performed in the space of mixed strategies, results in the set of all rationalizable strategies. In general, best response is undominated but not vice versa, so that rationalizable strategies are included in the set of iteratively strictly undominated strategies.

17 Nachbar (1990) analyzes the discrete time case. Monotone dynamics are also examined by Friedman (1991).

18 When selection dynamic (5) is not convex monotone, it cannot eliminate the dominated strategy D, when applied to the game in figure 8.4 for some parameter values.

19 The difference between (ii) and (iia) is that the latter measures perturbations by the distance the strategy distribution is moved, rather than the fraction of

entrants. For generic two-person extensive-form games, the difference is inconsequential (Swinkels (1992a)).

20 Swinkels (1992b) employs a weaker topological condition, which admits the case where the EES set is homomorphic to a convex set. He goes on to show that an EES set is always convex in a generic two-person extensive-form game.

21 Also see Ritzerburger and Weibull (1995) and Swinkels (1993) for the relationship between dynamic stability and strategic stability.

22 There is one more potential source of inefficiency. Consider a strategy which sends each message with an equal probability and plays the efficient action a (in the game in figure 5.1) if and only if *different* messages were sent. This inefficient equilibrim is an ESS essentially because mutants who send messages with uneven probabilities have less chance to achieve cooperation (a,a). Such an equilibrium is killed when the game is played by random role assignment, because mutants can send different messages in column and row player's role and always achieve cooperation among them.

23 The same conclusion holds if one replaces an ES set with an EES set or a CSS.

24 This assumes that a mutation always happens with the same probability ε. Bergin and Lipman (1996) point out that, if the mutation rate is state dependent, almost anything can happen in the long run.

25 A similar logic is utilized by a stochastic algorithm to find the global maximum ("*simulated annealing*" introduced by Kirkpatrick, Gelatt, Vecchi (1983)).

26 The present formulation incorporates various matching schemes, such as the n-population case, random role assignment with a single population, random matching with a single population for symmetric games, or non-uniform random matching (local interaction).

27 Canning has a series of works emphasizing this point (see (1992)).

28 The stated properties are known to hold for any irreducible and aperiodic finite Markov chain. A Markov chain is irreducible when all states are mutually reachable within finite periods. When the greatest common divisor of $\{t = 1, 2, \ldots \,|\, Pr(z(t) = i \,|\, z(0) = i) > 0\}$ is 1 for any state i, the Markov chain is called aperiodic. It is easy to check that these two conditions are satisfied when $\varepsilon > 0$.

29 The latter comes from the fact that the limit distribution is a stationary distribution for $\varepsilon = 0$.

30 Young (1993a) provides an example, which shows that the assertion is not true without the marginal bandwagon condition.

31 Undefeated equilibrium is introduced by Mailath, Okuno-Fujiwara, and Postlewaite (1993), and gives somewhat different predictions than strategic stability.

32 See Karlin and Taylor (1981) and Risken (1984).

References

Alchian, A. (1950). "Uncertainty, evolution and economic theory." *Journal of Political Economy*, 58: 211–22.

Amir, M. and Berninghaus, S. K. (1996). "Another approach to mutation and learning in games." *Games and Economic Behavior*, 14: 19–43.

An, M. and Kiefer, N. M. (1992). "Lattice games: evolution and equilibria selection." CAE Working Paper No. 92-11, Cornell University.

Anderlini, L. and Ianni, A. (1996). "Path dependence and learning from neighbours." *Games and Economic Behavior*, 13: 141–77.

Aoki, Masanao (1996). *Hierarchical State Space Evolutionary Dynamics and Mean Field Approximations*. Cambridge: Cambridge University Press.

Axelrod, R. (1984). *Evolution of Cooperation*. New York: Basic Books.

Axelrod, R. and Hamilton, W. (1981). "Evolution of cooperation." *Science*, 211: 1390–6.

Banerjee, A. and Weibull, J. (1992). "Evolution and rationality: some recent game-theoretic results." Working Paper No. 345, The Industrial Institute for Economic and Social Research, Stockholm.

(1995). "Evolutionary selection and rational behavior." In Kirman, A. and Salmon, M. (eds.), *Learning and Rationality in Economics*. Cambridge, MA: Blackwell.

Bergin, J. and Lipman, B. L. (1996). "Evolution with State-dependent mutations." *Econometrica*, 64: 943–56.

Bernheim, D. (1984). "Rationalizable strategic behavior." *Econometrica*, 52: 1007–28.

Bhaskar, V. (1994). "Noisy communication and the fast evolution of cooperation." CentER Discussion Paper No. 94112, Tilburg University.

Biais, B. and Shadur, R. (1993). "On the survival of irratonal traders: a Darwinian approach." Mimeo, Université de Toulouse and Tel Aviv University.

Binmore, K. and Samuelson, L. (1992). "Evolutionary stability in repeated games played by finite automata." *Journal of Economic Theory*, 57: 278–305.

(1993). "Muddling through: Noisy equilibrium selection." forthcoming in *Journal of Economic Theory*.

Binmore, K. Samuelson, L., and Vaughan, R. (1993). "Musical chairs: modeling noisy evolution." *Games and Economic Behaviour*, 11: 1–35.

Blume, L. (1993). "The statistical mechanics of strategic interaction." *Games and Economic Behavior*, 5: 387–424.

Blume, L. and Easley, D. (1992). "Evolution and market behavior." *Journal of Economic Theory*, 58: 9–40.

(1993). "Economic natural selection." *Economics Letters*, 42: 281–9.

(1995). "Evolution and rationality in competitive markets." In Kirman, A. and Salmon, M. (eds.), *Learning and Rationality in Economics*. Cambridge, MA: Blackwell.

Bomze, I. and Pötschner, B. (1988). *Game Theoretical Foundations of Evolutionary Stability*. Berlin: Springer Verlag.

Bomze, I. M. and van Damme, E. (1992). "A dynamical characterization of evolutionary stable states." *Annals of Operations Research*, 27: 229–44.

Börgers, T. and Sarin, R. (1993). "Learning through reinforcement and replicator dynamics." Working Paper, University College London.

Boylan, R. T. (1992). "Laws of large numbers for dynamical systems with randomly matched individuals." *Journal of Economic Theory*, 57: 473–506.

(1995). "Continuous approximation of dynamical systems with randomly matched individuals." *Journal of Economic Theory*, 66: 615–25.

Busch, R. R. and Mosteller, F. (1955). *Stochastic Models for Learning*. New York: Wiley.

Cabrales, A. (1994). "Stochastic replicator dynamics." Mimeo, University of California, San Diego.

Canning, D. (1992). "Average behavior in learning models." *Journal of Economic Theory*, 57: 442–72.

Carmichael, H. L. and MacLeod, W. B. (1995). "Territorial bargaining: an application to internal labour markets." Mimeo, Queen's University and University of Montreal.

Cho, I.-K. and Kreps, D. (1987). "Signaling games and stable equilibria." *Quarterly Journal of Economics*, 102: 179–222.

Cohen, D. (1966) "Optimizing reproduction in a randomly varying environment." *Journal of Theoretical Biology*, 12: 119–29.

Crawford, V. (1991). "An 'evolutionary' interpretation of Van Huyck, Battalio, and Beil's experimental results on coordination." *Games and Economic Behavior*, 3: 25–59.

Cressman, R. (1990). "Strong stability and density-dependent evolutionarily steable strategies." *Journal of Theoretical Biology*, 145: 319–30.

Dekel, E. and Scotchmer, S. (1992). "On the evolution of optimizing behavior." *Journal of Economic Theory*, 57: 392–406.

Durlauf, S. (1991). "Multiple equilibria and persistence in aggregate fluctuation." *American Economic Review*, 81: 70–4.

Ellison, G. (1993). "Learning, local interaction, and coordination." *Econometrica*, 61: 1047–72.

(1995). "Basins of attraction and long run equilibria and the speed of step-by-step evolution." MIT Working Paper No. 96-4.

Fisher, R. A. (1930). *The General Theory of Natural Selection*. Oxford: Clarendon Press.

Fosteer, D. and Young, P. (1990). "Stochastic evolutionary game dynamics." *Theoretical Population Biology*, 38: 219–32.

Frank, R. (1987). "If homo economicus could choose his own utility function, would he want one with a conscience?" *American Economic Review*, 77: 593–604.

(1988). *Passions Within Reason*. New York: Norton.

Freidlin, M. I. and Wentzell, A. D. (1984). *Random Perturbations of Dynamical Systems*. New York: Springer-Verlag, chapter 6.

Friedman, D. (1991). "Evolutionary games in economics." *Econometrica*, 59: 637–66.

Friedman, M. (1953). "The methodology of positive economics." In *Essays in Positive Economics*. Chicago: University of Chicago Press.

Fudenberg, D. (1992). "Explaining cooperation and commitment in repeated games." In Laffont, J.-J. (ed.), *Advances in Economic Theory*, Vol. I. Cambridge: Cambridge University Press.

Fudenberg, D. and Harris, C. (1992). "Evolutionary dynamics with aggregate shocks." *Journal of Economic Theory*, 57: 420–41.

Fudenberg, D. and Levine, D. (1995). "Theory of Learning in Games." Mimeo, Harvard University.

Fudenberg, D. and Maskin, E. (1990). "Evolution and cooperation in noisy repeated games." *American Economic Review*, 80: 274–9.

Gilboa, I. and Matsui, A. (1991). "Social stability and equilibrium." *Econometrica*, 59: 859–67.

Goyal, S. and Janssen, M. (1993). "Non-exclusive conventions and social coordination." Mimeo, Erasmus University, Netherlands.

Hamilton, W. D. (1967). "Extraordinary sex ratios." *Science*, 156: 477–88.

(1970). "Selfish and spiteful behavior in an evolutionary model." *Nature*, 228: 1218–20.

(1972). "Altruism and related phenomena, mainly in social insects." *Annual Review of Ecology and Systematics*, 3: 193–232.

Hammerstein, P. and Selten, R. (1994). "Game theory and evolutionary biology." In Aumann, R. and Hart, S. (eds.), *Handbook of Game Theory with Economic Applications*, Vol. II. Amsterdam: Elsevier.

Harsanyi, J. C. and Selten, R. (1988). *A General Theory of Equilibrium Selection in Games*. Cambridge, MA: MIT Press.

Hines, W. G. S. (1980). "Three characterizations of population strategy stability." *Journal of Applied Probability*, 17: 333–40.

(1987). "Evolutionary stable strategies: a review of basic theory." *Theoretical Population Biology*, 31: 195–272.

Hofbauer, J., Schuster, P., and Sigmund, K. (1979). "A note on evolutionary stable strategies and game dynamics." *Journal of Theoretical Biology*, 81: 609–12.

Hofbauer, J. and Sigmund, K. (1988). *The Theory of Evolution and Dynamical Systems*. Cambridge: Cambridge University Press.

Hofbauer, J. and Weibull, J. (1995). "Evolutionary selection against dominated strategies." forthcoming in *Journal of Economic Theory*.

Kandori, M., Mailath, G., and Rob, R. (1993). "Learning, mutation, and long run equilibria in games." *Econometrica*, 61: 29–56.

Kandori, M. and Rob, R. (1994). "Bandwagon effects and long run technology choice." forthcoming in *Games and Economic Behaviour*.

(1995). "Evolution of equilibria in the long run: a general theroy and applications." *Journal of Economic Theory*, 65: 383–414.

Karlin, S. and Taylor, H. M. (1981). *A Second Course in Stochastic Processes*. New York: Academic Press.

Kim, Y. and Sobel, J. (1995). "An evolutionary approach to pre-play communication." *Econometrica*, 63: 1181–94.

Kirkpatrick, S., Gelatt, C. D. Jr., and Vecchi, M. P. (1983). "Optimization by simulated annealing." *Science*, 220: 671–80.

Kohlberg, E. and Mertens, J.-F. (1986). "On the strategic stability of equilibria." *Econometrica*, 54: 1003–37.

Mailath, G. (1992). "Introduction: symposium on evolutionary game theory." *Journal of Economic Theory*, 57: 259–77.

(1993). "Perpetual randomness in evolutionary economics." *Economics Letters*, 42: 291–9.

(1995). "Recent developments in evolutionary game theory." Paper presented at 1995 AEA meetings.

Mailath, G., Okuno-Fujiwara, M., and Postlewaite, A. (1993). "Belief-based refinements in signaling games." *Journal of Economic Theory*, 60: 241–76.

Maruta, T. (1995). "On the relationships between risk-dominance and stochastic stability." Mimeo, MEDS, Northwestern University.

Matsui, A. (1991). "Cheap talk and cooperation in the society." *Journal of Economic Theory*, 54: 245–58.

(1992). "Best response dynamics and socially stable strategies." *Journal of Economic Theory*, 57: 343–62.

(1995). "On cultural evolution: toward a theoretical foundation of cultural diversity and interactions." Mimeo, University of Tsukuba, Japan.

Maynard Smith, J. (1982). *Evolution and the Theory of Games*. Cambridge: Cambridge University Press.

Maynard Smith, J. and Price, G. R. (1973). "The logic of animal conflicts." *Nature*, 246: 15–18.

Milgrom, P. and Roberts, J. (1991). "Adaptive and sophisticated learning in normal form games." *Games and Economic Behavior*, 3: 82–100.

Nachbar, J. H. (1990). "Evolutionary selection dynamics in games: convergence and limit properties." *International Journal of Game Theory*, 19: 59–89.

Nelson, R. and Winter, S. G. (1982). *An Evolutionary Theory of Economic Change*. Cambridge, MA: Belknap Press of Harvard University Press.

Nöldeke, G. and Samuelson, L. (1993). "An evolutionary analysis of backward and forward induction." *Games and Economic Behavior*, 5: 425–54.

(1995). "A dynamic model of equilibrium selection in signaling markets." Mimeo, University of Bonn.

Pearce, D. (1984). "Rationalizable strategic behavior and the problem of perfection." *Econometrica*, 52: 1029–50.

Rhode, P. and Stegeman, M. (1994). "Non-Nash equilibria of Darwinian dynamics (with applications to duopoly)." Mimeo, University of North Carolina, Chapel Hill.

Riskin, H. (1984). *The Fokker-Planck Equation*. Berlin: Springer.

Ritzerburger and Weibull, J. (1995). "Evolutionary selection in normal form games." *Econometrica*, 63: 1371–99.

Robson, A. (1990). "Efficiency in evolutionary games: Darwin, Nash, and the secret handshake." *Journal of Theoretical Biology*, 144: 379–96.

Samuelson, L. (1993). "Recent advances in evolutionary economics: comments." *Economics Letters*, 42: 313–19.

Samuelson, L. and Zhang, J. (1992). "Evolutionary stability in asymmetric games." *Journal of Economic Theory*, 57: 363–91.

Samuelson, P. A. (1948). *Economics*. New York: McGraw-Hill.

Schaffer, M. E. (1988). "Evolutionarily stable strategies for a finite population and a variable contest size." *Journal of Theoretical Biology*, 132: 469–78.

Schlag, K. (1994). "Why imitate, and if so, how?" Mimeo, University of Bonn.

Schuster, P., Sigmund, K., Hofbauer, J., and Wolff, R. (1981). "Selfregulation of behavior in animal societies, parts I, II and III." *Biological Cybernetics*, 40: 1–8,

9–15, 17–25.

Selten, R. (1980). "A note on evolutionary stable strategies in asymmetric animal conflicts." *Journal of Theoretical Biology*, 84: 93–101.

(1983). "Evolutionary stability in extensive two-person games." *Mathematical Social Sciences*, 5: 269–363.

(1991). "Evolution, learning, and economic behavior." *Games and Economic Behavior*, 3: 3–24.

Sobel, J. (1993). "Evolutionary stability and efficiency." *Economics Letters*, 42: 301–12.

Swinkels, J. (1992a). "Evolutionary stability with equilibrium entrants." *Journal of Economic Theory*, 57: 306–32.

(1992b). "Evolution and strategic stability: from Maynard Smith to Kohlberg and Mertens." *Journal of Economic Theory*, 57: 333–42.

(1993). "Adjustment dynamics and rational play in games." *Games and Economic Behavior*, 5: 455–84.

Taylor, P. D. and Jonker, L. B. (1978). "Evolutionarily stable strategies and game dynamics." *Mathematical Biosciences*, 40: 145–56.

Thomas, B. (1985). "On evolutionarily stable sets." *Journal of Mathematical Biology*, 22: 105–15.

van Damme, E. (1984). "A relation between perfect equilibria in extensive form games and proper equilibria in normal form games." *International Journal of Game Theory*, 13: 1–13.

(1987). *Stability and Perfection of Nash Equilibria*. Berlin: Springer Verlag, chapter 9.

(1993). "Evolutionary game theory." CentER Discussion Paper No. 9375, Tilburg University.

Vaughan, R. (1993). "Evolutive equilibrium selection I: symmetric two player binary choice games." Mimeo, University College London.

Vega-Redondo, F. (1995). "The evolution of Warlasian behavior." Mimeo, Universidad de Alicante.

(1996). *Evolution in Games: Theory and Economic Applications*. Oxford: Oxford University Press.

Wärneryd, K. (1991). "Evolutionary stability in unanimity games with cheap talk." *Economics Letters*, 36: 375–8.

Weibull, J. (1995). *Evolutionary Game Theory*. Cambridge, MA: MIT Press.

Weissing, F. J. (1990). "On the relation between evolutionary stability and discrete dynamic stability." Mimeo, University of Bielefeld, Germany.

Young, P. (1993a). "The evolution of conventions." *Econometrica*, 61: 57–84.

(1993b). "An evolutionary model of bargaining." *Journal of Economic Theory*, 59: 145–68.

(1995). "Equilibrium selection through adaptation and experimentation." In Kirman, A. and Salmon, M. (eds.), *Learning and Rationality in Economics*. Cambridge, MA: Blackwell.

Zeeman, E. C. (1981). "Dynamics of the evolution of animal conflicts." *Journal of Theoretical Biology*, 89: 249–70.

CHAPTER 9

Learning from learning in economics

Ramon Marimon

The process of learning,
of the growth of subjective knowledge,
is always fundamentally the same.
It is *imaginative criticism*.
(Karl Popper (1979), p. 148)

1   INTRODUCTION.

Learning and evolutionary theory in economics are two related research fields that have experienced exponential growth in the last five years. In a sense, this renewed interest in learning theory seems unjustified: the main questions beings addressed are not new. Nash himself wondered how agents would reach the equilibrium he proposed; Muth thought of the rational expectations hypothesis as an extreme counterpart to concurrent macroeconomic models with naive expectations formation, to mention two pioneer examples. In this chapter I review some of the recent contributions to learning theory in games and macroeconomic models. Such a closer look reveals that even if the old questions have not yet been fully answered and it remains difficult – if not impossible – to set a dividing line between rational and adaptive behavior, a *theory of the learnable in economics* is on its way.

To the question *why do we study learning in economics*, four main, non-mutually exclusive, answers have been put forward: (i) *Bounded rationality*; (ii) *Equilibrium justifications*; (iii) *Equilibrium selection*, and (iv) *Observed non-equilibrium behavior*. Let me briefly comment on each of them.

(*i*) *Bounded rationality* It is often argued that "our rationality assumptions are too strong, that our models must take into account human weaknesses such as limited ability to compute etc." In fact, recent developments in *decision theory* (see, Dekel and Gul's contribution to this volume) show how the theory of choice and equilibrium, can be founded in weaker rationality, and common knowledge, assumptions. Furthermore, as some recent work shows (see section 3), it is also possible to develop a theory based on "behavioral axioms" as a foundation for adaptive learning models. Nevertheless, such a *choice theoretical model of learning* would be of very limited interest if it only contributed in making our assumptions more realistic. As has been recognized by many, "realism" cannot be the object of economic modeling.

(*ii*) *Equilibrium justification* This was Nash's concern. Can we attain equilibria, not as a result of a fixed point argument (i.e., with the help of Adam Smith's "invisible hand"), but as the asymptotic outcome of a decentralized learning process? This remains a focal question and, as we will see in sections 4 and 5, substantial progress has been made in the last few years. Answers to this question link with applied econometric work: an *observed* social outcome must be *learnable* by agents. That is, positive answers to the above question can help to integrate theoretical and applied work. But, in this sense, learning theory plays a secondary or transitory role: once we have shown that we can *justify* a certain equilibrium outcome as the outcome of a learning process, we might as well leave learning aside and concentrate on equilibrium theory. In other words, for learning theory in economics to stand on its own we must look into other explanations.

(*iii*) *Equilibrium selection* If not all equilibrium outcomes are equally *justified* by learning, then learning theory can provide a much needed selection criteria. Owing to multiplicity – often, indeterminacy – of equilibria many of our theories have little predictable power. In contrast, experimental evidence shows that in many environments some equilibria are more likely to emerge than others, suggesting that our theories need more structure to capture these features. For example, in games not all Nash equilibria are equally played. A simple benchmark, that anyone can try, is the *Battle of the Sexes* game: the *mixed* Nash equilibrium typically does not emerge. Similarly, competitive rational expectations equilibrium models (REE) with incomplete market structure have, in general, a continuum of equilibria but experimental evidence shows that not all are equally likely to be observed. In fact, the outcomes observed in different experiments seem to be better characterized by the stability properties of learning algorithms.[1]

The natural step is to replace Nash equilibrium and rational expectations equilibrium with some suitable refinement. But, as we will see in sections 4 and 5, two problems arise. First, if some *stability* criteria are imposed to select among equilibria, then these criteria are not independent of the class of learning algorithms under consideration. Second, some games try to model relatively sophisticated agents (e.g., CEOs' managerial decisions, etc.) and some proposed refinement concepts are based on high levels of deduction by the players involved. Whether such levels of sophistication are achieved is, again, an empirical question, but learning models should allow for these forms of behavior when agents gain enough experience; that is, the "bound" on rationality should be displaced away as agents learn through experience.

Learning theory can help to systematically explore and explain evidence on *equilibrium selection* by providing more structure to the map that defines how agents form and coordinate their expectations and actions, based on their experience and capabilities. In particular, alternative consistency and behavior conditions on learning rules should "make falsifiable" the set of observed paths and, in turn, the set of *learnable equilibria.*

(*iv*) *Observed non-equilibrium behavior* While existing equilibrium theories must be "refined" to account for some economic facts, they should also be "extended" to account for others. While equilibrium conditions must be stringent to preclude certain unobserved multiplicities, at the same time, they may have to be weakened to account for observed persistent patterns that seem to show the complexity of attaining certain equilibrium outcomes. The evidence comes from different sources. The experimental lab provides a useful tool to isolate these phenomena.[1] There are, at least, three types of experimental facts that should be considered and a learning theory may help to explain them. First, "sensitivity to marginal payoffs," that is, typically agent's actions are affected by the relative performance of their actions, something not taken into account by a simple – marginalist – maximization point of view, which only considers that the best action is taken. Second, "experience or expectations across environments," seem to affect agents' behavior. In a theoretical model, agents' behavior (e.g., in which information, and how they should condition their decisions) is usually predetermined. Nevertheless, experience – and/or expectations – about other environments may result in well-defined "non-equilibrium" patterns when agents try to act rationally across different environments. Third, some equilibria seem to be "stable" in the large but "locally unstable". For example, equilibrium selection may occur for low frequency data, while high frequency data may show persistent volatility. As a result, observed patterns around the equilibrium are more complicated than standard theory prescribes; or may be misinterpreted, for example, by over randomizing the model.

Macroeconomic and, in particular, financial data also provide evidence which is difficult to reconcile with existing dynamic rational expectations equilibrium models, but may be explained by taking the learning process into account. For example, asset market data show that there is persistency of returns' volatility and of trading volume (and cross-correlation between absolute returns and trading volume); many inflationary spells cannot be counted as non-stationary rational expectations equilibrium paths (see, section 5).

The possibility of explaining *non-equilibrium behavior* raises an obvious question. Does learning theory account for any possible pattern? That is, does if *justify* "*everything goes*"? Unfortunately, there are examples that seem to point in this direction (e.g., convergence to fairly arbitrary "aspiration levels" or to indeterminate REE, etc.). However, a closer look at these examples shows that agents must *coordinate* in fairly arbitrary learning rules to achieve such outcomes. As we will see, when the learning process is considered as a decentralized process in which agents' learning rules can be arbitrarily chosen from a large class (satisfying basic behavioral and/or consistency conditions), then it does not justify *everything goes*. As we will see in sections 4 and 5, on the one hand, notions of equilibrium, which are weaker than Nash, or REE, may be defined by only requiring, for example, that agents' subjective beliefs are self-confirmed in equilibrium. With this notion, non-Nash (or REE) equilibrium patterns are possible, but not all patterns are possible. In particular, in "simple" environments only Nash (or REE) are equilibria. On the other hand, for large classes of adaptive learning rules it is possible to discriminate among Nash, or REE, equilibria.

The last two answers, which I would rank as more relevant, can be summarized by saying that the development of a *theory of the learnable in economics* can provide our equilibrium theories with more predictable power, by helping to reject some equilibria and by helping to account for other non-equilibrium patterns. But then, learning theory can also play other roles in economics:

(*v*) *The study of complex economic environments* If a class of learning models provides consistent results in well-understood environments, then such a class can be used as a tool to explore more complicated environments that we do not know how to characterize *ex ante*. For example, if the learning model converges, then it is usually possible to characterize *ex post* the resulting outcome, e.g., to see whether it is a particular type of equilibrium. Some models with Artificially Intelligent Agents (AIA) have been successfully applied in this way. In fact, in the last few years a growing number of computational (and estimation) algorithms based on learning and evolutionary principles have been developed. These algorithms have been used both as a "theorist tool" for study, for example, nonlinear stochastic rational expectations models or as an "applied economist, or a financial analyst, tool" for estimation and prediction. The development of learning theory can help to characterize the "learnable solutions" that such computational estimation procedures may attain (see, e.g., Sargent (1993) and White (1992)).

(*vi*) *As a normative theory* This is an area of research which has been little explored, but learning can contribute to our normative theories in different ways (see section 5 for some examples). First, a disturbing feature of models with multiplicity of equilibria is that the welfare implications of an economic policy usually are different across equilibria. If, for a large class of learning algorithms and initial conditions, the process converges to a particular equilibrium, then one can make policy prescriptions with high confidence. Second, new policies, or institutions, can be designed taking into account the fact that agents must learn from their experience; say, about the effects of different incentives or tax schemes. For example, many economic policies suffer from some form of indeterminacy since the effect of their announcement depends on agents' expectations. While there is an extended literature on "credibility problems" as incentive problems, reputation (inference from policy announcements given past experience) is also a learning problem and a better understanding of it can help policy design. Similarly, market and organizational forms can be designed taking into account how institutional arrangements affect the stability properties of equilibria and, therefore, affect welfare when the process of convergence to equilibrium is also taken into account. Third, the designer, or planner, may have to take into account that he, or the designed organization, has also to learn. In other words, the problem may not be of designing a contract, or organization, that it is efficient from a given period zero and is simply executed as uncertainties unfold, but the problem may be to design a contract that will adapt well to "unforeseen contingencies."

As can be seen, the scope of a *theory of the learnable in economics* goes well beyond the standard – and Nash's original question – of whether we can justify an equilibrium concept as being the result of a learning process. My aim in the remainder of this chapter is to summarize some of the recent results that, I think, are helping in building up such a theory. Given the rapid growth of this literature, I only report on some of the recent contributions on individual learning (section 3), learning in games (section 4) and learning in dynamic macroeconomic models (section 5).[2] In the next section, I introduce some notation and describe a basic framework.

2   BASIC FRAMEWORK

A large class of economic, and game theoretical, models can be cast in a relatively simple general framework. There is a *set of agents I*, time is discrete $(0, 1, \ldots)$. At each period of time there is an action set for each agent, A_i a public outcome set X, and a set of states of nature S. In period t, agent i's one-period *ex-post* payoff, is represented by $u_i(a_{i,t}, x_{t+1})$, and *ex-ante* present value payoffs by $(1 - \delta)E\Sigma_{n=0}^{\infty}d^n Eu(a_{i,t+n}, x_{t+1+n})$, where $\delta \in [0, 1)$ (notice that $\delta = 0$ corresponds to *myopic* behavior and the $\lim_{\delta \to 1}$ is given by the long-run average expected payoff: $\lim_{T \to \infty} \frac{1}{T}\Sigma_{n=0}^{T-1}Eu(a_{t+n}, x_{t+1+n}))$.

The public outcome evolves according to $x_t = \phi(g(a_t, \ldots, a_{t-m}), x_{t-1}, \ldots, x_{t-m}, s_t)$, where g aggregates the actions of all the agents, and $s_t \in S$ is an exogenous shock.

Within this framework we can consider several environments. (*i*) *Single agent without intertemporal feedback*: $I = \{i\}$ and $x_t = s_t$. This is the standard case of individual decision theory with uncertainty. (*ii*) *Single agent with intertemporal feedback*: $I = \{i\}$ and $x_t = \phi(g(a_{i,t-1}, \ldots, a_{i,t-m}), x_{t-1}, \ldots, x_{t-m}, s_t)$. Individual investment problems take this form and, as we will see in section 3, most learning difficulties, usually associated with multi-agent problems, already appear in these environments. (*iii*) *Multi-agent without intertemporal feedback*: $I = \{1, \ldots, n\xi$, and $x_t = \phi(g(a_{t-1}), s_t)$. The standard example is a *multi-stage game*:[3] $x_t = a_{-i,t-1}$ (notice that for every player a "public outcome" is defined). (*iv*) *Competitive with intertemporal feedback*: $I = [0, 1]$ (i.e., a continuum of agents) and $x_t = \phi(g(a_t, a_{t-1}), x_{t-1}, s_t)$. For example, in a deterministic *temporary equilibrium* model, such as the standard *overlapping generations model*, $x_t = g(a_t, a_{t-1})$.

In most of the above environments, the actions of agent i do not affect public outcome. Then, from the perspective of agent i, given the actions of other agents $\{a_{-i,t}\}$, the public outcome can be thought of as "the state of the outside world." The realizations of the stochastic process $\{x_t\}_{t=0}^{\infty}$ are governed by a probability measure v on $(X_{\infty}, \mathscr{F}_{\infty})$, where $X_{\infty} = \Pi_{n=0}^{t}X$ and $\mathscr{F}_t$ is the σ-field generated by $(x_0, \ldots, x_t)$, the corresponding empirical distribution – as it is perceived by agent i – is denoted by m_t (with subindex only when needed), i.e., m_t is a probability measure on $(X_t, \mathscr{F}_t)$. Even when agent i's actions affect the public outcome, as long as he does not take account of this dependence, he may still consider the public outcome as "the exogenous outside world."

Some further notation is needed to denote agents' decisions. At any point in time – say, t – the agent must take a (mixed) action, $\alpha_t \in \Delta(A)$, based on all his past information, represented by $h_t \in H_t$ (h_t may include

$(x_0, \ldots, x_t), (s_0, \ldots, s_{t-1})(a_0, \ldots, a_{t-1})$, as well as all the information that the agent has about $(A, X, S, u,$ and $v))$. A *behavioral rule* (or strategy), σ maps histories into (mixed) actions (i.e., $\sigma: H_\infty \to \Delta(A), \sigma_t$ is $\mathscr{H}_t$ measurable).

In the standard framework, $A, X, S, u,$ and v are assumed to be known, and the Savage or Anscombe and Aumann (1963) axioms prescribe that the agent will choose the path of actions that maximizes expected utility. In this case, it is irrelevant for the solution of the problem whether the agent is facing a "once and for all" problem or has accumulated "experience." The problem, even in its infinite-horizon formulation, is essentially a static problem that has a resolution in period zero by choosing the optimal behavioral rule. In the general equilibrium framework, this corresponds to solving for Arrow–Debreu contingent plans in period zero. As is well known, even in this context the characterization, and computation, of optimal behavioral rules is greatly simplified if they have a *recursive structure*. This is, whether there is an "optimal policy" R, such that optimal σ^* satisfy $\sigma_t^*(h_t) = R(x_t, \theta_t)$, where θ_t is some vector statistic from h_t which follows a pre-specified law of motion $\theta_t = \psi(x_{t-1}, \theta_{t-1})$ (with initial conditions).

In a learning process, *experience* is essential and so is some form of recursivity that explicitly defines how experience is accumulated. As we will see, when $\sigma_t^*(h_t) = R(x_t, \theta_t)$, R may be a fairly complicated object, which may include a selection procedure among simpler recursive rules, an internal accounting system, etc. In many economic problems, however, a relatively simple behavioral rule R is assumed. For example, $\sigma_t^*(h_t) = BR(x_{t+1}^e)$, where $BR(x_{t+1}^e)$ is – a selection from – an agent's *best reply* to his expectations about the public outcome x_{t+1}^e, and $x_{t+1}^e = f(x_t, \theta_t)$, where f is a forecasting rule. For example, $\theta_t = (x_t^e, \alpha_t), f(x_t, x_t^e, \alpha_t) = x_t^e + \alpha_t(x_t - x_t^e)$, and $\alpha_t = \dfrac{\alpha_{t-1}}{\alpha_{t-1} + 1}$; that is, if $\alpha_0 = 1$ then x_{t+1}^e is the empirical mean. Notice that, in this case, $R \equiv BR \cdot f$ and $\psi(x_t, \theta_t) \equiv (f(x_t, x_t^e, \alpha_t), \alpha_t + 1)$. More generally, one can consider R as an element of a class of learning rules $\mathscr{R}$. In this case, the agent may "choose how to learn," that is, select which learning rule $R \in \mathscr{R}$ fits better his learning needs. For example, in the last formulation, the class of learning rules, $\mathscr{R}$, may be defined by two parameters (a, α_0) characterizing the *step size* sequence $\alpha_t = \dfrac{\alpha_{t-1}}{\alpha_{t-1} + a}$ (e.g., if $a = (1 - \alpha_0)$ then $\alpha_t = \alpha_0$ for all t) or by having a finite memory with some parametric form.

It is standard to separate decision models, according to the number of agents, that is whether it is an individual choice model, a finite agent, or a competitive equilibrium model. I will follow this classical separation in the following sections. However, from the point of view of learning theory, what matters is how agents actions *feedback* into, or are correlated with, the public outcome. In a sense, *learnable equilibria are solutions to multi-agent problems achieved without recursion to a fixed point argument.* For an equilibrium to be the asymptotic outcome of a learning process (i.e., a *learnable equilibrium*) it is required that for every individual agent his expectations about the public outcome are *self-confirmed,* and that his resulting actions do not disturb such expectations. Different forms of *feedback* – together with the *complexity* of the "outside world" and of the decision process – make such convergence more or less difficult to achieve. This will be a recurrent theme through the following sections.

3   LEARNING TO CHOOSE

Ad-hoc learning economic models have been around for a long time without building up to a theory of adaptive learning. In contrast, Bayesian statistical methods have given foundation to a well-developed theory of *Bayesian learning.* While the basic elements of the theory date back to the development of the corresponding statistical theory (see, e.g., de Groot (1970)), the theory was "put in use" in the seventies and eighties as a learning foundation of rational expectations equilibria by Jordan and Blume and Easley, among others (see Blume and Easley (1995)), and in the early nineties as a learning foundation of Nash and Correlated equilibria by Jordan (1991), Kalai and Lehrer (1993a, 1993b, and 1995), and Nyarko (1994), among others.

3.1   Rational learning?

Bayesian learning has been labeled "rational learning" since *within* the Bayesian framework, the Bayesian learner satisfies the standard rationality axioms. In particular, along the learning process, the agent follows "optimal statistical procedures" and his views of the world "cannot be contradicted," if anything, they become "more accurate." However, as is well known, the quotation marks cannot be dismissed. In relatively complex environments the optimal procedures are optimal only by reference to the agent's simplified view of the environment, not in relation to the actual environment; the agent's simplified view may be highly counterfactual, although the agent may not perceive this, and, as a result, the agent's predictions may be far from converging to the right predictions. It is for these reasons that Bayesian learning will only be a first short stop in our search for a theory of the learnable in economics (see Blume and Easley (1995) for a more complete account).

A Bayesian learner summarizes his uncertainty about the aspects of the economy that are unknown to him with an appropriate prior distribution. That is, the *agent knows what he does not know*. For example, if payoffs are unknown the prior must also be defined over possible payoff functions. To make the problem manageable, most Bayesian learning models reduce learning to a forecasting problem. The Bayesian learner starts with a prior μ on $(X_\infty, \mathcal{F}_\infty)$, and follows a process of Bayesian updating $\mu(x_{t+1} | x^t)$. The question is whether these updated beliefs converge to the real distribution $v(x_{t+1} | x^t)$. If such convergence is achieved then forecasted beliefs and the objective distribution are said to *strongly merge*. The basic result in which this literature builds is a theorem by Blackwell and Dubins (1962) which says that if v is *absolutely continuous* with respect to μ (denoted $v \ll \mu$), then the forecasts of the corresponding conditional distributions *strongly merge* ($v \ll \mu$ if for any subset D of X_∞, $v(D) > 0$ implies $\mu(D) > 0$). That is, the forecaster cannot place *ex-ante* zero probability to paths that have positive probability in the environment (see Kalai and Lehrer (1993a) and Nyarko (1994)).

Blackwell and Dubins's theorem exemplifies the strengths and weaknesses of Bayesian learning theory. The theorem, as many analytic learning results, is based on the martingale convergence theorem (and the Radon–Nikodyn theorem; see Blackwell and Dubins (1962)) and it provides a very strong tool for convergence theorems. However, it also shows how the learner must "show his cards" *ex-ante* by committing himself to a prior μ and follow the Bayesian rules of the game. To see this, consider a simple environment where $X = \{0, 1\}$. Let v define a sequence of Bernoulli trials (i.e., Prob$\{x_t = 1\} = p \in (0, 1)$ for all $t \geq 1$) and let the Bayesian's prior distribution on $(0, 1), \mu(p_0)$, be a *Beta* distribution with parameters $(q_0, 1 - q_0)$. Then the Bayesian process of updating posteriors $\mu(p_{t+1} | x^t)$ is – almost – that of a *frequentalist* in the sense that, $p^e_{t+1} = q_t$, and, for

$$t > 0, q_t = q_{t-1} + \frac{1}{t+1}(x_t - q_{t-1}) \text{ and } \mu_t \to \delta_p. \text{ That is, his forecasts are}$$

accurate in the limit.[4]

Two small variations of the above endowment are enough to question the "rationality" of the Bayesian learner. First, suppose that $X = \{0, 1, 2\}$, but that the agent thinks that $X = \{0, 1\}$ and behaves as before. The unexpected event $x_t = 2$ will be ignored by the dogmatic Bayesian while it will be easily accounted for by the frequentalist. Second, consider that $X = \{0, 1\}$, but that v defines a deterministic sequence $(0, 1, 0, 1, \ldots, 0, 1 \ldots)$. Both, the Bayesian and the frequentalists described above will converge to the belief $p^e = 1/2$, disregarding the "obvious" cycling *pattern*.

These last examples show the importance of some form of *absolute continuity* condition on the prior beliefs with respect to the "true" environment in order to achieve accurate forecasts (*strong merging*). But, as Nachbar (1995) has recently shown, even when such absolute continuity conditions are satisfied, there is another limitation with the "rational learning" approach that must be taken into account. An idea underlying "rational learning" is that, if an agent knows how to *best reply* to his forecast, then *strong merging* of beliefs results in *optimal* outcomes against *accurate predictions*. This is correct if one considers stationary environments in which the actions of the individual agent do not affect the distribution of the public outcome, but when such distribution is affected by the agent's actions then this property of "rational learning" may be too much to ask for.

To better understand this difficulty consider the following example. Let $X = \{0, 1\}$, $A = \{a^1, a^2\}$, $u(a^1, 1) = u(a^2, 0) = 0$, $u(a^1, 0) = u(a^2, 1) = 1$. Suppose that a Bayesian learner starts with a prior μ satisfying the absolute continuity condition with respect to a class of environments $v \in \mathcal{N}$. His prior and the process of Bayesian updating will result in a *best reply* behavioral strategy, σ, for *any* environment $v \in \mathcal{N}$. Suppose that such strategy is a pure strategy, that is $\forall h_t, \sigma_t(h_t) \in A$. Now consider a class of "miscoordination environments" defined by $\text{Prob}\{x_t = 0 \mid x^{t-1}\} > 1/2$ if $\sigma_t(x^{t-1}) = a^2$ and $\text{Prob}\{x_t = 1 \mid x^{t-1}\} \geq 1/2$ if $\sigma_t(x^{t-1}) = a^1$. If these environments are in $\mathcal{N}$ then the agent will, eventually learn to forecast, but then σ will no longer be his optimal strategy. Associated with the new *best reply* strategy there are other "miscoordination environments," etc. The problem is that, in general, one cannot "close" this process. That is, in general, one cannot have an optimal strategy for all environments in $\mathcal{N}$ and, at the same time, remain within this class $\mathcal{N}$ when the *feedback* from the optimal strategy is taken into account. For example, if, moving ahead, we consider the public outcome as the resulting action of a second player in a *Battle of the Sexes* game, then the lack of "closedness' means that, if $\mathcal{N}$ is "rich enough," it cannot simultaneously be the set of *plausible* strategies of the opponent and the set to which best reply strategies belong.

Nachbar's warning is in the spirit of the *impossibility theorems* that, since Göedel's theorem, have been common in the "logician's approach" to learning theory and, as Binmore (1988) has shown, are also present in our context. These results do not show "impossibility of learning", but they are warnings against making excessive "rationality and completeness" demands.[5] With this lesson of humility, a first direction to pursue is to be less demanding about what is meant by a learnable outcome.

3.2 Rational, calibrated beliefs and other consistency conditions

Strong merging of beliefs requires that even tail events are forecasted correctly. This is a very *strong consistency* condition. A weaker, and reasonable, condition is to require only accurate forecasts over arbitrarily long but finite future horizons. If this property is satisfied, then it is said that forecasts *weakly merge* with the true environment (see, Lehrer and Smordinsky (1993)). Therefore, in non-stationary environments, tail events may prevent forecasts from being accurate and, in multiple agent environments, may prevent agents from asymptotically agreeing.

Similar ideas have been formalized by Kurz (1994a, 1994b) as a basis for his concept of *rational belief equilibria*. A rational belief is one that is "consistent" with the observed long-run empirical distribution. That is, even if v does not define a stationary process, as long as as the long-run empirical distribution is well defined – say, m – then the environment is considered to be *stable*. *Rational beliefs*, μ, are those which are "compatible with the data," in the sense of generating the same empirical distribution m, which must also be absolutely continuous with respect to beliefs (i.e., $m \ll \mu$; see Kurz (1994a) for details). Since many measures on $(X_\infty, \mathscr{F}_\infty)$ are compatible with the same empirical distribution, heterogeneity of beliefs (at the tail!) is allowed. A rational believer can be thought of as a Bayesian learner that is born with experience, and forced to use the empirical distribution as a prior, and for which forecast *weakly merge* with the environment.

A similar – and weaker – concept is that of a "well-calibrated forecaster" (see, Dawid (1982)). A well-calibrated forecaster is one whose forecasts – asymptotically – conform with the empirical distribution. For example, the stock price should go up 2/3 of the periods that it is forecasted that it will go up with probability 2/3. Foster and Vohra (1995) have recently further developed this idea and applied it to study convergence of calibrated learning schemes to correlated equilibria (see section 4).

It should be clear that "calibrated forecasts" may be far from accurate. Consider again the cyclic environment $X = \{0, 1\}$ with v generating $(0, 1, 0, 1, \ldots, 0, 1, \ldots)$. A forecast of $x_t = 1$ with probability one half will be well calibrated while an accurate forecast for v^1 will make a prediction of x_t conditioned on x_{t-1}; or conditioned on whether t is odd or even.

As in statistical inference, alternative *consistency conditions* provide different convergence tests. In line with statistical tests, Fudenberg and Levine (1995a) propose a weak asymptotic consistency test to assess the "fitness" of a behavioral rule. A behavioral rule σ is said to be $(\varepsilon - \delta)$ *consistent* if there exist a T such that for *any i.i.d. environment* v, and for $t \geq T$ with *confidence* δ the realized long-run average payoff (up to t) is, within an *error* ε, at least as good as the optimal – one period – mixed strategy against the empirical distribution m_t.[6]

In other words, Fudenberg and Levine (1995) take the empirical distribution – not the "true environment" – as reference and require that the behavioral rule performs almost as well as optimal play against the empirical distribution. Immediately comes to mind a simple generalization of the *frequentalist forecaster*. The well-known *fictitious play* rule: compute the empirical distribution of the opponents' play and best reply against such empirical distribution. The problem is that while the fictitious player in *i.i.d.* environments may attain accurate forecasts and almost maximal payoffs, one can also construct "miscoordination" (non-*i.i.d.*) environments to trick a fictitious player. However, Fudenberg and Levine show that an exponential version of fictitious play is ($\varepsilon - \delta$)-consistent for *any environment*; they call such property *universal consistency*.

To base consistency tests on the *empirical* distribution, instead of on the *true* distribution, is a necessary step for a *theory of the learnable*. However, two difficulties must be considered. First, the fact that *the agent perceives the marginal empirical distribution* and in environments with *feedback*, the actual – correlated – distribution may be difficult to recover from such a partial picture. Second, the problem, already mentioned, of *pattern recognition* of the empirical distribution, that is, it may be difficult to find the right conditioning of the data. The following example illustrates these difficulties.

Example 1 There are three actions and three possible states. Payoffs are given by

	x^1	x^2	x^3
a^1	0	2	1
a^2	1	0	2
a^3	2	1	0

I consider two environments, in the first environment, private actions and public outcomes are correlated in the following form: $\text{Prob}\{x_t = x^1 \,|\, a_t = a^1\} = \text{Prob}\{x_t = x^2 \,|\, a_t = a^2\} = \text{Prob}\{x_t = x^3 \,|\, a_t = a^3\} = 0$, and $\text{Prob}\{x_t = x^2 \,|\, a_t = a^1\} = \text{Prob}\{x_t = x^3 \,|\, a_t = a^1\} = \text{Prob}\{x_t = x^1 \,|\, a_t = a^2\} = \text{Prob}\{x_t = x^3 \,|\, a_t = a^2\} = \text{Prob}\{x_t = x^1 \,|\, a_t = a^3\} = \text{Prob}\{x_t = x^2 \,|\, a_t = a^3\} = 1/2$. Notice that if the agent plays the three actions with (almost) equal probability, the empirical distribution, m, can converge to the uniform distribution, well-calibrated (universally consistent) beliefs will be *self-confirmed*, and the agent will receive an average payoff close to 1. Nevertheless, if the agent conditions on his own actions, or if he simply sticks to one action, he can receive a payoff of almost

1.5 and with respect to such (conditioned) empirical distribution be a well-calibrated forecaster. In the second environment (a one agent version of Shapley's (1964) example), there is the following *intertemporal feedback*: $\text{Prob}\{x_t = x^1 \,|\, a_{t-1} = a^2\} = \text{Prob}\{x_t = x^2 \,|\, a_{t-1} = a^3\} = \text{Prob}\{x_t = x^3 \,|\, a_{t-1} = a^1\} = 1$. If the agent behaves as a well-calibrated (unconditional) forecaster, the history of play will cycle and the perceived distribution can approximate the uniform distribution. Again, almost equal weight to all three actions can be a consistent behavior. But then, the agent does not take into account two important elements. First, within any (countable) history, the agent infinitely often assigns positive probability to zero probability events (see Jordan 1993 for a similar remark). Second, at the beginning of period t, there is a much better sufficient statistic to predict the future outcome, x_t: the last action of the agent a_{t-1}. That is, with the same information – and different conditioning – the agent can receive an average payoff of almost 2.

In a sense, Fudenberg and Levine's *universal consistency* condition tests a behavioral rule against an econometrician who knows how to adopt the optimal action with respect to the empirical distribution. That is, there still is an external element of reference. However, it may be that either the agent is constrained to a set of behavioral rules, $\mathcal{R}$, or that the problem is complex enough that the econometrician is not in a better position than the learning agent. In these contexts, one may have to consider an *internal consistency* condition with respect to a class of behavioral rules, $\mathcal{R}$. This is, for example, the approach taken by Evans and Ramey (1994), Brock and Hommes (1995), and Marcet and Nicolini (1995) (see section 5). Brock and Hommes consider learning agents as consumers of forecasting services who are willing to tradeoff accuracy for lower forecasting fees. Marcet and Nicolini consider agents that choose, among a class of adaptive learning rules, the one that better tracks the possible non-stationarities of their economic environment. Consistency is then defined in relative terms within such a class. In these models agents "choose how to learn." Consistency is not defined only asymptotically, since agents keep testing different rules, and which one is the best rule may keep changing in a non-stationary environment.

We have been moving away from the set frame of Bayesian learning. Considering classes of rules and, particularly, studying their "consistency" opens two obvious questions (see Kreps (1990)): Can we characterize a broad class of adaptive learning algorithms based on a few behavioral assumptions? Does such behavior result in "standard" optimal, or equilibrium, choices in relatively simple environments?

3.3 Learnable choice

In the context of games, Milgrom and Roberts (1991) have provided a first characterization of a learning class based on a weak monotonicity condition: "an adaptive rule must only play strategies that, in relation to the observed finite history, are undominated." Marimon and McGrattan (1995) consider a general class of learning rules based on a stronger monotonicity condition (together with *experimentation* and *inertia*): an adaptive learning rule must move in the direction of the – possibly, unknown – best reply map, that is, must follow the evolutionary principle of assigning more weight to actions that have been shown to work better in the past.

Recently, Easley and Rustichini (1995) have "rationalized" replicator type dynamics. They consider a class of finite memory simple rules – say, a pure strategy – and adaptive rules $\mathscr{R}$ which select – or weight – different simple rules. They impose basic "axioms" on the selection procedure $\mathscr{R}$: (*i*) a *monotonicity* condition: increase the weight on rules that have relatively high payoffs; (*ii*) a *symmetry* condition: selection procedures should not be affected by relabeling, and (*iii*) an *independence* (of irrelevant alternatives) condition: the effect of a payoff on the weight of a simple rule should be independent of other payoffs. In the context of single agent problems without intertemporal feedback, they show that: first, an adaptive rule $\mathscr{R}$ satisfying these three axioms asymptotically selects rules which are objective expected utility maximizers, among the set of simple rules; second, any expected utility maximizer rule can be selected by a procedure satisfying the axioms; and, third, the class of selection procedures, $\mathscr{R}$, satisfying these axioms are, at least asymptotically, strict monotone transforms of replicator dynamics.

In particular, the family of *exponential fictitious play* rules, which, as we have mentioned before, Fudenberg and Levine (1995a) show to be $(\varepsilon - \delta)$-*universally consistent*, is representative of the class of rules satisfying Easley and Rustichini's axioms. In other words, the universal consistency condition is satisfied for a class of behavioral rules characterized by a few "behavioral axioms." Furthermore, a representative of such a class can be constructed.

Unfortunately, in more complex environments, these basic axioms may not be enough for learning. First, either when the learning problem is not just a forecasting problem, and the agent must also learn about his payoffs or the set of actions at his disposal, or in non-stationary environments, *experimentation* is an essential feature of the learning process. Second, in environments with *intertemporal feedback* from individual agents, there may be a problem of *overreactions* resulting in agents never learning the final consequences of their actions. *Inertia*, that is to stick to the same action with some probability, is a form of *building stationarity* into the environment on the part of the agent. In summary, in addition to a *strong monotonicity condition* – say, of the replicator dynamics type – *experimentation* and *inertia* characterize a general class of learning rules and a more general theory of *learnable choice* must take them into account (Marimon and McGrattan (1995); see also Fudenberg and Levine (1995a) and Kaniovski and Young (1995)).

3.4   Explicit behavioral rules

Learnable outcomes must be achieved by explicit behavioral rules. Experimental economics, applied decision theory, and behavioral sciences may help us understand how economic subjects actually learn from their experiences, but in the same way as we need explicit functional forms representing preferences and technologies to test and develop our economic theories and as econometricians need explicit estimation programs, a theory of the *learnable in economics* needs explicit behavior rules: recursive rules suitable for computational experimentation. *Fictitious play*, and its variants, are examples of explicit adaptive rules. As recursive estimation procedures, fictitious play is an example of a *stochastic approximation algorithm*. As *recursive meta-rules* that chooses among simple rules or actions, it is an example of an *artificially intelligent agent*. I finish this section with a brief discussion of these general classes of explicit behavioral rules (see, Sargent (1993), for other economic examples).

Adaptive learning as a stochastic approximation algorithm

The frequentalist methods of computing the sample mean or the empirical distribution, are simple examples of stochastic approximation methods. The following example (a variant of *fictitious play*) illustrates the strength of these algorithms (see, Arthur (1993), Easley and Rustichini (1995), and Marimon and McGrattan (1995)).

Example 2 The agent only knows his set of actions $A = (a^1, \ldots, a^n)$ and only observes his realized payoffs, i.e., he does not observe $\{x_t\}$. We assume that $\{x_t\}$ is (strictly) stationary and that payoffs are strictly positive and bounded ($\bar{u} \geq u(a, x) \geq \underline{u} > 0$). A Bayesian learner would have to form a prior over possible payoff matrices, in addition to the prior on μ, etc. The adaptive agent, instead, defines his behavioral strategy by randomly choosing among actions according to some measure of relative strength. Let S_t^k be the strength attached to action a^k in period t and $S = \Sigma_{k=1}^n S_t^k$. Fix $S_1 \in \mathcal{R}_{++}$ (*i.e.*,

$S_1^k > 0, \forall k)$ (this is the extent in which our adaptive agent has a prior). Then strengths evolve according to the rule

$$S_{t+1}^k = S_t^k + \begin{cases} u(a^k, x_t) & \text{if } a^k \text{ is used at } t, \\ 0 & \text{otherwise.} \end{cases}$$

Then actions are randomly selected according to $\alpha_t(a^k) = \dfrac{S_t^k}{S_t}$. To express this behavioral rule in stochastic approximation form, let $z_t^k \equiv \alpha_t(a^k)$, and $v(a^k, x_t)$ be a random variable that takes value 0 with probability $(1 - z_t^k)$ and $u(a^k, x)$ with probability $z_t^k v_t(x)$. Then, we have that mixed actions evolve according to

$$z_{t+1}^k = z_t^k + \frac{1}{S_{t+1}}[v(a^k, x_t) - (S_{t+1} - S_t)z_t^k].$$

This is an example of a stochastic process of the form

$$z_{t+1} = z_t + \alpha_t[h(a_t, z_t)], \tag{1}$$

where z is the object to be learned and $h(a_t, z_t)$ is a random variable, which depends on the parameter z, and, possibly, on the action a taken by the agent. If "the gain sequence" (for simplification taken to be deterministic) $\{\alpha_t\}$ satisfies a "decay condition" ($\Sigma_{t=1}^\infty \alpha_t = \infty, \Sigma_{t=1}^\infty \alpha_t^p < \infty$ for some $p > 1$), and z_t is a stationary process, then the steady states of the system of stochastic difference equations (1) are given by the solutions of $E[h(a, z_t)] = 0.$[7] A specially useful result is that the corresponding asymptotic behavior of $\{z_t\}$ is characterized by the solutions of the *ordinary difference equation*

$$\frac{dz}{d\tau}(\tau) = E[h(a, z(\tau))]. \tag{2}$$

Returning to our Example 2, the corresponding ODE is

$$\frac{dz^k}{d\tau}(\tau) = (1 - z^k(t))z^k(t)\left[e[u(a^k, x)] - E\sum_{j \neq k} z^j(t)[u(a^j, x)]\right].$$

This is a form of the *replicator dynamics* and the stable stationary point of the ODE corresponds to assigning all the weight to the actions with highest expected payoff. That is, with very little information, and fairly simple behavioral rules, the agent learns to choose actions that maximize the objective expected utility of the one-period decision problems. Although this may take a long time! As Arthur (1993) shows, comparing his artificial agents with results on human subjects reported by Busch and Mosteller (1955), the rates of convergence, and convergence itself, is very sensitive to the degree of disparity of payoffs.

As we have seen, a frequentalist who computes the empirical distribution of a process $\{x_t\}, x_t \in \{0, 1\}$ can completely miss a well-defined cycling pattern. This is a general problem in defining learning processes as stochastic approximation algorithms (or any type of algorithm). The underlying environment prescribes which algorithm is better suited for learning (in terms of a *consistency condition*). For example, in the cycling case would be enough to properly condition the algorithm (e.g., have a forecast for odd periods and another for even periods). Similarly, one may want to adjust the "gain sequence" to the environment (see, e.g., Benveniste *et al.* (1990)). It is well understood that there is a tradeoff between *tracking* and *accuracy*: a decrease of the gain α reduces variance of the error (allows for more accuracy), but, at the same time, may increase the bias of the forecast since it tends to underestimate the possible drift or non-stationarity of the underlying process (may not "track" the process well). This, which is a standard problem in statistical inference, shows the type of tradeoffs that are common in learning dynamics and that a learning theory must account for.

Artificially intelligent agents

Example 2 of an adaptive decisionmaker selecting rules according to their relative strength, can be seen as a very simplified brain of an *artificially intelligent agent* using Holland's *classifier systems* (CS) (see, e.g., Holland 1995). Classifier systems, based on genetic algorithms, were designed as an "all purpose adaptive algorithm." That is, in contrast with *experts systems* specially designed for a task or problem, and in contrast with learning machines, such as *neural networks* (NN), not designed for a particular task but in need of external training within an environment before they could appropriately perform, CS could – in principle – adapt to alternative tasks and learn from the beginning. In fact, some of the CS principles – mainly, selection of rules by genetic algorithm operations – have been incorporated in *neural network* architecture. *Recurrent neural networks* (RNN) share many things in common with classifier systems.

It is not possible to describe here these different classes of recursive algorithms (see, e.g., Holland (1995), Sargent (1993), Cho and Sargent (1995), and White (1992)), but only to point out some features that characterize their "higher adaptability": (i) Decisions, as languages, are decomposed into basic components ("if . . . then" statements, neurons, etc.); (ii) the "building blocks" structure means that there is "parallel learning" of different components (*schemata* in CS); (iii) an *internal accounting system* allows aggregation and internal transmission of information, which may result in building up "internal models" (e.g., some forms of endogenous pattern recognition); (iv) even if certain "tuning to the environment" is needed, stochastic search can result in "discoveries," that is, "unforeseen contingencies" may be accounted for. These features of *artificial intelligent agents* allow them to learn through relatively complex environments generating interesting – nonlinear – feedback. For this reason, an economy with *feedback* populated by *artificial intelligent agents* is labeled a *complex adaptive system*. At the same time, such sophistication makes their analytical study more difficult and computational simulations are an integral part of the development of these models.

4 LEARNING IN GAMES

From the perspective of learning theory, game theory provides a set of models where *feedback* effects may be specially perverse, except that they are governed by the norms of behavior that characterize individual learning. I discuss some of the recent contributions to the theory of learning in games (see also Fudenberg and Levine (1995b)). Broadly speaking, I proceed from weaker behavioral assumptions and solutions to stronger ones.

Monotonicity and rationalizable solutions

As we have seen, adaptive behavior can be characterized by a monotonicity condition. Milgrom and Roberts' (1991) condition of only playing strategies which, in relation to a finite past history of play, are not strictly dominated, is a fairly weak monotonicity condition. Nevertheless, as they have shown, it is enough to guarantee that, in the long run, only *rationalizable strategies* will be played, i.e., only strategies that survive an iterated process of elimination of strictly dominated strategies. This result has an immediate corollary, if agents' behavior satisfies their monotonicity condition and play converges to a single strategy profile, σ^*, then it must be a pure strategy Nash equilibrium.

If an agent is not fully aware of his feedback in the environment, or not all actions are observable and experimentation is costly enough, then he may converge to play an action which does not maximize objective expected utility, but maximizes his subjective expected utility. In a sense, Milgrom and Roberts' result is "too strong" since if their monotonicity condition is expressed in terms of subjective beliefs, then only *subjective rationalizability* may be achieved.

4.1 Subjective equilibrium notions

A process of iterated elimination of strategies which are not a best reply to subjective beliefs may converge to a situation where every player i adopts a behavioral strategy σ_i that is optimal, given his subjective beliefs μ_i of other agents' play (of the environment), and his beliefs are not contradicted. That is, μ_i coincides with v_i, where v_i is the objective marginal distribution induced on player i's path of play (i.e., $v = (\sigma_1 \times \cdots \times \sigma_I)$). In other words, agent i's beliefs may not coincide with the objective distribution outside his path of play, as is required in a Nash equilibrium.

Subjective equilibrium notions in economics go back to Hayek (1945). Hahn (1973) defined a *conjectural equilibrium* as a situation where agents' subjective beliefs (agents' *models*) about the economy were self-fulfilled and agents had no incentive to change their policies. This notion has been formalized, in the context of games, by Battigalli (see Battigalli *et al.* (1992)). Fudenberg and Levine (1993) and Fudenberg and Kreps (1995) have proposed the notion of *self-confirming equilibrium* and – independently – Kalai and Lehrer (1993b, 1995) the notion of *subjective equilibrium*. In a *subjective equilibrium* agents may misperceive their *feedback* in the social outcome. For example, in an oligopolistic market, with a large number of firms, a competitive equilibrium would correspond to a *subjective equilibrium* where firms do not take into account their individual effect on prices (see also Brousseau and Kirman (1995)).

Even if agents observe the actions of their opponents and know how to *best reply* to them, non-objective beliefs can be *self-confirmed*. For example, in an extensive game with limited experimentation, two players can have inconsistent beliefs about a third player and never realize this, since the information that would show such inconsistency is never revealed (see, Fudenberg and Kreps (1995)).

Kalai and Lehrer (1993b, 1995), Fudenberg and Levine (1993), and Fudenberg and Kreps (1995 and 1994) provide conditions under which such subjective equilibria are, in fact, Nash equilibria. For instance, in a one stage game *self-confirming* equilibria are Nash equilibria since all information sets are reached. The convergence of Bayesian learning in repeated games to Nash equilibria has also been established by Nyarko (see, Nyarko (1994)), and, recently, Sandroni (1995) has extended these results to finitely repeated games.

Subjectivism, marginal best replies and correlated equilibria

As seen in section 3, if the distribution of outcomes, x_t, is correlated with the agent's actions, a_t, then learning can converge to different subjective solutions, depending on how the agent conditions his forecasts. In a repeated game, correlations are likely to occur since agents respond to each other's past actions. The question is whether such correlations result in a distribution of play which is a – possibly, subjective – *correlated equilibrium*.

In a *subjective correlated equilibrium*, agents' subjective beliefs may contemplate correlated play by other players and these beliefs can be different while playing different pure strategies (non-unitary beliefs). That is, agents' best replies can be subjective *conditional* best replies.

There are several reasons why correlated equilibrium, and not Nash equilibrium, seems to emerge as the central reference equilibrium concept in learning theory. First, as has been said, correlations naturally arise in repeated play. Second, as Aumann (1987) has argued, Bayesian rationality in a multi-agent context (without common priors) is equivalent to a *subjective correlated equilibrium*. Third, as Hart and Schmeidler (1989) have shown, in a correlated equilibrium every agent can be viewed as playing a *zero sum game* against the opponents. This has two related implications. The first is that the existence of correlated equilibria can be derived using standard separation arguments (i.e., without the recall to a fixed-point argument); the second is that, as we will see, the simple zero-sum games, such as that between a player and the environment, has been known to be learnable. The question is whether players condition properly, to guarantee that the joint solution of this learning process results in a correlated equilibrium.

In the context of repeated games, Kalai and Lehrer (1995) and, independently, Nyarko (1994) have shown that Bayesian learning leads, eventually, to approximate subjective correlated equilibria when beliefs satisfy an absolute continuity condition. They also provide conditions that guarantee that such convergence is to an objective correlated equilibrium. That is, *strong merging* (or *weak merging*) of beliefs translate into objective (subjective) equilibrium outcomes. But, as we have seen, these consistency conditions require strong absolute continuity assumptions. The question is whether weaker consistency conditions result in some form of equilibrium outcome.

Recently, Foster and Vohra (1995), in the context of a two-player repeated stage game (with myopic payoffs), have proved a remarkable result. They show that, if both players behave as *well-calibrated forecasters*, then the asymptotic distribution of forecasts, or *calibrated beliefs* is a correlated equilibrium, and that – for almost every game – any correlated equilibrium is learnable by well-calibrated players. Unfortunately, their existence proof of well-calibrated players, based on the zero-sum characterization of correlated equilibria, is not constructive.

As has been seen in example 1, if the actions of players are correlated, players may correctly perceive the marginal distribution, but this does not mean that the product of these marginal distributions is the joint distribution (a basic and well-known fact about joint distributions). Example 1 translates into the famous Shapley example. That is:

Example 1′ (Shapley)

	b^1	b^2	b^3
a^1	0, 0	2, 1	1, 2
a^2	1, 2	0, 0	2, 1
a^3	2, 0	1, 2	0, 0

Fudenberg and Levine (1995a) show that the long-run play of *universally consistent* behavioral rules are (infinitely often) correlated distributions that have a marginal best-response property, i.e., agents' – subjectively – best reply to the empirical marginal distributions. For instance, in example 1′, it is known that fictitious play cycles along the strategy vectors with positive payoffs and that these cycling patterns slow down. The asymptotic distribution has the *marginal best-reply* property, but the joint distribution is not a correlated equilibrium.

The convergence of learning processes to subjective non-Nash, or correlated, equilibria (or, just *marginal best-reply* solutions) is directly related to the *complexity* of the game and the potential benefits that players may get from reaching "objective" beliefs. Three possible sources of *subjectivism* are: (i) the lack of enough *experimentation*; (ii) the existence of correlations that may occur through the game, and (iii) the "misspecification" of the model. While the experimentation costs are easy to measure (for example, "enough experimentation" in an extensive form game means that all nodes are "tested infinitely often"; Fudenberg and Kreps (1994, 1995), Hendon *et al.* (1995)), it is less obvious how to measure the "complexity" of correlated patterns or of possible model misspecifications. Such "complexity" measures could help us to understand the gap between subjective and objective equilibrium outcomes.

4.2   The learnability of Nash equilibria

As has been seen, under relatively weak monotonicity assumptions, *if the learning process converges, it will converge* to a Nash equilibrium. Also, under the appropriate absolute continuity (and independence) assumptions, Bayesian learning converges to Nash equilibrium in repeated games (see also footnote 5). Furthermore, it has been known for some time that, for some classes of games, convergence to Nash equilibria is guaranteed for certain classes of learning algorithms. For instance, in addition to Milgrom and Roberts' adaptive play in (strict) dominance solvable games, convergence to Nash has been shown for fictitious play in zero-sum games (Robinson (1951) and Brown (1951)) and in 2 × 2 games (with a prespecified "breaking ties" rule; Miyasawa (1961)). These results (as well as Foster and Vohra's (1995) convergence to correlated equilibrium) are in terms of *beliefs*. It is well known that convergence of beliefs does not imply convergence of the empirical distributions of play (see, e.g., Jordan (1993)). As we have also seen, Fudenberg and Levine (1995a) show that, if players' behavioral rules satisfy their asymptotic *universal consistency* condition, then players can only be playing infinitely often strategies that satisfy the *marginal best-reply* property.

Fudenberg and Kreps (1993) provide a – sharper – global convergence result for fictitious play in 2 × 2 games (with a unique totally mixed Nash equilibrium) by considering an augmented game in which payoffs are perturbed. This work has been extended by Benhaïm and Hirsch (1994), and, recently, Kaniovski and Young (1995) have shown that, in the same context of 2 × 2 games, if both agents' learning rules are of fictitious play type – with perturbations – then the learning process converges almost surely to a *stable Nash equilibrium*, either mixed or pure (in fact, arbitrarily close to a *dynamically stable equilibrium*). For example, in the *Battle of the Sexes* game the learning process converges to one of the two pure strategy equilibria with probability one. All these global convergence results for 2 × 2 games use stochastic approximation techniques and, as Kaniovski and Young point out, they can also be interpreted as the output of an evolutionary process with two populations where agents are fictitious players with random sampling (as in Young 1993). These results, however, do not generalize to more than two-action games since Shapley's (1964) example (example 1′) remains a counterexample to global convergence of play.

With respect to *local stability* results, it has also been known that *strict Nash equilibria* (that is, Nash equilibria with single-valued best replies) are *learnable equilibria* in the sense that they are asymptotically locally stable to some process of adaptive learning – say, satisfying Milgrom and Roberts' monotonicity condition (see, e.g., Fudenberg and Kreps (1993)). As we have seen, Foster and Vohra (1995) also provide a local stability result for correlated equilibrium (i.e., any correlated equilibrium can be *forecasted* by calibrated forecasters). Fudenberg and Kreps (1993) provide a local stability result for Nash equilibrium. They consider "convergence of behavioral strategies" instead of the previously used "convergence of beliefs (or empirical frequencies)." More specifically, they consider a strategy profile, σ^*, *locally stable* if the following *weak asymptotic consistency* conditions are satisfied: (i) the beliefs (assessments) of all the players converge to the empirical distribution of play; (ii) for every player, the mixed strategy played at $t, \sigma^i_t(h_t)$ (not necessarily all the pure strategies in its support) is within an $\varepsilon_t > 0$ of being the best reply, where $\varepsilon_t \to 0$; and (iii) for every $\delta > 0$, there is a t such that $\text{Prob}\{h_t \mid \lim_{t' \to \infty} \sigma^i_{t'}(h'_t) = \sigma^*\} > 1 - \delta$. They show that every Nash equilibrium is locally stable and that any non-Nash equilibrium strategy profile is not locally stable (in particular, correlated equilibria that are not Nash equilibria are not locally stable).

Fudenberg and Kreps (1993) results can be viewed as a *learning justification* of Nash equilibria. Loosely speaking, in repeated play finite games, "every Nash equilibrium is learnable and the only learnable strategy profiles are Nash equilibria." As I remarked, however, their asymptotic consistency condition – that is, their *learnability* concept – is very weak, and it must be since, for example, it prescribes that, Nash equilibria where agents play *weakly dominated* strategies, or the mixed Nash equilibrium in the *Battle of the Sexes*, are *learnable*. However, for most learning algorithms that have any chance of learning in relatively complicated environments, such equilibria do not emerge as the outcome of the learning process. For example, as we have just seen, in 2×2 games, Kaniovski and Young's "perturbated learners" learn such – non-*dynamically stable* – equilibria with zero probability. Of course, the same remark applies to the local belief stability concept of Foster and Vohra (1995).

4.3   The "support" of attraction

As we have seen, for a large class of learning algorithms, *when play converges*, it must be to a Nash equilibrium and, when agents learn with experimentation (or other forms of perturbations), it must converge to a refinement of Nash equilibrium. We have also seen some global convergence results for 2×2 games. A characterization for general strategic form games is available if only the "support of play" is considered. This is the approach taken by Marimon and McGrattan (1995) and by Hurkens (1994). The basic idea is that if a learning algorithm satisfies a monotonicity condition, then "learning processes move in the direction of the best reply map." Furthermore, if agents *experiment*, individual best replies are perturbated. As a result, the support of the attractors of large classes of learning rules can be characterized.

Hurkens (1994) considers a learning model where players are members of classes and at each period of time a player of a class is randomly selected to play (as in Young (1993)). These players have fixed finite memory and satisfy Milgrom and Roberts' monotonicity condition. Given the finiteness assumptions the learning process has a Markovian structure. He then shows that, if memory is long enough, play eventually sets into a *curb set*. A *curb set* is one that it is closed under best replies and a curb* set is one that it is closed under undominated best replies.[8] Curb sets may include Nash equilibria with dominated strategies. However, Hurkens extends the same result to minimal curb* sets, by strengthening the monotonicity condition.

Marimon and McGrattan (1995) (see section 3) consider variations of *persistent retracts*. A persistent retract is minimal with respect to the property of being closed under perturbed best replies.[8] A *robust equilibrium* is a singleton persistent retract. For example, in a *matching pennies* game all the strategies define a persistent retract, but in the *Battle of the Sexes*, only the pure strategy Nash equilibria are robust equilibria (and curb* sets; but there are robust equilibria which are not curb* sets). They also extend these concepts to correlated equilibria, to capture correlated cycles, such as the one of Shapley's example. Long-run dynamics of these learning algorithms either converge to a *robust equilibrium* or *the support* of the asymptotic play is a *robust correlated cycle*. In 2 × 2 games, Posch (1995) shows how "perturbed learning" can result in well-defined cycles, i.e., a cycle (of the joint distribution of play) with support in a *robust correlated cycle*, as in the *matching pennies game*.

As we see, when agents use learning algorithms satisfying basic behavioral assumptions (monotonicity, inertia and experimentation), then play converges – if it does – to a refinement of Nash equilibria (robust equilibria). The problem arises when agents' feedback translate into correlated cycling behavior. Such patterns may not result in well-defined cycles and then it is not clear how agents condition their actions on the observed play. This problem does not arise in – say, *supermodular* – games where convergence is monotone. In such cases, *pattern recognition* of the asymptotic play does not disrupt the convergence process. Recently, Sonsino (1995) has extended adaptive behavior to allow for certain degrees of pattern recognition. He shows how agents may learn and sustain a cycle, such as "take turns in playing pure strategy equilibria" in the *Battle of the Sexes*, but he also shows that unbounded memory is needed to *pattern recognize and converge* to a mixed strategy profile.

4.4 Neural nets rediscover the Folk Theorem

There is one more lesson to learn from the recent literature on learning in games. In all of the above discussion, learning agents did not have a final goal. The learning problem, however, can be greatly simplified if agents "know what they want." For example, at any point in time, an agent can *discriminate* whether his "aspiration" level has been achieved or not. Cho (1994, 1995) develops a model in which two artificially intelligent agents (AIA), with *neural network* capabilities, play repeated games. He recovers the *Folk Theorem*. That is, any individually rational payoff can be achieved as the long-run payoff of the AIA game (with or without discount). He also extends this result (without discounting) to games with imperfect monitoring.

5   LEARNING DYNAMIC RATIONAL EXPECTATIONS EQUILIBRIA

In competitive environments an individual agent does not affect the social outcome and, therefore, does not create strange correlations out of his optimal actions and mistakes. Furthermore, most learning models only address the problem of forecasting a public outcome, such as prices. These features simplify the learning problem. In competitive environments, however, we typically study intertemporal problems with continuous action sets. This feature complicates again the learning problem.

5.1   Learnable rational expectations equilibria

Most macroeconomic models are examples of the general competitive model with intertemporal feedback, where there is a continuum of agents – say, $I = [0, 1]$ – and a public outcome evolves according to $x_t = \phi(g(a_t, a_{t-1}), x_{t-1}, s_t)$ (see section 2). Furthermore, in many models, $a_{i,t} = BR_i(x_{t+1}^{e_i})$ where $x_{t+1}^{e_i}$ is agent i's expectation of x_{t+1}, at t. In this case, there is a well-defined mapping $\Gamma: X_\infty^{[0,1]} \to X_\infty$, such that $\{x_t\} = \Gamma(\{x_{i,t}^e\}_{i \in I})$. Rational expectations equilibria are fixed points of Γ, in the sense that $\{x_t^*\} = \Gamma(\{x_t^*\}_{i \in I})$. That is, agents *agree on the right forecast*, even when this means agreeing on a non-stationary path. Most existing learning models take three important short cuts. First, they assume a *representative agent*; second, the model is reduced to a "temporary equilibrium" model of the form $x_t = \gamma(x_{t+1}^e)$, where $\gamma = \phi \cdot g \cdot BR$ (see, e.g., Grandmont, 1994); and, third, the learnability question is limited to the fixed points of the temporary equilibrium map, $x^* = \gamma(x^*)$, that is to the stationary fixed points of $\Gamma(\cdot)$. In addition to a fixed point, there can be the stationary fixed cycles, which are stationary rational expectations equilibria (SREE).[9] Of these "short cuts," probably the most "distorting" one is the *representative agent*. It violates a basic *learnability principle*: agents may imitate others (social learning), but "agents learn independently." In a REE different agents must share the same beliefs about public outcomes, but learning is supposed to study how such a coordination of beliefs takes place. Furthermore, the *representative agent* introduces *feedback* effects (e.g., his mistakes are not smoothed out by others) that are not present in historical competitive economies.

Subjectivist and rational belief equilibria

As in games, self-fulfilling expectations may not imply rational expectations. In fact, as I mentioned in section 3, some "subjectivist" concepts, such as Kurz's "rational beliefs," have been postulated as a – weaker than REE – solution to dynamic competitive models. Nevertheless, some of the sources for "subjectivism," discussed in section 4, disappear in competitive environments. In particular, the agent should not be misled about his effects on public outcomes, which are nil, nor be concerned about individual correlations. This, however, does not mean that *subjective competitive equilibria* cannot exist. For example, in Kurz's (1994a and 1994b) *rational belief* equilibria, it is only required that all agents' beliefs must be "compatible with the data." That is, they must satisfy the absolute continuity property of only assigning zero probability to unobserved events. In his examples, non-REE *rational belief equilibria* exist by having agents disagree with the objective REE distribution – v – in its non-stationary component. In other words, agents agree in "pattern recognizing" stationary public events, but fail to grasp the complexity of the underlying – possibly, non-stationary – economy.

One way to get disagreement between REE and *rational belief* equilibria is by having some non-stationarity built into the environment – say, an important tail event. But then, it is not clear that there should be any loss of efficiency from not reaching REE. In fact, continuity of infinitely lived agents' preferences implies that tail events should have no effect on prices, otherwise (without continuity) the same existence of REE is at stake. This suggests an interesting relationship between *learnability of equilibria* and *market completeness*.

Araujo and Sandroni (1994) show that, in an exchange economy with *dynamically complete markets*, Bayesian learners *always* converge to rational expectations; a remarkable result. As is standard in this literature, they appeal to the Blackwell–Dubins theorem (see, section 3) and the facts that agents' preferences are continuous and all public information – that is, prices – is endogenous. Nevertheless, it has been known, since, for example, the work of Townsend (1983) that in stationary economies – with incomplete markets – the learning process may result in generating non-stationary prices, which presumably could result in rational belief equilibria which are not REE.

There is another source of *subjectivism*, which has already been mentioned, of which we have a number of examples: *model misspecification*. An example, can be that all agents use a linear forecasting model when REE prices have non-linearities and the economy converges to a "linear rational belief equilibrium." Most of these models, however, maintain a *representative agent* assumption or assume agents share similar learning rules (models). Both assumptions impose a high degree of "coordinated subjectivism."

E-stability

The *learnability* of the SREE with fixed learning rules has been well studied. In particular, the following classes of learning rules have been studied: (i) finite memory forecasting rules $x_{t+1}^e = f(x_{t-1}, \ldots, x_{t-m})$, where the class $f(\cdot)$ satisfies certain basic assumptions, such as the ability to forecast stationary paths (i.e., $\bar{x} = f(\bar{x}, \ldots, \bar{x})$) (see, for examples, Grandmont and Laroque, (1991) and Grandmont (1994)); (ii) Cagan's adaptive learning rules: $x_{t+1}^e = x_t^e + \alpha(x_{t-1} - x_t^e)$, with a *constant gain* $\alpha \in (0, 1)$ (see, for example, Guesnerie and Woodford (1991) and Evans and Honkapohja (1995a)); and (iii) learning rules with a stochastic approximation representation of the form $x_{t+1}^e = x_t^e + \alpha_t(x_{t-1} - x_t^e)$, such as recursive least-square rules (the *gain sequence* satisfies the "decay condition," mentioned in section 3.4, $\{\alpha_t\}, \alpha_t \in (0, 1)\Sigma_{t=0}^{\infty}\alpha_t = +\infty$ and $\Sigma_{t=0}^{\infty}\alpha_t^p < +\infty, p > 1$) (see, Bray (1983), Marcet and Sargent (1989a, 1989b), Woodford (1990), Evans and Honkapohja (1994, 1995a, 1995b) among others). Some of this work studies the relation between the "determinacy" (local uniqueness) of the SREE, or of the corresponding REE sunspot cycle, and the *learnability* of the corresponding equilibrium using adaptive learning rules (see, e.g., Guesnerie and Woodford (1991)).

By using specific classes of forecasting rules the concept of *learnable equilibrium* is well defined. The learnability of a SREE, $x^* = \gamma(x^*)$, is given by the interaction of the γ map and the forecasting map (assuming a representative agent). That is, for finite memory rules (i) or for Cagan rules (ii) one can use standard stability theory (i.e., characterizing the asymptotic stability by linearization around the steady state, etc.), and for rules of the form (iii), stochastic approximation theory provides the necessary characterization. In particular, if the corresponding ODE (recall section 3),

$$\frac{dx}{d\tau} = E[\gamma(x(\tau)) - x(\tau)],$$ is locally asymptotically stable at x^*, then the SREE

is called *E-stable*.[10] In models with constant gain, (ii), the asymptotic stability properties also depend on α being small enough. That is, if agents place enough weight on current events (α close to one) the SREE may not be learnable, even if the ODE is locally asymptotically stable and, therefore, *learnable* with rules with decreasing gain. These conditions generalize to "determinate" SREE cycles.

Woodford (1990) was the first to show that sunspot cycles could be *learnable* equilibria. In a sense, this result created skepticism for the idea that learning can help to "select" among REE. In fact, there are examples where adaptive learning agents' beliefs converge to *indeterminate* REE (Evans and Honkapohja (1994), Duffy (1994)).[11] Does this mean that *any REE is learnable*?

As we have seen in relation to Fudenberg and Kreps' (1993) results (*any Nash equilibrium is learnable*), the answer to the above question depends on the definition that we use of learnability. For instance, a closer look at the "convergence to indeterminate equilibria" examples reveals that a very weak concept of learnability is being used: they are either not robust to over-parametrizations of the learning rule or require an "overreactive" agent – usually, a representative – with important *feedback* effects. Similarly, a closer look at the "convergence to cycles" models shows that learnability of, say, a k-cycle requires that agents follow rules of the form $x_{t+k}^e = x_t^e + \alpha_t(x_t - x_t^e)$. In other words, the cycle must be "pattern recognized" before it can be learned. For example, Evans, Honkapohja, and Sargent (1993) study a model of REE sunspot k-cycles populated by a fraction of perfect foresight agents and a fraction of agents that do not recognize cycles (e.g., they treat price fluctuations like noise). They show that, if the fraction of non-"perfect foresighters" is large enough, all the cycles of period $k \geq 2$ disappear. In other words, cycles may exist only if enough agents are simultaneously "tuned" to them.

Ultimately, however, *learnability* is an empirical matter. The experimental evidence shows well-defined regularities. In particular, non-stationary REE and non-stable SREE have never been observed (see, for example, Marimon and Sunder (1995)). Similarly, with respect to *sunspot* cycles, the experimental evidence is revealing: purely belief driven cycles have never been observed; however, when agents share a common experience with a real cycle, perfectly correlated with a sunspot cycle, the E-stable sunspot cycle may persist after the real shock, driving the real cycle, disappears (Marimon, Spear, and Sunder (1993)).

5.2   Global stability and local instability?

The macroexperimental evidence is consistent with the theoretical (and experimental) results in games. When learning is not "tuned to an equilibrium" but agents must experiment and coordinate based on past experience, then many REE dynamics may be disregarded. In particular, *dynamic stability* criteria for large classes of learning rules, provide a good global characterization of observed paths (e.g., inflation paths tend to cluster around a E-stable SREE; as in the *Battle of the Sexes* agents converge to play pure strategy equilibria). Nevertheless, experimental evidence also shows that local dynamics, around a E-stable SREE, may be fairly complicated and not well predicted by the local stability properties of simple learning algorithms. This phenomena is particularly true when there are fluctuations around the steady state (e.g., there are complex roots). Subjects tend to react to such fluctuations (see, Marimon and Sunder (1995)), as in games players tend to react to cycling patterns. As a result, the local convergence properties depend on how agents "pattern recognize" such high frequency fluctuations and how their behavior "feeds back" into the economy. This dichotomy between the predictability of *low frequency* data and the difficulty to predict *high frequency* data is, in turn, consistent with macroeconomic and financial data and, therefore, learning models not only help to explain it but also help to design economic policies.

Stabilization policies with learning

Agents expectations always play an important role in the successful implementation of economic policies, and this is particularly true of stabilization policies. Unfortunately, most macroeconomic models have either made an *ad-hoc* treatment of expectations precluding agents from anticipating the effects of policies or, as a healthy reaction to such models, assumed *rational expectations* precluding agents from *learning* the possible consequences of policies. Recently learning models have started to fill this gap.

Evans, Honkapohja, and Marimon (1996) show how introducing a (credible) bound on the amount of deficit to GDP ratio that can be financed by seignorage can be a powerful instrument for stabilization policy, resulting in *global stability*, in an overlapping generations model with learning by heterogeneous agents. Such a policy, however, only makes more acute the problem of indeterminacy of REE equilibria. In other words, a policy which is often proposed (for example, in the Maastricht Treaty) is an advisable policy only when learning is taken into account. They also provide experimental data showing how subjects learn to foresee the effects of policies, but in their model this results in making the stabilization policies even more effective.

Similarly, Marcet and Nicolini (1995) show that recurrent inflationary episodes interrupted by *pegging exchange rates policies*, such as the ones experienced in several South American countries in the last twenty years, can be explained by an adaptive learning model, where agents endogenously change the weight placed on current events (the "tracking" parameter α discussed in section 3). Again, incorporating learning not only allows to explain some macrodata, but also provides a different evaluation of an often-proposed stabilization policy.

5.2.2 *Volatility, persistent correlations and complicated dynamics around the steady state*

Learning models are increasingly used to explain patterns which do not seem to satisfy REE restrictions. From long-run development trends (Arifovic *et al.* (1995)) to short-term trade and price volatility in financial and exchange markets (see, e.g., Hussman (1992), Brock and LeBaron (1995), de Fontnouvelle (1995)), some of these "high frequency" models exploit the fact that, around the steady state, variability may be high, and correlations persistent, in an adaptive learning model. In fact, it is well understood that the *speed of convergence* near equilibrium depends on the sophistication of learning rules (again, the tradeoff between *tracking* and *accuracy* discussed in section 3).

A claim, often made, is that final convergence to a competitive equilibrium can be difficult to achieve since "near equilibrium competitive forces may soften." This claim goes back to the problem studied by Grossman and Stiglitz, among others, of who has an incentive to purchase information if equilibrium prices are fully revealing. Brock and Hommes (1995) have recently developed an interesting model that addresses this issue. A simple example of their economies goes as follows. Agents can either forecast using their, relatively myopic, forecasting rules or purchase the services of a more sophisticated forecaster. All forecasting rules are of the stochastic approximation type, however the corresponding ODE is unstable if agents use their "free" rules, while it is stable if they use the – more accurate – costly rule. Far from the steady state most agents buy the forecasting services, pushing the economy towards the steady state; however, near the steady state it is not worth paying for forecasting services. This implies local instability (as in Grandmont and Laroque (1991)) and, at the same time, non-divergence from a neighborhood of the steady state. As a result adaptive paths may be fairly complicated; they prove the existence of *homoclinic orbits* and of *strange chaotic attractors* for a class of predictor rules.

In the experiential lab, we have observed similar "complicated dynamics" around the steady state. There are, however, two distinct underlying phenomena. One is that, as in Brock and Hommes, agents lose the incentive to sharpen their decisions rules so as to finally converge to equilibrium, and learning paths only "cluster around" the E-stable SREE (see Marimon and Sunder (1993)). The other is that around the SREE there may be fluctuations and agents try to follow and enforce the fluctuations in order to capture possible short-run rents even if they can appropriately guess the SREE (e.g., the announced policy identifies the SREE) (Marimon and Sunder (1995)). In other words, a trader in the stock market may not be interested in "fundamentals."

5.3   Social planners as AIA

As in games, there are macroeconomic problems where it seems appropriate to think that the learner has the "right pattern and equilibrium in mind." These are planner's problems in which the planner (or principal) is concerned that the agent follows a contract as planned. The resulting optimal strategies in these type of problems are fairly complicated history-dependent contracts. Nevertheless building on the work of Cho on *neural nets* playing repeated games (section 4), Cho and Sargent (1996), show how relatively sophisticated planner's problems (e.g., an optimal capital accumulation problem with private information) can be implemented by *artificially intelligent planners* with neural nets capabilities.

6   CONCLUDING REMARK

As I mentioned in the introduction, to build a *theory of the learnable in economics* goes way beyond some standard justifications for the study of learning in economics. According to this view, I have placed the emphasis in this abridged survey on several lines of inquiry: (i) the characterization of *adaptive learning*, of broad classes of rules, based on behavioral assumptions and resulting in learning processes which are "well behaved" (i.e., satisfy certain *consistency conditions*) in well-understood environments; (ii) parallel to the definition of alternative *consistency conditions*, the definition of *subjective forms of equilibria*; (iii) the characterization of the asymptotic properties of certain classes of learning algorithms and their ability to *select among equilibria*; (iv) the ability of learning models *to explain observed data* which are not properly accounted for by existing equilibrium theories; and (v) the use of learning models as *normative models* to help the design of economic policy and of political and economic institutions.

Although – possibly, for sociological reasons – research in *learning in games* and in *learning in macro* have been conducted fairly separately, as sometimes has been the case between *learning theory* and *experimental evidence*, I have tried to bring these different lines together, showing how progress in all the above lines of inquiry "crosses field lines." In summary, I hope this chapter will help others, as it has helped me, to go to the original sources and *learn from learning in economics*.

Notes

I would like to thank Buz Brock, Drew Fudenberg, Ed Green, Seppo Honkapohja, Larry Jones, Ehud Kalai, Ehud Lehrer, David Levine, Albert Marcet, Ellen McGrattan, John Nachbar, Hamid Sabourian, Thomas Sargent, and, specially, Giorgia Giovannetti for their comments on previous drafts, David Kreps, for his patience and encouragement, and all of those who have sent me their current work. Of course, the opinions and remaining misunderstandings can only be attributed to me.

1 For an overview of experimental evidence see Kagel and Roth (1995). For games, see also Crawford's contribution to this volume, and for evidence on macro-economic models see section 5.

2 See Kandori's contribution to this volume for a review of the, closely related, *evolutionary* and *social learning* models.

3 I use the following standard notation: if a_t denotes the actions of all the agents in period t, then $a_t = (a_{i,t}, a_{-i,t})$, where $a_{-i,t}$ denotes the actions of "all agents but i." Furthermore, $a^t = (a_0, \ldots, a_t)$; similarly for other variables. Also, when there is no confusion, $u(\alpha, m)$ denotes expected utility with respect to the mixed action α and the distribution m.

4 Here δ_p denotes the (Dirac) distribution with point-mass at p. Notice that a *frequentalist* will have *point expectations* $p_{t+1}^e = p_t^e + \dfrac{1}{t}(x_t - p_t^e)$ for $t > 0$. That is, the mean forecasts of a Bayesian with an appropriate beta prior distribution are those of a *frequentalist* with a prior q_0 (see de Groot (1970)).

5 In the context of evolutionary repeated games, Anderlini and Sobourian (1995) provide a global convergence result for computable environments which contrasts with Nachbar's (1995) negative results. We can translate an informal version of their results to our context. Now instead of having a single behavioral rule, the agent will be considering a large number of rules and, as in an evolutionary process, give more weight to those rules that are performing better. Anderlini and Sabourian (1995) show that asymptotically an optimal rule will be selected, which, in the context of games, means there is *global convergence* to a Nash equilibrium. Anderlini and Sabourian's result does not contradict Nachbar's since the selected rule will depend on the environment, which does not mean that such a specific rule could not be tricked in another environment.

6 That is, $v\left\{ h_t \mid \dfrac{1}{t} \sum_{n=0}^{t} u(a_n, x_n) + \varepsilon \geq \max_\alpha u(\alpha, m_t) \right\} \geq (1 - \delta)$. Valiant's (1984) *Probably Approximately Correct* (*PAC*) learning theory relates the $(\varepsilon - \delta)$ and T consistency requirements with the *complexity* of the class of concepts to be learned (*sample complexity*) and with the *computational complexity* of the learning algorithm (see, Natarajan (1991)).

7 See, Benveniste *et al.* (1990) and Ljung *et al.* (1992) for an account of Stochastic Approximation Theory. In particular, when the process has a fixed α, then it is a Markovian process, and, with enough perturbations (experimentations), the process is ergodic. That is, there is an ergodic distribution $m(\alpha)$ characterizing the

asymptotic behavior of the process $\{z_t\}$. We can then take the limit of these distributions $m(\alpha)$ as $\alpha \to 0$ at the right rate. This is the approach taken by *simulated annealing* methods which have been widely applied in *evolutionary models* (see Kandori's contribution to this volume). This shows that, as long as adaptation and evolution are governed by similar rules, differences in asymptotic behavior can only be attributed to different forms in which perturbations and limits of α interact.

8 Formally, let $PB_i(\sigma_{-i})$ denote the set of non-dominated pure strategies which are i's best replies to σ_{-i}, and $PB(\sigma)$ the corresponding joint best reply correspondence. A set $D = \Pi_I D_i$ is a *curb set* if $PB(\Pi_I \Delta(D_i)) \subset D$. Such a set is called a *minimal curb set* if it does not properly contain a curb set. Curb* sets are similarly defined by considering only undominated best replies. Furthermore, D is a persistent retract if it is minimal with respect to the property: $PB(\Pi_I \Delta(D_i^\varepsilon)) \subset D$, where D_i^ε is an open neighborhood of D_i.

9 A fixed cycle – say of period k – is a vector $(x_1^*, \ldots, x_k^*)$ such that, $x_1^* = \gamma(x_2^*), \ldots, x_{k-1}^* = \gamma(x_k^*), x_k^* = \gamma(x_1^*)$.

10 Evans and Honkapohja (1995a), call an E-stable equilibrium that is stable to overparametrizations of the learning rule *strongly* E-stable, otherwise they call it *weakly* E-stable. (Overparametrizations examples are: in a k cycle, consider $k \cdot n$ cycles; in an ARMA(k, n) model, consider increasing (k, n), etc.)

11 In their examples where a "representative agent" learns an indeterminate equilibrium with an ARMA rule, such equilibrium is only *weakly* E-stable. In Duffy's example the "representative agent" only reacts to current events and his behavior immediately *feeds back* into the economy: his forecasting rule is $\pi_{t+1}^e = [1 + (b-1)\pi_t]/b$ where $b > 1$ parameterizes the continuum of REE!

12 Unfortunately, space limitations have prevented me from properly quoting many interesting contributions. The interested reader can find a more complete list of references in my www page at http://www.eui.it/eco/marimon.

References[12]

Anderlini, Luca and Sabourian, Hamid (1995). "The evolution of algorithmic learning rules: a global stability result." Mimeo, Cambridge University.

Anscombe, F. and Aumann, Robert (1963). "A definition of subjective probability." *Annals of Mathematics and Statistics*, 34: 199–205.

Araujo, Aloisio and Sandroni, Alvaro (1994). "On the convergence to rational expectations when markets are complete." Mimeo, IMPA, Rio de Janeiro.

Arifovic, Jasmina, Bullard, James, and Duffy, John (1995). "Learning in a model of economic growth and development." Mimeo, Department of Economics, University of Pittsburgh.

Arthur, Brian W. (1993). "On designing economic agents that behave like human agents." *Journal of Evolutionary Economics*, 3: 1–22.

(1995). "Complexity in eocnomic and financial markets." *Journal of Complexity*, 1.

Aumann, Robert J. (1987). "Correlated equilibrium as an expression of Bayesian rationality." *Econometrica*, 55; 1–18.

Battigalli, P., Gilli, M., and Molinari, M. C. (1992). "Learning convergence to equilibrium in repeated strategic interactions: an introductory survey." *Ricerche Economiche*, 46; 335–378.

Benhaïm, M. and Hirsch, M. W. (1994). "Learning processes, mixed equilibria and dynamical systems arising from repeated games." Mimeo, Department of Mathematics, University of California at Berkeley.

Benveniste, Albert, Métivier, Michel, and Priouret, Pierre (1990). *Adaptive Algorithms and Stochastic Approximations*. Berlin: Springer-Verlag.

Binmore, K. (1988). "Modeling rational players: part II." *Economics and Philosophy*, 4: 9–55.

Blackwell, D. and Dubins, L. (1962). "Merging of opinions with increasing information." *Annual of Mathematical Statistics*, 33: 882–6.

Blume, Lawrence E. and Easley, David (1995). "What has the rational learning literature taught us?" In Kirman, A. and Salmon, M. (eds.), pp. 12–39.

Bray, Margaret M. (1982). "Learning estimation and the stability of rational expectations." *Journal of Economic Theory*, 26: 318–39.

Bray, Margaret M. and Kreps, David (1987). "Rational learning and rational expectations." In Feiwel, George (ed.), *Arrows and the Ascent of Modern Economic Theory*. New York: New York University Press, pp. 597–625.

Brock, William A. and Hommes, Cars H. (1995). "Rational routes to randomness." SSRI Working Paper No. 9506, Department of Economics, University of Wisconsin.

Brock, William A. and LeBaron, Blake (1995). "A dynamic structural model for stock return volatility and trading volume." NBER Working Paper No. 4988.

Brousseau, Vincent and Kirman, Alan (1995). "The dynamics of learning in *N*-person games with the wrong *N*." In Kirman, A. and Salmon, M. (eds.).

Brown, G. (1951). "Iterated solution of games by fictitious play." In Koopmans, T. C. (ed.), *Activity Analysis of Production and Allocation*. New York: Wiley, pp. 374–6.

Bullard, James (1994). "Learning equilibria." *Journal of Economic Theory*, 64(2): 468–85.

Busch, R. R. and Mosteller, R. (1955). *Stochastic Models of Learning*. New York: Wiley.

Canning, David (1992). "Average behavior in learning models." *Journal of Economic Theory*, 57: 442–72.

Cho, In-Koo (1994). "Bounded rationality, neural networks and folk theorem in repeated games with discounting." *Economic Theory*, 4(6): 935–57.

(1995). "Perceptrons play repeated games with imperfect monitoring." Mimeo, University of Chicago.

Cho, In-Koo and Sargent, Thomas (1996). "Neural networks for encoding and adapting in dynamic economies." In Amman, H. H. Kendrick, D. A. and Rust, J. (eds.), *Handbook of Computational Economics*. vol 1. Amsterdam, Elsevier Science, North Holland.

Dawid, A. P. (1982). "The well calibrated Bayesian." *Journal of The American Statistical Association,* 77: 605–13.

de Fontnouvelle, Patrick (1995). "Informational strategies in financial markets: the implications for volatility and trading volume dynamics." Mimeo, Iowa State University.

de Groot, Morris, H. (1970). *Optimal Statistical Decisions.* New York: McGraw-Hill.

Duffy, John (1994). "On learning and the nonuniqueness of equilibrium in an overlapping generations model with fiat money." *Journal of Economic Theory,* 64(2): 541–53.

Easley, David and Rustichini, Aldo (1995). "Choice without belief." Mimeo, Cornell University.

Evans, George W. and Honkapohja, Seppo (1994). "Convergence of least squares learning to a non-stationary equilibrium." *Economic Letters,* 46: 131–6.

(1995a). "Adaptive learning and expectational stability: an introduction." In Kirman, A. and Salmon, M. (eds.), pp. 102–26.

(1995b). "Local convergence of recursive learning to steady states and cycles in stochastic nonlinear models." *Econometrica,* 63(1): 195–206.

Evans, George W., Honkapohja, Seppo, and Marimon, Ramon (1996). "Convergence in monetary models with heterogeneous learning rules." CEPR WP 1310.

Evans, George W., Honkapohja, Seppo, and Sargent, Thomas (1993). "On the preservation of deterministic cycles when some agents perceive them to be random fluctuations." *Journal of Economic Dynamics and Control,* 17: 705–21.

Evans, George W. and Ramey, Gary (1994). "Expectation calculation, hyperinflation and currency collapse." Forthcoming in Dixon, H. and Rankin, N. (eds.), *The New Macroeconomics: Imperfect Markets and Policy Effectiveness.* Cambridge: Cambridge University Press.

Foster, Dean and Vohra, Rakesh V. (1995). "Calibrated learning and correlated equilibrium." Mimeo, University of Pennsylvania.

Fudenberg, Drew and Kreps, David (1993). "Learning mixed equilibria." *Games and Economic Behavior,* 5: 320–367.

(1994). "Learning in extensive games, II: experimentation and Nash equilibrium." Economic Theory Discussion Paper No. 20, Harvard Institute for Economic Research, Harvard University.

(1995). "Learning in extensive games, I: self confirming equilibrium." *Games and Economic Behavior,* 8: 20–55.

Fudenberg, Drew and Levine, David (1993). "Self-confirming equilibria." *Econometrica,* 61(3): 523–46.

(1995a). "Universal consistency and cautious fictitious play." *Journal of Economic Dynamics and Control,* 19: 1065–89.

(1995b). "Theory of learning in games." Manuscript, UCLA.

Grandmont, Jean-Michael (1994). "Expectations formation and stability of large socioeconomic systems." Working Paper No. 9424, CEPREMAP, Paris.

Grandmont, Jean-Michael and Laroque, Guy (1991). "Economic dynamics with learning: some instability examples." In Barnett, W. A. *et al.* (eds.), *Equilibrium*

Theory and Application, Proceedings of the Sixth International Symposium in Economic Theory and Econometrics. Cambridge: Cambridge University Press, pp. 247–73.

Guesnerie, Roger and Woodford, Michael (1991). "Stability of cycles with adaptive learning rules." In Barnett, W. A. *et al.* (eds.), *Equilibrium Theory and Applications.* Cambridge: Cambridge University Press.

Hahn, Frank (1973). *On the Notion of Equilibrium in Economics: An Inaugural Lecture.* Cambridge: Cambridge University Press.

Hart, Sergiu and Schmeidler, David (1989). "Existence of correlated equilibria." *Mathematics of Operations Research,* 14.

Hayek, Frederik A. (1945). "The use of knowledge in society." *American Economic Review,* 35: 519–30.

Hendon, Ebbe, Jacobsen, Hans J., and Sloth, Birgitte (1995). "Adaptive learning in extensive form games and sequential equilibrium." Mimeo, Institute of Economics, University of Copenhagen.

Holland, John (1995). *Hidden Order: How Adaptation Builds Complexity.* Menlo Park, CA: Addison-Wesley.

Howitt, Peter (1992). "Interest rate control and nonconvergence of rational expectations." *Journal of Political Economy,* 100: 776–800.

Hurkens, Sjaak (1994). "Learning by forgetful players: from primitive formations to persistent retracts." Working Paper No. 9437, Center, Tilburg University.

Hussman, John (1992). "Market efficiency and inefficiency in rational expectations equilibria." *Journal of Economic Dynamics and Control,* 16: 655–80.

Jordan, James S. (1991). "Bayesian learning in normal form games." *Games and Economic Behavior,* 3: 60–81.

 (1993). "Three problems in learning mixed-strategy Nash equilibria." *Games and Economic Behavior,* 5: 368–86.

Kagel, John H. and Roth, Alvin E. (1995). *The Handbook of Experimental Economics.* Princeton, NJ: Princeton University Press.

Kalai, Ehud and Lehrer, Ehud (1993a). "Rational learning leads to Nash equilibrium." *Econometrica,* 61(5): 1019–46.

 (1993b). "Subjective equilibria in repeated games." *Econometrica,* 61: 1231–40.

 (1995). "Subjective games and equilibria." *Games and Economic Behavior,* 8: 123–63.

Kaniovski, Yuri M. and Young, H. Peyton (1995). "Learning dynamics in games with stochastic perturbations." *Games and Economic Behavior,* 11: 330–63.

Kirman, Alan and Salmon, Mark (eds.) (1995). *Learning and Rationality in Economics.* Oxford: Blackwell.

Kreps, David (1990). *Game Theory and Economic Modeling.* Oxford: Clarendon Press.

Kurz, Mordecai (1994a). "On the structure and diversity of rational beliefs." *Economic Theory,* 4(6): 877–900.

 (1994b). "On rational belief equilibria." *Economic Theory,* 4(6): 859–76.

Lehrer, Ehud and Smordinsky, R. (1993). "Compatible measures and learning." Preprint, Tel Aviv University.

Ljung, Lennart, Pflug, George, and Walk, Harro (1992). *Stochastic Approximation and Optimization of Random Systems*. Basel: Birkhauser.

Marcet, Albert and Nicolini, Juan P. (1995). "Recurrent hyperinflations and learning." Mimeo, Universitat Pompeu Fabra.

Marcet, Albert and Sargent, Thomas (1989a). "Convergence of least squares learning mechanisms in self referential, linear stochastic models." *Journal of Economic Theory*, 48: 337–68.

(1989b). "Convergence of least squares learning in environments with hidden state variables and private information." *Journal of Political Economy*, 97: 1306–22.

Marimon, Ramon and McGrattan, Ellen (1995). "On adaptive learning in strategic games." In Kirman, A. and Salmon, M. (eds.), pp. 63–101.

Marimon, Ramon, McGrattan, Ellen, and Sargent, Thomas (1990). "Money as a medium of exchange in an economy with artificially intelligent agents." *Journal of Economic Dynamics and Control*, 47: 282–366.

Marimon, Ramon and Sunder, Shyam (1993). "Indeterminacy of equilibria in an hyperinflationary world: experimental evidence." *Econometrica*, 61(5): 1073–108.

(1995). "Does a constant money growth rule help stabilize inflation?: experimental evidence." Carnegie-Rochester Conference Series on Public Policy, 43: 111–156.

Marimon, Ramon, Spear, Stephen, and Sunder, Shyam (1993). "Expectationally-driven market volatility: an experimental study." *Journal of Economic Theory*, 61: 74–103..

Milgrom, Paul and Roberts, John (1991). "Adaptive and sophisticated learning in normal form games." *Games and Economic Behavior*, 3: 82–100.

Miyasawa, K. (1961). "On the convergence of the learning process in a 2×2 non-zero-sum game." Econometric Research Program, Research Memorandum No. 33, Princeton University.

Muth, John F. (1960). "Optimal properties of exponentially weighted forecasts." *Journal of the American Statistical Association*, 55: 299–306.

Nachbar, John H. (1995). "Prediction, optimization and rational learning in games." Mimeo, Washington University, St. Louis.

Nash, John F. (1950). "Equilibrium points in n-person games." *Proc. Nat. Acad. Sci. USA*, 36: 48–9.

Natarajan, Balas K. (1991). *Machine Learning*. San Mateo, California: Morgan Kaufmann Publishers.

Nyarko, Yaw (1994). "Bayesian learning leads to correlated equilibria in normal form games." *Economic Theory*, 4(6): 821–42.

Popper, Karl R. (1979). *Objective Knowledge: An Evolutionary Approach*. Oxford: Oxford University Press.

Posch, Martin (1995). "Cycling in stochastic learning algorithms for normal form games." Mimeo, University of Vienna.

Robinson, J. (1951). "An iterative method of solving a game." *Annals of Mathematics*, 54: 296–301.

Sandroni, Alvaro (1995). "Does rational learning lead to Nash equilibrium in finitely repeated games?" Mimeo, University of Pennsylvania.

Sargent, Thomas J. (1993). *Bounded Rationality in Macroeconomics*. Oxford: Claredon.

Shapley, Lloyd (1964). "Some topics in two-person games." *In Advances in Game Theory, Annals of Mathematical Studies*, 5: 1–28.

Sonsino, Doron (1995). "Learning to learn, pattern recognition, and Nash equilibrium." Mimeo, GSB Stanford University.

Swinkels, Jeroen M. (1993). "Adjustment dynamics and rational play in games." *Games and Economic Behavior*, 5: 455–84.

Timmermann, Alan (1993). "How learning in financial markets generates excess volatility and predictability of excess returns." *Quarterly Journal of Economics*, 108: 1135–45.

Townsend, Robert M. (1983). "Forecasting the forecasts of others." *Journal of Political Economy*, 91: 546–88.

Valiant, L. G. (1984). "A theory of the learnable." *Communications of the ACM*, **27** (11): 1134–42.

van Huyck, John, Battalio, Raymond, and Cook, Joseph (1994). "Selection dynamics, asymptotic stability, and adaptive behavior." *Journal of Political Economy*, **102**: 975–1005.

White, Halbert (1992). *Artificial Neural Networks. Approximation and Learning Theory*. Oxford: Blackwell.

Woodford, Michael (1990). "Learning to believe in sunspots." *Econometrica*, **58** (2): 277–308.

Young, H. Peyton (1993). "The evolution of conventions." *Econometrica*, **61** (1): 57–84.

Index